# Reading St. Luke's Text and Theology:
## Pentecostal Voices

# Reading St. Luke's Text and Theology: Pentecostal Voices

*Essays in Honor of Professor Roger Stronstad*

EDITED BY Riku P. Tuppurainen

PICKWICK *Publications* • Eugene, Oregon

READING ST. LUKE'S TEXT AND THEOLOGY: PENTECOSTAL VOICES
Essays in Honor of Professor Roger Stronstad

Copyright © 2019 Wipf and Stock. All rights reserved. Except for brief quotations in critical publications or reviews, no part of this book may be reproduced in any manner without prior written permission from the publisher. Write: Permissions, Wipf and Stock Publishers, 199 W. 8th Ave., Suite 3, Eugene, OR 97401.

Pickwick Publications
An Imprint of Wipf and Stock Publishers
199 W. 8th Ave., Suite 3
Eugene, OR 97401

www.wipfandstock.com

PAPERBACK ISBN: 978-1-5326-1984-7
HARDCOVER ISBN: 978-1-5326-1986-1
EBOOK ISBN: 978-1-5326-1985-4

*Cataloguing-in-Publication data:*

Names: Tuppurainen, Riku, editor.

Title: Reading St. Luke's text and theology : Pentecostal voices : essays in honor of Professor Roger Stronstad / edited by Riku Tuppurainen.

Description: Eugene, OR: Pickwick Publications, 2019 | Includes bibliographical references and index.

Identifiers: ISBN 978-1-5326-1984-7 (paperback) | ISBN 978-1-5326-1986-1 (hardcover) | ISBN 978-1-5326-1985-4 (ebook)

Subjects: LCSH: Bible. Luke—Criticism, interpretation, etc. | Bible. Luke—Theology | Stronstad, Roger. | Pentecostalism.

Classification: BS2589 R43 2019 (print) | BS2589 (ebook)

Manufactured in the U.S.A.                                                  OCTOBER 9, 2019

Scripture taken from THE HOLY BIBLE, NEW INTERNATIONAL VERSION®, NIV® Copyright © 1973, 1978, 1984, 2011 by Biblica, Inc.™ Used by permission. All rights reserved worldwide.

Scripture taken from the New American Standard Bible®, Copyright © 1960, 1962, 1963, 1968, 1971, 1972, 1973, 1975, 1977, 1995 by The Lockman Foundation. Used by permission.

Scripture quotations marked (ESV) are from The ESV® Bible (The Holy Bible, English Standard Version®), copyright © 2001 by Crossway, a publishing ministry of Good News Publishers. Used by permission. All rights reserved.

Scripture quotations are from Common Bible: New Revised Standard Version Bible, copyright © 1989 National Council of the Churches of Christ in the United States of America. Used by permission. All rights reserved worldwide.

**Roger Jonathan Stronstad**

1944−

# Contents

*Contributors* | xi

*Preface* | xv

*Abbreviations* | xviii

*Comprehensive Bibliography of Roger Stronstad's Published Works* | xxix
    PREPARED BY ALFORD DEELEY

## PART I—ROGER STRONSTAD AS BIBLICAL SCHOLAR, PENTECOSTAL THEOLOGIAN, AND EDUCATOR | 1

**1** Roger Stronstad | 3
*The Creation of a Pentecostal Biblical Scholar*
MARTIN W. MITTELSTADT

**2** Roger Stronstad as a Pentecostal Theologian | 12
DAVID WELLS

**3** Roger Stronstad as Theological Educator | 17
DAVE DEMCHUK

## PART II—READING ST. LUKE'S TEXT: HERMENEUTICAL CONSIDERATIONS | 21

**4** The Role of Tongues in Luke-Acts | 23
*A Pentecostal Reading of St. Luke's Spirit-Narratives*
ROBERT MENZIES

**5** Pentecostals and Luke-Acts | 35
*Reading St. Luke in the Pre- and Post-Stronstad Eras*
VAN JOHNSON

**6** Reading St. Luke's Narrative as "Texture" | 48
*Acts 2:1–4 in the Light of Socio-Rhetorical Criticism*
RIKU P. TUPPURAINEN

7  Experiencing the Meaning of St. Luke's Text | 61
   SCOTT ELLINGTON

8  Nothing to Sneeze at | 73
   *Receiving Acts 19:11–12 in the Canadian Pentecostal Tradition*
   MARTIN W. MITTELSTADT

9  St. Luke's Text and Postmodern Pentecostal Hermeneutics | 85
   BRADLEY TRUMAN NOEL

## PART III—READING ST. LUKE'S THEOLOGY: PNEUMATOLOGICAL AMBIENCES | 99

10 The Charismatic Ecclesiology of St. Luke | 101
   *Biblical and Systematic Theology in Tandem*
   DAVID COUREY

11 Prayer for the Spirit in Luke 11:1–13 | 114
   CRAIG S. KEENER

12 Tracing St. Luke's Pneumatology | 135
   *A Theological Study of Bezae's Textual Readings*
   BOB WELCH

13 Charismatic Ministries in St. Luke's Theology | 147
   JOHN W. WYCKOFF

14 Sin, Science, and the Spirit | 159
   *A Pentecostal Reading of St. Luke*
   AMOS YONG

15 Towards Pentecostal Missional Pneumatology | 173
   *An Affirmation and an Assessment*
   VELI-MATTI KÄRKKÄINEN

## PART IV—READING ST. LUKE'S PNEUMATOLOGY WITH OTHER TEXTS | 183

16 The Charismatic Spirit in the Torah and Former Prophets | 185
   LEE ROY MARTIN

17 Man Shall Not Live on Bread Alone | 197
   *The Burden of Prophetic Leadership in Numbers 11*
   WILF HILDEBRANDT

## CONTENTS

**18** Restoring Righteousness to Creation | 209
*An Overview of Matthew's Theology of the Spirit*
BLAINE CHARETTE

**19** The Holy Spirit in Mark | 220
RIKK WATTS

**20** The Paraclete | 231
*The Spirit of Prophecy in the Johannine Community*
BENNY AKER

**21** What Does It Mean—According to the Book of Acts and the Letter to the Ephesians—to Be "Filled with" / "Full of" the Holy Spirit? | 243
SVEN SODERLUND

**22** The Spirit in the Book of Revelation | 254
*A Narrative Hearing*
JOHN CHRISTOPHER THOMAS

*Bibliography* | 265

# Contributors

*Benny Aker* (PhD, St. Louis University)
Professor Emeritus of New Testament Exegesis, Assemblies of God Theological Seminary, Springfield, MO.

*Blaine Charette* (PhD, University of Sheffield)
Professor of New Testament, Northwest University, Kirkland, WA.

*David Courey* (PhD, McMaster Divinity College)
Guest Professor of Systematic Theology, Evangelical Theological Faculty, Leuven, Belgium; Lecturer, Continental Theological Seminary, Sint-Pieters-Leeuw, Belgium.

*Alford Deeley* (MA, Regent College)
Roger J. Stronstad Chair of Biblical Theology, Summit Pacific College, Abbotsford, BC.

*Dave Demchuk* (DMin, Trinity Evangelical Divinity School)
President and Professor, Summit Pacific College, Abbotsford, BC.

*Scott Ellington* (PhD, University of Sheffield)
Professor of Christian Ministries, Emmanuel College, Franklin Springs, GA.

*Wilf Hildebrandt* (DTh, University of South Africa)
Dean of Education and Professor, Summit Pacific College, Abbotsford, BC.

*Van Johnson* (ThD, Wycliffe College / University of Toronto)
Dean and Professor at Master's Seminary, Toronto, ON; Adjunct Professor, Tyndale Seminary, Toronto, ON.

*Veli-Matti Kärkkäinen* (DTheo & Habil, DTheo, University of Helsinki)
Professor of Systematic Theology, Fuller Theological Seminary, Pasadena, CA; Docent of Ecumenics at University of Helsinki, Finland.

## CONTRIBUTORS

*Craig S. Keener* (PhD, Duke University)
F. M. and Ada Thompson Professor of the New Testament, Asbury Theological Seminary, Wilmore, KY.

*Lee Roy Martin* (DTh, University of South Africa)
Professor of Old Testament and Biblical Languages, Pentecostal Theological Seminary, Cleveland, TN.

*Robert Menzies* (PhD, University of Aberdeen)
Adjunct Professor, Asia Pacific Theological Seminary, Baguio City, Philippines; Director of Synergy, a rural service organization, Kunming, China.

*Martin Mittelstadt* (PhD, Marquette University)
Professor of New Testament, Evangel University, Springfield, MO.

*Bradley Truman Noel* (DTh, University of South Africa; DMin, Acadia Divinity College)
Director of Pentecostal Studies and Associate Professor of Christian Ministries, Tyndale University College, Toronto, ON.

*Sven Soderlund* (PhD, University of Glasgow)
Professor Emeritus, Biblical Studies, Regent College, Vancouver, BC.

*John Christopher Thomas* (PhD, University of Sheffield)
Clarence J. Abbott Professor of Biblical Studies, Pentecostal Theological Seminary, Cleveland, TN; Director, Centre for Pentecostal and Charismatic Studies, School of History, Philosophy, and Social Sciences, Bangor University, Bangor, UK.

*Riku P. Tuppurainen* (DTh, University of South Africa)
Dean of Graduate Studies, Summit Pacific College, Abbotsford, BC; Senior Pastor, Finnish Bethel Church, Vancouver, BC.

*Rikk Watts* (PhD, University of Cambridge)
Dean of Theology, Professor, Alphacrucis College, Sydney, Australia; Research Faculty of New Testament, Regent College, Vancouver, BC.

*David Wells* (DD, McMaster Divinity College; Briercrest; Pentecostal Bible and Leadership Institute)
General Superintendent of the Pentecostal Assemblies of Canada.

CONTRIBUTORS

*Bob Welch* (PhD, Bangor University)
Lecturer and Chairman of Practical Theology
Continental Theological Seminary, Sint-Pieters-Leeuw, Belgium.

*John Wyckoff* (PhD, Baylor University)
Professor of Bible and Theology, Southwestern Assemblies of God University, Waxahachie, TX.

*Amos Yong* (PhD, Boston University)
Professor of Theology and Mission and Dean of the School of Theology and the School of Intercultural Studies, Fuller Theological Seminary, Pasadena, CA.

# Preface

Roger Stronstad has enjoyed a lengthy career as a Pentecostal theologian, biblical scholar, educator, and author. He has served the scholarly and the church communities vigorously over the past several decades; his service commenced even before the publication of his most well-known work, *The Charismatic Theology of St. Luke* (1984). This and his several other publications in the area of Luke-Acts, pneumatology and biblical theology have made significant contributions to biblical scholarship in general and Pentecostal scholarship and theology in particular. Stronstad and his scholarship has touched numerous minds and hearts, including my own.

Stronstad's less noticed scholarly interest and contribution is in the area of C. S. Lewis studies. He contributed to the C. S. Lewis Society for years, for example, as an editor for *The Canadian C. S. Lewis Journal*.

Early one morning in the fall of 2016, I had a unique experience during my routine devotional time at home. In the middle of a quiet prayer my mind was filled with a clear and strong idea to honor Roger Stronstad on the occasion of his 75th birthday by leading a *festschrift* project. Later that week, I found myself in his office at Summit Pacific College, Abbotsford, BC sharing my experience and my proposal. Roger humbly turned down the suggestion. "I don't think that it is necessary," he said, "I have just served. . . . I am not worthy of anything like that." After some persuasion, however, Roger agreed to give the idea prayerful consideration. Within a few weeks he acknowledged, after all, that this was a fine idea.

I thank Wipf and Stock (Pickwick) for publishing this volume as well as all the scholars who readily accepted the invitation to contribute to this *festschrift*. The contributors' constructive critiques and suggestions have been a great help in the process of finalizing the manuscript for publication. I want to recognize Laurence Van Kleek, the librarian at the Hudson Library, for serving as a proofreader and preparing indexes.[1] Finally, I want to extent my special thanks to the Summit Pacific College and my family for great support during the preparation of this volume.

The content of the *festschrift* reflects the area in which Dr. Stronstad spent most of his academic career. His focus has been, albeit not exclusively limited to, Lukan writings and especially Lukan pneumatology. It is not an overstatement to say that Roger

---

1. Also, he indexes *The Pneuma Review* for *Christian Periodical Index*.

Stronstad systematized Lukan pneumatology from and for a Pentecostal perspective. While laboring in this field, he inevitably touched another equally important area; namely, hermeneutics. His hermeneutical endeavors have strengthened Pentecostal scholarship, which acknowledges that there is a pre-Stronstad and a post-Stronstad era for Pentecostal Luke-Acts studies, as David Wells and Van Johnson highlight in their essays.

*Reading St. Luke's Text and Theology: Pentecostal Voices* aims to voice current Pentecostal scholarship on the selected topic in relation to the above-mentioned areas. The volume's title reflects Roger's first book by adopting the terminology of "St. Luke," which is also used in the chapter titles throughout the book. The content is divided into four parts: (1) Roger Stronstad: Biblical scholar, Pentecostal theologian, and educator; (2) Reading St. Luke's Text: Hermeneutical Considerations; (3) Reading St. Luke's Theology: Pneumatological Ambiences; and (4) Reading St. Luke's Pneumatology with other Texts. Thus, the essay collection contributes both to Lukan pneumatology and hermeneutics from a Pentecostal perspective as well as to pneumatological topics in other writings in the selected canonical books. In addition, the volume includes a comprehensive bibliography of Roger Stronstad's published works.

Part one consists of three essays. The first essay, by Martin Mittelstadt, a biblical scholar from Evangel University, is a reflection of Stronstad as a Pentecostal biblical scholar including his leading hermeneutical views. The second essay by David Wells, the General Superintendent of the Pentecostal Assemblies of Canada (PAOC), reflects on Stronstad as a Pentecostal theologian and his theological contribution within the global Pentecostal movement in general and within the PAOC fellowship in particular. The final essay in this part by Dave Demchuk, the President of the Summit Pacific College, presents his personal insights on Stronstad as a theological educator and his contribution to this field, especially in the context of Summit Pacific College where Stronstad served in a variety of educational roles before retiring in 2017.

Part two is a collection of articles that relate to hermeneutical questions in relation to the Lukan corpus, Pentecostal theology and hermeneutics. Stronstad's works touch on hermeneutical issues, which continue as topics of discussion and research among Pentecostals. These essays address many current issues, such as Pentecostal reception history, theology, experience, community, postmodernism, and questions of methodology.

The next six essays in part three focus on Luke's pneumatology. Contributors to this section include international Pentecostal biblical and systematic scholars who have done significant work in this area. Topics under which Lukan pneumatology is presented vary from ecclesiology to missions and from science to biblical theology. It is especially in this section, yet not limited only to this part of the book, where it becomes obvious that Pentecostal scholarship in relation to Lukan studies has still much to discover. These essays reveal new areas of study and, thus, introduce new evidence or suggest new conclusions and research areas.

## PREFACE

Part four deals with various other NT and OT texts which gives Pentecostal voice to larger pneumatological content in the scriptures. These contributions focus on pneumatology in respective texts, which are also compared implicitly or explicitly with Lukan pneumatology. Two essays are looking into the Spirit in the OT writings from a fresh angle. The NT texts include the other three gospels, as well as selected texts from the Pauline corpus and Revelation. These essays take the discussion beyond traditional topics in Pentecostal distinctive pneumatology, which proves that current biblical Pentecostal scholarship is not reading extra Lukan pneumatology merely through the Lukan lenses.

This collection of essays testifies of at least three major realities in current Pentecostal scholarship. First, the powerful influence of Dr. Stronstad's life and work in the area of Lukan theology and hermeneutics has been, and still is, obvious. A devoted scholar, like Stronstad, can make a huge difference in a world wild movement. Secondly, this volume demonstrates that there is no uniformity among Pentecostal thinking. Pentecostal scholarship continues to revisit old topics from new perspectives; at the same time, new areas of research have emerged in Pentecostal dialogue. Yet, there is an underpinning common denominator; the Spirit has a vital part—perhaps even a more vital part than we have previously noticed—in the life of the contemporary church. Finally, Biblical theology and Pentecostal pneumatology are intertwined with hermeneutics. This is demonstrated by the fact that some essays in this volume, which are placed under the "hermeneutic" section, could have also been placed under the "pneumatology" section and vice versa. Clearly hermeneutics should continually be a point of interest among Pentecostal academia and churches also in the future.

In this volume, we indeed hear various Pentecostal voices, which are, in one way or another, linked to the work of our honoree. Yet, my hope is that this volume will not only serve the current and the upcoming Pentecostal generation within the movement, but will also find a voice among other Christian traditions, as we all are journeying together on the road of Emmaus pondering the events in the past, the present and the future. I am convinced that this is also the prayer of our honoree, Dr. Stronstad.

Riku Tuppurainen
Vancouver, BC
June 4, 2019

# Abbreviations

## General Abbreviations

| | |
|---|---|
| ℵ01 | Sinaiticus |
| AB | Anchor Bible |
| *AF* | *The Apostolic Faith* |
| A/G | Assemblies of God |
| *AJPS* | *Asian Journal of Pentecostal Studies* |
| ALUOS | *Annual of Leeds University Oriental Society* |
| AYBRL | Anchor Yale Bible Reference Library |
| B03 | Vaticanus |
| *BA* | *Biblical Archaeologist* |
| BCE | Before common era |
| BDAG | Danker, Frederick W., Water Baur, William F. Arndt, and F. Wilbur Gingrich. *Greek-English Lexicon of the New Testament and Other Early Christian Literature*. 3rd ed. Chicago: University of Chicago Press, 2000. |
| *BEB* | *Baker Encyclopedia of the Bible*. Edited by Walter A. Elwell. 2. vols. Grand Rapids: Baker, 1988. |
| BECNT | Baker Exegetical Commentary on the New Testament |
| *BegC* | *The Beginning of Christianity.* Part 1: *The Acts of the Apostles*. Edited by Frederic J. Foakes-Jackson and Kirsopp Lake. 5 vols. London: Macmillan, 1922. Repr. under the subtitle, Grand Rapids: Baker, 1977. |

| | |
|---|---|
| BETL | Bibliotheca Ephemeridum Theologicarum Lovaniensium |
| *bis* | twice |
| BSC | Bible Student's Commentary |
| CBC | Cambridge Bible Commentary |
| *CBQ* | *Catholic Biblical Quarterly* |
| cf. | confer (compare or consult) |
| ch./chs. | Chapter/chapters |
| *CIJ* | *Corpus Inscriptionum Judaicarum* |
| *CTJ* | *Calvin Theological Journal* |
| D05 | Manuscript Bezae (Gospels and Acts) |
| diss. | Dissertation |
| *DJG* | *Dictionary of Jesus and the Gospels.* Edited by Joel B. Green, Jeannine K. Brown, and Nicholas Perrin. 2nd ed. Downers Grove, IL: InterVarsity, 1992, 2013. |
| esp. | especially |
| ESV | English Standard Version |
| ET | English translation |
| etc. | *et cetera,* and so forth |
| *EvQ* | *The Evangelical Quarterly* |
| *ExpT* | *Expository Times* |
| fn. | Footnote |
| Gr. | Greek |
| Heb. | Hebrew |
| *HTR* | *Harvard Theological Review* |
| ICC | International Critical Commentary |
| i.e. | *id est,* that is |
| IFPHC | International Flower Pentecostal Heritage Center, Assemblies of God Archives, Springfield, MO. |

| | |
|---|---|
| IJSCC | *International Journal for the Study of the Christian Church* |
| JBL | *Journal of Biblical Literature* |
| JBPR | *Journal of Biblical and Pneumatological Research* |
| JES | *Journal of Ecumenical Studies* |
| JETS | *Journal of the Evangelical Theological Society* |
| JPT | *Journal of Pentecostal Theology* |
| JPTSup | *Journal of Pentecostal Theology Supplement Series* |
| JSNTSup | *Journal for the Study of the New Testament Supplement Series* |
| JSOTSup | *Journal for the Study of the Old Testament Supplement Series* |
| JTS | *Journal of Theological Studies* |
| LNTS | The Library of New Testament Studies |
| LXX | Septuagint |
| MCS | Master of Christian Studies |
| MT | Masoretic Text |
| n./nn. | note/notes |
| NAC | The New American Commentary |
| NASB | New American Standard Bible |
| *Neot* | *Neotestamentica* |
| NICOT | New International Commentary on the Old Testament |
| *NIDB* | *New Interpreter's Biblical Commenatry* |
| NIV | New International Version |
| *NovT* | *Novum Testamentum* |
| n.p. | no place |
| NRSV | New Revised Standard Version |
| NT | New Testament |
| *NTS* | *New Testament Studies* |
| NV | New Version |

| | |
|---|---|
| OT | Old Testament |
| OTL | Old Testament Library |
| OTM | Old Testament Message |
| P | Papyri |
| p./pp. | page/pages |
| PAOC | Pentecostal Assemblies of Canada |
| pl. | plural |
| *PT* | *Pentecostal Testimony* |
| repr. | reprint |
| *ResQ* | *Restoration Quarterly* |
| rev. | revised |
| *RevQ* | *Revue de Qumran* |
| Sanh. | Sanhedrin |
| SBLDS | Society of Biblical Literature Dissertation Series |
| *SBT* | *Studies in Biblical Theology* |
| *SJT* | *Scottish Journal of Theology* |
| SNTSMS | Society for New Testament Studies Monograph Series |
| SPS | Society for Pentecostal Studies |
| SRC | Socio-rhetorical criticism |
| *ST* | *Studia Theologica* |
| *TDNT* | *Theological Dictionary of the New Testament*. Edited by Gerhard Kittel and Gerhard Friedrich. Translated by Geoffrey W. Bromiley. Electronic Edition. 10 vols. Grand Rapids: Eerdmans, 1964–1976. |
| THNTC | The Two Horizons New Testament Commentary |
| TIS | Theological Interpretation of the Scriptures |
| TNTC | Tyndale New Testament Commenatries |
| *TS* | *Theological Studies* |

| | |
|---|---|
| TWOT | *Theological Wordbook of the Old Testament*. Edited by R. Laird Harris, Gleason L. Archer Jr., and Bruce K. Waltke. 2 vols. Chicago: Moody, 1980, 1999. |
| UBS | United Bible Society |
| UBS4 | United Bible Society, fourth revised edition |
| v./vv. | verse/verses |
| VE | *Vox Evangelica* |
| vol./vols. | volume/volumes |
| VT | *Vetus Testamentum* |
| WBC | Word Biblical Commentary |
| WTS | *Westminster Theological Journal* |

## Old Testament / Hebrew Bible

| | |
|---|---|
| Gen | Genesis |
| Exod | Exodus |
| Lev | Leviticus |
| Num | Numbers |
| Deut | Deuteronomy |
| Judg | Judges |
| 1–2 Kgs | 1–2 Kings |
| Ruth | Ruth |
| 1–2 Sam | 1–2 Samuel |
| 1–2 Chr | 1–2 Chronicles |
| Ezra | Ezra |
| Job | Job |
| Ps (Pss) | Psalm (Psalms) |
| Prov | Proverbs |
| Eccl | Ecclesiastes |
| Song | Song of Songs |
| Isa | Isaiah |

| | |
|---|---|
| Jer | Jeremiah |
| Lam | Lamentation |
| Ezek | Ezekiel |
| Dan | Daniel |
| Hos | Hosea |
| Joel | Joel |
| Mic | Micah |
| Hab | Habakkuk |
| Hag | Haggai |
| Zech | Zechariah |
| Mal | Malachi |

## New Testament

| | |
|---|---|
| Matt | Matthew |
| Mark | Mark |
| Luke | Luke |
| John | John |
| Acts | Acts |
| Rom | Romans |
| 1–2 Cor | 1–2 Corinthians |
| Gal | Galatians |
| Eph | Ephesians |
| Phil | Philippians |
| Col | Colossians |
| 1–2 Thess | 1–2 Thessalonians |
| Heb | Hebrews |
| 1–2 Pet | 1–2 Peter |
| 1–2–3 John | 1–2–3 John |
| Jude | Jude |

| | |
|---|---|
| Rev | Revelation |

## LXX / Deuterocanonical Books

| | |
|---|---|
| Sir | Sirach |
| Wis | Wisdom of Solomon |

## Old Testament Pseudepigrapha

| | |
|---|---|
| 1 En. | 1 Enoch |
| 2 Bar. | 2 Baruch |
| Jub. | Jubilees |
| Let. Aris. | Letters of Aristeas |
| Ps. Sol. | Psalm of Solomon |
| Sib. Or. | Sibylline Oracles |
| T. Ab. | Testament of Abraham |
| T. Ash. | Testament of Asher |
| T. Benj. | Testament of Benjamin |
| T. Sim. | Testament of Simeon |
| T. Iss. | Testament of Issachar |
| T. Jos. | Testament of Joseph |
| T. Jud. | Testament of Judah |
| T. Levi | Testament of Levi |

## Other Jewish Writings

| | |
|---|---|
| 1QH | Thanksgiving Hymns |
| 1QM | War Scroll |
| 1QS | Rule of the Community |
| 1QpHab | Pesher Habakkuk |
| 4Q | Qumran cave four fragments |
| 4Q504 | Words of the Luminaries |

## ABBREVIATIONS

| | |
|---|---|
| 4Q521 | Messianic Apocalypse |
| 4Q558 | papVisionb ar |
| *Ant.* | Josephus, *Jewish Antiquities* |
| A.Z. | *Abodah Zarah* |
| bar. | baraita |
| B. B. | Bava Batra |
| *Behuq. pq.* | *Ehuaqotai; pereq* |
| b. Ber | Berakhot (Babylonian tractate) |
| b. Giṭ | Gittin (Babylonian tractate) |
| b. Pes. | Pesahim (Babylonian tractate) |
| b. Sanh. | Sanhedrin (Babylonian tractate) |
| b. Shab. | Shabbat (Babylonian tractate) |
| b. Ta'an. | Taanit (Babylonian tractate) |
| b. Yeb. | Yevamot (Babylonian tractate) |
| b. Yoma | Yoma (Babylonian tractate) |
| *CD* | *Cairo Genizah* copy of the *Damascus Document* |
| Deut. Rab. | Deuteronomy Rabbah |
| Did. | Didache |
| Eccl. Rab. | Ecclesiastes Rabbah |
| Gen. Apoc. | Genesis Apocryphon |
| Gen. Rab. | Genesis Rabba |
| Ḥag. | Hagigah |
| Ḥul. | Hullin |
| *J.W.* | Josephus, *Jewish Wars* |
| Lam. Rab. | Lamentations Rabbah |
| Lev. Rab. | Leviticus Rabbah |
| m. Ber. | Berakhot (Mishnah tractate) |
| Meg. | Megillah |
| Mek. | Mekilta |
| Mek. Shir. | Mekilta Shirata |

| | |
|---|---|
| Midr. | Midrash |
| m. Ḳid. | mishna Kiddushin |
| m. R. H. | Rosh Hashanah (Mishnah tractate) |
| m. Sanh. | Sanhedrin (Mishnah tractate) |
| m. Sot. | Sotah (Mishnah tractate) |
| Num. Rab. | Numbers Rabbah |
| Pes. | Pesahim |
| Pesiq. Rab. | Pesiqta Rabbati |
| Pesiq. Rab Kah. | Pesiqta of Rab Kahana |
| Q | Qumran |
| Rab. | Rabbah |
| R. H. | Rosh Hashanah |
| Shab. | Shabbat |
| Sipra *Qed. pq.* | Sipra (Sifra) *Qedoshim; pereq* |
| Sot. | Sotah |
| Suk. | Sukkah |
| *Tanḥ.* | Tanhuma |
| t. Ber | Berakhot (Tosefta tractate) |
| Tem. | Temurah |
| Tg. | Targumic text |
| Tg. Neof. | Targum Neofiti |
| Tg. Ps.-J. | Targum Pseudo-Jonathan |
| tos. Ber. | tosefta Berakhot |
| Zeb. | Zevahim |

## Other Christian Writings

| | |
|---|---|
| *1 Apol.* | Justin Martyr, *1 Apology* |
| copmeg | Coptic, Middle Egyptian |
| *Dial.* | Justin Martyr, *Dialogue with Trypho* |

*ABBREVIATIONS*

| | |
|---|---|
| Dio Chrysostom *Or.* 36. | Dio Chrysostom, *Borysthenitica (Or. 36)* |
| it(ar) | Old Latin 61 |
| P38 | Papyri 38 |
| P41 | Papyri 41 |
| *Phil.* | Polycarp, *To the Philippians* |
| syrhmg | Syriac, a Syriac variant reading in the margin |

## Other Ancient Literature

| | |
|---|---|
| *Acharn.* | Aristophanes, *Acharnenses* |
| *Aet.* | Philo, *De aeternitate mundi* |
| *Alleg. Interp.* | Philo, *Allegorical Interpretation* |
| *Conf.* | Philo, *De confusion linguarum* |
| *Contempl.* | Philo, *De vita contemplative* |
| *Decal.* | Philo, *De decalogo* |
| *Det.* | Philo, *Quod deterius potiori insidari soleat* |
| *Dial.* | Seneca, *Dialogi* |
| *Disc.* | Epictetus, *Discourses* |
| *Dysk.* | Menander, *Dyskolos* |
| *Epig.* | Martial, *Epigrams* |
| *Fug.* | Philo, *De fuga et invention* |
| *Her.* | Philo, *Quis rerum divinarium heres sit* |
| *Il.* | Homer, *Iliad* |
| *Isthm.* | Pindar, *Isthmionikai* |
| *Leg.* | Philo, *Legum allegoriae* |
| *Migr.* | Philo, *De migration Abrahami* |
| *Mos.* | Philo, *De vita Mosis* |
| *Nem.* | Pindar, *Nemeonbikai* |
| *Oed. Tyr.* | Sophocles, *Oedipus tyrannus* |
| *Op.* | Philo, *De opificio mundi* |

## ABBREVIATIONS

| | |
|---|---|
| *Phaen.* | Aratus, *Phaennomena* |
| *Praem.* | Philo, *De Praemiis et poenis* |
| *Prov.* | Philo, *De providentia* |
| *QG* | Philo, *Quaestiones et solutions in Genesin* |
| *Sobr.* | Philo, *De sobrietate* |
| *Spec.* | Philo, *De specialibus legibus* |
| *Virt.* | Philo, *De virtutibus* |
| *Worse* | Philo, *That the Worse Attacks the Better* |

# Comprehensive Bibliography of Roger Stronstad's Published Works

## *Prepared by Alford Deeley*

The *Charismatic Theology of St. Luke* is much cherished and the most well-known work among all of Roger Stronstad's publications. A seminal work, this highly rewarded title[1] had its humble beginnings as an unpublished master's thesis entitled, "The Holy Spirit in Luke-Acts."[2] Like Stronstad's thesis, among his published works, are many that began as unpublished papers presented at conferences or lectureships. While of interest, only Stronstad's published material is listed herein.

Stronstad's works appear in chronological order under the categories of books, book chapters and articles, journal articles, popular magazine articles, book reviews, book endorsements, and finally, works published or edited by Stronstad.

## Books

*Models for Christian Living: A Commentary on the First Epistle of Peter*. Vancouver, BC: CLM Educational Society, 1983.
*The Charismatic Theology of St. Luke*. Peabody, MA: Hendrickson, 1984.[3]
*Spirit, Scripture, and Theology: A Pentecostal Perspective*. Baguio, Philippines: Asia Pacific Theological Seminary Press, 1995.[4]
*The Prophethood of All Believers: A Study in Luke's Charismatic Theology*. Sheffield: Sheffield Academic, 1999.
*Signs on the Earth Beneath: A Commentary on Acts 2:1–21*. Springfield, MO: Life Publishers International, 2003.
*Baptized and Filled with the Holy Spirit*. Springfield, MO: Life Publishers International, 2006.[5]

---

1. The Foundation for Pentecostal Scholarship awarded the 2013 Book Award of Excellence to Roger Stronstad for his *Charismatic Theology of St. Luke* after it appeared in its 2nd edition in 2012.

2. See Stronstad, "Holy Spirit in Luke-Acts."

3. Since its initial publication Stronstad's *The Charismatic Theology of St. Luke* has been translated into Finnish (1989), Spanish (1994), Chinese (2001), Romanian (2003) and French (2006).

4. *Spirit, Scripture, and Theology* has been translated into Chinese (2003).

5. *Baptized and Filled with the Holy Spirit* has been translated into Burmese (2015).

*The Prophethood of All Believers: A Study in Luke's Charismatic Theology*. Rev. ed. Cleveland, TN: Center for Pentecostal Theology, 2010.

*The Charismatic Theology of St. Luke: Trajectories from the Old Testament to Luke-Acts*. 2nd ed. Grand Rapids: Baker Academic, 2012.[6]

*A Pentecostal Biblical Theology: Turning Points in the Story of Redemption*. Cleveland, TN: Center for Pentecostal Theology, 2016.

*Mark: A Commentary*. Cleveland, TN: Center for Pentecostal Theology, 2018.

*Spirit, Scripture, and Theology: A Pentecostal Perspective*. 2nd ed. Baguio, Philippines: Asia Pacific Theological Seminary Press, 2018.

## Book Chapters/Articles

"Homologia." In *The New Testament Greek-English Dictionary: Lambda to Omicron*, edited by Thoralf Gilbrant and Ralph W. Harris. Vol 14 of *The Complete Biblical Library*. Springfield, MO: Gospel, 1986.

"Oninemi" In *The New Testament Greek-English Dictionary: Lambda to Omicron*, edited by Thoralf Gilbrant and Ralph W. Harris. Vol 14 of *The Complete Biblical Library*. Springfield, MO: Gospel, 1986.

"Onomazo." In *The New Testament Greek-English Dictionary: Lambda to Omicron*, edited by Thoralf Gilbrant and Ralph W. Harris. Vol 14 of *The Complete Biblical Library*. Springfield, MO: Gospel, 1986.

"'Filled with the Holy Spirit': Terminology in Luke-Acts." In *The Holy Spirit in the Scriptures and the Church: Essays Presented to Leslie Thomas Holdcroft*, edited by Roger Stronstad, and Laurence M. Van Kleek. Clayburn, BC: Western Pentecostal Bible College, 1987.

"The Holy Spirit at Pentecost: The Charismatic Community." In *A Reader on the Holy Spirit: Anointing, Equipping and Empowering for Service*, edited by Eloise Clarno. Los Angeles: International Church of the Foursquare Gospel, 1993.

"The Holy Spirit in the Acts of the Apostles: The Charismatic Community in Mission." In *A Reader on the Holy Spirit: Anointing, Equipping and Empowering for Service*, edited by Eloise Clarno. Los Angeles: International Church of the Foursquare Gospel, 1993.

"The Prophethood of all Believers: A Study in Luke's Charismatic Theology." In *Pentecostalism in Context: Essays in Honor of William W. Menzies*, edited by Wonsuk Ma and Robert P. Menzies. Sheffield: Sheffield Academic, 1997.

"First and Second Peter." In *Full Life Bible Commentary to the New Testament*, edited by French L. Arrington and Roger Stronstad. Grand Rapids: Zondervan, 1999.[7]

"Jude." In *Full Life Bible Commentary to the New Testament*, edited by French L. Arrington and Roger Stronstad. Grand Rapids: Zondervan, 1999.

"The Charismatic Theology of St. Luke: Revisited." In *Defining Issues in Pentecostalism: Classical and Emergent*, edited by Steven M. Studebaker. Eugene, OR: Pickwick, 2008.

---

6. This second edition of Stronstad's *The Charismatic Theology of St. Luke* has been translated into Chinese (2014).

7. Since its initial publication, *Full Life Bible Commentary to the New Testament* has been republished as *Life in the Spirit New Testament Commentary* (2003) and *Life in the Spirit Bible Commentary to the New Testament* (2016).

"A Baker's Dozen and Many More." In *Contemporary Issues in Pneumatology: Festschrift in Honor of George M. Flattery*, edited by James E. Richardson. Springfield, MO: Global University, 2010.

"Christ Our Baptizer: The Spirit-Baptized Life (Ministry)." In *Authentically Pentecostal: Here's What We See—A Conversation*, edited by David Wells and Van Johnson. Mississauga, ON: Pentecostal Assemblies of Canada, 2010.

"On Being Baptized in the Holy Spirit: A Pentecostal Perspective." In *Trajectories in the Book of Acts: Essays in Honor of John Wesley Wyckoff*, edited by Paul Alexander, Jordan Daniel May, and Robert G. Reid. Eugene, OR: Wipf and Stock, 2010.

"Acts of the Apostles." In *Handbook of Pentecostal Christianity*, edited by Adam Stewart. KeKalb: Northern Illinois University Press, 2012.

"Baptism of the Holy Spirit." In *Handbook of Pentecostal Christianity*, edited by Adam Stewart. KeKalb: Northern Illinois University Press, 2012.

"Initial Evidence." In *Handbook of Pentecostal Christianity*, edited by Adam Stewart. KeKalb: Northern Illinois University Press, 2012.

"Travels of Triumph and Tragedy (Acts 9:1–22:21)." In *Serving God's Community: Studies in Honor of W. Ward Gasque*, edited by Susan S. Phillips and Soo-Inn Tan. Vancouver, BC: Regent College Publishing, 2014.

"A Lukan Model of Pneumatic Hermeneutics." In *Holy Spirit: Unfinished Agenda*, edited by Johnson K. Lim. Singapore: Armour, 2015.

"Some Aspects of Hermeneutics in the Pentecostal Tradition." In *Pentecostals in the Twenty-First Century: Identity, Beliefs, Praxis*, edited by Corneliu Constantineanu, and Christopher J. Scobie. Eugene, OR: Cascade, 2018.[8]

## Journal Articles

"The Influence of the Old Testament on the Charismatic Theology of St. Luke." *Pneuma* 2.1 (1980).
"Trends in Pentecostal Hermeneutics." *Paraclete* 22.3 (1988).
"The Hermeneutics of Lukan Historiography." *Paraclete* 22.4 (1988).
"The Holy Spirit in Luke-Acts." *Paraclete* 23.1 (1989).
"The Holy Spirit in Luke-Acts: A Synthesis of Luke's Pneumatology." *Paraclete* 23.2 (1989).
"Unity and Diversity: New Testament Perspectives on the Holy Spirit." *Paraclete* 23.3 (1989).
"Pentecostal Experience and Hermeneutics." *Paraclete* 26.1 (1992).
"The Biblical Precedent for Historical Precedent." *Paraclete* 27.3 (1993).
"Affirming Diversity: God's People as a Community of Prophets." *Pneuma* 17.2 (1995).
"The Rebirth of Prophecy: Trajectories from Moses to Jesus and his Followers." *Journal of Biblical and Pneumatological Research* 5 (2013).
"They Spoke with Tongues and Prophesied." *Enrichment* 10.1 (2005).

## Magazine Articles

"Prophets and Pentecost." *Pentecostal Testimony*, March, 1976.
"On Thinking Christianly." *Pentecostal Testimony*, August, 1977.

---

8. *Pentecostals in the Twenty-First Century* with Stronstad's "Some Aspects of Hermeneutics in the Pentecostal Tradition" was originally translated and presented in Slovene (2016).

"Mark in Mawchi: A Story of Bible Translation in India." *Pentecostal Testimony*, November, 1977.
"Table Fellowship with Jesus." *Pentecostal Testimony*, February, 1978.
"Cautions for Calamity." *Pentecostal Testimony*, May, 1978.
"Worship in Heaven and on Earth." *Pentecostal Testimony*, October, 1978.
"Faith's Lifestyle Today." *Pentecostal Testimony*, February, 1979.
"I'm Not a Nineveh Man." *Pentecostal Testimony*, August, 1979.
"Assessing Emphases on Health, Wealth and Happiness." *Pentecostal Testimony*, November, 1979.
"Saul, David and Solomon and Today's Tarnish Problems." *Pentecostal Testimony*, March, 1980.
"How God's Promises Challenge Faith." *Pentecostal Testimony*, August, 1980.
"The Lord of the Harvest." *Pentecostal Testimony*, October, 1980.
"Blobs and Beanpoles." *Pentecostal Testimony*, August, 1981.
"No Woven Image." *Pentecostal Testimony*, October, 1981.
"Responding to Comment about that 'Woven Image.'" *Pentecostal Testimony*, January, 1982.
"Can Israel Do No Wrong?" *Pentecostal Testimony*, November, 1982.
"The Secular Celebration of Christmas." *Pentecostal Testimony*, December, 1982.
"Faith in the Balances." *Pentecostal Testimony*, February, 1983.
"On the Care and Feeding of Oxen: Some Ruminations on the Care of Pastors." *Pentecostal Testimony*, October, 1983.
"A Filipino Feast." *Pentecostal Testimony*, December, 1984.
"Pentecostal Power Politics." *Pentecostal Testimony*, June, 1985.
"C. S. Lewis: Mere Christian; His Books Have Sold over 100,000,000 Copies." *Resource*, September/October, 1995.
"Staying Strong Intellectually or Reading for Renewal." *Resource*, January/February, 1998.
"What it Means to be Pentecostal." *Testimony*, June, 2001.

## Book Reviews

"Pentecostal Hermeneutics." Review of *Gospel and Spirit: Issues in New Testament Hermeneutics*, by Gordon D. Fee. *Pneuma* 15.2 (1993).
Review of *Empowered for Witness: The Spirit in Luke-Acts*, by Robert P. Menzies. *Pneuma* 20.1 (1998).
Review of *A Challenge to C. S. Lewis*, by Peter Milward, SJ. *Canadian C. S. Lewis Journal* 88 (1995).
Review of *Not A Tame Lion: The Spiritual Legacy of C. S. Lewis*, by Terry W. Glaspey. *Canadian C. S. Lewis Journal* 93 (1998).
Review of *Simply C. S. Lewis: A Beginner's Guide to the Life and Works of C. S. Lewis*, by Thomas C. Peters. *Canadian C. S. Lewis Journal* 93 (1998).
Review of *C. S. Lewis: Writer, Dreamer and Mentor*, by Lionel Adey, *Living Church* 217 (1998).
"Christian Mythmakers." Review of *The Harmony Within: The Spiritual Vision of George MacDonald*, by Roland Hein; *Bright Shadow of Reality: Spiritual Longing in C. S. Lewis*, by Corbin Scott Carnell; *The Lord of the Rings: One Volume Edition*, by J. R. R. Tolkien; *Roverandom*, by J. R. R. Tolkien; *Tolkien: Man and Myth*, by Joseph Pearce. *The Living Church* 219 (1999).
"Forty Years On." Review of *Baptism in the Holy Spirit*, by James D. G. Dunn. *JPT* 19.1 (2010).

Review of *Filled with the Spirit*, by John R. Levison. *JPT* 20.2 (2011).
Review of *Prophetic Jesus, Prophetic Church*, by Luke Timothy Johnson. *JPT* 22.1 (2013).
Review of *Who Is the Holy Spirit? A Walk with the Apostles*, by Amos Yong. *JPT* 22.2 (2013).
Review of *Living in the Supernatural Dimension*, by John Abraham. *Enrich* (Spring/Summer, 2013).
Review of *Luke-Acts and Jewish Historiography: A Study on the Theology, Literature, and Ideology of Luke-Acts*, by Samson Uytanlet. *The Pentecostal Educator* 2.1 (2015).

## Book Endorsements

Endorsement of *Baptism in the Spirit: Luke-Acts and the Dunn Debate*, by William P. Atkinson. Eugene, OR: Pickwick, 2011.
Endorsement of *Empowered Believers: The Holy Spirit in the Book of Acts*, by Gonzalo Haya-Prats. Eugene, OR: Cascade, 2011.
Endorsement of *The Holy Spirit in Mission: Prophetic Speech and Action in Christian Witness*, by Gary Tyra. Downers Grove, IL: InterVarsity, 2012.
Endorsement of *Pentecost: This Story Is Our Story*, by Robert P. Menzies. Springfield, MO: Gospel, 2013.
Endorsement of *Speaking in Tongues*, by Robert P. Menzies. Cleveland, TN: Center for Pentecostal Theology, 2016.

## Books/Journals Edited

*The Holy Spirit in the Scriptures and the Church: Essays Presented to Leslie Thomas Holdcroft.* Edited by Roger Stronstad and Laurence M. Van Kleek. Clayburn, BC: Western Pentecostal Bible College, 1987.
*The Full Life Study Bible: New International Version; An International Study Bible for Pentecostal and Charismatic Christians.* Edited by Don Stamps and Roger Stronstad. Grand Rapids: Zondervan, 1993.[9]
*The Full Life Bible Commentary to the New Testament.* Edited by French L. Arrington, and Roger Stronstad. Grand Rapids: Zondervan, 1999.[10]
*The Canadian C. S. Lewis Journal.* Edited by Roger Stronstad. 17 vols. Abbotsford, BC: Western Pentecostal Bible College, 1993–2001.[11]

---

9. Since its initial publication, *The Full Life Study Bible* has been republished as *Life in the Spirit Study Bible* (2003).

10. Since its initial publication, *The Full Life Bible Commentary to the New Testament* has been republished as *Life in the Spirit New Testament Commentary* (2003) and *Life in the Spirit Bible Commentary to the New Testament* (2016).

11. As editor of *The Canadian C. S. Lewis Journal* from 1993–2001, Stronstad was responsible for volumes 84–100.

# PART I

# Roger Stronstad as Biblical Scholar, Pentecostal Theologian, and Educator

"The experience of being baptized with the Holy Spirit did not cease when the story of Acts ended. Countless numbers of identifiable and anonymous Christians down through the centuries have been baptized in the Holy Spirit by Jesus to empower their witness about Jesus."

—ROGER STRONSTAD, *SIGNS ON THE EARTH BENEATH*, 46.

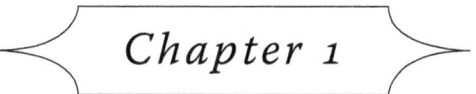

# Chapter 1

## Roger Stronstad
### *The Creation of a Pentecostal Biblical Scholar*

MARTIN W. MITTELSTADT

The time had come to mark the influence of our fellow Canadian Pentecostal scholars. In 2010, the second Canadian symposium at the Society for Pentecostal Studies set out to express appreciation to four Canadian Pentecostal academicians revered at home and around the world. We honored Ronald Kydd, David Reed, the late Clark Pinnock, and Roger Stronstad. I had the privilege of paying tribute to Roger Stronstad. Since I first sought out Stronstad in 1993 during the early stages of my dissertation, his scholarship and friendship have inspired my career. In this essay, I reflect yet again on the pioneering contributions of a Canadian Pentecostal academician.[1] I suggest that Stronstad's accomplishments produce at least four enduring results, many of them on display in this volume: (1) in his *magnum opus*, the ground-breaking *The Charismatic Theology of St. Luke*, Stronstad rescues Luke from the chains of Pauline interpreters and returns Luke to his rightful place as a contributor to biblical theology; (2) in his *Prophethood of All Believers*, Stronstad reveals an ever-maturing scholarship by strengthening the language of his earlier volume; (3) in a one-volume commentary, Stronstad and co-editor French Arrington explore canonical order by producing the first Luke-Acts commentary; and (4) in numerous articles on hermeneutics, Stronstad defends and extends the views the above. In so doing, Stronstad models for many burgeoning and seasoned Pentecostal scholars the convergence of academic rigour with pastoral concern.

---

1. This essay is a synopsis of Mittelstadt, "Academic and Pentecostal: An Appreciation of Roger Stronstad," published in the inaugural issue of *Canadian Journal of Pentecostal-Charismatic Christianity* 1 (2010) 31–64.

## A Classic in the Making: The Charismatic Theology of St. Luke

Stronstad embarks on a MCS in theology at Regent College with one specific purpose: "I wanted to write a thesis in which I might refute the common anti-Pentecostal clichés which characterized evangelical Protestantism through the sixties and the seventies."[2] Stronstad wrestles with recently released works such as *A Theology of the Holy Spirit* by Frederick Dale Bruner, *Baptism in the Holy Spirit* by James D. G. Dunn and, on a more popular level, *The Baptism and Fullness of the Holy Spirit* by influential British preacher John Stott.[3] These scholars inspire Stronstad to embark upon an ever-converging career around pneumatology, Luke-Acts (particularly alongside Pauline literature), and hermeneutics. With his solid Pentecostal foundation and an encouraging and exploratory academic environment at Regent College, Stronstad completes his master's thesis with what he called "the mundane title" of *The Holy Spirit in Luke-Acts*.[4]

Stronstad searches in vain for a publisher until Benny Aker, then of Hendrickson Publishers, paves the way for a thesis that remains in print at the time of this publication. Who would have predicted that a revised master's thesis would become Stronstad's signature *Charismatic Theology*, first published in 1984 and revised and republished in 2012? By way of his first and enduring publication, Stronstad initiates a breakthrough for Pentecostals.

Stronstad draws heavily on Ward Gasque, his thesis supervisor, and, not coincidentally, Clark Pinnock, who joined the Regent College faculty during Stronstad's tenure as a student. With flare, the influential Pinnock would write the prophetic foreword not only to *The Charismatic Theology of St. Luke*, but also for all promising Pentecostal theologians:

> Watch out you evangelicals—the young Pentecostal scholars are coming! . . . We cannot consider Pentecostalism to be an aberration born of experiential excesses but a twentieth-century revival of New Testament theology and religion. It has not only restored joy and power to the church but a clearer reading of the Bible as well. So with gladness of heart I say, "Welcome to this book and peace to the Pentecostal communities." We should let Stronstad help us grow together in the unity of the faith in the Son of God.[5]

James Dunn's revised dissertation, *Baptism in the Spirit*, stirred Pentecostals in a way that he could have hardly imagined; his subtitle, *A Re-examination of the NT Teaching on the Gift of the Spirit in Relation to Pentecostalism Today*, sets up his dispute with classical Pentecostals. Published in 1970, Dunn's volume undergoes numerous printings and not only launches his career, but also lures Pentecostals into the world

---

2. From my email correspondence with Stronstad between January 22–30, 2010.
3. Bruner, *Theology of the Holy Spirit*; Dunn, *Baptism in the Holy Spirit*; Stott, *Baptism and Fullness*.
4. Stronstad, "Charismatic Theology: Revisited," vii.
5. Stronstad, "Charismatic Theology: Revisited," vii.

of critical scholarship. Dunn typifies the larger Evangelical community and becomes the primary conversation partner for "young" Pentecostals looking to "join the big leagues."[6] Dunn's deductions concerning Spirit baptism stimulate further interest surrounding hermeneutics and the disposition of Evangelicals and Fundamentalists toward cessationism. Stronstad and emerging scholars, such as James Shelton and Howard Ervin, respond (directly or indirectly) to Dunn and consequently bring Pentecostal theology and praxis into the academic marketplace.[7]

In his *Charismatic Theology*, Stronstad keeps Dunn's conclusions in view. Given Pentecostal adherence to post-conversion experience of Spirit baptism, Dunn's view equating Spirit baptism with regeneration becomes an inevitable target for Pentecostal response. Stronstad notes Paul's singular use of the phrases "baptism in the Spirit" (1 Cor 12:13) and "filled with the Spirit" (Eph 5:18) compared to Luke's twelve references to the same two phrases.[8] Stronstad accuses Dunn (and others) of an illegitimate identity transfer that silences Luke's pneumatology.[9] He pays close attention to Luke's use of these terms and, unlike Dunn, argues that readers should deem Luke's pneumatology as charismatic, vocational, and prophetic.[10] Stronstad employs the term *charismatic* as experience(s) of the Holy Spirit to enable individuals to speak *prophetically* and thereby fulfill their *vocation* as ministers of the word.

According to Stronstad, Luke's multi-layered purposes follow the septuagintal tradition and resonate with the didactic methodologies of chroniclers of Israel's sacred history.[11] Stronstad roots Lukan pneumatology to OT transfer of the charismatic Spirit from leader to successor(s), like Moses to his elders (Num 11:14–17, 25) and subsequently to Joshua (Num 27:16–20; Deut 34:9), Elijah to Elisha (2 Kgs 2:9, 15), and the sobering account of Saul (1 Sam 10:10) to David (1 Sam 16:13–14). As Luke turns to his own era, Jesus transfers the same Spirit that rests upon him and empowers his entire mission (Luke 4:18–21) to the disciples at Pentecost (Acts 2:1–21).[12] This

---

6. Early Pentecostals looked consistently to the Lukan narratives for evidence and affirmation of the charismatic experiences of their participants, the standardization of primary doctrine, and navigation of the movement through dissent. Subsequent generations of preachers and teachers within classical Pentecostalism then worked hard to preserve teachings for contemporary application. They wrote myriad pamphlets and devotionals for congregants and textbooks for students preparing for ministry. They demonstrated little interest in the scholarly battles that mark the twentieth century. The arrival of Dunn's dissertation proves pivotal.

7. On responses to Dunn, see Atkinson, "Pentecostal Responses: Luke-Acts"; "Pentecostal Responses: Pauline Literature"; Mittelstadt, *Reading Luke-Acts*, 46–63.

8. Luke uses nine times the phrase "filled with the Holy Spirit" (Luke 1:15, 41, 67; Acts 2:4; 4:8, 31; 9:17; 13:9, 52) and three times the phrase "baptism in the Holy Spirit" (Luke 3:16; Acts 1:5; 11:16).

9. Stronstad, *Charismatic Theology*, 9.

10. See further Stronstad, "Unity and Diversity."

11. Stronstad incorporates material from his "Influence of the Old Testament." He finds continuity between the majority of verbs used by Luke and Greek translators of the Hebrew Scriptures to describe the charismatic activity of the Spirit (Stronstad, "Influence of the Old Testament," 44–45).

12. Stronstad, *Charismatic Theology*, 45, 52.

transfer becomes a paradigmatic experience for the eschatological people of God. According to Stronstad, these accounts also include various *signs*, that is, a Lukan motif that authenticates and guarantees readers that God's hand rests upon chosen leaders. Various phenomena, whether a voice from heaven, wind, fire, tongues, praise, and/or prophecy, provide visible and/or audible witness to Spirit enablement (Luke 3:22; Acts 2:1–4; 8:18; 10:45; 15:8; 19:6).

Stronstad emphasizes further that the Lukan Jesus not only functions as the consummate man of the Spirit, but also instructs the disciples with future promises of the Holy Spirit for the advancement of Jesus's mission following his ascension. Jesus's promise and encouragement concerning reliance upon the Holy Spirit during difficult times (Luke 11:13; 12:12; 21:14–15; Acts 1:4–5, 8) finds ongoing fulfillment through the authoritative witness of the Apostles, Stephen, and Paul. Stronstad stresses that Spirit enablement, available to all Christians, produces wisdom and faith as well as the ability to perform miracles; engage in persuasive and bold witness (Acts 2:41; 4:31); prophesy via invasive speeches of worship, witness, and judgment; and receive guidance through visions and dreams (Acts 6:3, 5; 11:24).

Stronstad's radical conclusions pave the way for future methodological advances. Early in *Charismatic Theology*, Stronstad builds upon hermeneutical developments that take shape in the seventies. Stronstad argues persuasively that a fresh critical approach liberates Luke from the primary role of historian and primer for the historical Paul; instead, Stronstad's Luke serves as a "theologian in his own right."[13] In so doing, Stronstad provides Pentecostals a credible foundation for their theology and experience. Academic circles could no longer ignore what Pentecostals believed and practised since the beginning of the twentieth century; Luke's historical analysis includes didactic *and* theological dimensions. Luke writes not only to narrate the events relating to Christianity's origin, but also to instruct Theophilus and subsequent readers. Luke produces a theological narrative designed to offer instruction on matters such as christology, soteriology, missiology, and, most importantly, for Pentecostals, pneumatology. Given the current triumph of literary criticism, these methodological advances may not appear monumental, but Stronstad's efforts placed him well ahead of the curve. The enduring influence of *Charismatic Theology* demonstrates the pioneering nature of his work.

Finally, the pastoral import of Stronstad's contribution becomes immediately apparent. Through his emphasis is upon divine enablement, Stronstad argues that Luke's understanding of Spirit-reception is devoid of Dunn's (and Bruner's) soteriological connotations.[14] Instead, the church described by Luke becomes a charismatic community, called and empowered for mission through the Spirit.[15] Given Luke's charismatic

---

13. Stronstad, *Charismatic Theology*, 7–9. Stronstad leans heavily on Marshall, *Gospel of Luke*; Hengel, *Acts*.

14. Stronstad, *Charismatic Theology*, 63–69.

15. Once again, Stronstad roots Luke's use of the vocation motif in the septuagintal tradition. See

theology, Stronstad calls upon Pentecostals to revisit the doctrine and experience of the Spirit: "Pentecostals and Charismatics must remember that the gift of the Spirit is not just a spiritual blessing; it is a responsibility. Its meaning extends beyond the prayer room and the worship service to a world which needs to hear a prophetic voice in concert with the demonstration of the power of the Spirit."[16]

## From Priesthood to Prophethood

In his *The Prophethood of All Believers*, Stronstad expands Luther's and the subsequent Protestant axiom "priesthood of all believers."[17] Along with a calling to serve as a kingdom of priests, believers receive the vocation to serve God as a nation of prophets. According to Stronstad, Luke's story of Jesus in his Gospel and the community Jesus inaugurates in Acts establish the theological, functional, and experiential "prophethood of all believers." Published in 1999, Stronstad builds on his earlier work. He positions the new community as a permanent, though only partially restored eschatological community of individual and collective prophets.

Stronstad roots his thesis in Moses's "earnest desire" that all God's people would be prophets (Num 11:29). Moses finds the Israelites difficult to lead and distributes his leadership among seventy Israelite elders. With this transfer of leadership, God also provides critical transfer of the Spirit. Following the prophecy of two elders, Moses responds by expressing his prayer that Israel be not only a kingdom of priests, but also, ideally, one of prophets.

Stronstad turns to the fulfillment of Moses's vision in Luke's birth narrative. Numerous prophetic oracles herald the arrival of John the Baptist and Jesus, the royal prophet. Between Jesus's reception of the Spirit at his baptism and Jesus's release of the Spirit on the day of Pentecost, everything Jesus says and does functions as the work and words of a Spirit-anointed, Spirit-filled, and Spirit-empowered prophet. At Pentecost, the Lukan Jesus transfers the Spirit to the disciples gathered in Jerusalem. Prophetic words by the resurrected Jesus (Luke 24:48; Acts 1:4–5, 8) signal Luke's desire to establish a new community of prophets who will proclaim Jesus to the ends of the earth. In fulfillment of Moses's earnest desire and Joel's prophecy that "your sons and your daughters shall prophesy" (Joel 2:28–29), a small community of prophets grows into a new and eschatological nation of prophets.

Stronstad argues that Acts charts the journeys of six charismatic prophets who typify and illustrate various components of the prophethood of all believers. Peter sets

---

Stronstad, *Charismatic Theology*, 23. For example, artisans and craftsman are filled with the Spirit to work on the Tabernacle (Exod 28:3; 31:3; 35:31), and during the Judges period, the Spirit enables various leaders with military prowess (Othniel [Judg 3:10]; Gideon [Judg 6:34]; Jephthah [Judg 11:29]; and Samson [Judg 14:6, 19; 15:14]).

16. Stronstad, *Charismatic Theology*, 83.
17. Stronstad, *Prophethood of All Believers*.

the standard for prophetic ministry and stands with Paul as Luke's co-heroes of the prophetic community in action. Peter not only experiences the Spirit of prophecy but also proclaims the Spirit's universal availability. He offers inspired witness not only in Jerusalem, but also Samaria and throughout Judea, particularly in the western communities of Lydda and Joppa. Like Peter, Paul is "filled with the Holy Spirit" (Acts 9:17; 13:9, 52) and identified as a prophet (Acts 13:1), who performs similar "signs and wonders" (Acts 14:3). According to Stronstad, Luke discusses charismatic prophets in pairs. Peter and Paul, the two charismatic apostles, minister in concert with two charismatic deacons, Stephen and Philip. Under the Spirit's direction, Stephen serves God's people by bringing unity to a divided community and then speaks with wisdom that confounds the gospel's opponents. Stephen's martyrdom places the deacon in good company; he dies in continuity with a long line of rejected prophets, most recently the rejected prophet Jesus. Like Stephen, Philip not only functions as a charismatic deacon, but also gives inspired witness in Samaria and Ethiopia. The third pair consists of Barnabas and Agabus. Luke begins with Barnabas, a leader among the "prophets and teachers" in the church of Antioch (Acts 13:1). Alongside Paul, Barnabas embarks on a successful evangelistic and teaching ministry. Finally, Agabus enters the story as an agent of social justice. Through the Spirit, Agabus predicts a great famine and inspires the Antioch disciples to launch a famine relief project.

In summary, Luke's story portrays God's people as an eschatological community upon whom Jesus liberally graces the Spirit of prophecy. Moses's desire (representative of numerous prophets, including Isaiah, Elijah, and Elisha) finds fulfillment in Jesus, the "prophet mighty in word and deed in the sight of God and of all the people" (Luke 24:19), and extends from Jesus to disciples (Acts 1:1). As in *Charismatic Theology*, Stronstad produces poignant contemporary application; he implores readers to embrace Luke's vision for the current day. On one hand, Stronstad laments the cessation of prophetic life and ministry in the church, and he longs for restoration of the prophethood of all believers. On the other hand, Stronstad celebrates the arrival of the Pentecostal and Charismatic movements as recovery of a prophetic heritage, but he does not refrain from criticizing fellow Pentecostals. Stronstad chastises any overzealous trivialization and commercialization of self-seeking experience, emotion, and private blessing that lessens the prophetic witness and service envisioned by Luke.[18]

## The Life in the Spirit New Testament Commentary: A Challenge to Canonical Chronology

Though Stronstad himself never embarks on a thoroughgoing commentary on Luke, Acts, or Luke-Acts, he and French Arrington (Church of God, Cleveland, TN) play

---

18. See Turner, "Does Luke Believe?" Though he finds general agreement with Stronstad's emphasis on the dynamic nature of the Spirit in Luke-Acts, Turner suggests Stronstad's "prophethood of all believers" extends beyond Luke's vision for prophetic life and ministry.

a critical role as editors of the one-volume *Life in the Spirit New Testament Commentary*.[19] In an unprecedented move, Stronstad and Arrington reorder canonical sequence and produce a commentary beginning with John and continuing with Matthew, Mark, Luke, Acts, and Romans.[20] In the preface they offer their reasoning: "(1) to link Luke and Acts together, so that they can be seen as a continuous unified account . . . (2) to retain Acts adjacent to the Pauline letters; and (3) to keep the Synoptic Gospels together."[21] Arrington reiterates numerous structural parallels and connections to Stronstad's earlier work: (1) the prefaces with dedication to Theophilus (Luke 1:1–4; Acts 1:1–5); (2) comparable fillings with the Spirit as ministry inauguration (Luke 3:21–22; Acts 2:1–4); (3) forty-day periods of preparation and ministry (Luke 4:2; Acts 1:3); (4) inaugural homilies (Luke 4:16–30; Acts 2:14–40); (5) various words and deeds provoking conflict, unbelief, and rejection (Luke 4:31–8:56; Acts 3:1–12:17); (6) evangelization of Gentiles (Luke 10:1–12; Acts 13:1–19:20); and (7) the extended journeys of Jesus and Paul (Luke 9:51–22:53; Acts 19:21–21:26).[22]

Though this commentary receives little attention from scholars, including Pentecostals, it warrants consideration for at least two reasons. Given Pentecostal interest in the continuity between the Spirit-led Jesus and the Spirit-empowered community, Stronstad and Arrington's vision paves the way for future scholars and publishers to consider thoroughgoing Luke-Acts commentaries.[23] On the other hand, though Pentecostals certainly reap the dividends of literary criticism, they must also engage in canonical analysis. In other words, how might Stronstad (and others) address the re-contextualized function of Luke and Acts via canonical separation? How might/should the insertion of John's Gospel between Luke and Acts impact Pentecostal interpretation? What might Pentecostals glean from the canonical order of the biblical text?

## Hermeneutical Debate

Since Stronstad prompts significant implications for hermeneuticians, I must offer final observations on this enduring mark.[24] First, in an early assessment of Pentecostals

---

19. Arrington and Stronstad, *Life in the Spirit*.

20. Arrington and Stronstad, *Life in the Spirit*, 375–693.

21. Stronstad and Arrington move John's Gospel to the front with the following comment: "As we meet these objectives, John has been moved to stand first. This location is appropriate since its prologue opens with the preexistence of Christ" (Arrington and Stronstad, *Life in the Spirit*, vii). Other early hints at interest in a Luke-Acts commentary come from Michaels, "Luke-Acts." The decision of the editors to combine the Third Gospel and Acts marks the beginning a two-volume literary approach. Around the same time, see the influential literary analyses by Tannehill, *Narrative Unity*; Talbert, *Reading Luke*; *Reading Acts*.

22. Arrington and Stronstad, *Life in the Spirit*, 385.

23. See Smith, *Canonical*; Robinson and Wall, *Called*.

24. Length restrictions require select representation. For a more thorough history of this debate,

and hermeneutics, Stronstad offers a historical overview of interpretative trends. He charts and evaluates four Pentecostal readings of Luke-Acts, namely, the "pragmatic" approach of Charles Parham and Carl Brumback, the "genre" approach of Gordon Fee, the "pneumatic" approach of Howard Ervin, and the "holistic" approach of William Menzies. Stronstad recognizes value in early Pentecostal pursuit of first-century experience and empowerment, Fee's emphasis upon the distinctive genre of Luke-Acts, Ervin's ability to bring experience into the interpretative process, and Menzies's combination of inductive, deductive, and verification levels.[25]

In subsequent essays, as Stronstad begins to assess specific components of these approaches, Fee emerges as Stronstad's primary target. Though Fee surely stands as the best-known Pentecostal representative to the Evangelical community, Stronstad accuses Fee of limiting the "normative or precedent value of historical narrative."[26] Stronstad demonstrates that, "for Luke, historical narrative can and does have a didactic purpose or instructional intentionality."[27] Luke introduces key theological themes and then re-establishes, illustrates, and reinforces those themes through further historical episodes.[28] As in *Charismatic Theology*, Stronstad argues that Luke models his narrative on the Old Testament historical narratives; both are "episodic and function, either individually or in combination, as exemplary, typological, programmatic and paradigmatic elements in the story."[29]

In still another essay, Stronstad addresses the convergence of "Pentecostal Experience and Hermeneutics" and concedes some of the inherent concern directed toward certain Pentecostals for uncritical and emotional flaunting of experience. For example, in response to Donald Carson's deprecation of Pentecostals as exegetes of their own experience, Stronstad suggests that Carson and certain Evangelical (particularly Cessationist) critics similarly exegete their non-experience.[30] Stronstad strives to balance the role of "charismatic experiential presuppositions" and "experiential verification" in the hermeneutical process. He implores fellow Pentecostals to employ

---

see Mittelstadt, *Reading Luke-Acts*.

25. Stronstad, "Trends in Pentecostal Hermeneutics."

26. Stronstad, "Hermeneutics of Lukan Historiography," 9. Fee develops his position in Fee and Stuart, *How to Read the Bible*, 94–112; Fee, "Baptism in the Holy Spirit." See Stronstad's further evaluation in Stronstad, "Pentecostal Hermeneutics."

27. Stronstad, *Spirit, Scripture and Theology*, 41. Stronstad cites F. F. Bruce: "History writing in antiquity had a didactic quality and aim" (Bruce, "First Church Historian," 13). David Aune adds, "Luke-Acts provided historical definition and identity as well as theological legitimation for the author's conception of *normative* Christianity" (Aune, *New Testament*, 137).

28. Stronstad, "Hermeneutics of Lukan Historiography," 16. See also Stronstad, "Biblical Precedent."

29. Stronstad, *Spirit, Scripture, and Theology*, 42.

30. Stronstad, "Pentecostal Experience." See the critique of Pentecostals in Carson, *Showing the Spirit*, 12.

complementary tension between grammatico-historical exegesis and contemporary experience.[31]

## Celebrating the Life and Scholarship of Roger Stronstad

Roger Stronstad stands as a Pentecostal scholar *par excellence*. He opens the door for Pentecostals to enter the larger academic world. Where Pentecostals speak openly about their experience and receive accusations of unjustifiable exegesis, Stronstad emerges as a much-needed bridge builder for Pentecostal theologians and practitioners.

For example, surveyors of Lukan scholarship in the previous generation give little recognition to emerging Pentecostal scholars. Gasque (1989) and Mark Alan Powell (1989; 1991) include Stronstad's *Charismatic Theology* as the lone Pentecostal contribution.[32] In his third and most recent survey of Luke-Acts scholarship (2006), however, Francois Bovon reflects on current trends and retreats on conclusions made in 1976:

> As a first conclusion to these pages on the Spirit I note that the number of books published marks the arrival of Pentecostal scholars in the field of New Testament scholarship. As a second conclusion, I regret that I have not investigated whether or not this wave of publication represents true scholarly progress. In my survey published in 1976, I suggested that the study of Lukan pneumatology had reached an end. Was I wrong?[33]

Bovon offers slow, but sure, recognition of a gradual awakening to Pentecostal scholarship, particularly with respect to contributions on the Holy Spirit's role in Luke-Acts. By 2006, Bovon recognizes not only of Stronstad's contributions, but also those of James Shelton and John Michael Penney (alongside dialogue partners James Dunn and Max Turner) under the category of Luke and the Holy Spirit and of Matthias Wenk under Luke and social justice. In terms of the larger academy, it is no overstatement to submit that the entry of Pentecostals to Lukan scholarship stands squarely on Stronstad's foundational career.

Many Pentecostal biblical scholars advance in their careers because of Roger Stronstad's prophetic career. Like Luke, Stronstad creates courage necessary to believe that scholarship is an essential form of witness. Contributors to this volume speak with me and celebrate a model scholar and disciple, who stands in the wake of Luke's revelatory literature and before a company of Pentecostal commentators.

---

31. Stronstad, "Pentecostalism."

32. Gasque, *History*; Powell, *What are They Saying About Luke?*; *What are They Saying About Acts?*

33. Bovon, *Luke the Theologian*, 540. In this and two earlier editions (1979, 1987), Bovon documents the proliferation of scholarship on Luke-Acts.

## Chapter 2

# Roger Stronstad as a Pentecostal Theologian

### DAVID WELLS

In the foreword to Roger Stronstad's *The Charismatic Theology of St. Luke*, Clark Pinnock wrote: "With the appearance of this book, we may be seeing the first motions of a wave of intellectually convincing Pentecostal theology which will sweep in upon us in the next decades."[1]

Pinnock was correct in his intuition. Many of us, as Pentecostal pastors, leaders, and academics, comprehend that in Pentecostal theology—and especially Pentecostal reading of Lukan theology—there stands before us a pre-Stronstad and a post-Stronstad era.

I do not say this lightly. Following the publication of *The Charismatic Theology of St. Luke* and Roger's subsequent works, such as *Spirit, Scripture, and Theology: A Pentecostal Perspective* and *The Prophethood of All Believers: A Study in Luke's Charismatic Theology*, the very essence of how Pentecostal theology and its distinctions were taught changed markedly. A total renewal of how the Spirit's narrative in Scripture is explained—especially in prophetic and Lukan literature—took place.

I was instructed in Pentecostal theology and pneumatology "pre-Stronstad." While academically and experientially embracing the Spirit's work for empowerment and witness, there was always a sense that there was more in the biblical narrative to be mined. This would enable a deeper presentation of the person and work of the Spirit for the young people I was leading or for the friends in the broader body of Christ with whom I was in a relationship. Through his writing and teaching, Roger led the way for persons like me to comprehend more fully and experience the Spirit-baptized, Spirit-empowered life evidenced in the prophets, taught and demonstrated by Jesus, and lived out by the apostles and those in the first church. As a result, I preach, teach, converse, and live differently.

---

1. Stronstad, *Charismatic Theology*, vii.

To comprehend why I would write in this almost hyperbolic way, one must understand the accountability that a Pentecostal leader in my role carries for the theological vitality of our churches, pastors and credential holders. Historically, the Pentecostal Assemblies of Canada (PAOC) holds a high view of Scripture with a commitment to relational discipleship, theological education, and proclamation of the Word. With all of this comes a conviction that an essential aspect of our future vitality depends upon recognizing that God's Word is alive and active in our individual lives, homes, and churches.

During the past two decades as I have served in district and national leadership, however, there has been a definite concern in our leadership circles that the Word of God has not been engaged in a living, active way in many lives or contexts within our family of churches. The evidence, anecdotal and at times confirmed scientifically,[2] has challenged us as leaders to take proactive steps.

As an overseer, I have always welcomed our theologians, teachers, and academics to be fully engaged as coparticipants in our efforts to fulfill our mission. One step was to identify the priority of theological vitality as one of three areas of focus and strategic action that would be emphasized in the PAOC's 2020 Initiative.[3]

This initiative identifies strategic responses that were expected of our network of churches and leaders, including corporate prayer, Scripture engagement, and equipping for Spirit-empowered living.

Consistent with these desired outcomes, the PAOC's General Executive reached a decision to ensure that theological engagement was consistently facilitated as one of our Fellowship's strategic priorities. Shortly after I became General Superintendent, a Theological Study Commission (TSC) was formed and began its work. Not surprisingly, Roger was one of those initially appointed to this commission. All other members of the commission had been informed and influenced by Roger through his writing and lectures and welcomed his participation during the initial stages of the TSC's work.

Though Roger has had to step back from the TSC, I am convinced we continue to need his ongoing, active influence. This is especially true regarding Scripture's authority, its interpretation, and the Spirit-empowered living and speech that will produce vital believers and churches who give witness of their Lord. I am grateful this influence continues through his ongoing scholarship, his books and articles, and the imprint he has left on many of us through his teaching, mentoring and relationship.

---

2. The PAOC and other evangelical organizations in Canada have widely studied and circulated the Canadian Bible Engagement Study (CBES), which addresses concerning trends related to Bible engagement and discipleship.

3. The PAOC's 2020 Initiative is an integrated strategy focused on the denomination's spiritual, theological and missional vitality. Members of the Theology Study Commission have actively led the PAOC's engagement with theology through regional and national conversations, the publishing of articles and books, and by facilitating the process authorized by the General Executive to "review and refresh" the PAOC's *Statement of Fundamental and Essential Truths*.

This Festschrift offers specific evidence of the ways that many lives have been imprinted with the undeniably unique Roger Stronstad stamp. Each writer goes into far greater depth in explaining the individual areas of theological impact that Dr. Stronstad has made. As the overseer of a Pentecostal Fellowship, I, and those with whom I serve, keenly desire that churches, families, and individuals experience theological vitality. Moreover, we feel responsible for our Pentecostal "flock." I conclude with some specific points of gratitude detailing how Roger Stronstad, as a Pentecostal theologian, has contributed to our meeting this awesome responsibility.

First, Roger embodies the passion that truth matters. His writings, conversations, and lectures, while solid theologically, were never focused simply on academics. Dr. Stronstad's passion—whether for students, our church fellowship, or the broader body of Christ—was that they would fully engage the great narrative of God's mission[4] with the proper interpretation of Scripture and be fully equipped by the Spirit's empowering presence and baptism.

To behold the purity of this passion firsthand was a beautiful sight and, on occasion, a fearful thing. I recall being with Roger in credential interviews for graduating students at Summit Pacific College. More than once, a student would wrestle to elucidate his pneumatological understanding of the person and work of the Spirit, and Spirit baptism—all this while in the presence of their teacher and mentor. I marveled as Dr. Stronstad would wisely come alongside that student conversationally and reengage the entire narrative of Lukan theology with them in five to seven minutes. His calming support ignited their clarity, and their understanding of the person and work of the Spirit was greatly strengthened. With that, another credential applicant was confident to move on to Pentecostal ministry within the PAOC!

In a different vein, I have personally received correspondence and phone calls from Roger when he felt that a district-sponsored conference speaker or ministry was compromising our students' understanding of Scripture and our shared ethics, both as a college and as a fellowship. While not enjoying the immediate dialogue, deep respect was forged between us, along with a shared passion that truth spoken in love matters.

Secondly, I am very grateful as a church overseer for the "post-Stronstad" era of pneumatological understandings rooted in Lukan theology. As one reviewer notes regarding *The Charismatic Theology of St. Luke*, "Stronstad offers a cogent and thought-provoking study of Luke as a charismatic theologian whose understanding of the Spirit [was] shaped wholly [by] his understanding of Jesus and the nature of the early church. Writing in the spirit of the finest of biblical scholarship, Stronstad challenges, indeed forces, traditional Protestants to reexamine and reconsider the impact of Pentecost."[5]

---

4. See Stronstad, *Pentecostal Biblical Theology*.
5. From the back cover of the first edition of Stronstad, *Charismatic Theology*.

My first appreciation, however, as the PAOC's General Superintendent is not that this and other writings have challenged and forced other Christian communities to reexamine and reconsider the impact of Pentecost, but that they have challenged and demanded response within our circles. We need the dynamic of the Spirit working in and through us every day. To settle for mere mental assent to a doctrinal statement that affirms classical Pentecostal understandings of pneumatology is putrid, unappealing and unconvincing. The trajectory of Lukan theology, as taught and illustrated in a defined progression by the prophets, Jesus and the first church, demands total buy-in by all of God's people for Jesus to be known and to be made known.

Beyond Pentecostal circles, I am actively engaged in interdenominational conversations, networks, and ecumenical dialogues, where I am continually grateful for the scholarly work done by Dr. Stronstad. With confidence, we may present the fact that the "Pentecostalization" of the global church does have solid theological moorings.

Finally, through Roger's writings and relational engagement with him, I have noted the distinct inclusivity of Pentecost. The Spirit's presence and gifts are for everyone. As a teacher, mentor and colleague, Roger has always demonstrated his openness to engage young and old, male and female, from whatever background or ethnicity. His desire has been to see the life of Christ formed in a person's life by the dynamic of the Word and the Spirit.

In his *The Prophethood of All Believers: A Study in Luke's Charismatic Theology*, Dr. Stronstad demonstrates that people of the Spirit are to be "prophetic communities" which bear witness of Jesus in every dimension that the mission of God entails. With empowered lives and speech, we show that, like Jesus, the Spirit of the Lord is on every one of us to bring about the redemptive, transformative work of the kingdom.

Those we are privileged to be in a relationship with and to influence must know they are welcomed into a prophetic community. This is not a community birthed in the esoteric, theoretical inclusivity of Western-based "progressive" values. It is a Spirit-birthed, Word-based community whose inclusivity is made possible by its Lord, who welcomes us by His reconciling work on the cross to experience new life together. As Luke's charismatic theology demonstrates, this community is not left to its own devices, but is empowered prophetically in word and action to take the gospel to all regardless of age, status, gender or ethnicity. This vision of the people of God is critical in the context in which I serve today, especially among those who are half my age or younger.

With deep affection, I have sought to reflect the respect and appreciation that we, as a Pentecostal Fellowship in Canada, have for our colleague and friend, Roger Stronstad. As a theologian, he has strengthened the church, as one gifted as a teacher should do. He has deepened, clarified, challenged and encouraged us to grow in our Lord's grace and knowledge. He has reinvigorated us regarding the person and work of the Spirit. As a colleague, he has been supportive and loyal, while at times "sharpening iron with iron." He has made us better. As a friend, he has been a brother who, along the way, has prayed for us and been willing to share his needs and for which he has requested prayer. His wife, Laurel, is a valued member of our Fellowship. What a gift from God for the PAOC to have Roger Stronstad as a theologian, teacher, colleague, and friend!

# Chapter 3

## Roger Stronstad as Theological Educator

### DAVE DEMCHUK

It is an honor to reflect on the career of a dear friend, mentor, and associate, Dr. Roger Stronstad on the occasion of his seventy-fifth birthday. My association with Roger began in the fall of 1978, which was Roger's first full-time year teaching at Summit Pacific College (then known as Western Pentecostal Bible College). That friendship continues to this day. Like many of Roger's former students who have now become his colleagues, our friendship with Roger, and, his role as a theological educator, can be seen in three distinct stages: as an instructor, a mentor, and finally, as a colleague.

My first introduction to Roger was as a second-year student at Bible college. I enrolled in the prescribed courses for a three-year diploma in English Bible. Among the offerings was a three-credit course on the book of Romans. It was taught by, at that time, a relatively unknown instructor, Roger Stronstad. He had previously taught an afternoon course on Hebrews as an adjunct instructor, but aside from that, none of us knew much about him.

As thirty of us assembled for our first class session on Monday morning at eight o'clock, Roger was already in the classroom awaiting our arrival. After a short introduction and review of the syllabus, Roger began with an introduction to Romans. His understanding of the pivotal role of this Pauline letter in the broader Christian history sold me on the study of the book. Once we moved into the exegesis of the text, I found both his logical presentation of the flow of Paul's argument and his exposition of the text to be very compelling.

The usual posture of students in what came to be known as a "Roger class" was head down, feverishly trying to capture the material that was being lectured, with a periodic "surface for air," and to capture the next major heading to be copied. For Romans, the class assignments included a 10–12-page exegesis paper on an 8–10 verse excerpt from the book, as well as a review of F. F. Bruce's new volume *Paul: Apostle of the Heart Set Free*. Bruce was somewhat of a favorite scholar for Roger—and through Roger's influence, he became so for many of his students as well. The exam for the course consisted of 2–3 questions, whose answers occupied the better part of 4–5 pages of foolscap. The course felt like "heavy-lifting" from an academic perspective, but it whetted my appetite for Biblical studies and set a foundation for what has been a lifetime of study within the Pauline letters of the New Testament.

During the course of the next two years, "Roger" courses were pretty standard fare for many of us students. In the Old and New Testament theology courses, he introduced us to the discipline of Biblical Theology—and the ground-breaking NT theology work of George Eldon Ladd. Roger integrated the works of contemporary evangelical scholarship effectively into his teaching, while giving pride of place to Pentecostal theological formulation. He taught Historical Literature (which came to be known by students as "Hysterical Lit"—perhaps indicative of the workload it entailed). As well, he taught Wisdom Literature, General Epistles and Eschatological Literature, rounding out the courses for those of us in our second and third years. Freshmen were introduced to Roger through the Gospels and Pentateuch. All in all, Roger taught a total of twenty-nine different courses at Summit, all linked to the main discipline of Biblical Theology (except his course on Contemporary Christian Literature)!

Along with his gifting as a teacher, Roger played a significant leadership role on our campus from the start. This was primarily through his influence as a shaper of college culture. In a formal world, where instructors were referred to as "brother" or "sister" or perhaps the revered "Doctor," Roger brought a breath of fresh air with his informality. He simply wanted to be called "Roger" and gently insisted that students call him by his first name. He and his wife Laurel served as our class faculty representatives and hosted periodic gatherings at their home on Saturday evenings, which included dinner and a Canadian tradition—Hockey Night in Canada. Some of us took the opportunity to check out Roger's personal library and gained a few suggestions as to how to build our own biblical studies libraries.

Roger regularly advocated for his students. He provided early opportunities for some of us to serve as teaching assistants—a role that sometimes even involved participating as a class lecturer. He encouraged many to pursue further studies, especially at his alma mater, Regent College, in Vancouver. Not a small number of his former students can recall the place and occasion where he affirmed our abilities and suggested that graduate studies would be a logical next step. And every now and again there was the gift of a book or two from the generous heart of our friend that has now become legendary. *Apostolic History and the Gospel*, the F. F. Bruce *festschrift*, remains a cherished gift for my graduation from Bible College in 1980 from Roger and Laurel.

The role of a theological educator extends far beyond the reach of the classroom, and long past the time of graduation. To appreciate fully Roger's contribution to theological education, it is helpful to understand him as an individual. As a mentor to many, Roger exemplified a lifestyle worthy of imitation.

Roger has always been an individual whose life was rounded out by many interests and hobbies. As an avid photographer, he amassed an enviable collection of vintage cameras. Spring and summer automobile shows were regularly scheduled events on his calendar. While his professional library was enviable, he had accumulated a fair number of first editions, many with the author's signatures in a wide range of disciplines. Roger's interest also extends to collecting books that pertain to British Columbia history, including a collection of First Nations' artwork.

Roger has been responsible for making his students aware of the rich contribution of contemporary Christian literature. Through his course, he introduced a couple of generations of students to authors like G. K. Chesterton, C. S. Lewis, Charles Williams, George MacDonald, Dorothy L. Sayers, and of course, J. R. R. Tolkien. He edited *The Canadian C. S. Lewis Journal* through the nineties, and in the Spring of 2000 traveled to Oxford to visit many of the haunts of Lewis and the "Inklings." His extensive library of these Christian authors has been donated by him and placed in the Hudson Library at Summit Pacific College.

Over the years, Roger has lived out his advice that students become life-long learners. He continues to study and read, keeping abreast of new developments—especially in the area of the study of Luke-Acts. Of course, the publication of *The Charismatic Theology of Luke-Acts* (1984) was something of a "game-changer" in its contribution to Pentecostal Theology. In 2009, George Wood, the General Superintendent of the Assemblies of God, noted at a meeting of the Society for Pentecostal Studies, that anyone who wanted to engage Luke-Acts from a Pentecostal perspective had to "go through the door of Roger Stronstad." Roger's contribution to the broader world of Pentecostal studies has continued since the publication of *The Charismatic Theology of St. Luke*, with several books and articles on issues of Biblical Theology and Pentecostal hermeneutics. Along with French Arrington, he edited *The Full-Life: Bible Commentary to the New Testament*—the first single-volume commentary on the New Testament written by Pentecostal scholars from a variety of traditions. Over his career, Roger contributed to world-wide Pentecostal education by serving in many guest lectureships. For four years, he served on the executive of the Society for Pentecostal Studies, serving as its President in 1994.

During this busy season, Roger still found ample time for his current and former students. His door was always open to dialogue, counsel and reflect. For those wishing to pursue a teaching career, there were often opportunities to test classroom giftings through adjunct assignments Roger delegated. I do recall his advice during a particularly difficult season in my ministry career. I found myself wondering how God would weave together the disparate pieces of my experiences and education. His reminder, delivered with the confident assurance of a seasoned preacher, was that God would use every experience and bit of education for his glory as you dedicate it to Him. This was timeless advice that I have seen come to bear in my own life, and something I continue to pass on to my students.

Roger has regularly reminded all of us of the significant role that his dear wife Laurel has played in his many achievements. This is transpired even though, throughout much of their married life, Laurel has suffered from a chronic, and sometimes debilitating illness. Roger has dedicated as much time to her care and companionship as to any of his other pursuits. Pentecostals have often been stereotyped as being overly triumphalistic in their understanding of how the Christian life was to unfold. For our broader community, Roger models Godly character and commitment in the face of their on-going seasons of suffering. He exemplifies the Pauline admonition to the husband to "Love their wives as Christ loved the Church."

In December of 2006, I assumed the role of President of Summit Pacific College. It has been during this latter season of our friendship that I have gained an even greater appreciation of the contribution Roger has made to Bible College education. Along with a stellar contribution in the classroom, Roger served as Summit's Academic Dean for twenty years. In 2015, he transitioned back to full-time teaching, continuing as the college's director of the Biblical Theology program (a position in fact he held since 1981). Under Roger's leadership, many of Summit's current program offerings were developed. As well, long-lasting ties with Trinity Western University were forged. This relationship has greatly benefited our graduates whose Bachelor of Arts in Religious Studies was strengthened by the courses taught by the university.

Roger's career at Summit spanned three presidents. Every new instructor (up to this day) has benefited through formal and informal coaching moments with him. As the unofficial keeper of the college "corporate memory," his assistance has been invaluable. This memory, combined with the fact that he established many of the procedures and processes that guide the details of the college, he has played a pivotal role in maintaining the college's accreditation status (not to mention keeping a rookie President on track!).

In 2011, Roger retired from full-time teaching to become Summit's first Scholar-in-Residence, a position he held until 2017. During this time, he continued with some adjunct teaching responsibilities, but focused more on his writing. The second edition of *The Charismatic Theology of St. Luke* was published (2012) and *A Pentecostal Biblical Theology: Turning Points in the Story of Redemption* followed in 2016. This latter work synthesized his years of teaching both Old and New Testament Theology at Summit. The second edition of *Spirit, Scripture, and Theology: A Pentecostal Perspective* was released in 2018, along with a commentary on the book of Mark. In this new role, Roger continued many of his recognizable routines, opening his office early in the morning, and welcoming team members with a cup of strongly brewed coffee, and attending to writing.

Students of intertextuality will undoubtedly recognize that the hymn writer's use of the phrase "Great things he hath taught us, great things he hath done" was penned in reference to our Lord. But with apologies to Fanny Crosby, many of us would feel it an appropriate phrase to summarize Roger's life's work as a theological educator. We thank God for him, pray God's strength in the days ahead, and honor him for a rich contribution to Pentecostal theological education.

# PART II

# Reading St. Luke's Text: Hermeneutical Considerations

"It is probable that the emerging consensus about Luke-Acts: . . . will put an end to the all-too-common artificial, arbitrary, and altogether false dichotomy which is made between history and theology in Luke-Acts; . . . will jettison the 'cannon within a cannon' approach to theology whereby Paul determines what is normative and also determines what Luke means, and . . . will accord to Luke-Acts the unity of genre and the complementary unity of authorial theological intent from Luke's first to his second accounts about the origin and spread of Christianity."

—ROGER STRONSTAD, "SOME ASPECTS OF HERMENEUTICS IN THE PENTECOSTAL TRADITION," IN *PENTECOSTALS IN THE TWENTY-FIRST CENTURY*, 40.

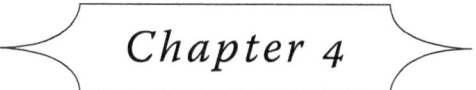

# Chapter 4

## The Role of Tongues in Luke-Acts
### *A Pentecostal Reading of St. Luke's Spirit-Narratives*

ROBERT MENZIES[1]

Pentecostals have a distinctive hermeneutic, a particular way of reading the Bible.[2] Pentecostals have always read the narrative of Acts, and particularly the account of the outpouring of the Holy Spirit, narrated in Acts 2, as a model for the church. The stories of Acts are our stories; we read them with a sense of expectation. I am convinced that this straightforward hermeneutical approach is one of the key reasons why an emphasis on speaking in tongues played such an important role in the formation of the modern Pentecostal movement. Certainly, the link between speaking in tongues and baptism in the Holy Spirit has marked the modern Pentecostal movement since its inception and without this linkage it is doubtful whether the movement would have seen the light of day, let alone survived.[3]

Glossolalia has been crucially important for Pentecostals for many reasons, but I would suggest that two are of particular importance.[4] First, speaking in tongues highlights and validates the unique way that Pentecostals read the book of Acts: Acts is not simply a historical document; rather, Acts presents a model for the life of the contemporary church. Thus, tongues serve as a sign that "their experience" is "our

---

1. I am delighted to contribute to this volume honoring my friend, Roger Stronstad. Roger's writings, insightful words, and friendship have been a tremendous encouragement to me. I remember with great fondness sharing a week of discussion and fellowship with Roger in Fiji just before I embarked on my PhD studies. Those conversations were a precious gift.

2. This essay is a modified version of a paper that I presented by request in Mandarin Chinese to a group of Assemblies of God ministers in Taiwan. Also, this essay draws material, without constant referencing, from "The Role of Tongues in Luke-Acts" (Menzies, *Pentecost*, 67–101). Published by permission.

3. Synan, "Role of Tongues," 67–82.

4. I could give other illustrations of a keen interest in and commitment to speaking in tongues and the "initial evidence" doctrine from the Philippines, Singapore, Malaysia, and China.

experience" and that all the gifts of the Spirit (including the "sign gifts") are valid for the church today. Secondly, tongues call the church to recognize and remember its true identity: the church is nothing less than a community of end-time prophets called and empowered to bear bold witness for Jesus. In short, the Pentecostal approach to tongues symbolizes significant aspects of the movement: (1) its unique hermeneutic, namely that Acts and the apostolic church represent a model for the church today, and (2) its distinctive pneumatological emphasis, namely the prophetic and missionary nature of the Pentecostal gift. For Pentecostals, then, tongues serve as a sign that the calling and power of the apostolic church are valid for contemporary believers.

In this essay I explore, from Luke's perspective, the role of tongues in the life of the church and the individual believer. I shall do this by analyzing two texts from Luke's Gospel that are often overlooked in this discussion: Luke 10:1 and 11:13. We shall begin our inquiry, however, by describing an important aspect of Luke's narrative. This, in turn, will enable us to place these two key passages in the larger context of Luke's two-volume work.

## Acts 2:4 and Luke's Narrative

Luke describes the initial coming of the Spirit on four occasions (Acts 2:4; 8:17; 10:46; 19:6). Many scholars include Paul's reception of the Spirit (Acts 9:17–19) in this list; thus they argue that Luke only refers to tongues in three out of five instances. They then conclude that 60 percent is good as a batting average in baseball, but not sufficient proof that Luke intended to establish a normative pattern. If we are to understand Luke's purposes, however, I believe that a deeper probing into Luke's narrative is required.

First, it should be noted that Luke nowhere actually describes the Spirit coming upon Paul. This is simply implied in the narrative (Acts 9:17–19). So, we only have four episodes that actually describe the initial reception of the Spirit in the book of Acts. Of the four instances in the book of Acts where Luke actually describes the initial coming of the Spirit, three explicitly cite glossolalia as the immediate result (Acts 2:4; 10:46; 19:6) and the other one (Acts 8:14–19) strongly implies it. Even the ineptest reader can hardly miss the point in Acts 8:14–19 that something striking and apparent took place when the Samaritans received the Spirit. In light of the larger context of Luke-Acts, the striking sign that encouraged the magician Simon to seek to purchase the ability to dispense the gift of the Spirit can only be glossolalia.

So, let us examine these three, central texts. What is immediately eye-catching is the consistent manner in which Luke describes the Spirit-inspired speech that accompanies the coming of the Spirit in these three passages. In each of these passages, Acts 2:4; 10:46; 19:6, Luke uses the words *laleō* and *glōssais* to refer to Spirit-inspired utterances. How should we understand these words? The usage of the phrase *laleō glōssais* in the New Testament is instructive.

In 1 Corinthians 12–14 Paul refers to the gift of tongues (*glōssais*)[5] and uses the phrase *laleō glōssais* to designate unintelligible utterances inspired by the Spirit.[6] The fact that this gift of tongues refers to unintelligible utterances (e.g., the glossolalia experienced in contemporary Pentecostal churches), rather than known human languages, is confirmed by the fact that Paul explicitly states that these tongues must be interpreted by one spiritually gifted if they are to be understood (1 Cor 14:6–19, 28; cf. 12:10, 30).

In Acts 10:46 and 19:6 Luke also uses the phrase *laleō glōssais* to designate utterances inspired by the Spirit. In Acts 10:46 Peter and his colleagues hear Cornelius and his household "speaking in tongues and praising God." Acts 19:6 states that the Ephesian disciples "spoke in tongues and prophesied." The literary parallels between the descriptions of speaking in tongues in these passages and 1 Corinthians 12–14 are impressive. All of these texts: (1) associate speaking in tongues with the inspiration of the Holy Spirit; (2) utilize similar vocabulary (*laleō glōssais*); and (3) describe inspired speech associated with worship and prophetic pronouncements. Additionally, since 1 Corinthians 12–14 clearly speaks of unintelligible utterances and there is no indication in either of the Acts passages that known languages are being spoken—indeed, there is no apparent need for a miracle of xenolalia in either instance (what foreign language would they have spoken?)—most English translations (including the NRSV) translate the occurrences of *laleō glōssais* in these texts with reference to speaking in tongues.

The references to *glōssais* in Acts 2:4, however, raise interesting questions for those seeking to understand this passage. In Acts 2:4 we read that those present were all filled with the Holy Spirit and began to "speak in other tongues [*lalein heterais glōssais*] as the Spirit enabled them." This phenomenon creates confusion among the Jews of the crowd who, we are told, represent "every nation under heaven" (Acts 2:5). The crowd gathered in astonishment because "each one heard them speaking in his own language" (*dialektō*; Acts 2:6). These details are repeated as Luke narrates the response of the astonished group: "Are not all these men who are speaking Galileans? Then how is it that each of us hears them in his own native language" (*dialektō*; Acts 2:7–8)? After the crowd lists in amazement the various nations represented by those present, they declare, "we hear them declaring the wonders of God in our own tongues" (*glōssais*; Acts 2:11)!

Since Acts 2:11 clearly relates *glōssais* to the various human languages of those present in the crowd, most scholars interpret the "tongues" (*glōssais*) of Acts 2:4 and 2:11 as referring to intelligible speech. The disciples are enabled by the Spirit to declare "the wonders of God" in human languages that they had not previously learned. This reading of the text has encouraged some translators, including those who produced

---

5. 1 Cor 12:10, 28; 13:8; 14:22, 26.
6. 1 Cor 12:30; 13:1; 14:2, 4, 6, 13, 18, 23, 27, 39.

the NRSV, to translate the *glōssais* of Acts 2:4 and 2:11 with the term "language" rather than "tongue."

While we can understand why translators are tempted to translate the same words in these passages differently—they actually refer to different activities (xenolalia in Acts 2:4 and glossolalia in Acts 10:46; 19:6)—this sort of translation creates a real problem. It obscures the fact that Luke uses the same Greek terms to describe what takes place when the Spirit is received in Acts 2:4; 10:46; 19:6. Why, we may ask, does Luke use the same language to describe each of these events even though they actually refer to different activities? This striking literary connection suggests that Luke has intentionally shaped his narrative to highlight this linkage. In other words, the pattern is important to him. Luke *desired* to make the connection: he *desired* to establish Acts 2 as a model.

The significance of the verbal connections between the *glōssais* (tongues) of these three passages becomes apparent when we examine Luke's understanding of the role of tongues in the life of the church. A close reading of Luke's narrative reveals that he views speaking in tongues as a special type of prophetic speech and, as such, an important sign. Speaking in tongues is associated with prophecy and presented as a significant sign in each of the three passages which describe this phenomenon in Acts. The stage is set, the model unveiled, in Acts 2.

In Acts 2:17–18 (cf. Acts 2:4) speaking in tongues is specifically described as a fulfillment of Joel's prophecy that in the last days all of God's people will prophesy. The strange sounds of the disciples' tongues-speech, Peter declares, are in fact not the ramblings of drunkards; rather, they represent prophetic utterances issued by God's end-time messengers (Acts 2:13, 15–17). The meaning of the symbolism of the speaking "in other tongues," which enables "the Jews from even nation under heaven" to hear the message in their "own language" (Acts 2:5–6), is clearly explained. It marks this group as members of Joel's end-time prophetic band and indicates that the "last days" and the salvation associated with it have arrived. Thus, Luke narrates Peter's powerful declaration concerning Jesus, "Exalted to the right hand of God . . . he [Jesus] has poured out *what you now see and hear*" (Acts 2:33). "Therefore," Peter declares, "let all Israel be assured of this: God has made this Jesus, whom you crucified, both Lord and Christ" (Acts 2:36). The logic of the narrative is transparent: Since the Spirit of prophecy is only given to the "servants" of God (Acts 2:18)—that is, the true people of God, the heirs of the promise God made to Israel (Joel 2:28–32)—and, since the disciples of Jesus are those who are now receiving this gift, it follows that Jesus is Lord (Acts 2:33) and that his disciples constitute the true people of God. In Acts 2 tongues speech, then, serves as a sign that both validates the disciples' claim that Jesus is Lord and confirms their status as members of Joel's end-time prophetic band.[7]

---

7. Schweizer concludes that the phrase, "and you will receive the gift of the Holy Spirit" (Acts 2:38), should be interpreted as a promise that the Spirit shall be "imparted to those who are already converted and baptized" (Schweizer, "πνεῦμα," *TDNT* 6:412). Note also the judgment offered by Brown:

The association with prophecy is made again in Acts 10:42–48. During Peter's sermon to Cornelius and his household, the Holy Spirit "came on all those who heard the message" (Acts 10:44). Peter's colleagues "were astonished that the gift of the Holy Spirit had been poured out even on the Gentiles, for they heard them speaking in tongues and praising God" (Acts 10:45–46). It is instructive to note that the Holy Spirit interrupts Peter just as he has declared, "He [Jesus] commanded us to preach to the people and to testify that he is the one whom God appointed as judge of the living and the dead. *All the prophets testify about him* that everyone who believes in him receives forgiveness of sins through his name" (Acts 10:42–43).

In view of Luke's emphasis on prophetic inspiration throughout his two-volume work and, more specifically, his description of speaking in tongues as prophetic speech in Acts 2:17–18, it can hardly be coincidental that the Holy Spirit breaks in and inspires glossolalia precisely at this point in Peter's sermon. Indeed, as the context makes clear, Peter's colleagues are astonished at what transpires because it testifies to the fact that God has accepted uncircumcised Gentiles. Again, the connection between speaking in tongues and prophecy is crucial for Luke's narrative. In Acts 2:17–18 we are informed that reception of the Spirit of prophecy (i.e., the Pentecostal gift) is the exclusive privilege of "the servants" of God and that it typically results in miraculous and audible speech.[8] Speaking in tongues is presented as one manifestation of this miraculous, Spirit-inspired speech (Acts 2:4, 17–18). So, when Cornelius and his household burst forth in tongues, this act provides demonstrative proof that they are in fact part of the end-time prophetic band of which Joel prophesied. They, too, are connected to the prophets who "testify" about Jesus (Acts 10:43). This astonishes Peter's colleagues, because they recognize the clear implications that flow from this dramatic event: since Cornelius and his household are prophets, they must also be "servants" of the Lord (that is, members of the people of God). How, then, can Peter and the others withhold baptism from them? (Acts 10:47–48).

The importance of this connection in the narrative is highlighted further in Acts 11:15–18. Here, as Peter recounts the events associated with the conversion of Cornelius and his household, he emphasizes that "the Holy Spirit came on them as he had come on us at the beginning" (Acts 11:15) and then declares, "God gave them the same gift as he gave us" (Acts 11:17). The fact that Jewish disciples at Pentecost and Gentile believers at Caesarea all spoke in tongues is not incidental to Luke's purposes;

---

"Surely it is preferable to interpret the passage in accordance with all the other texts which we have considered and to understand the words 'you shall receive' to point to an event subsequent to baptism" (Brown, "'Water-Baptism' and 'Spirit-Baptism,'" 14).

8. Of the eight instances where Luke describes or refers to the initial reception of the Spirit by a person or group, five specifically allude to some form of inspired speech as an immediate result (Luke 1:41, 67; Acts 2:4; 10:46; 19:6) and one implies the occurrence of such activity (Acts 8:15, 18). In the remaining two instances, although inspired speech is absent from Luke's account (Luke 3:22; Acts 9:17), it is a prominent feature in the pericopes that follow (Luke 4:14, 18–19; Acts 9:20).

rather, it represents a significant theme in his story of the movement of the gospel from Jews in Jerusalem to Gentiles in Rome and beyond.

Finally, in Acts 19:6 the connection between prophecy and speaking in tongues is again explicitly stated. When Paul laid hands on the Ephesian disciples, the Holy Spirit "came on them, and they spoke in tongues and prophesied." Here, again, tongues serve as a significant sign. Paul's prior question posed to the Ephesian "disciples," "Did you receive the Holy Spirit when you believed?" (Acts 19:2), implies another question, "How would we know?" Of course, the pattern and literary connections that Luke has created enable us to answer this question and anticipate the outcome that follows.

All of this demonstrates that Luke has carefully crafted his narrative to highlight the connections between Acts 2:4; 10:46; and 19:6. Luke creates this literary linkage by presenting, in each instance, "speaking in tongues" as the definitive and expected sign for reception of the Spirit of prophesy promised by Joel. This sign confirms that the disciples are the true people of God and also validates their proclamation that Jesus is Lord. I would add that this sort of apologetic suggests that Luke's readers routinely experienced this sign themselves. If "speaking in tongues" was relatively unknown to Luke's readers, this message—that tongues validated their proclamation and standing before God—would carry little encouragement. If they, too, experienced glossolalia, however, then the dialogue in Luke's narrative takes on fresh meaning. Peter's declaration that "They have received the Holy Spirit just as we have" (Acts 10:47) speaks directly to them and reminds them of the apostolic calling and power that is also theirs. Paul's question, "Did you receive the Holy Spirit when you believed?" encourages Luke's readers to reflect on their experiences of Spirit-inspired rapture and recognize that their own expressions of tongues-speech mark them as end-time prophets, people called and empowered to bear witness for Jesus.

These literary connections, which hinge on the phrase "to speak in tongues," challenge us to take a fresh look at two additional passages. Although these texts are vitally important for this discussion, they have been largely over-looked.

## Luke 10:1–16

Our first passage, the Sending of the Seventy (Luke 10:1–16), is a text unique to Luke's Gospel. While all three Synoptic Gospels record Jesus's words of instruction to the Twelve as he sends them out on their mission, only Luke records a second, larger sending of disciples (Luke 10:1–16). In Luke 10:1 we read, "After this the Lord appointed seventy-two [some MSS read, 'seventy'] others and sent them two by two ahead of him to every town and place where he was about to go." It should be noted that this number has symbolic significance. Jesus's selection of the Twelve was certainly not a coincidence. He did not choose twelve disciples simply because there were twelve men particularly suited for the task. The number twelve was full of symbolic meaning. It evoked the twelve sons of Jacob and thus symbolized the twelve tribes of

Israel (Gen 35:23–26). So, Jesus's selection of the Twelve was a declaration that he was reconstituting Israel, the people of God.

This suggests that the number seventy is also rooted in the OT narrative and has symbolic meaning. But what OT background and symbolic meaning should we attach to this event? Although a variety of proposals have been put forward, I am convinced that the background for this sending of the "seventy" is to be found in Numbers 11:24–30. This passage describes how the Lord "took of the Spirit that was on [Moses] and put the Spirit on the seventy elders" (Num 11:25). This resulted in the seventy elders, who had gathered around the Tent, prophesying for a short duration. Two other elders, Eldad and Medad, did not go to the Tent; rather, they remained in the camp and they continued to prophesy. When Joshua heard of this, he rushed to Moses and urged him to stop them. But Moses replied, "Are you jealous for my sake? I wish that all the Lord's people were prophets and that the Lord would put his Spirit on them!" (Num 11:29).

The Numbers 11 proposal has a number of significant advantages over other explanations: (1) it accounts for the two textual traditions underlying Luke 10:1 (How many actually prophesied in Numbers 11?); (2) it finds explicit fulfillment in the narrative of Acts; (3) it ties into one of the great themes of Luke-Acts, the work of the Holy Spirit; and (4) numerous allusions to Moses and his actions in Luke's travel narrative support our suggestion that the symbolism for Luke's reference to the Seventy should be found in Numbers 11.[9]

With this background in mind, the significance of the symbolism is found in the expansion of the number of disciples "sent out" into mission from the Twelve to the Seventy. The reference to the Seventy, then, evokes memories of Moses's wish that "all the Lord's people were prophets," and, in this way, points ahead to Pentecost (Acts 2), where this wish is initially fulfilled. Of course, this wish continues to be fulfilled throughout the narrative of Acts. This reference to the Seventy, then, foreshadows the outpouring of the Spirit on all the servants of the Lord and their universal participation in the mission of God (Acts 2:17–18; cf. 4:31).[10] According to Luke, every follower of Jesus is called and promised the requisite power to be a prophet.

It is important to note that the ecstatic speech of the elders in Numbers 11 constitutes the backdrop against which Luke interprets the Pentecostal and subsequent outpourings of the Spirit.[11] It would appear that Luke views every believer as (at least potentially) an end-time prophet, and that he anticipates that they, too, will issue forth

---

9. For more detailed support of this position, see Menzies, *Language of the Spirit*, 73–82.

10. Nickle says, "The 'Seventy' is the church in its entirety, including Luke's own community, announcing the in-breaking of God's royal rule throughout the length and breadth of God's creation" (Nickle, *Preaching*, 117).

11. Wenham describes the prophesying narrated in Numbers 11:24–30 as an instance of "unintelligible ecstatic utterance, what the New Testament terms speaking in tongues" (Wenham, *Numbers*, 109).

in Spirit-inspired ecstatic speech.[12] This is the clear implication of his narrative, which includes repetitive fulfillments of Moses's wish that reference glossolalia.

We have already noted that of the four instances in Acts where Luke actually describes the initial coming of the Spirit, three explicitly cite tongues speech as the immediate result and the other one strongly implies it. This is the case, even though Luke could have easily used other language, particularly in Acts 2, to describe what had transpired. The Acts 8 passage has various purposes. When it is viewed in the context of Luke's larger narrative, however, there can be little doubt in the reader's mind concerning the cause of Simon's ill-fated attempt to purchase the ability to dispense the Spirit. The motif is transparent; Luke's point is made: the Pentecostal gift, as a fulfillment of Moses's wish (Num 11:29) and Joel's prophecy (Joel 2:28–32), is a prophetic anointing that enables its recipient to bear bold witness for Jesus and, this being the case, *it is marked by the ecstatic speech characteristic of prophets*. Luke affirms that this ecstatic speech will include glossolalia.

This prophetic orientation explains why Luke considered tongues to be a sign of the reception of the Pentecostal gift. Certainly, as we have noted, Luke does present tongues as evidence of the Spirit's coming. On the day of Pentecost, Peter declares that the tongues of the disciples served as a sign. Their tongues not only established the fact that they, the disciples of Jesus, were the end-time prophets of which Joel prophesied; but also their tongues marked the arrival of the last days (Acts 2:17–21) and served to establish the fact that Jesus had risen from the dead and is Lord (Acts 2:33–36). In Acts 10:44–48, "speaking in tongues" is again "depicted as proof positive and sufficient to convince Peter's companions" that the Spirit had been poured out on the Gentiles.[13] Indeed, when Peter hears Cornelius and his household speak in tongues, he declares, "They have received the Holy Spirit just as we have" (Acts 10:47). In Acts 19:6 tongues and prophecy are cited as the immediate results of the coming of the Spirit, the incontrovertible evidence of an affirmative answer to Paul's question posed earlier in the narrative: "Did you receive the Holy Spirit when you believed?"

It is interesting to note that Luke does not share the angst of many modern Christians concerning the possibility of false tongues. Luke does not offer guidelines for discerning whether tongues are genuine or fake, from God or from some other source.[14] Rather, Luke assumes that the Christian community will know and experience that which is needed and good.

---

12. With the term, "ecstatic," I mean "pertaining to or flowing from an experience of intense joy." I do not wish to imply a loss of control with this term. While glossolalia transcends our reasoning faculties, the experience does not render them useless (cf. 1 Cor 14:28, 32–33).

13. Dunn, *Jesus and the Spirit*, 189.

14. Dunn, *Jesus and the Spirit*, 191, 195. This sort of lacuna led Dunn, over thirty years ago, to describe Luke's perspective as "lop-sided." Given the dramatic rise of the Pentecostal movement and the sad state of many traditional churches, one wonders if Dunn might now be more sympathetic to Luke's enthusiastic approach. Perhaps the church can regain its balance by listening more carefully to Luke.

At this point, some may say, "This all sounds reasonable and good, but is this really enough to support the claim that Luke expected every believer, when baptized in the Spirit, to speak in tongues?" I believe that our next text provides exactly what we need to answer this question with an unqualified "yes."

## Luke 11:9–13

Another text that reflects Luke's desire to encourage his church to experience the prophetic inspiration of the Spirit and all that entails (i.e., joyful praise, glossolalia, and bold witness) is found in Luke 11:13. This verse, which forms the climax to Jesus's teaching on prayer, again testifies to the fact that Luke views the work of the Holy Spirit described in Acts as relevant for the life of his church. Luke is not writing wistfully about an era of charismatic activity in the distant past.[15] Luke 11:13 reads, "If you then, though you are evil, know how to give good gifts to your children, how much more will your Father in heaven give the Holy Spirit to those who ask Him!" It is instructive to note that the parallel passage in Matthew's Gospel contains slightly different phrasing: "how much more will your Father in heaven give good gifts to those who ask Him!" (Matt 7:11). It is virtually certain that Luke has interpreted the "good gifts" in his source material with a reference to the "Holy Spirit."[16] Luke, then, provides us with a Spirit-inspired, authoritative commentary on this saying of Jesus. Three important implications follow:

First, Luke's alteration of the Matthean form of the saying anticipates the post-resurrection experience of the church.[17] This is evident from the fact that the promise that the Father will give the Holy Spirit to those who ask begins to be realized only at Pentecost. By contemporizing the text in this way, Luke stresses the relevance of the saying for the post-Pentecostal community to which he writes. It would seem that for Luke there is no neat line of separation dividing the apostolic church from his church or ours. Quite the contrary, Luke calls his readers to follow in their footsteps.

Second, the context indicates that the promise is made to disciples (Luke 11:1). Thus, Luke's contemporized version of the saying is clearly directed to the members of the Christian community.[18] Since it is addressed to Christians, the promise cannot refer to an initiatory or life-giving gift.[19] This judgment finds confirmation in the re-

---

15. Contra the judgment of Conzelmann, *Acts of the Apostles*, 15, 159–60.

16. Reasons for this conclusion include: (1) the fact that the reference to the Holy Spirit breaks the parallelism of the "good gifts" given by earthly fathers and "the good gifts" given by our heavenly Father; (2) Luke often inserts references to the Holy Spirit into his source material; (3) Matthew never omits or adds references to the Holy Spirit in his sources.

17. Fitzmyer, *Gospel According to Luke*, 916; Ellis, *Gospel of Luke*, 164; Stronstad, *Charismatic Theology*, 46.

18. The scholarly consensus affirms that Luke-Acts was addressed primarily to Christians.

19. Montague, *Holy Spirit*, 259–60.

petitive character of the exhortations to pray in Luke 11:9;[20] prayer for the Spirit (and, in light of the promise, we may presume this includes the reception of the Spirit) is to be an ongoing practice. The gift of the Holy Spirit, to which Luke refers, neither initiates one into the new age, nor is it to be received only once;[21] rather, this pneumatic gift is given to disciples and it is to be experienced on an ongoing basis.

Third, Luke's usage elsewhere indicates that he viewed the gift of the Holy Spirit in 11:13 as a prophetic enabling. On two occasions in Luke-Acts the Spirit is given to those praying;[22] in both the Spirit is portrayed as the source of prophetic activity. Luke's account of Jesus's baptism indicates that Jesus received the Spirit after his baptism while praying (Luke 3:21). This gift of the Spirit, portrayed principally as the source of prophetic power (Luke 4:18–19), equipped Jesus for his messianic task. Later, in Acts 4:31 the disciples, after having prayed, "were all filled with the Holy Spirit and spoke the word of God boldly." Again, the Spirit given in response to prayer is the impetus for prophetic activity.

What sort of prophetic activity did Luke anticipate would accompany this bestowal of the Spirit? Certainly, a reading of Luke's narrative would suggest a wide range of possibilities: joyful praise, glossolalia, visions, bold witness in the face of persecution, to name a few. Several aspects of Luke's narrative suggest, however, that glossolalia was one of the expected outcomes in Luke's mind and in the minds of his readers.

First, as we noted, Luke's narrative suggests that glossolalia typically accompanies the initial reception of the Spirit. Furthermore, Luke highlights the fact that glossolalia serves as an external sign of the prophetic gift. These elements of Luke's account would undoubtedly encourage readers in Luke's church, like they have with contemporary readers, to seek the prophetic gift, *complete with its accompanying external sign.*

Secondly, in view of the emphasis in this passage on asking (v. 9) and the Father's willingness to respond (v. 13), it would seem natural for Luke's readers to ask a question that again is often asked by contemporary Christians, how will we know when we have received this gift? Here we hear echoes of Paul's question in Acts 19:2. Of course, Luke has provided a clear answer. The arrival of prophetic power has a visible, external sign: glossolalia. This is not to say that there are not other ways in which the Spirit's power and presence are made known to us. This is simply to affirm that Luke's

---

20. Note the repetitive or continuous action implicit in the verbs in 11:9: *aiteite* (ask), *zēteite* (seek), *krouete* (knock).

21. Cf. Büchsel, *Der Geist Gottes im Neuen Testament*, 189–90. See also Montague, *Holy Spirit*, 259–60.

22. Acts 8:15, 17, represents the only instance in Luke-Acts (apart from the two texts discussed above) where reception of the Spirit is explicitly associated with prayer. Here, however, the Spirit is bestowed on the Samaritans in response to the prayer of Peter and John. While the situation in Acts 8:15, 17, is not a true parallel to Luke 11:13, in Acts 8:15, 17, the Spirit is also portrayed in prophetic terms. Prayer is implicitly associated with the reception of the Spirit at Pentecost (Acts 1:14; 2:4). Here also the gift of the Spirit is presented as a prophetic endowment. So also Acts 9:17, though here the actual reception of the Spirit is not described.

narrative indicates that a visible, external sign does exist and that he and his readers would naturally expect to manifest this sign.

I would add that this sign must have been tremendously encouraging for Luke's church as it is for countless contemporary Christians. It signified their connection with the apostolic church and confirmed their identity as end-time prophets. I find it interesting that so many believers from traditional churches today react negatively to the notion of glossolalia as a visible sign. They often ask, should we really emphasize a visible sign like tongues? Yet these same Christians participate in a liturgical form of worship that is filled with sacraments and imagery, a form of worship that emphasizes visible signs. Signs are valuable when they point to something significant. Luke and his church clearly understood this.

Finally, the question should be asked, why would Luke need to encourage his readers not to be afraid of receiving a bad or harmful gift (note the snake and scorpion of vv. 11–12)?[23] Why would he need to encourage his church to pursue this gift of the Spirit? If the gift is quiet, internal, and ethereal, why would there be any concern? If the gift includes glossolalia, however, which is noisy, unintelligible, and has many pagan counterparts,[24] then the concerns make sense.[25] Luke's response is designed to quell any fears. The Father gives good gifts. We need not fret or fear.

In short, through his skillful editing of this saying of Jesus (Luke 11:13), Luke encourages post-Pentecostal disciples to pray for a prophetic anointing, an experience of spiritual rapture that will produce power and praise in their lives, an experience like those modeled by Jesus (Luke 3:21–22; 10:21) and the early church (Acts 2:4; 10:46; 19:6). The reader would naturally expect glossolalia to be a normal, frequent, and expected part of this experience. The fact that Luke viewed glossolalia as a significant component of this bestowal of the Spirit is suggested by the larger context of Luke-Acts, which portrays tongues as an external sign of the Spirit's coming, and also by the more immediate context, which indicates Luke's encouragement to pray for the Holy Spirit is a response to the fears of some within his community. This text, then, indicates that Luke viewed tongues as positive and available to every disciple of Jesus.

---

23. It is perhaps significant that Luke's comparisons feature dangerous objects ("snake" and "scorpion" [Luke 11:11–12]), whereas Matthew's comparisons include one that is simply useless ("stone" and "snake" [Matthew 7:9–10]). This might suggest that Luke was consciously seeking to help his readers overcome their fear.

24. For Jewish and pagan examples of ecstasy and inspired utterances see Dunn, *Jesus and the Spirit*, 304–5.

25. Note that the Beelzebub controversy immediately follows (Luke 11:14–28). Some accused Jesus of being demon-possessed (Luke 11:15). The early Christians were undoubtedly confronted with similar charges. It is thus not surprising that Luke "takes pains to show [that] Christianity [is] both different from and superior to magic" (Vinson, *Luke*, 380; cf. Acts 8:9–24; 16:16–18; 19:11–20).

## Conclusion

I have argued that, according to Luke, tongues played a significant role in the life of the apostolic church. Furthermore, Luke expected that tongues would continue to play a positive role in his church and ours, both of which are located in "these last days." In Luke's view, every believer can manifest this spiritual gift. So, Luke encourages every believer to pray for prophetic anointings (Luke 11:13), experiences of Spirit-inspired exultation from which power and praise flow; and experiences similar to those modeled by Jesus (Luke 3:21–22; 10:21) and the early church (Acts 2:4; 10:46; 19:6). Luke believed that these experiences would typically include glossolalia, which he considered a special form of prophetic speech and a sign that the Pentecostal gift had been received.

These conclusions are based on a number of interrelated arguments that might be summarized as follows:

1. Luke's narrative reveals that he views speaking in tongues as a special type of prophetic speech.

2. Luke indicates that glossolalia, as a special type of prophetic speech, has an ongoing role to play in the life of the church.

3. Glossolalia was well known and widely practiced in the churches for which Luke writes.

4. Luke views the Pentecostal outpouring of the Spirit as a fulfillment of Moses's wish (Num 11:29) and Joel's prophecy (Joel 2:28–32). Thus, it is a prophetic anointing that is marked by the ecstatic speech characteristic of prophets (i.e., glossolalia).

5. According to Luke, the gift of tongues is available to every disciple of Jesus; thus, Luke encourages believers to pray for a prophetic anointing, which he envisions will include glossolalia.

These conclusions suggest that Luke presents a challenge to the contemporary church—a church that has all too often lost sight of its apostolic calling and charismatic roots. Glossolalia, in a unique way, symbolizes this challenge. It reminds us of our calling and our need of divine enabling. This was true of Luke's church and it is equally true of ours. Put another way, tongues remind us of our true identity; we are to be a community of prophets, called and empowered to bear bold witness for Jesus and to declare his mighty deeds.

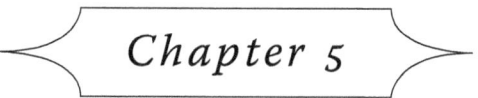

# Chapter 5

## Pentecostals and Luke-Acts
*Reading St. Luke in the Pre- and Post-Stronstad Eras*

VAN JOHNSON[1]

Roger Stronstad loves patterns. When I arrived at Western Pentecostal Bible College in January of 1994 as a new faculty member, Roger's warm welcome was extended to including me in his carpool. One morning stands out: as we turned into the lower parking lot, the driver groaned and stopped the vehicle. Roger was frozen at the wheel. "*Now* where I am going to park?" He was staring at a row of empty parking spots save for one, but the car was in Roger's spot. Every day Roger ate a cheese sandwich for lunch. Without fail he took his daily breaks with the rest of the staff at 10 a.m. and 3 p.m. One weekend I called his house at 10 a.m., and he was on a coffee break. Roger connected productivity with good habits and considering his prodigious productivity as an administrator, teacher, and writer; patterns fit him.

Is it any wonder, then, that Roger would spot the patterns in Luke-Acts and write the book that would influence scholarship in so many directions? He found a kindred spirit in the author of Luke-Acts, who employed patterns to great effect. The book he told me that primed his mind was *Literary Patterns, Theological Themes, and the Genre of Luke-Acts* (1974) by Charles Talbert. An exploration of the NT as literature was in its early stages, and Roger was one of the first to take the literary nature of Luke-Acts seriously. In so doing, he identified a trajectory from the prophetic tradition about the Holy Spirit in the OT that carried through Luke and Acts, shaping their form and content. The church becomes a charismatic community of prophets who continue the work of Jesus. To his credit, he showed how an interpretation of Acts was so much broader than the exegesis of the Spirit Baptism passages.

---

1. I am deeply grateful for professor Roger Stronstad's contribution to my life and scholarship. Roger, I wish you all the best at your 75th birthday.

## Introduction: What Text?

From its beginning, the Pentecostal movement has grounded its self-identity in the book of Acts, with Acts 2 as the starting point. There it found both the explanation for its shared experience of Spirit Baptism as empowerment for witness, and her identity as a last days revival movement. Speaking in tongues was a sign that the community had been equipped to proclaim the gospel before the soon return of Jesus.

Other Christian spiritual traditions prioritize certain biblical texts as essential to their ethos: Romans and Galatians for the Reformed; the Sermon on the Mount for the Anabaptists. Pentecostals need not apologize for having a preferential text. With the recent trend in biblical studies to consider Luke and Acts as a whole, however, it now seems odd that their spiritual formation was centered on the latter without regard for the former. If both volumes comprise Luke's grand narrative of the coming reign of the kingdom of God, Pentecostals have only been avid readers of the "latter reign."[2] While showing great interest in the gospels generally, they have demonstrated no more interest in Luke's gospel than any of the others.[3] The canonical layout is one reason for this.

The separation of Luke and Acts with the gospel of John rammed in-between disguises their literary and theological unity. I do wonder how much theological damage the canonical order has caused the historic church.[4] If the order had preserved the unity of Luke's writings, would the church have been better positioned to see herself as continuing the charismatic mission of Jesus and the apostles, which Paul described in a very Lukan way in Rom 15:19 as: "by the power of signs and miracles, through the power of the Spirit"?[5]

Apropos to a consideration of Luke's writings, this essay will have two parts, but in this instance, I will take up the two parts in reverse order. Before addressing certain areas of Pentecostal theology that are informed by Stronstad's work, I want to argue that the early Pentecostals read Acts well exegetically and responded to its message appropriately—even pre-Stronstad.

## Pentecostals and Acts: Pre-Stronstad

The earliest Pentecostals absorbed the Acts narrative as a whole and attempted to live out its story in ways generated by it, even though they preceded the emergence of narrative criticism and other literary methodologies by more than half a century. If Acts

---

2. From my commutes with Roger, I know he loves a play on words. This one is for him.

3. Other than frequent references to Luke 24:49, where Jesus reminds his disciples that they will be clothed with power, the early Canadian Pentecostal newsletters show no particular concern to cite Lukan passages when gospel references are cited.

4. Johnson calls the consequences "momentous," devoting the opening pages of *Prophetic Jesus, Prophetic Church* to its ramifications. See Johnson, *Prophetic Jesus, Prophetic Church*, 1–4.

5. All Scripture references are from the NIV (1984).

were a jazz standard, the Pentecostals played the traditional melody, but improvised with riffs appropriate to their space and time. It is safe to say, in general, that the evangelical community is not an appreciative audience for the Pentecostal rendition: Pentecostals do not respect the historical distance between the world of the text and their own (and certainly Pentecostals perceived no distance), and so their sight-reading of the melody of Acts is impaired. This view, however, that the only appropriate way to read the biblical text is with the historical-critical method is becoming increasingly rare in scholarly circles: shifts in emphases in biblical studies over the last half-century invite a positive re-evaluation of a traditional Pentecostal reading.

To discuss the factors that informed an early Pentecostal reading of Acts, we begin with the nature of the text itself (both the world depicted in the narrative and the social world behind it) and then consider what theological and social backgrounds Pentecostals brought to it. The apocalyptic worldview of Acts is our entry point. What we find in the NT is a Christianized version of the eschatological worldview found in Jewish Apocalyptic Literature of Second Temple Judaism.[6] Such a worldview encompasses an outlook, not only about this world, but also a transcendent one above and beyond it that shapes belief and behavior in here and now.

The belief system of Jewish apocalyptic writings is shaped by a reconfiguration of space and time, in which time and space undergo a quantitative reduction. This counter-intuitive perspective derives from revelation. The epistemological premise of the apocalyptic worldview (which is indicated by the term "apocalypse," or "revelation") is that the true nature of reality is revealed by God through means that bypass human reason. The distance between God's ways that are higher than ours is reduced as He vouchsafes His purposes for humankind and all creation through prophetic utterances, dreams and visions. Heaven is open for those who have an eye to see and an ear to hear.[7]

Whereas in Jewish apocalyptic writings angels were the intermediaries between God and humanity in disclosing heavenly wisdom, their role in that regard is overshadowed in the NT by the revelatory work of the Holy Spirit—a pneumatic epistemology. Angels and demons, nevertheless, remain active players in a world with no barrier between heaven and earth. Heavenly beings, both benevolent and malevolent, influence life in every part of God's creation.

The temporal dimension of apocalyptic hope, i.e., the brevity of time before the end of the world and the judgment, was an essential element for the Jewish writers of the historical apocalypses.[8] As time is reduced, so is the significance of earthly space:

---

6. For background on Jewish apocalyptic, see Collins, *Apocalyptic Imagination*.

7. I credit the idea of an open heaven to Rowland's book on Jewish and Christian apocalyptic—Rowland, *Open Heaven*.

8. Historical apocalypses track world/cosmic history (e.g., Daniel; 4 Ezra; 2 Bar).

the locus for promise-fulfillment is shifted to another world. Calls for repentance and perseverance pervade the literature.[9]

In NT apocalyptic, with the death and resurrection of the Messiah, the hope was for his imminent return. Paul would not have been alone in reckoning that he would still be alive when that happened (1Thess 4:15). If no generation expected the soon return of Jesus more fervently than the first Christians, then first generation Pentecostals came a close second. Since the activity of the Spirit signaled the final days of history in the Acts narrative, then the reappearance of the charismata signaled the last of the last days for Pentecostals. For both groups, the shortness of time was fundamental for their beliefs and behaviors. In the NT writings and in early Pentecostal newsletters, the exhortations were for repentance, perseverance, and urgent witness.

The latter's rugged adherence to such expectation was inscribed in the fourth element of the Fourfold Gospel: Christ as Coming King. Donald Dayton's *Theological Roots of Pentecostalism* established the wide-ranging influence of the Fourfold Gospel on early Pentecostalism, and I would like to consider how this theological framework informed their reading of Acts.

The effects of their belief in Christ as (soon) Coming King were many. It readied them to accept Jesus's call to be last-day witnesses, it confirmed that the reappearance of healing (Christ as healer) and the other gifts of the Spirit were signs of the end, and true to the nature of apocalyptic eschatology where a reduction of time is combined with a devaluation of space, it focused their hope and energies on the world to come. While witnessing to save souls was paramount, they did not disregard the human condition around them because they were the poor, too. The reputation they have gained over the years as unconcerned about social issues is valid historically, only if one is looking for organized social action, which demands what they did not have: appropriate social positioning that would provide access to the levers of power.

They improvised the Fourfold Gospel by re-arranging Christ as Sanctifier to Christ as Baptizer to align themselves more closely with the theme of Acts, but they retained the chorus line that salvation precedes the experience of Pentecost. It was the emphasis in some sectors of the Holiness movement on baptism in the Holy Spirit as power for service and witness that captured the imagination of early Pentecostals, and their belief, that time was short, set their imagination on fire.

A. B. Simpson's influence on Pentecostals exceeded his advocacy of the Fourfold Gospel. His teaching that the promised "latter rain" was beginning to fall among Holiness people gave them a label. When the Pentecostals adopted "latter rain" for themselves, it was an announcement that their ancestry was the apostolic community and a declaration that they had superseded the Holiness people before them.

---

9. This is distinct from OT hope that expects God to keep his promises within history to a nation on a piece of sacred land, what Hanson has called "prophetic eschatology" as opposed to "apocalyptic eschatology." See Hanson, *Dawn of Apocalyptic*.

The worldview of Acts is that of apocalyptic eschatology, and the world behind the text is an oral culture. As opposed to a literate culture, an oral one preferences what is spoken rather than what is written, and values who is doing the communicating as much, if not more than, what is being spoken.[10] Wisdom resides in people of experience, whose gift to the community is not just knowing the stories, parables, or proverbs of the group, but knowing what story to tell in any given situation.[11] Due to widespread illiteracy, the biblical texts were engaged by the first Christians as they gathered together to hear them read. When Pentecostals gathered to hear sermons, and many of them were based on narrative passages, their orality predisposed them to learn from and apply to themselves the parables of Jesus and the experiences of those who encountered him. This disposition was also part of their heritage in the holiness tradition, where experience played a role in religious life.

In a literate culture, reason and logic determine truth; the merits of an argument are weighed, rather than the character of the person making it. Naturally, then, the Reformed tradition favors the systematic teaching of Paul's letters over the historical/theological events in Acts (and perhaps, the Gospels in general). From Paul, propositional statements of truth can be collated, and theological systems erected. No wonder, then, that more literate Christian traditions often have an ambivalent theological relationship with Acts. Their suspicion of NT narrative is cultural as well as theological.[12] Although this view may be losing ground in evangelical schools, too often Acts is still sectioned off from other portions of the NT as historical, rendering it inspirational, but of limited value for the formulation of doctrine or the construction of church life. At work is the hermeneutical principle of *sola* didactic: belief and practice are to be derived from didactic texts alone. Pentecostals, oblivious to this distinction, did not view Acts as a museum exhibit; they thought they were part of the exhibit.

There is too little space to say much here about the social dynamics of the world behind the text of Luke-Acts and how these dynamics continue to resonate among the global Pentecostal community, except to note them: the dyadic, non-individualistic, orientation of relationships, where value and meaning are oriented around the other rather than the self; the importance of the extended family (instead of the modern variant of the nuclear one); the precariousness of everyday life for the majority that is associated with subsistence living.[13] Compare this with David Barrett's composite sketch of the global Pentecostal:

> More urban than rural, more female than male, more children (under 18 years) than adults, more third-world (66 percent) than western world (32 percent),

---

10. The contrast between an oral culture and a literate one is not between illiterate and literate, although in the first century illiteracy was widespread, and would be until the modern period.

11. Sample, *Ministry in an Oral Culture*.

12. It is telling that such a distinction does not apply to OT narratives.

13. The book to read is Neyrey, *Social World of Luke-Acts*.

more living in poverty (87 percent) than affluence (13 percent), more family-related than individualist.[14]

These affinities with the early church community are significant for their reading of Acts, and Luke for that matter.

On account of their theological and social make-up, it is germane to inquire whether Pentecostals are better positioned to interpret Acts than other groups whose orientation is more literate than oral, or, more modern than pre-modern. The issue is not which perspective is objective instead of subjective, but which subjectivity is more appropriate to reading and responding to the intent of the text. Pentecostals have long been accused of engaging in the illicit hermeneutical method of *eisegesis*, that is, a reading that imposes meaning from outside the text. Such a charge ignores the cultural preferences behind the accusation, and it runs counter to newer perspectives in biblical studies that incorporate the reader into the interpretive event. Without denying the importance of authorial intent and the historical-critical quest to discover it, the intent of the Spirit who forms and aids communities of faith in interpretation should not be disregarded.

Reader response theory, although rightly criticized for its insistence that texts have no meaning other than the meaning the reader brings to it, prompted a reconsideration in biblical studies of the hermeneutical maxim that the meaning of a text resides solely in authorial intent. While there is certainly no consensus among biblical scholars on this, it has become more acceptable to factor into the hermeneutical process the inevitability that every community brings a perspective to the text. The world of the reader interacts with the world of the text.

In this regard, it is worth noting how the texts themselves invite interaction, which raises the issue of audience response as part of the reading process. Of note is the field of socio-rhetorical analysis pioneered by Vernon K. Robbins. His socio-rhetorical approach examines the way that texts, even narrative ones, have textures that facilitate their persuasive purposes. So what was the purpose toward which Luke used his persuasive methods of communication?

If it is granted that the issue of the delay of the *parousia* was a motivating factor for the author, and one doesn't have to follow all of the permutations of Hans Conzelmann's arguments about how Luke responds to the delay to recognize the tension of unrealized eschatological hope underlying the Lukan compositions.[15] Luke is almost certainly writing about beginnings, not for historical interest, but to encourage the furtherance of the mission before Christ's return. If Luke is writing to shift the focus from why he has not returned to what should be done in the meantime (and I think this is almost certain, too), then the Lukan texts are a prophetic call for more witnesses to arise.

14. Cited in Land, *Pentecostal Spirituality*, 10.
15. Conzelmann, *Theology of St. Luke*.

J. Darr argues that the effect intended by the author is to make its readers into *the ideal witnesses* of what is recorded in Luke-Acts:

> Its rhetorical strategies are largely designed to persuade readers to be certain kinds of hearers (attentive, receptive, discerning, committed, tenacious) and retellers (accurate, bold, effective, persistent) of "the things that have been fulfilled among us" (Luke 1:1).[16]

While no sensible Pentecostal would adopt the word "ideal" as an appropriate self-description, the list of adjectives in parentheses seems an apt description of Pentecostalism's characteristic responses to the Acts narrative. While we may fault Pentecostals for errors in judgment in interpreting Acts, they have done so by entering into the narrative and its apocalyptic worldview. As Robert Fulford, a noted Canadian journalist and media critic, stated in one of his Massey Lectures on *The Triumph of Narrative*:

> A master narrative that we find convincing and persuasive differs from other stories in an important way: it swallows us. It is not a play we can see performed, or a painting we can view, or a city we can visit. A master narrative is a dwelling place. We are intended to live in it.[17]

## Pentecostals and Luke-Acts: Post-Stronstad

In 1970 James Dunn's *Baptism in the Holy Spirit* was published, which was a response to the Pentecostal interpretation of Baptism in the Holy Spirit as a charismatic event. The work was a recasting of a standard position of the church that the coming of the Spirit in Acts 2 was salvific, which he described with a phrase that has circulated widely: "conversion-initiation." According to Dunn, the Spirit's work is salvific in Acts as it is in the Pauline letters. It was this work that called out directly Pentecostal scholarship; note the subtitle: "A Re-examination of the New Testament Teaching on the Gift of the Spirit in Relation to Pentecostalism Today." One of the respondents was Stronstad (and special mention should be made here of Robert Menzies),[18] who argued that the Acts' references to Spirit baptism and filling must be interpreted in light of the Spirit-empowerment of Jesus in Luke and the charismatic traditions associated with the OT prophets. The Spirit's work in Luke-Acts is vocational rather than salvific.

In what follows, I would like to explore the implications for Pentecostal theology of Stronstad's writing and the recognition that Luke and Acts are two parts of one narrative.

---

16. Darr, "Watch How You Listen," 87.
17. Fulford, *Triumph of Narrative*, 32.
18. Menzies, *Development of Early Christian Pneumatology*.

PART II—READING ST. LUKE'S TEXT: HERMENEUTICAL CONSIDERATIONS

## The Nature of Spirit Baptism—How Many Evidences Do We Need?

To defend their insistence that tongues were *the* indicator of Spirit Baptism, Pentecostals used Acts 2 as the template for subsequent references to the experience (Acts 8–10, 19). Whether stated explicitly or not, tongues were assumed to be present in all instances of Spirit Baptism in Acts because it was present at Pentecost. The plausibility of this hermeneutic is increased when the pattern approach of the author of Luke-Acts is considered.

As Luke Timothy Johnson has noted about the style of Luke-Acts, it is the placement of a term or idea that is just as important as what is said.[19] For example, the audience is told early on that Jesus speaks and performs miracles in the power of the Spirit (Luke 4:14, 18–19, 36; 5:17), but the writer doesn't remind the audience of the Spirit's presence every time a miracle occurs. This is just good story-telling. The scriptwriters of superhero movies do not bore the audience by reminding them of the source of the hero's power every time something "super-heroic" happens. Similarly, the first description of Spirit Baptism at Pentecost in Acts 2 is the fullest account of Spirit Baptism. In later Spirit Baptism scenes, the details are fewer because the writer has already set the expectation as to the nature of the event described.

In that light, it is significant that Luke mentions tongues as much as he does in subsequent passages; the audience has already been told that speaking in tongues accompanies the experience in the account of Pentecost (Acts 2). The repetition conveys emphasis. It would be the same mistake, then, to search for theological significance in the number of times that the author specifies that the Spirit is involved in the miracles of Jesus, as it would be to tally how often tongues is mentioned in connection with Spirit Baptism. Repetitions are for emphases not statistics.

The descriptive terminology that early Pentecostals used to define the role of tongues would vary early on—starting with "Bible evidence,"[20] and then later "initial evidence," or "initial physical sign/evidence"—but the unique and privileged role of tongues in Spirit Baptism did not. That the original phrasing was "Bible evidence" testifies to their attempt to remain true to the Scriptures. Once the adjective "initial" was placed in front of "evidence," the existence of other signs or evidences was officially recognized. In my opinion, this 'many evidences' concept was an unfortunate choice because it left the function of the multiple evidences undefined; it made no clear distinction between what indicates reception and the phenomena associated with the gift itself.

My denomination, the Pentecostal Assemblies of Canada (PAOC), has commissioned its Theological Study Commission to refresh its *Statement of Fundamental and Essential Truths*. Stronstad's work has influenced our committee in two ways. He insists that there is something unique about the first experience of tongue-speech in

---

19. Johnson, *Prophetic Jesus*, 20.
20. This goes back to Charles Parham. See Jacobsen, *Thinking in the Spirit*, 48.

that it confirms in a public manner the call of God to perform a divine task (and here he draws on similarities between the anointing of Jesus and the baptism of his followers). As well, he argues that the Spirit comes upon us to enable inspired or prophetic speech.[21]

Our proposed refresh seeks to clarify the sign value of tongues, and in so doing, distinguish it from the many effects or outcomes of Spirit Baptism. The gift is not tongues; the gift is Spirit Baptism.[22] One sign indicates the reception of a gift with one primary outcome: power to witness by the power of the Spirit. While we recognize the many wonderful side-effects of Spirit Baptism, we do not want to lose its purpose as conveyed in Luke-Acts. During the sixties and seventies, the Charismatic Movement shifted the conversation about the Spirit from revival (salvation) toward domestication of the Holy Spirit for renewal—not that there is anything wrong with that if you are a Charismatic. The after-effects are still being felt among Pentecostals, perhaps most critically in their general acceptance of tongues as prayer language with personal benefits, rather than as a sign of benefit for others. It is this social dimension that lies at the heart of the movement.

In addition, the committee is emphasizing the nature of tongues-speech as an indication not just *that* something has occurred but also *what* has occurred. The embodied response to the coming of the Spirit at Pentecost was a vocal one, indicating the nature of the gift itself as enablement to communicate the kingdom of God. Here the reader of Luke-Acts is at a hermeneutical advantage: it would have been shocking to someone who had just read Luke if the 120 had done anything other than speak based on the precedent set in Luke's Gospel. When the Spirit comes, prophetic speech results in both volumes.[23]

Speaking in tongues was the sign for the 120 that the promised Spirit had come, and how they responded was stereotypical in Luke-Acts. In the Gospel, the crowds react regularly to the miracles of Jesus by praising God (e.g., Luke 5:26; 7:16; 18:43). When the 120 were filled they praised God, too, albeit this time with xenolalic praise. Although tongues as praise are significant for other discussions of the nature of tongues-speech,[24] what is crucial here is that in Acts 2 it supports the Lukan emphasis on witness. For the crowd gathered that day, they heard a Spirit-prompted testimony to the presence of God among them.

---

21. Stronstad, *Charismatic Theology*, 68.

22. Pentecostals, early on and repeatedly, differentiated tongues as evidence or sign of Spirit Baptism from the gift of tongues in 1 Cor 12. See, e.g., McAlister, "Difference," 4.

23. See Stronstad, *Charismatic Theology*, 60–61.

24. Similar to 1 Cor 14:14–17.

PART II—READING ST. LUKE'S TEXT: HERMENEUTICAL CONSIDERATIONS

## The Nature of Prophetic Speech/Witness: Declaring the Kingdom of God

Spirit Baptism as prophetic enablement is a major theme in Stronstad's work, carrying over from *The Charismatic Theology of St. Luke* into *The Prophethood of All Believers*. It must be gratifying to him that one of the best newer works on Luke-Acts is entitled *Prophetic Jesus, Prophetic Church*.[25] More work needs to be done in Pentecostal circles to connect Stronstad's emphasis on prophetic speech with what prophetic speech concerns: the kingdom of God, which includes both the presence of the kingdom actualized in the present and its future realization. The classic expression for this dual temporality is "already" and "not yet."

The strategic placement of references to the kingdom in Luke-Acts shows its thematic centrality. Not only is the kingdom of God *the* message of Jesus in Luke (e.g., "I must preach the good news of the kingdom of God to other towns also, because that is why I was sent" [Luke 4:43]), but also it is reiterated as the primary theme of his post-resurrection instruction at the outset of Acts. "He appeared to them over a period of forty days and spoke about the kingdom of God" (Acts 1:3). In the last verse of the book, Paul is depicted as preaching the kingdom of God from Rome (Acts 28:31). Two brief observations are in order about the significance of the kingdom as the message of Spirit Baptism.

First, we must listen to Jesus to know what Spirit-baptized speech about the kingdom of God sounds like. The tone is set when he reads Isa 61:1–2a in his hometown synagogue: "The Spirit of the Lord is on me, because he has anointed me to preach good news to the poor. He has sent me to proclaim freedom for the prisoners and recovery of sight for the blind, to release the oppressed, to proclaim the year of the Lord's favour" (Luke 4:18–19). What we hear are calls for repentance, but also speech that calls out sickness and the demonic, that calls for the poor to be favored, that calls for entrance into the kingdom by becoming less, rather than grasping to become more. That is to say, witness Lukan-style is more than leaning over the back-fence post when the timing seems right to invite someone to Alpha.

Second, what can easily be missed because the apostles and Paul have become legendary is that the power of their witness resided not in their personal attributes. Lest we forget, the kingdom in Luke-Acts is proclaimed by the most unlikely people: no one particularly impressive among the original twelve in Luke, and Paul was a Jewish zealot persecuting the church. "The Empowered Witness of the Unlikely" would be an apt subtitle for Acts. It was Peter's Joel reference that "all flesh" are candidates for Spirit Baptism that has resonated loudly through the last century. May we not lose our confidence. I am particularly concerned that the next generation of Pentecostals would find their voice and communicate with boldness whenever the Spirit prompts and whatever the venue.

---

25. See Johnson, *Prophetic Jesus, Prophetic Church*.

## Pentecost and the Continuation of the Church

A reading of Luke before Acts reinforces the continuity of the mission to declare the kingdom of God: as Acts 1:1 says, what Jesus began his followers carry on. This is because the same Spirit empowers the pre- and post-Pentecost church. According to Stronstad, Pentecost signals that the church has become a charismatic community capable of furthering Jesus's prophetic mission.[26]

If this interpretation captures the gist of Luke-Acts, where the symmetry of structure reinforces continuance rather than fresh beginnings, then the abiding affection of many Pentecostals for the notion that Acts marks the beginning of the church appears misplaced. A Pauline reading of the Spirit into Luke-Acts (what might be labeled a form of *eisegesis*) is one reason, and another is the lingering influence of Dispensationalism—a modern riff on ancient apocalyptic eschatology that Pentecostals imported into the Acts narrative. This modern system teaches that the salvation history of Israel and the church move on separate paths. The church cannot emerge until Israel has rejected Jesus's offer of the kingdom; the church age begins after his ascension with the coming of the Spirit. The arrival of the Spirit marks the institution of the church.

Yet as strange as it may seem, in lieu of the Pauline association of the Spirit with salvation and the believer's incorporation into the church, to imagine the church in existence without the Spirit, it is equally so to imagine that the church only exists when Jesus her head is not physically present. K. Giles in his article, "The Church in the Gospel of Luke," asserts that it is "divine presence" that constitutes the community as the church, whether it is Jesus in Luke's gospel or the Spirit in Acts.[27] Further, if we are to believe that Acts 2 is the moment of salvation, then we are left with the conundrum that the 12 and 70 witnesses engage just as successfully in the mission of Jesus—preaching the kingdom with signs and wonders—as his followers do after the Day of Pentecost. This begs the question: Who needs salvation or Pentecost, or the Spirit for that matter? Or, is the Spirit enabling them pre-Pentecost to fulfill their short-term missions? There is an argument to be made for this.

In the introduction to Dunn's commentary on Acts, he mentions Luke's proclivity to leave certain themes out of his gospel which are found in Mark, a source he used, because he wanted to save their impact until his second volume. To cite examples, the discussion of clean/unclean in Mark 7 appears in Acts 10 as part of the Cornelius episode, and Luke reserves the account of John the Baptist's death found in Mark 6 until Acts 13.[28] What Dunn does not mention may be the most significant example of all (which omission has something to do with his interpretation of Acts 2 as salvific)—the pre-Pentecost empowerment of the Spirit on both missionary teams.

---

26. Stronstad, *Charismatic Theology*, 69.
27. Giles, "Church in the Gospel of Luke," 121.
28. Dunn, *Acts of the Apostles*, 11.

## PART II—READING ST. LUKE'S TEXT: HERMENEUTICAL CONSIDERATIONS

To begin with, it is not as if Spirit empowerment is unprecedented in Luke's gospel for anyone other than Jesus. An entire family is filled with the Spirit, Zechariah, Elizabeth, and their son, John—and that is just in the first chapter! When Jesus sends out the 12, he gives them power and authority (Luke 9:1). While not explicitly stated, the reader should assume that the 70 receive the same combination, and the presence of authority is mentioned in their debriefing (Luke 10:19). After all, both groups perform the same tasks with equal effectiveness. Why is the Spirit not mentioned as the source of their power? The answer that Jesus gives them *his* power is complicated by the fact that there is no other category for divine power in Luke's Gospel other than the Spirit; the Spirit is the power of the Lord (Luke 4:14; 5:17). If Jesus gives them power, then it is the power of the Spirit.

It seems to me that the Spirit is not mentioned explicitly as the power behind the two missions because the author wanted to save its impact until Acts 2. It was there he could emphasize the point that the post-Easter Day of Pentecost was about scope and magnitude, a quantitative expansion as an answer to prayer in which the number of workers would exceed those whom Jesus had sent out personally.

Furthermore, the sending out of the 70 (the textual variant of 72 suggests not just an alternate number but a variant interpretation)[29] has distinct Spirit overtones. Stronstad locates the typological background for Acts 10 in the transfer of the Spirit from Moses to the 70 elders in Numbers 11.[30] This view has weight because of the strategic way the author uses Moses throughout Luke and Acts.[31] Stronstad, though he rarely hesitates to push a parallel as far as biblically possible, backs away from identifying the Spirit as involved in the transfer scene of the 70 in Luke 10, presumably because he is saving that event for Acts 2. Yet, the prominence of the Spirit in the Mosaic transfer motif is highly suggestive that Luke intended an implicit reference to the Spirit. The explicit identification, of course, was reserved for volume two.

There is an additional connection between Luke 10 and Acts 2; that is, between prayer request and prayer answered. Before Jesus sends out of the 70, he calls for prayer that the Lord of the harvest would send out more workers because the harvest is ready and abundant (Luke 10:2). The word "harvest" appears three times in this one verse, a typical Lukan convention of repetition to highlight something for a listening audience.[32] The prayer finds its initial answer at the Feast of Harvest itself,[33] celebrating the harvest first-fruits. That festival, also known as Pentecost, is when 120 witnesses emerge as the Spirit is transferred to them, and by the end of the day, the result was a

---

29. It is common to read the variant of 72 as a representative number for the nations (LXX of Gen 10), so that the sending out of 72 in the gospel prefigures the extension of the mission beyond Jewish territory in Acts.

30. Stronstad, *Charismatic Theology*, 51.

31. Johnson also sees the Mosaic motif as prominent in typifying the prophetic ministry of Jesus. See Johnson, *Prophetic Jesus*, 34–5.

32. For example, the Spirit is referred to three times in the pericope about Simeon (Luke 2:25–27).

33. Exod 23:16.

dizzying increase of the community by 3,000. To these Peter declared that the same promise of the Spirit would apply (Acts 2:39). The import behind the Acts record of the successive places where the gospel moves geographically is of the same ilk, where the emphasis is on increasing the number of witnesses to the kingdom among the unlikely—Paul, and Samaritans, and of course, Gentiles. In short, the parallelism between Luke and Acts and its overriding proclamation of an ever-expanding kingdom makes the Acts 2 experience resemble more of a reboot than a start-up.

## Conclusion: Future Pentecostal Scholarship and Luke-Acts

What is the lay of the land for future Pentecostal scholarly engagement? There has never been a better time to be a Pentecostal biblical scholar. Pick a methodology. The NT fields are ripe for harvest. The benefits of the traditional methodology of historical criticism in search of authorial intent have been demonstrated, and here I mention the exemplary work of Robert Menzies. With redaction criticism of the post-WWII era and the breaking down of the didactic/narrative distinction, the focus has moved to the theology of Luke and the other gospel writers. In particular, now that Luke and Acts have been reunited, there is a great opportunity for further exploration.

Some of the areas of biblical studies mentioned above are part of a larger trend that focuses on the text itself. With the advent of literary criticism that incorporates the interpreting community into interpretation, there is a new appreciation of the value of the traditional Pentecostal method, where text and community are incorporated.[34]

The social world of Luke-Acts has come to the fore with the contribution of social scientific perspectives, and this approach holds great promise as well. In highlighting the social dynamics of first-century life as more dyadic than an individual, it reminds Pentecostals of their roots, when the Spirit was understood to be given for the sake of the other rather than the individual. It also recalls an earlier time, when texts of the NT were read out loud to groups of believers, who interpreted and responded to them together. This sounds like the Pentecostal community in which I grew up.

Then there is reception history, which looks at how texts have been interpreted historically. For our purposes in this essay, it is irrelevant: there is a reception history for a Pentecostal reading of Acts already, but for Luke-Acts, not yet.

---

34. For a primer on this see Martin, *Pentecostal Hermeneutics*.

## Chapter 6

# Reading St. Luke's Narrative as "Texture"
## Acts 2:1–4 in the Light of Socio-Rhetorical Criticism

RIKU P. TUPPURAINEN[1]

Lukan narratives are read in different ways for a variety of reasons. The recent debate around Luke-Acts focusing on Lukan pneumatology, a debate in which Pentecostal scholarship has participated vigorously, serves as an example. Walter Brueggemann points out that a person's reading of the biblical texts is easily influenced by one's thought-systems that permit "one text to judge and evaluate another, and often to eliminate the 'lesser' text,"[2] and that the method "in which we have been schooled inevitably operates within hidden criteria . . . that decide beforehand what would be included in a text."[3] These hermeneutical challenges impact readers in their exegetical and hermeneutical efforts and direct how they read—that is, what they include in the text's meaning effects.[4] Readers' thought-systems and preferred methodology influence their capacity to see what the text may or may not communicate (hermeneutics of expectations). Therefore, every reader should ask self-critical

---

1. I have enjoyed and used Roger Stronstad's writings in my teaching, so much so that my students at Continental Theological Seminary, Belgium, often asked if I knew him personally. My response was that I have not met him, but one day, I will! When I finally met Roger, I met a committed follower of Christ, whose life is a living demonstration of the biblical message that he has devoted to study and explain. I want to express my sincere gratitude to him for his scholarship and friendship. His contributions continue to be a great blessing to my students and me.

2. This resonates with one of Luther's "hermeneutical" keys, namely, *scriptura sacra sui ipsius interpres*, according to which more unambiguous texts should interpret obscure texts. See McKim, *Historical Handbook*, 218.

3. Brueggemann, *Texts Under Negotiation*, 58.

4. By the phrase "text's meaning effects" I refer to textual and extratextual components and aspects that are related to a passage and influence how the text is understood, i.e., what we include in a text, using Brueggemann's words.

questions: Which meaning effects inform my understanding of a particular passage and how does my chosen methodology direct my reading?

There have been many attempts in the past to overcome these hermeneutical challenges. Martin Luther's *Sola Scriptura* reading and, much more recently, Stephen Motyer's development of James Dunn's "Points of Sensitivity" reading serve as examples.[5] These attempts were motivated by the desire to avoid the limitations of previous thought-systems and methodologies.

In this essay, I suggest that Vernon K. Robbins's model of Socio-Rhetorical Criticism (SRC)[6] is helpful for readers of NT narratives in seeking to overcome some aspects of these challenges. Robbins's approach to SRC views a text as a texture (see the following section below). SRC reading opens up a new horizon for determining a text's meaning effects—a horizon that is broader than the reader's horizon—thus taking the reader closer to the text's horizon.

I am not arguing for this method with a naïve claim that this (or any other) method ensures the final reading.[7] No method can do that. Instead, I argue that even a Spirit-sensitive reading[8] needs to be cast into a methodological framework that offers a pathway for understanding. I also argue that SRC is a valuable tool that can provide a comprehensive examination of the text that leads readers to recognize a text's meaning effects, which perhaps otherwise would go unnoticed.

In this essay, I shall first outline Robbins's model of SRC. Secondly, I shall present selected examples of how it may help readers to appreciate various meaning effects as applied to Acts 2:1–4. A more complete application of this method to Luke-Acts, and even to Acts 2:1–4, should be done elsewhere.[9]

## Text as Texture

SRC views a text as a thick texture, a multi-dimensional presentation of the author's persuasive (rhetorical) communication that includes multiple meaning effects. "Thick texture" analogy conveys the idea that the text is a combination of different textures like a tapestry. A tapestry has various kinds of surfaces, colors, knitting styles, and materials. If one examines a tapestry only from the flat surface, like on a computer screen, one certainly would miss some of its aesthetic effects, and perhaps also its historical

---

5. Motyer, *Your Father the Devil?*, esp. 35–73.

6. Socio-rhetorical criticism is the analytical model of studying ancient texts developed by Vernon K. Robbins. Its application may vary from one practitioner to another, and therefore, my application of the model may not strictly follow his presentation. Robbins two works that explain his model are Robbins, *Tapestry of Early Christian Discourse*; *Exploring the Texture of Texts*.

7. See Gadamer, *Truth and Method*.

8. I use this term to describe readers who recognize the Spirit's role in the act of writing (inspiration), in the text (message), and the act of reading (illumination).

9. See my attempt in Tuppurainen, "Contribution of Socio-Rhetorical Criticism." Another such attempt is Witherington, *Acts of the Apostles*.

aspect and technical insights. SRC leads the reader to learn from the various textures of the text. As I have observed elsewhere, "The text is not read only as a collection of literary signs . . . but rather as a flow of signs connected to the socio-ideological web of people and events in all their richness of textures and colours."[10]

It is evident that the reader who learns from the text's textures, not only cognitively but also experientially, is influenced by the text's rhetoric. Thus, a socio-rhetorical reading does not celebrate the idea that the interpreter is an objective observer outside of the text and its persuasion (rhetoric). The older ideology that the reader is (and can be) an objective observer of the text was built on a philosophy of language that took the text as a self-expression, that is, the self-expression of a biblical writer/community which does not have (or which should not have) transformational capacity on a reader today. Anthony C. Thiselton argues "that to view texts as no more than mirrors of the human individual self or even of a community presupposes an inadequate philosophy of language and cannot do justice to a theology of the biblical writings."[11] SRC does not view biblical texts that way. Instead, the interpreter is directed to become an object of the text's persuasion.[12] Becoming an object of the text's persuasion, the reader's horizon gets closer to the horizon of the narrative and its author.

In summary, a SRC reader is guided to recognize and use the text's meaning effects and to feel the text's rhetoric for a better understanding of the message. SRC interpretation leads, therefore, to an understanding that is based on a reader's cognitive and emotive/experiential understanding, which is more impact-making than understanding based on mere cognitive information.

## Study of Thick Texture of the Text: An Overview

How does a person study the thick texture of a text? Robbins's model helps the reader to approach a narrative from different angles and to ask various sets of questions as textures require. The reader engages one texture at a time, continually encountering the text with his/her previous understanding while, at the same time, fresh insights and information are discovered and new feelings are evoked. In this kind of reading, the reader is not only asking questions and receiving answers from the text, its co-texts, and contexts, but he/she is also invited to become a (silent) character in the narrative who may sympathize with certain narrative characters and distance him/herself from others. At the end of the reading, the reader brings together all findings, information, and even experiences and feelings. Robbins presents the following textures consideration.[13]

10. Tuppurainen, "Role(s) of the Spirit-Paraclete," 78.
11. Thiselton, "Retrospective Reappraisal," 519.
12. Paddison, "Theological Interpretation," 30.
13. The following explanation of the textures are based on Robbins, *Exploring the Texture of Texts*; *Tapestry of Early Christian Discourse*, without further referencing.

## Inner Texture

The reader starts with the text's flat surface. First, the reader assesses the narrative unit, including its opening, middle, and closing, and how the parts of the narrative function in relation to the entire text. Then, aesthetical and rhetorical textures, like human emotions and feelings, as well as, repetition, progression, and argumentation, are examined. Questions asked from these textures include: What is repeated, and how is repetition presented in the text? What is argued for, and how does the text present the argument? How does the text progress and which direction does the progression take? What kinds of senses or emotions do the narrative evoke?

## Intertexture

Here the reader is looking for the text's connection to other texts (intertextuality) as well as for social, cultural, and historical aspects which are found as a textualized form in the text. For example, the following questions could be asked from a text: What is the relation of the data in the text with phenomena outside of it? Are there references or echoes in the text which are related to religion or culture? What kind of historical event or period is referenced (textualized) in the text? Intertexture, even though still working with the text, also takes a look beyond the text; it has a point of connection with the world within which it was written.

## Social and Cultural Texture

Here the reader finds out what kind of people were those who lived in the world that the text presents. The reader should ask questions like: What kind of social and cultural systems does the text both presuppose and evoke? Also, how is the dominant culture interacting with other culture such as countercultures and contra-cultures? This texture leads the reader to examine religious aspects by asking how various religious groups act and react towards each other.

## Ideological Texture

One of the reader's tasks here is to find out the biblical author's ideology, which he/she reveals in the text. Today's readers are certainly not free from ideological influence while reading. There is, therefore, a need to study the ideology of the author, the author's text, as well as the ideologies of previous interpreters.[14] Also, the reader is required to examine his/her own and his/her community's ideology (e.g., beliefs, values, and presumptions) and compare it to the ideology embedded in the text. Thus, a question like, What kinds of presuppositions, interests, commitments, desires,

---

14. See Watson, "Why We Need Socio-Rhetorical Commentary," 136.

privileges, and constraints do I, as a reader, and the ecclesiastical community of which I am a part bring into my reading? The examination of ideological texture may help lead the reader to move closer to the ideology of the text.

## Sacred texture

Sacred texture focuses on the study of divine and spirit beings, holy persons, and the like. The reader's task is to learn how divine/spirit/holy beings function in the text—what they communicate. The sacred texture leads also the reader to investigate what is the relation between divine beings and humans. For example, questions like, Who or what are holy persons? How are people in general or God's people, in particular, related to God? What are transactions from the divine to humans? How is the believing community formed and how does it move forward?

The above five textures are not limited to one particular world or dimension of the text as the sample questions also demonstrate. Using Manfred Oeming's phraseology, SRC does not limit the text to "author and his world," "narrative world," or "reader and his world."[15] It takes into account all three "worlds" employing their meaning effects for understanding of the text. The historical world of the text, the narrative world, and the reader's world receive attention in the process of SRC reading.[16]

These three worlds have been emphasized in various ways in the past,[17] including in the Pentecostal hermeneutical tradition. In the Pentecostal tradition, narratives have been read in ways which reflect, not only Pentecostal distinctives, but also hermeneutical eras in which the reading took place. These approaches include reader-response, historical-grammatical and, more recently, narrative-critical readings. Such approaches emphasize one or two of the three worlds.

What SRC tries to accomplish is that it leads the reader to a balanced and thorough study of all these three worlds through the examination of the text's textures. This kind of reading is helping the reader avoid his/her limited horizon caused by the personal/communal thought-systems and/or preferred hermeneutical approach.

In the following section I have chosen to limit my application of SRC to Acts 2:1–4 by using the three worlds mentioned above. I want to emphasize how important it is to allow meaning effects from all these worlds to inform our reading. Also, the presentation below demonstrates how SRC reads the text as texture and how it directs the reader to move from one's own horizon towards the text's horizon.

---

15. Oeming, *Contemporary Biblical Hermeneutics*.

16. We could also add "divine dimension" to our discussion, which is a part of the SRC agenda. This dimension is mainly observed through the sacred texture of the text that gives readers a possibility to encounter the divine realities as presented in the text.

17. Lategan, "Current Issues in the Hermeneutical Debate," 1–4.

# Acts 2:1–4 as Texture: Historical, Narrative, and Reading Worlds

## Historical Worlds: Examples of Historical Settings

The study of historical worlds includes the event, the time of recording the event, and the time between the event and reading the record. Here we will take a look at the time of the event and the recording of that event.

First, we note that the event of Pentecost took place fifty days after Jesus's ascension. During that time, the believing community in Jerusalem obeyed Jesus's instructions as given in Acts 1:4 and endeavored to make sense of their new situation as they were now "on their own" without Jesus's physical presence (Acts 1:12–26). This was the time when Jewish leaders in Jerusalem were relieved since the Nazarenes' leader had been eliminated. Perhaps they were wondering how the movement was going to express itself and how long it might survive without a leader (cf. Acts 5:36).[18]

Secondly, this event took place on the day of Pentecost, a significant Jewish pilgrim feast—the worst possible time from the Jewish leaders' perspective—which also relates to the Spirit-event's theological meaning.[19] Also, it likely occurred on the temple mount,[20] which also adds another meaning effect to the Spirit-filling event's significance.

Thirdly, the time of writing evokes some meaning effects. We have good reason to believe that Luke wrote Acts after AD 70.[21] At that time, Jews were feeling "the trauma resulting from the destruction of the Temple and cessation of its worship."[22] Luke, however, did not share that trauma. On the contrary, Luke wrote from the vantage point of a surviving and vigorously alive church. The gospel had advanced "to the ends of the earth" in the presence of the Spirit.[23] Yet, there was a dispute between the synagogue and the church. The situation of writing, therefore, was quite different from the time when the event took place.

How do these historical meaning effects inform the reader? It is reasonable to say that the historical realities at the time of the event and writing motivated Luke to define carefully who are the people of God, namely those who receive the Spirit. Acts 2:1–4 seems to be directed to that end as well, since it sits at the historical intersection of the post-resurrection era when Jewish-Christian topics were high on the agenda. The sense we get at this point is that Acts 2:1–4 is Jewish-Christian in its focus. This sketch also demonstrates how valuable historical meaning effects are for interpretation,[24] as they lead readers to avoid ahistorical, ethnocentric, and/or mere synchronic readings.

---

18. See Tuppurainen, "Role(s) of the Spirit-Paraclete," 152–53.
19. See Witherington, *Acts of the Apostles*, 131.
20. See Keener, *Acts*, 1:796–97.
21. Keener, *Acts*, 1:400–401.
22. Cf. Motyer, *Your Father the Devil?*, 37–39.
23. Acts 1:8. See also Acts 6:7; 9:31; 12:24; 16:5; 19:20; 28:30–31.
24. See Bartholomew, *Introducing Biblical Hermeneutics*, 118.

If readers move directly from the narrative to today's reading context, the questions that are asked from the text are often those which are motivated by the readers' own concerns and their world (horizon). That kind of reading runs a high risk of being colored by a hermeneutical approach limited to a certain thought-system.

## Narrative World: Examples of Structure, Repetition, and Progression

SRC employs narrative-critical components like Saymor Chatman's theory of a story. The components include implied author, characters, narrator, narratee, story time, actions, dialogues, and implied reader, with other narrative critical aspects, such as plot and commentary.[25] The purpose is to understand how the narrative develops, argues, persuades, and how various characters function in it. Here elements that are part of the inner texture, such as opening-middle-closing, argumentation, and progression, are studied. Also, aspects from the sacred texture are included in this study.

As a preliminary observation, we note that the Spirit-filling in Acts 2:1–4 is embedded in Luke-Acts, the story of God's promised Savior and salvation. In the immediately preceding narrative context (Acts 1) the reader finds themes that are vital parts of Acts 2:1–4 and the narrative that follows it. That context introduces the kingdom of God motif (1:3), the faithful believing community (1:4–5, 12–14), the witness motif (1:8, 15–26), and the succession motif (cf. 1:5–8, 9–10, 21–26). In Acts 2, Jesus's faithful followers became persons in whom the Spirit resides (Spirit-baptized, Spirit-empowered, Spirit-filled, and Spirit-led, as Stronstad puts it),[26] and who now are Jesus's successors on earth. As such, Spirit-filled people are the empowered people in God's kingdom—Jesus's witnesses. Not only do they now have more strength/boldness to witness, but also they have received a new identity as Jesus's *witnesses* in the world.

This narrative (2:1–4) is located in the middle of Luke-Acts, where the believing community (as well as the reader) is pondering the question how the community can possibly continue without Jesus's physical presence. The leader of the group is gone! Under Peter's leadership, the believing community was able to solve one of their dilemmas, namely, to fill the vacant place left by Judas Iscariot with another eyewitness, Matthias. But more than that was needed; eyewitnesses were going to last only so far. Who would become valid witnesses of these things thereafter? The answer is found in the fulfillment of the promise Jesus had given (Luke 24:49; Acts 1:4–5, 8) and which is now realized in Acts 2:1–4. The narrative from this point forward tells a story of God's kingdom people, the people of the Spirit (the church). The people of the Spirit form a new "nation" of God's people (*laos*),[27] who represent Jesus on earth as his witnesses in a similar fashion as the first eyewitnesses bore witness to Jesus. What happens after

---

25. See Culpepper, *Anatomy of the Fourth Gospel*, 6.

26. Stronstad, *Pentecostal Biblical Theology*, 162.

27. Jervell points out that for Luke there is only one Israel, namely, the people (*laos*) of God. See Jervell, *Theology of Acts of the Apostles*, 13.

Acts 2:1–4 is a demonstration of what Jesus continued to do, i.e., how the community of God's Spirit-people as the witnesses penetrated into the unbelieving Jewish and Gentile worlds by words, deeds, sufferings, and even martyrdoms. Even those who did not enjoy an eyewitness status, like the apostle Paul, became valid witnesses as they were recipients of the Spirit. These witnesses crossed geographical, ethnic, religious, social, economic, gender, generational, and cultural boundaries.

The inner texture, an examination of the narrative world, also pays attention to repetition, rhetorical progression, and argumentation. As for repetition and progression two words of "wind/Spirit" [*pnoē* and *pneuma*], two verbs of "to fill" [*pleroō* and *pimplēmi*] and two occurrences of a noun "tongue" [*glōssa*] suggest progression in Acts 2:1–4.

*Pnoē* in verse two might have been chosen to differentiate between the physical phenomenon "wind" (v. 2) from the coming of the Spirit, *pneuma* (v. 4). This word choice can be argued by the fact that *pnoē* is not used for the (Holy) Spirit in Luke-Acts. More importantly, however, this points to a progression from the Hebrew Scriptures to the Pentecostal event. *Pnoē* in the Septuagint is used not only for moving air (wind), but also for breath (of life) given by God. In Genesis 2:7, *pnoē* is employed for God's breath (i.e., the breath of life) that he placed in Adam. We remember that *pneuma* is also a word for the life-giving "breath" or "wind," (cf. Ezek. 37:5–6), which Luke employs distinctively for the Holy Spirit.[28] Also these words force readers to picture God as a source of a (new) life in this context. There is neither life nor a Spirit-filled life outside of him. The coming of the Spirit tells the Jewish audience that the last days have dawned. Now God's Spirit was blowing among his people (cf. Acts 5:32).

The other word pair, *pleroō* and *pimplēmi*, shares the same meaning "to fill / to satisfy."[29] Both words are used in "Spirit filling" texts.[30] Here a noise, like a violent rushing wind, *filled* (*pleroō*) the *entire* house and the Spirit *filled* (*pimplēmi*) *every* follower of Jesus.[31] We may argue that Luke used two different verbs for stylistic reasons. Alternatively, Luke may have chosen these words to emphasize the difference between the phenomena and the actual Spirit filling in this context. When the rushing-wind sound filled the room, it was unintelligible. It came from heaven, that is, from God. When the 120 were filled with the Spirit, however, the sound that they produced was the intelligible proclamation of God's works (cf. Acts 2:6, 11b). This, too, suggests a progression.

Rhetorical power in this narrative is directed, however, more importantly towards the progression from outward to inward. This progression reminds us of Jesus's

---

28. Keener, *Acts*, 1:783.

29. They translate the same Hebrew word in the LXX. See, Delling, "πίμπλημι," TDNT 6:128–31; "πληρόω," TDNT 6:286–98. See also Stronstad, "Filled with the Holy Spirit," 1–3.

30. Stronstad, "Filled with the Holy Spirit," 1–3.

31. See Ezek 37:11–14, where the whole *oikos* of Israel is described as dry bones without hope and being cut off but also receiving *pneuma* of God that makes them alive again restoring their hope.

teaching in Luke 11 and his statement in Luke 11:13b, "how much more will the heavenly Father give the Holy Spirit to those who ask him!"[32] Earthly fathers may provide earthly goods for their children, but only God can provide the Spirit—the Spirit that enables his kingdom rule in his people (Luke 11:2). In addition, there is a striking progression here because this took place in the context of the Temple. The presence of God had filled the Temple in the past. Now, however, an even greater event took place when the Spirit filled Jesus's followers—something that had not been anticipated by Jews. In short, the progression from outward to inward suggests God's complete rule in Spirit-filled people.

Rhetorical progression is also observed when comparing God's previous Spirit-fillings with the Acts 2:1–4 event. The filling vocabulary in Acts is employed to expand the horizon of memory of God's dealings with his people in the past (e.g., Exod 28:3; 31:3; 35:31; Isa 11:1–3). This connection between past and present is also established between the Pentecostal event of "Spirit filling" and several OT narratives even when "filling" vocabulary is not employed (e.g., Ezek 37; Num 11).

Finally, the word *glōssa* (tongue) is used in two different ways. First, it refers to an optical phenomenon of tongues "like fire." Fire is related to God's presence as well as God's guidance during the Exodus (e.g., Exod 13:21–22;19:18; see also Luke 3:16), also to God's judgment (e.g., Isa 34:9; 29:6; 66:16; Joel 2:3). The second usage refers to an audio phenomenon of spoken languages. Luke uses *glōssais* (in plural, feminine, dative) only in the context of "language speaking" under the influence of the Spirit (Acts 2:4, 11; 10:46; 19:6). Progression is from a visible and unarticulated phenomenon of "tongues" to the action of producing an intelligent utterance (vv. 6, 11). The content of that Spirit-inspired speech might have related to the fire concepts present in the Hebrew scriptures such as God's presence, guidance, and judgment. In any case, the outward phenomena function as signs in this particular context—the signs of God's involvement—but the Spirit himself is the evidence that these are God's people, the new witnessing nation for God's work in Jesus Christ (Acts 2:11, 22–36).[33]

Repetition of "filling" and "tongues" creates the following pattern:

A1 verse 2    . . . suddenly there came . . . a sound . . . and it *filled* the entire house . . .
    B1 verse 3    . . . divided *tongues* as of fire appeared to them and rested on each one of them.
A2 verse 4a    . . . they were all *filled* with the Holy Spirit . . .
    B2 verse 4b    . . . began to speak in other *tongues* as the Spirit gave them utterance.

Three further observations are pertinent: First, the Spirit is mentioned both times when "filling" and "tongues" are mentioned the second time in lines A2 and B2. The force of this progression would become more evident if the intertexture were

---

32. Scripture quotations are taken from the ESV.
33. See Michaels, "Evidences."

studied more in detail. Secondly, there is no chiasm in this unit. Instead, here the progression increases toward the end of the narrative unit where the promise of the Spirit is fulfilled. Thirdly, the event was inclusive: note the reference to "entire house" (A1), "each one" (B1), "all" (A2, and implied in B2). All of Jesus's followers were recipients of the Spirit.

Does this short portion from Luke-Acts's narrative make a particular argument? Based on this study of historical and text worlds, Acts 2:1–4 argues that the coming of the Spirit on/in Jesus's followers was God's doing as promised. Also, these studies confirm that the Spirit *is* the evidence that Jesus's followers *are* God's people and thus, his empowered witnesses (cf. Acts 5:32). Phenomena, rushing wind-sound and fire-tongues, that preceded this (vv. 2–3) and what followed (vv. 5–11), namely that they spoke of the mighty works of God in various tongues, are directed towards Jewish bystanders to connect their previous understanding of God's doing with the current event. Here the reader, I suggest, begins to feel this passage's embeddedness in its historical Jewish-Christian meaningfulness as well as its rhetorical power for expressing its universal and timeless importance.

To summarize: the reader has learned various meaning effects while studying these textures. Today's readers are persuaded, like the bystanders in the narrative, to accept the view that the coming of the Spirit is indeed God's doing, which changes lives by giving them Jesus's witness status. The witness status, including a variety of the Spirit's activities, is extended to those who had never been eyewitnesses of Jesus themselves. The readers today may expect that they, too, can receive the same status in the same Spirit.

## Reader's World: Examples of Readers' Reading Context and Ideology

We are reading the narrative of Acts 2:1–4 in the twenty-first-century pluralistic world. Our world does not necessarily include the Jewish-Christian question in the same way that it did in the Lukan world. Yet our world certainly includes dichotomies between various kinds of religions/ideologies/politics and Christian faith. How, then, does this reading context inform our reading? I suggest that similarity between the historical setting of Acts 2 and our reading context finds similarity in the need to demonstrate who God's people are: As they were then, so are they today Jesus's empowered witnesses in this world—people marked by the Spirit. This narrative of the coming of the Spirit speaks, therefore, to a larger theological-spiritual reality than the mere phenomena of the arrival of the Spirit or the Jewish-Christian question.

The reader's ideology is a part of the readers' world as well. In SRC reading, ideological texture of the text "investigates people: the reader, the author, and previous interpreters."[34] Examination of the reader's ideological world should include the ex-

---

34. Tuppurainen, "Role(s) of the Spirit-Paraclete," 158.

amination of the biblical author's worldview that is revealed in the text (cf. ideological texture). This is a necessary exercise to avoid ahistorical and ethnocentric readings. When observing Luke's overall ideology presented in Acts, it is fair to say that his worldview is dualistic in the sense that he divides people into two categories: people who have the Spirit (and everything that it includes, such as salvation in Jesus Christ) and people who do not have the Spirit. Luke's worldview is presented in the initial coming of the Spirit (Acts 2:1–4) and its aftermath, as well as in many other places in Acts, such as 3:38–39; 5:29–32. Luke does not, however, present the Spirit as a boundary keeper in the sense that outsiders are hopelessly beyond the pale of becoming insiders. On the contrary, the Spirit is available for all who turn from their sinful ways to God (Acts 2:38–39).

Examination of the readers' world should pay attention to the limitations, prejudices, assumptions, stereotypes, as well as the similarities and differences of their ideology in comparison to the ideology found in the text. It needs to be noted, also, that the readers' previous spiritual experiences (reflected in ideology) are easily used as a meaning effect. Therefore, experiences should also be submitted to evaluation. For example, Pentecostal and Reformed readers, by virtue of their ideological/theological/experiential differences, emphasize certain meaning effects and ignore some others when reading Acts 2:1–4. As important as the contemporary community might be for biblical hermeneutics,[35] SRC reminds us that one's community and its ideology (including experiences) should also be compared and contrasted with the text's ideology and submitted to its persuasion. It helps readers to do that if they "step in" the narrative world, allowing its rhetoric to persuade, rather than trying to stand outside of the text as "objective" readers. In the case of Acts 2, this would mean that readers place themselves as submissive agents of the Spirit's filling (Acts 2:1–4, 37–38).

The readers' ecclesial-ideological context, a context that includes previous cognitive, empirical, and emotional components, influences what the text is for them. Therefore, the following questions arise for the SRC reader: In which context and for what purpose did previous interpreters read Acts 2:1–4? As an example, many studies by Pentecostal scholars of Acts 2:1–4 and related Spirit-passages during the last two or three decades were prompted by the Dunn-Menzies dialogue in which Pentecostal scholars, such as Roger Stronstad, Howard Ervin, David Petts, James Shelton, and William Atkinson participated. The debate has produced various studies (and readings) of the Spirit passages that concentrate on Spirit-baptism and its separability from salvation, Spirit and power, and *glossolalia*.[36]

The ongoing discussion of Pentecostal hermeneutic(s) has also included the question of the reader and one's community's ideology. A recent survey among credential holders of the Pentecostal Assemblies of Canada indicates a less unanimous view of how normatively "tongues" should be connected to Spirit baptism as the initial

---

35. Archer, *Pentecostal Hermeneutic*.
36. See Mittelstadt, *Reading Luke-Acts*, 46–80.

evidence in comparison with the viewpoint held three decades ago.[37] Although the survey questions were not directly linked to Acts 2:1–4, the responses suggest the direction which the reading of this passage might be taking in the contemporary Canadian Pentecostal context. The point I wish to make is simply this: SRC acknowledges ideological and ecclesial factors, as well as ideological changes that have influenced previous approaches to what meaning effects have been emphasized and which meaning effects have been allowed to inform these readings.

In summary, a reader's self-examination, peer-examination, dialogue with one's own and other ecclesial traditions, as well as an examination of the biblical author's ideology, are necessary exercises if one desires to follow the lead of the SRC. Here we have seen, for example, that Acts 2:1–4 benefits from observations of the contemporary world that remind us that the coming of the Spirit is not focused on ecclesiastical (internal) matters. We have also noticed that previous and current ideologies often bring various limitations to what may be included in the text's meaning effect. Sometimes reading is closely linked to the current context and "views of today" whereas on other occasions reading may be left to the historical past having no, or little, value for today.

## Concluding Remarks

I have tried to demonstrate with a few examples how SRC may help readers to grasp the text in a holistic and comprehensive way, thus protecting such readers from the limitations of their personal and/or communal thought-systems, preferred hermeneutical approaches and expectations. Examination of the historical, narrative, and reading worlds by applying the five SRC textures has suggested meaning effects that have contributed to our understanding of Lukan rhetoric, not only at the level of history or narrative, but also in our contemporary context. In this brief study we have approached the text from many angles and have seen not only persuasion *in* the text, but also felt the persuasion *of* the text.

This study shows that Acts 2:1–4 is neither a mere proof text for the initial evidence doctrine, nor a text that differentiates various church traditions from each other. The study also demonstrates that Acts 2:1–4 is much more than a mere historical record of a past event, which is sometimes interpreted to have no (experiential) value for us today. What the text does is that it persuades and ensures (not just informs) its readers that they, too, as Jesus's followers, are the people of the Spirit. That is to say, they are Jesus's witnesses, not just by imagination but by the Spirit's coming in/on them. In a unique historical setting and by the exercise of narrative-rhetoric, we have seen how the Holy Spirit fills Jesus's followers and become differentiated from the rest of the people. From that moment on Luke demonstrates that only Spirit-people

---

37. See, Gabriel et al., "Changing Conceptions of Speaking in Tongues," 3–4, 6.

were Jesus's witnesses. Today, the Spirit's presence is needed for that same purpose. The Spirit is for all Jesus's disciples who come to salvation by repenting (Acts 2:38). The Spirit is today, as it was in Acts, the evidence of who Jesus's empowered witnesses are in this world (not just witnesses within the church). The Spirit also expresses his power and presence in a variety of ways, in and through his people, as Luke demonstrates throughout Acts following Acts 2:1–4.

My suggestion is that the text functions to define and demonstrate who are God's people. They are those to whom he has granted authority to be Jesus's witnesses by giving them the Spirit. Luke's point of view with reference to the coming of the Spirit is, therefore, not only vocational, referring certain kinds of actions to be accomplished by the power of the Spirit, but also ontological, referring to the believers' empowered status. The Spirit in Acts 2:1–4 gives believers and the believing community not only power to witness, but also the status to be Jesus's empowered witnesses, even for those disciples of Jesus who had never been his eyewitnesses. Glory to God—I, too, then, can be Jesus's Spirit-empowered witness!

# Chapter 7

## Experiencing the Meaning of St. Luke's Text

### Scott Ellington[1]

Roger Stronstad's *The Charismatic Theology of St. Luke: Trajectories from the Old Testament to Luke-Acts* captures elemental insights into the modern experience of Pentecost and the touchstone texts from which participants sought to understand the fresh move of the Spirit that opened the twentieth century. All books are products of their time, but great ones such as *Charismatic Theology* transcend the confines of the moment of their creation and continue to illumine and to provoke discussion in new and unfolding contexts. For this particular discussion, I will draw on three points that Stronstrad raises that I have found particularly useful in considering the challenges and opportunities of global Pentecostalism in the twenty-first century.

First is the legitimacy, and at times superiority, of narrative biblical texts for formulating Pentecostal doctrine rather than the didactic passages more often favored in articulating Evangelical theologies. For Pentecostals, the interpretive distance between personal experience and biblical story is shorter and more easily traversed, particularly in oral cultures at home with storytelling, than it is between those experiences and didactic texts. Stronstad made a compelling case for settling Pentecostal doctrine on the dynamic and open-ended foundation of stories. Stories manifest a clear preferencing of human experience and resistance to codification and settled final meaning.

Second is his observation, inherent in the book's subtitle, of both a continuity of Spirit movement through the twin canons of Scripture and an evolving of the Spirit's activity, so that the Acts' Pentecost both builds on and moves beyond the prophetic empowerments described in the Old Testament. The Spirit is present and active

---

1. Professor Stronstad's work has had a tremendous influence on my own thinking about Pentecostal theology and hermeneutics, and their importance in our tradition of testimony. We identify with the stories in the Bible and our own testimonies of experiencing God's presence in our lives mirror and add to those biblical narratives. Roger Stronstad's groundbreaking work has helped me to understand that our theology begins with the stories that we tell about God.

throughout the full canon of Scripture, yet the Spirit does not confine herself[2] simply to endlessly repeating the past. Spirit movement is in harmony with, but is not simply a passive replicating of, earlier movements. This recognizes the unfolding nature of God's redemptive plan and the reality that the architect and builder of that plan remain involved in its manifestation.

Third is his identification of five hallmark passages in Acts that continue to provide a primary interpretive lens for those who share in global Pentecost; the original outpouring among the upper room disciples (2:1–13), the conversion of the deeply suspect Samaritans (8:14–19), Saul's Damascus road about face (9:17–18), the God-propelled conversion of the first gentile, Cornelius, together with his household (10:44–46), and the revived spiritual journey of the Ephesian disciples (19:1–7). Together, these passages record a diversity of experiences and perspectives, and suggest resistance to a reductionist or formulaic understanding of what the Baptism in the Holy Spirit should or, indeed, must look like.

In the brief discussion that follows, I will consider two trajectories emanating from Stronstad's work. First, I wish to explore a *traditioning* process in which the central hallmark that still gives continuity to an increasingly diverse global Pentecostal movement, namely the experience of charismatic empowerment, continues to be interpreted in new and contextually relevant ways as variations on that experience are read in dialogue with these biblical stories told about the first Pentecost. I propose to discuss first the nature of this traditioning process that, I will argue, describes the shape of Pentecostal hermeneutics. Pentecostals have always brought their stories with them to the biblical text, offering their own testimonies in conversation with those of the Bible's writers. Pentecostal doctrine, then, is distilled from conversations overheard by the congregation between attestations. Also, because Pentecostal doctrine plants its feet on shared experience, it must, by its very nature, be more vibrant and fluid in order to reflect new experiences offered in different times and contexts.

I would then like to consider three interpretive intersections of Pentecostal experience with Acts narratives in the twenty-first century. First, I wish to consider the new paradigm within which we all experience and read, that is, from within a postmodern worldview with its emphasis on the reader as a creator of meaning. I will consider ways in which Pentecostals are both more at home with and at times fundamentally at odds with a reading trajectory that gives the reader's experience a central role in hearing Scripture. Secondly, I would like to consider briefly the breadth of perspective offered in what is increasingly a global, non-western movement, so that what was once perhaps thought of as "the" Pentecostal perspective is increasingly revealed to be but one thread in a rich and growing tapestry of cultures, contexts, and stories. Thirdly, I would like to consider the ways in which even the story of United States Pentecostals

---

2. Masculine pronouns do not fully describe God's nature, and therefore, rather than avoid using personal pronouns all together, I've elected to describe the Spirit as "she" in acknowledgement of the fact that the image of God in humanity includes both genders.

in the original context of the modern world is itself challenged and transformed by fresh experiences and new stories coming amidst a transitioning worldview. A central question that provides a foil for this last consideration is the place that altered views of gender identity increasingly occupy on the broader church. As a tradition that leads with experience and says with Peter "this is that," what do Pentecostals do when a new and unfamiliar "this" is offered and affirmed?

## Reading as Traditioning

Kenneth Archer has grounded his Pentecostal hermeneutic in a particular historical narrative, that told by the first generation of modern US Pentecostals. Specifically, Archer argues the story the Pentecostal community of the early twentieth century told about itself makes up that community's Central Narrative Convictions and it is those convictions that, for Archer, allow for a specifically Pentecostal reading.[3] This "Latter Rain" narrative, says Archer, provides the primary reading lens for Pentecostal interpretation and is characterized by a renewed experience of charismatic gifting after a long "spiritual drought" precipitated by the apostasy of the Church.[4] The experience of an Acts-like encounter with the Spirit shapes contemporary Pentecostals' readings of scripture, providing according to Archer, not a particular interpretive method, but rather a distinctive narrative that resonates with the biblical narratives.

One critique of Archer's approach, though, is the extent to which global Pentecostalism can be described as a range of movements that share in common a Latter Rain narrative motif. Certainly, the eschatological urgency provoked by a global outpouring of the Spirit in the twentieth century suggested, just as it did in the first century, the immediacy of the anticipated eschaton. But just as with first-century believers, Pentecostals in the twenty-first century have found that the "soon return" of Christ has not meant in the first decade or the first generation or, indeed, the first century of the modern Pentecostal outpouring, so that the eschatological focus of the Spirit's outpouring may play less of a central role in Pentecostal theologies than it once did. Put differently, while Pentecostals may share in common a narrative of charismatic empowerment for ministry, the eschatological expectation may well occupy a somewhat different place in that defining narrative than it did a century ago.

Archer describes the interplay of narratives in dialogical terms, as the testimony of individual experience in the context of the community is brought into dialogue with scripture.[5] This discussion is better understood, I suggest, as a trialogue, with the Spirit as an active partner to be listened for and to whom to be yielded. So, the Pentecostal tendency to minimize the historical distance between the biblical narratives and their own testimonies is legitimized by both the shared experience of charismatic

---

3. Archer, *Pentecostal Hermeneutic*, 156.
4. Archer, *Pentecostal Hermeneutic*, 159.
5. Archer, *Pentecostal Hermeneutic*, 135, 144.

empowering and by the presence of the author of both narratives, of scripture and personal testimony, participating in the conversation.

I have described previously a traditioning process modeled in the Psalter. Israel's root memories are drawn on in times of crisis, reminding both those praying and God of those identifying narratives. So, when God answers and delivers, it is the frequent practice, even the obligation of the one saved to testify before the "Great Assembly," thus locating their particular experience in Israel's larger story and adding to that story. Reading the Psalms, though, it becomes clear that both the memories that the psalmist evokes and the testimony she or he offers are by no means fixed, but their telling of both memory and testimony is fluid, adapting to the needs and perspective of the moment. Experience is both shaped by and shapes the way that the one praying remembers Israel's story, and the renewed encounter with God forms that which they will add to the story. Israel's story with Yahweh grows and journeys to new places and, while it is a coherent tale, it is certainly more than the endless reiteration of the past.

Traditioning also describes Pentecostal readings in scripture. Testimony to experience is brought to the Bible as similar stories are sought and textual meaning and experience illumine and shape one another in the trialogue that ensues. Meaning is dependent upon and is shaped by the experiences of those who encounter God and write about it under the inspiration of the Spirit in scripture and by those who encounter the Spirit and offer testimony to that encounter in the community yielding to the same Spirit. Pentecostals are among those who (1) read with keen awareness and privileging of their own experiences of the Spirit and (2) anticipate that that same Spirit will speak not only in the "past tense" of the biblical writer, but in the active voice of one present with the reading community.

Pentecostal doctrine is shaped by this trialogue between experience, text, and Spirit, and as such while it remains coherent it should not be seen as simply static and uniform. Doctrine, which is not the inspired Word of God but rather conceptual renderings of that word in a particular context and from a particular worldview, must by its very nature be open to some level of movement since it reflects a conversation that is ongoing. The prominent place given to experiences of encounter by Pentecostals ensures that efforts to quantify meaning through the articulation of doctrine must remain incomplete. The first two doctrinal divisions in classic Pentecostalism, "Finished Work" which denies that sanctification is distinct work of the Spirit's grace and "Oneness" or "Jesus Only" Pentecostalism that denies Trinitarian doctrine, serve to illustrate this point. In my own generation, the doctrine of sanctification as a distinct crisis event thought to precede Holy Spirit baptism has lost much of the significance that it had for early Pentecostals emerging as they were from a holiness tradition. Moreover, while the majority of western Pentecostals remain Trinitarian, Allan Anderson points out that Oneness Pentecostals make up the largest grass root expression of classic Pentecostalism in China.[6]

---

6. Anderson, *Introduction to Pentecostalism*, 13.

Also, largely as a result of the broadening experiences resulting from the Charismatic movement of the sixties and seventies the doctrine of "initial evidence," that speaking in tongues is the necessary proof of the baptism in the Spirit, has been increasingly questioned, not because the five core Acts narratives have changed, but because of a growing number of testimonies to charismatic encounters with the Spirit that are not marked by that particular manifestation. When doctrine derives from a narrative rather than didactic portions of scripture and when those biblical narratives are accessed and interpreted through experience, of necessity, any resulting doctrine that seeks to codify those encounters must be open to re-evaluation in light of fresh experiences of the Spirit. Put differently; as important as doctrine is for guiding the faith and challenging that which divides and diverts the church from Christ and his cross, it is for Pentecostals the describer, rather than the determiner of the testimony/text/Spirit trialogue. Doctrine does not prescribe what God must be and how he must work, but rather it describes for Pentecostals this trialogical exchange as they seek to find their place in the larger narrative that includes both scripture and subsequent experiences of the Spirit. Doctrine arises, from and is responsive to, this traditioning process.

## Reading Acts at the Crossroads

Stronstad has reminded us of the central role played by those Acts narratives that describe varied experiences of Holy Spirit baptism in the first church and with three of those root narratives as conversation partners I would like to consider three narrative intersections in the many trajectories that are Pentecostalism in the coming decades; (1) the move to a postmodern, reader-centered worldview, (2) the multiplicity of indigenous Pentecostal communities globally with their own experiences, testimonies, and theological understandings, and (3) the challenge for western Pentecostals to hear the Spirit's voice as the shadow cast by Azusa street lengthens.

### Reader-Centered Postmodern Worldview

We read the Bible having stepped (or for some, having been dragged) into a postmodern milieu that has as its central tenet the denial of any single universal authority or the telling of any reality defining metanarrative, with a resulting focus on the local context and individual reading as the locus for generating meaning and truth. The voice of the reader eclipses that of the writer in determining the import of the biblical text. During the few decades that I have taught in Pentecostal institutions, the basic relationship of the student to the Bible has changed. Two or three decades ago the conversations revolved around what the Bible said and, if the inquiry ran a bit deeper, how correctly to interpret what was said. But having arrived at the one "right" reading, the only remaining question was "Will we or won't we do what God says do?" Today the Bible is less well known by students, but that in itself is not such a difficult problem to overcome. A far more durable shift has taken place in the assumptions that younger readers now bring to their study of the text. A conversation in a conservative Pentecostal college classroom today is much more likely to go, "I know that that's what the Bible says, but I think and I've experienced." Contemporary college students are much more ready to appeal to personal experience and to see their own perspective as valid, without feeling the need to relate it to a universal dictum equally authoritative for all believers. The question is not "Will the next generation of Pentecostal readers become postmodern in their thinking about the Bible?" In many ways they already are.

There is much in this shift that commends itself to classic Pentecostalism, such as the emphasis on personal experience, the preferencing of orality and narrative, and the insistence that meaning must be validated by relevance and applicability, so that some have argued for an easy relationship by Pentecostals with a postmodern hermeneutic.[7] But our jumping on the "postmodern bandwagon"[8] is held in check by the nature of the narrative itself, so that some scholars advocate a more moderate exchange rather than a wholehearted adoption or an adversarial avoidance of postmodern hermeneutical assumptions and practices.[9] Postmodernism, by definition, cannot countenance the exclusive and exclusionary claims of any metanarrative. The "no other gods before me" and "no other name under heaven given among mortals by which we must be saved" immediately press the postmodern reader outside the story, so that they observe selectively, being unwilling and unable to inhabit on its own terms a story that negates other stories. Such a stark reader-centered hearing can only listen from a distance because, metanarratives, such as the Bible, offer invasive testimonies that change or invalidate some stories while offering and affirming others.

It is, then, the voice of the "other" that a postmodern reading marginalizes or excludes altogether. The Spirit challenges and threatens to qualify and even annul some testimonies of experience and it is this voice that Pentecostals embrace, keeping them finally at odds with a thoroughgoing postmodern approach to scripture. If I have emphasized the voice of the reader's experience, it is also the case that the voice of the Spirit, listened for both in the biblical text and in the expectation of the Spirit's presence and participation in the trialogue, places limits on reader-response readings. The challenge common to all readers of the Bible is, however, particularly acute for Pentecostals who attribute so much to the Spirit's leading, namely, how best to distinguish the Spirit's voice from a Feuerbachian projection of our own voice into the heavens. How do we allow for the Spirit's voice to be truly other than our own?

Paul's encounter with the Spirit on the road to Damascus offers a poignant example of a Spirit-encounter transforming the reader's world dramatically. Though he learned no new passages and had the same knowledge base after his encounter with

---

7. Cargal, "Fundamentalist-Modernist Controversy."
8. Menzies, "Postmodern Bandwagon."
9. Noel, *Postmodern Hermeneutics*; Johns, "Postmodern Worldview."

Jesus and with a man guided by the Spirit as he had before, Paul's reading of the text was nevertheless, changed foundationally by his encounter with the Spirit as, to use his own words some years later, the veil was taken away.[10] The text had not changed, but its meaning had been stood on its head, so that it now spoke to Paul with a markedly different voice. On the one hand, this affirms a tenet of postmodern reading by underscoring the reality that the text's meaning was derived not simply from authorial intent, but was constituted by what Paul, the reader, brought to his readings, presumably both before and after his Damascus road encounter. On the other hand, however, his encounter with the voice of the "Other" in the person of Christ both shattered Paul's own reading perspective and situated him to hear the voice of the text very differently. In any true conversation, one speaks and influences, but one also hears and is shaped by their conversation partners. The assumptions of Paul's reading world and those of our own postmodern paradigm must be open to critique and transformation by the voice of the Spirit both in and along with the Bible. Pentecostals are familiar with having their reading world shifted by the experience of Spirit baptism. The question is worth asking, though, whether Pentecostal theology a century on is still open to the voice of the Other, so that we hold of both doctrine and our readings of the text loosely?

## Indigenous Global Pentecostal Communities and Experiences

A second intersection with the Acts narratives is occasioned by the globalization of Pentecostalism that has led to the Bible being read and its meaning understood in a rich array of contexts and cultural perspectives. Given the disparate nature of human experience, it would be unreasonable to expect that the living Spirit would be experienced in precisely the same way by every reader of the Bible, without regard to their culture and reading-world. My own experience teaching the Bible in classes made up of students from a dozen or more different cultures helped me to realize how very different the "obvious" meaning of a particular biblical text can be, depending on the culture that shaped its reader. The twenty-first century is witnessing a coming of age of non-western biblical scholarship as academics from the majority world are offering interpretations that are truer to their own perspectives and concerns.

On the day of Pentecost Jews from around the Hellenistic world heard the gospel in their own languages. It's unclear from the narrative whether they witnessed a miracle of speaking or of hearing. Did the disciples speak in all those languages or did the Spirit whisper into the ears of hearers, interpreting the tongues with comfortably familiar words? To learn a language is to discover something of the way that people think, express their emotions, order their social exchanges, and construct their understanding of the world. And every translator discovers quickly that there are words that

---

10. McKay offers a compelling contemporary example of the worldview changing effect of Spirit baptism on one's understanding of the Bible in his article. See McKay, "When the Veil is Taken Away."

simply do not translate fully and clearly from one language to another, so that meaning is never wholly transferable between languages. Regardless of the mechanism, though, the miracle at Pentecost was not simply that everyone understood the words, but that they truly heard them, that is that they experienced the Spirit's message as transformed from a foreign to a familiar word. An encounter with the Spirit of God, the creator of all peoples and cultures, is fully hearable linguistically and culturally. It is the difference between typing words into a translation software and hearing a native speaker, with all that she says and does not say with her nuanced choice of words. It would be the most extravagant ethnocentricity, then, to suppose that every people and culture would experience the Spirit in the same way.

Thus, the twenty-first century, much more than its predecessor, will witness the diversity of Spirit encounters from around our world. The relationship between human beings and the rest of God's creation, the role of the ancestors as those who continue to shape the lives of the current generation, and the place of the individual in the broader community are all cultural perspectives which will shape conversations with the Word and the Spirit. Indeed, some cultures engaging in this trialogue will find the interpretive distance between their own culture and those that wrote the Bible to be significantly shorter than is the case for a western culture just now emerging from modernism.

Foundational texts like Acts 1:8, "But you will receive power when the Holy Spirit has come upon you; and you will be my witnesses in Jerusalem, and in all Judea and Samaria, and to the ends of the earth,"[11] find substantively different meanings in disparate cultural settings. Historically in the United States, this verse has meant for many that signs and wonders offer a compelling endorsement of the gospel message, so that like the proconsul of Paphos, seeing the sign leads to believing the teaching. John Gallegos suggests a rather different interpretive emphasis in an Africa context. "There are three fundamental orientations of the African Pentecostal worldview," says Gallegos, "that determine how African Pentecostals engage Scripture: a spiritual orientation, an orientation toward wholeness, and a power orientation."[12] Power in this and many non-western contexts centers on the reality that spiritual forces are encountered on a daily basis so that the question becomes "Is this God more powerful than those that already dominate daily life?" Power for evangelism includes power superior to the spirits and spells of native healers, a power that restores health and wholeness to individuals and to the community. Connie Au, however, maintains that in the context of Chinese house churches where so much of their history and experience centers on persecution, the power to endure and overcome through suffering is a central gift of the Spirit.

---

11. Quotation is from the NIV translation (1984).
12. Gallegos, *African Pentecostal Hermeneutics*, 48.

> In the context of house churches in China, Pentecostalism is not just about the manifestations, but more importantly, about suffering for the faith and the praxis of these manifestations and other fundamental doctrines. . . . If gifts demonstrate the power of the Spirit, then suffering is certainly a gift as it requires the power of the Spirit to endure.[13]

In a Latin American context, religion and politics are often inextricably bound together, so that Liberation theology has interpreted salvation in terms of political action for social transformation. Karl-Wilhelm Westmeier, though, argues that in a Latin American context Pentecostals respond to political power with passivity. "Obviously, then, Pentecostals do not necessarily support the status quo. Rather, Pentecostals support the status quo and either traditional or revolutionary governments to the extent that these governments permit 'breathing space' for their churches."[14] Often denied the mechanism of a democratic process, spiritual power for Latin American Pentecostals can orient toward a pragmatic separation of church and state, challenging directly the historic fellowship between the two since the first contact with European powers.

Charismatic experience is also interpreted and expressed in ways that relate to and build upon pre-existing religious experiences.[15] So, for example, Allan Anderson points to the spiritual worldview that stands behind the prayer mountain phenomenon in Korean culture.

> Traditionally, the many mountains of Korea were believed to be places where good spirits lived, and both shamans and ordinary pilgrims would receive power from the particular spirit on each mountain. At the risk of oversimplification, the Prayer Mountain movement may be said to be a culturally relevant form of Christian practice that reflects the ancient spirituality of Korean people.[16]

Often in non-western cultures, various forms of shamanism predate the birth and spread of Pentecostalism, so that healing and deliverance ministries both supplant and to an extent, mirror these familiar forms of spiritual warfare. Westmeier reports that "Stoll finds that Pentecostalism functions to 'rechannel [the] popular religiosity of folk Catholicism' into a more truly Christian framework."[17] The miracle of hearing in one's own language on the day of Pentecost, far from being a one-time inaugural phenomenon, is better understood as archetypal, characterizing the ongoing encounter with the Spirit that calls for, even demands, an inculturated hearing.

---

13. Au, "Pentecostalism and Suffering," 96.

14. Westmeier, "Pentecostal Expansion," 73.

15. Keener, *Spirit Hermeneutics*, 80, points out that this process took place within the Bible itself, with views of Satan and bodily resurrection being influenced by the Persian cultures in which Jews found themselves.

16. Anderson, "Pentecostalism in East Asia," 126–27.

17. Westmeier, "Pentecostal Expansion," 76.

## Challenge of Hearing the Spirit's Voice Today

A third intersection with the Acts narratives that continue to shape our understanding of Pentecost can be found globally and is certainly prominent in my own US culture. A range of gender issues, from the legalization of same-sex marriage to the recognition of a variety of transgender choices, has caused and will continue to cause debate and division in the Christian church, and Pentecostals should not wish to remain aloof from the effects of such discussions. Another marked change that has taken place in my years of teaching is the answer to one of the survey questions that I routinely ask at the beginning of my Christian Ethics course, namely, "Can a person be a practicing homosexual and still be a Christian, filled with the Holy Spirit and in a living relationship with Christ?" The number of students who confess themselves both Christian and Pentecostal and who affirm that a person can be both of these has grown appreciably in recent years and I find myself wondering to what extent the Church's somewhat confused approach to addressing sexuality and sexual sin has contributed to the shift.

The Acts narrative of the first gentile conversion sheds light on a distinction that my generation of Pentecostals has not always made, the distinction between the categories "uncleanness" and "sin." In this almost comical story Peter is virtually dragged by the Spirit into the house of an unclean gentile who, together with all gentiles, has been declared clean by the Spirit. Indeed, it takes a heavenly vision, repeated three times, to get Peter to enter the house. Lest we think that Peter's strong reluctance stemmed from something other than his perception of gentile uncleanness, Paul's rebuke of him in Galatians 2 for refusing to eat with gentile believers reminds us that old prejudices die hard and that Peter would have made a poor choice to be God's evangelist to the Gentiles. Having entered Cornelius's house and begun to talk, the Spirit hijacks the conversation, baptizing Cornelius and his household in the Spirit so that they speak in tongues. Whatever one might think of the doctrine of initial evidence, in this instance at least, it was critically important that the gentiles did speak in tongues, because in the very next chapter Peter had to defend his decision to baptize them. Cornelius was a virtuous man, a Godfearer, so that the issue for Peter and many of his Jewish fellow believers was not his sinfulness, but rather his uncleanness, and the Spirit had taken Peter to task over his unwillingness easily to relinquish his belief in the latter. Indeed, the form of the vision, challenging as it did the Mosaic dietary laws, suggests that with the coming of Pentecost not simply gentile uncleanness, but the old covenant categories of purity and cleanness generally had been transformed in the new covenant. It is my contention that in discussing the question of sexual sin and its role in separating the sinner from Christ, it is distracting and counterproductive to cling to a category of separation that the Spirit so clearly sets aside in Pentecost, the separation between Israel (or the church) and all that it "unclean."

I have had the good providence for many years to have several same-sex couples, often in monogamous, decades-long relationships, as neighbors and friends. Like many of my students and colleagues, I have family members that I love and whose company I enjoy who are gay. Some are good, generous, and loving; some have very pronounced faults and frailties. Yet all of them, like everyone else before they meet Christ, have sins that separate them from God. Put differently, I have come to understand that, just as Peter could and should break bread with gentiles, Pentecostals can and should break bread with people of different gender choices, and yet, that to do so is not to offer endorsement for the sinfulness of their life choices. Just as Jesus ate with tax collectors and sinner, so, too, must his church do. A fear of "contamination" or guilt by association with them says more about our wrong motives and perceptions than it does about Christ's desire that all renounce their sins and come to him.

The story of Cornelius being declared clean, of course, does not address the issue of sin, but it does suggest that we are mistaken to confuse or equate sin with the morally neutral notion of uncleanness or impurity. The reality that everything from women in menstruation to persons born with physical disabilities to persons with leprosy to eating shrimp was unclean under the old covenant, does not in any way offer comment on the sinfulness of those persons (or foods). While it is the case that uncleanness is occasionally associated with sin, such as in the testing of an unfaithful wife in Numbers 5, the vast majority of the uses of the Hebrew *tame* refer to separation from persons and situations who are not in and of themselves sinful. It was this notion that some types of persons are unclean, then, that the Spirit is at pains to wash away in the Pentecostal outpouring.

Academic discussion among Pentecostals of gender issues is still in its infancy, so that dialogue partners are hard to come by. In one such study, though, Adriaan Klinken observes among Zambian Pentecostals a strong tendency, in that context, to associate religion, nationalism, and anti-homosexual politics.[18] Zambia in its constitution has declared itself to be a "Christian nation" and external pressure to legalize homosexuality and to grant equal rights and protection under the law to persons regardless of their sexual orientation is seen to be symptomatic of a Satanic attack on the nation that threatens its spiritual purity. Without commenting on the sinfulness of homosexuality, Klinken notes the unique treatment that that particular life choice receives in Zambia's moral image of itself, "with so many 'un-Christian practices'—such as drunkenness, prostitution, corruption and witchcraft—occurring and being tolerated or accepted in the country while homosexuality is singled out." Nor are many of the other sins mentioned in the Bible criminalized in Zambian society.[19] Klinken's study demonstrates a propensity among Pentecostals in that context to attach, uncritically, categorizations that were transformed by the coming of Christ and by Pentecost to their understanding of a particular sin.

18. Klinken, "Homosexuality," 260.
19. Klinken, "Homosexuality," 272.

If Pentecostals believe that homosexuality is a sin, as I do, then relating to homosexuals and transgenders as somehow fundamentally different from others separated from God by sin by invoking Old Testament categories of purity and separation is counterproductive to our goal of loving them and sharing the gospel with them. Also, I wonder if some of my students who struggle with the issue of whether or not homosexuality is a sin owe at least part of their uncertainty to having been told, either implicitly or explicitly, that gays are "unclean," only to learn from personal experiences and through relationships that they are, after all, simply people in need of Christ.

## Concluding Remarks

Pentecostals are known for their testimonies, for the stories they tell of the God who they meet. Also, they do not simply read the stories of the Bible but seek to find a place in them. Like the psalmists we read, we, too, tell the old stories, we encounter God anew, and we stand before the assembly and add to the tale. Pentecostals, and indeed all Christians, are called not simply to understand biblical stories, but to bring to them their own experiences of encounter with God and to attest to the reality that in the same Spirit we all live and move and have our being.

## Chapter 8

## Nothing to Sneeze at

*Receiving Acts 19:11–12 in the Canadian Pentecostal Tradition*

MARTIN W. MITTELSTADT

God did extraordinary miracles through Paul, so that even handkerchiefs and aprons that had touched him were taken to the sick, and their illnesses were cured and the evil spirits left them. (Acts 19:11–12)

---

WORLD-WIDE DAY OF PRAYER—2ND WEDNESDAY OF EACH MONTH
DAILY PRAYER MEETING AT HEAD OFFICE EACH MORNING AT 8:45
– SEND PRAYER REQUESTS –
ANOINTED HANDKERCHIEFS SENT TO SICK UPON REQUEST[1]

When my father-in-law passed away in the fall of 2001, my wife Evelyn and I discovered among the family keepsakes an anointed cloth previously distributed by Evelyn's great-aunt, Regina Dudman. Since I had become somewhat jaded by the shenanigans of preachers and their hankies, I thought little of the cloth and tucked it away. A few years ago, I rummaged through the family ephemera in search of the handkerchief. On the envelope, Auntie Dudman wrote: "In Jesus Name. Anointed Kerchief. Acts 19:11 & 12. Return to Regina Dudman when used enough, kindly," and on the back, she directed, "not to be sent around from one place to another as it is for the person only." I questioned family members and learned that the handkerchief dates to the early 1960s. While family members enjoyed lengthy conversations concerning the handkerchief, little did they know that the handkerchief would provide

---

1. *PT* (April 1, 1943–November 15, 1944).

the impetus for this study, my first attempt to examine a biblical text through the lens of reception history.

Anthony C. Thiselton defines reception history as the Bible's *nachleben* (literally, its "afterlife" or post-history), and Ulrich Luz speaks of the Bible's "history of influence," specifically, the "actualizing of text in media other than a commentary; e.g., in sermons, canonical law, hymnody, art and in the actions of sufferings of the church."[2] Given the recent success of period-based reception histories, such as the Ancient Christian Commentary on Scripture and Reformation Commentary on Scripture, and Pentecostal's irrefutable impact upon twentieth-century Christianity, the time is ripe for Pentecostals to share our contributions to the ongoing life of a biblical text.[3]

My interest in reception history parallels my growing dissatisfaction with the never-ending exegetical quest for original meaning and binding application. As I move further into reception history, I find the adventure incredibly refreshing, but not without its challenges. At times, I remember my struggle to own the Pentecostal heritage of my youth, not least because we live in a tradition marked by teachings founded upon narrative texts, such as Luke-Acts. In his *Charismatic Theology of St. Luke*, Roger Stronstad, not only helped me survive as a Pentecostal, but also opened my theological eyes to a new world. By introducing me to Luke the theologian, possibilities of normativity, and narrative's didactic potential, Stronstad provided me with the foundational resources to stave off Pentecostal opponents unwilling to allow the cumulative outcome of Lukan stories to serve as a basis for doctrine and practice. Pentecostals, like Stronstad, worked hard to defend normative doctrines and practices based upon narrative. Reception history, however, forces scholars to assess Pentecostal beliefs and practices based upon narratives that fail to meet his criteria. In this essay, I reflect on *one* such example. How is it that Luke's single and descriptive reference to the use of handkerchiefs for healing provides the impetus for Pentecostal practices?[4] As a tribute to Roger and his native land (and length restrictions), I limit my survey to accounts among Canadian Pentecostals.

## Canadian Pentecostals and Their Handkerchiefs

Luz is obviously not a Pentecostal. I say this because his media list for reception analysis of biblical texts fails to include "testimonies." For my examination of Pentecostal use of handkerchiefs, I turn first and primarily to testimonies in newsletters; in so doing, I seek veiled exegesis and insight in stories told for edification. In *The Apostolic Faith* (*AF*), the official newsletter of the Azusa Street revival, editors report receiving

---

2. Thiselton, "Holy Spirit," 209; Luz, *Matthew 1–7*, 95.

3. See Mittelstadt, "Receiving Luke-Acts."

4. I began collecting such stories before I stumbled on the invaluable essay by Thomas, "Anointed Cloths." I not only add to the primary data on Acts 19:11–12, but accept his invitation to further this conversation.

daily prayer requests from around the world. In response, they and participants at Azusa Street assure readers that in return, "Handkerchiefs are sent in letters to be anointed and blest for healing."[5] When readers respond with the practice's results, editors waste no time in sharing specific testimonies of such healing. A number of these accounts come from Canadians. S. A. Morrisburg of Ontario exclaims: "Received the handkerchief all right, and God sent two distinct waves of power over us. The lady had been recovering for some time and was helped by the laying on of the handkerchief. All glory be to God who does the work. She has taken no medicine, but is healed by faith. Hallelujah!"[6] Across the country, E. W. Johnson of Stockholm, SK, shouts:

> I feel led by the Holy Spirit to testify to the glory of God what He has done for me and my wife. The Lord has wonderfully healed me from catarrh of nine years standing. Glory! glory! glory! glory be to my dear Redeemer's name! Soon as I received the handkerchief, or as soon as I opened the letter, such power went through my whole being as I have never felt before, and I praise Him, I feel the healing balm just now go through soul and body. Glory to King Jesus, the great Physician of soul and body.[7]

Finally, a report on meetings in Manitoba:

> Winnipeg, Can.—There was a great Pentecostal Convention in Winnipeg beginning November 15th. Preachers and workers from all parts of Canada were present. A band of workers who were in Portland at the time received a call from God to go to Winnipeg, and they were present at the convention: Sister Crawford and Mildred, Sister Neal, Brother Conlee and Brother Trotter. About twenty were baptized with the Holy Ghost and many were healed. The people brought handkerchiefs and aprons to be blessed as in Acts 19:12, and the Lord did wonderful signs through the simple faith of the dear ones that brought them. The Lord healed one young man of the tobacco habit, taking all the desire for the stuff away from him, through an anointed handkerchief, and he was saved in his own room. Demons were cast out of those bound by them.[8]

These testimonies warrant initial comments. First, the practice of requesting, sending, and receiving handkerchiefs by mail finds early support at Azusa Street and at the Winnipeg convention. Second, though the editors publish only a handful of testimonies in conjunction with anointed handkerchiefs, nearly half come from Canada. Canadian readers responded favorably. Third, healing comes not only for physical ailments, but brings freedom from addiction and the demonic. Finally, neither those who submit testimonies, nor the editors, include instruction for or defense of the

---

5. *AF* 1.4 (1906) 1, 3; 1.5 (1907) 1; 1.6 (1907) 1.
6. *AF* 1.6 (1907) 3.
7. *AF* 1.9 (1908) 1.
8. *AF* 1.12 (1908) 1.

practice. Indeed, most of the reports do not reference Acts 19:11–12. The closest defense in the *AF* comes from the pen of Nora Wilcox of Denver, CO:

> People are being healed of scrofula, salt rheum, curvature of spine, locomotive ataxia, diseases of the eyes, ears, etc. . . . People of all ages with all manner of diseases are coming for healing, and the deaf, lame, and blind. *The Acts of the Apostles are being repeated here now*. Handkerchiefs are being blessed and sent to sick people in other places, and children of God are getting handkerchiefs blessed for unbelieving husbands and children and for sick folks here in and around Denver.[9]

Other American newsletters convey similar accounts. In *The Household of God* (Dayton, OH) editor (and traveling evangelist with roots in the Apostolic Faith Mission) William Manley receives and publishes the testimony of Mrs. Ellen Romilley of Toronto:

> Dear Sir:—Praise the dear Lord for His love to me for healing me while attending your meetings. I have had a very weak heart all my life and for years I have been suffering with an abscess in my left ankle.
>
> Two or three times a year I was forced to keep my room and bed for two weeks or longer at a time. Since you cast the demons out and laid hands on me in the name of Jesus I can truthfully tell every one I was healed while attending divine healing meetings. Praise the dear Lord, all pain has left me; not even the least soreness left for me to bear now.
>
> I was sure the Dear Lord wanted to heal me, because He has been so good to me in sending one of the sisters to my home to see me while I was suffering from this weak ankle. The dear sister told me to get up and come down to your meeting and get healed. I told her I would love to do so, only I could not walk. I gave her a handkerchief to take to you to pray over and to put the healing power into it.
>
> Two of the sisters returned about 5:30 p.m. with the handkerchief, blessed and pinned it upon my very sore ankle. The moment it was applied to the sore it seemed to make it better.
>
> Next day the sister was on her way to see me. I met her coming to my home. We went to the mission together. I went with the crowd to the upper room and there the Lord wonderfully healed me. Praise His dear name forever![10]

Still in Toronto, an ecstatic mother writes to *AF*, now highjacked to Portland, OR:

> Praise God for the wonderful cure! Some time past I mailed you a letter containing a handkerchief for a little girl. She had cataracts grown all over her eyes and her mother said she would spend her all if she could only cure her

---

9. *AF* 1.8 (1907) 1 (emphasis added).
10. Romilley, "Heart and Limb Healed," 10.

darling. She was brought to Toronto, and, oh, the torture those doctors gave that little baby. Six years passed and she was no better. I told my daughter that I was going to ask the saints to pray over the baby, and, praise our dear Lord, the Blood healed her and her lovely eyes are well and strong.[11]

And a reader from Collingwood, ON, reports, "God wonderfully blessed me when I received the anointed handkerchief and put it on my afflicted body, and now the healing stream abounded. My husband was afflicted in body and he put it on and got healed. I have been healed many times."[12] The final remark suggests the couple used the handkerchief repeatedly.

Since this newsletter installment receives an array of testimonies from the United States and Canada, *AF* offers explanation for use of a handkerchief. The issue includes a headline titled "Anointed Handkerchiefs for Healing," followed by an Acts 19:11–12 citation, and references to the use of handkerchiefs for healing and exorcism. The editors then draw the following parallel:

> The woman who had suffered with an issue of blood twelve years was perfectly healed by touching Jesus's clothes. And through faith and prayer and the laying on of hands of holy persons, filled with the Holy Ghost, a handkerchief or paper can be anointed with the same power today.[13]

As to the use of handkerchiefs received and sent out from the mission,

> The saints always lay them on the Bible, usually opening it to Acts because that is the foundation of our faith. They anoint it with anointing oil for the sick and lay their hands on it and pray the prayer of faith, and God honors His Word and heals a great many. They should be laid on in faith and prayer by one that is right with God. Some saints will wash them when soiled and lay them again on the sick and the power of God continues to heal. To God be all the glory.[14]

A turn to Canadian publications yields similar commentary. A. H. Argue, editor of the *Apostolic Messenger*, offers a pithy and polemical refrain: "Much is said against praying over handkerchiefs for the sick in this present day. Acts 19:12: 'So that from his body were brought unto the sick handkerchiefs or aprons, and the diseases departed from them and the evil spirits went out of them.' Verses 13–16 show that there was truly counterfeit and evil spirits to contend with just the same as today."[15] Though the lack of context for this statement makes it difficult to ascertain Argue's purpose, he appears to defend "extraordinary" healing in an ancient city marked by "extraordinary" forces.

---

11. *AF* 19 (1907) 3.
12. *AF* 19 (1907) 2.
13. *AF* 19 (1907) 2.
14. *AF* 19 (1907) 2.
15. *Apostolic Messenger* 1.1 (1908) 4.

PART II—READING ST. LUKE'S TEXT: HERMENEUTICAL CONSIDERATIONS

In 1927, the *Pentecostal Testimony* (*PT*), the official organ of the Pentecostal Assemblies of Canada (PAOC), recounts a successful evangelistic campaign at Sixth Avenue Pentecostal Tabernacle in Vancouver under Smith Wigglesworth and his daughter, Sister J. Salter. After reports of Spirit baptisms and healing, the commentary concludes: "At the final service, scores of handkerchiefs were anointed and prayed over," and participants returned home with ready-to-use handkerchiefs.[16] In his *Ever Increasing Faith*, Wigglesworth reflects briefly (not unlike Nora Wilcox) on the reason for this practice:

> In some places there are 200 or 300 who would like us to visit them, but we are not able to do so. But I am so glad that the Lord Jesus is always willing to come and heal. He longs to meet the sick ones. He loves to heal them of their afflictions. The Lord is healing many people today by means of handkerchiefs *as you read that He healed people in the days of Paul*. You can read this in Acts 19:12.[17]

Apparently, vast need gives rise to a straightforward reading and response based upon Acts.

A decade later, J. A. Hughes, District Superintendent of British Columbia, describes a mission under the leadership of Brother Stewart. Shortly after Stewart commits to faith, his wife contracts tuberculosis. When Stewart requests prayer from friends in Prince Rupert, BC, and Portland, OR, he receives an anointed handkerchief "with instructions that he and his wife should separate from all that was worldly and displeasing to God and come out and out for the Lord." After a week, Sister Stewart "was up and around and on her way to recovery."[18] The Stewarts soon received Spirit baptism and began a successful Pentecostal mission.

The use of anointed cloths also proves favorable among early PAOC leaders. In the minutes of an Eastern District Council held in 1932, the recorder remarks on the field report given by Bro. Wilson of Ayton, ON: "a handkerchief was anointed and prayed over by the conference on behalf of one of Bro. Wilson's assembly who was at the point of death. We believe that God still answers prayer."[19]

And what about the headline at the beginning of this essay? In thirty-seven consecutive issues on the inside cover of *PT* from April 4, 1943, until November 15, 1944, the PAOC executive leadership solicits prayer requests for a monthly day of prayer and distributes anointed handkerchiefs upon request.[20] At least two subsequent testimonies chronicled in *PT* refer directly to the efficacy of this practice. First, in an

---

16. "Vancouver Campaign," 2.
17. Wigglesworth, *Ever Increasing Faith*, 54–55 (emphasis added).
18. Hughes, "British Columbia's Indian Believers," 8.
19. The title of the document reads: "PAOC Eastern District Conference now convening in Calvary Tabernacle. Toronto," and serves as *Minutes* (August 23, 1932).
20. *PT* (April 1, 1943–November 15, 1944).

anonymous testimony in the May 1, 1943, publication, a woman from Caledonia, ON, describes persistent head pain, subsequent diagnosis of "poison in my system," and treatments that failed to bring relief. Satan further taunts her until: "One day as I was reading the Pentecostal Testimony, I saw where it said that they would send anointed handkerchiefs to the sick, as we find it in the Word of God, Acts 19:12." She chooses not to cite this verse, but continues: "When the handkerchief came, I put it on my forehead believing in our Lord Jesus that He would heal me, and the pain left. Praise the Lord for all His goodness toward me! I hope that some sick person will do the same, that God's Name may be glorified!"[21]

The second testimony appears in *PT*'s January 1, 1944, issue. Mr. Huskins of MacDowall, SK, recounts violent pains after a major surgery. He writes: "I am writing to let you know that I received the anointed handkerchief which you sent to me on request.... When I retired at night I placed the handkerchief on my body, and prayed in the Name of Jesus for healing. Next morning the pain was gone . . . and has not returned. Praise His Wonderful Name."[22]

Despite the early American and emerging Canadian newsletter accounts revealing the geographical reach of this practice among Canadian Pentecostals and the mid-century emphasis on the ritual by PAOC leaders, reports of anointed handkerchiefs wane in the second half of the twentieth century. Having said this, I discovered a recent account. On April 23, 2017, at Bethel Pentecostal Church in Sarnia, ON, pastor Tim Gibb and congregants prayed for two women. The congregation gathers around a man whose wife was watching live at home and suffering from a "tormenting" rash. Gibb, a PAOC minister, prays for the ailing woman and anoints a cloth to be placed upon the woman by her husband. Gibb then anoints and prays over a second cloth that he would take later in the week to a woman diagnosed with cancer. In his brief theological comments, Gibb suggests that Acts 19:11–12 should not be "confined for history books." Instead, the text presents a model for a contemporary "transfer of anointing." Gibb also proposes a parallel to Acts 5:15 and Peter's shadow: "every person here has a shadow . . . and the Lord wants to use you to touch them." According to Gibb, believers should not seek such agency, but he encourages openness to the "extraordinary."[23]

## Making Sense of Handkerchiefs

Historians have grappled with understanding the practice of anointing handkerchiefs. Canadian historian, James Opp, provides a socio-historical assessment. An outsider to Pentecostalism, Opp recounts a *Toronto Star* reporter's visit to meetings at Trinity Pentecostal Assembly in 1919. The reporter describes the two-hour experience akin to

---

21. "My Testimony of Healing," 17.
22. *PT* (January 1, 1944) 15.
23. Gibb, "April 23rd AM." Thanks to Caleb Courtney for alerting me to this event.

"'having visited another planet,' the 'strangest' yet 'happiest' sect he had ever visited."[24] He witnessed pre-service prayer, a rousing song service, a lengthy end-times sermon, and extended altar prayer. As the focus turned to the sick, the reporter continues:

> Three handkerchiefs were laid on a table on the platform, and three men laid their hands on them. There was another burst of vehement prayer from all sides. By the laying on of hands those handkerchiefs became charged with divine power, and when they are slipped beneath the pillow of the sufferers to whom they belong the patients will be cured or at least relieved of their maladies.[25]

Summarizing this and other newspaper reports, Opp concludes that participants show no interest in who prays, only that the cumulative effect of God's presence among the faithful is transferred to the handkerchief.

If Opp observes that "Handkerchiefs served to incorporate the bodies of others within this spiritually charged environment,"[26] R. Marie Griffith goes a step further. Griffith, a humanities professor at Washington University in St. Louis, MO, contends that when Pentecostals carry an everyday handkerchief "associated with wiping away tears or sweat or mundanely blowing one's nose" into sacred space, the consecrated cloth no longer functions to remove bodily excretions; it now serves as a carrier of divine power.[27] At the same time, Griffith views the shared handkerchief as an expression of "human kindness and generosity. You can see the power of asking someone for a handkerchief out of desperation—when you have tuberculosis or some degenerative disease—and all these handkerchiefs flood into you from this widespread community of people you may never have met before."[28] In summary, handkerchiefs move through the hands of a praying and hospitable community.

While Opp and Griffin provide insight into the practice, anointed handkerchiefs are notably absent in Canadian church historian Ronald Kydd's study of *Healing Through the Centuries*.[29] Kydd, a former Pentecostal-turned-Anglican, categorizes six types of healing. For examples of revelational healing (God-given insight), he refers to William Branham and Kathryn Kuhlman, and for soteriological healing (healing in the atonement), he points to Oral Roberts. In his turn to the reliquarial model (the use

---

24. Opp, *Lord for the Body*, 142.
25. Opp, *Lord for the Body*, 142.
26. Opp, *Lord for the Body*, 143.
27. Griffith, "Female Devotional Practices," 197. See also Griffith, "Prayer Cloths"; Hornik and Parsons, *Acts of the Apostles*, 206. From the various testimonies, Griffin offers a similar refrain. When women place or apply the cloth to their bodies, they often experience an immediate reaction. Also noteworthy, these handkerchiefs would not generally be associated with the hands of powerful Pentecostal preachers.
28. Griffith, "Prayer Cloths."
29. Kydd, *Healing*. He argues for six healing models: confrontational, intercessory, reliquarial, incubational, revelational, and soteriological.

of objects in conjunction with healing), however, Kydd marches through examples as early as the third century, follows with testimonies from Ambrose and Augustine, and provides a detailed account of healings at St. Médard on the grave of Jansenist François de Pâris (d. 1727). He includes, however, no examples of Pentecostals and their use of material objects. In my recent conversation with Kydd, he reflected: "I may have felt intuitively that assumptions underlying conventional (read 'Catholic') reliquarial practice and what Pents. [sic] have done were too dissimilar. However, I repeat, that never floated to the surface in my thinking as far as I can remember."[30] Kydd provides the first and most extensive study of healing by a Pentecostal, and admits his failure to draw on a healing category well-known across the Pentecostal spectrum.

## Pentecostals, Handkerchiefs, and Modern Hermeneutics

With the reflections of historians in the background, I remain most intrigued by implications for biblical studies. I cannot help but consider this practice alongside the evolving hermeneutics over the last one hundred years. As mid-twentieth-century Pentecostals, whether for good or ill, begin their quest for acceptance among Evangelicals, they slowly find their way into Evangelical institutions of higher learning, where they encounter Evangelical methodologies and battles. On the one hand, Pentecostals align with emerging Evangelicals to defy Enlightenment-like challenges to core Christian beliefs, such as the nature of revelation, Jesus's virgin birth, and resurrection. On the other hand, these same Evangelicals champion cessationism. Though Pentecostal students and future educators under such influence reject cessationism, they certainly embrace the Evangelical quest for the biblical story's historical reliability and the subsequent pursuit of moving from "what the text meant" to "what it means today," For many of these Evangelicals, if reliability meant that "then" included miracles, "now" no longer requires them. When biblical scholars begin to read the Scriptures through the lens of formalism in the 1970s, perhaps no tradition benefits more from this turn than Pentecostals. Even if a pioneer like Stronstad shows little methodological interaction with formalists across university hallways, he, nonetheless, reads Luke-Acts, not only for historical reliability, but also as theological story. Though Stronstad and fellow Pentecostal scholar Gordon Fee battle over questions of narrative as theology and the possibility of patterns and normativity, the Stronstadian impulse prevails, and Pentecostals join with narrative critics across the academy in a quest to read Luke-Acts for theology and praxis. Surely a victory for Pentecostal scholars![31]

This trajectory applies straightforwardly to Acts 19:11–12. Should Luke's account of healing through use of Paul's handkerchiefs be taken at face value? While many "enlightened readers" would dismiss this account as an impossibility, Evangelical

---

30. Ronald Kydd, email with the author, January 31, 2018. See further Kydd, "Healing in the Christian Church."

31. See Mittelstadt, *Reading Luke-Acts*, 46–80.

cessationists would defend the account's reliability, but deny modern equivalency. In response to such denial, I need not give a grand review of the Pentecostal penchant for healing, but state simply the "Jesus did it then, and he can do it now" approach.[32] With literary criticism's arrival, Pentecostal scholars defend modern-day healing as normative by way of the Gospels and Acts; Jesus's paradigmatic healing ministry extends to the new apostolic community, and subsequent—including contemporary—faith communities. For these defenders of contemporary healing, conversation and debate generally centers on questions such as the importance of faith, the healing agent's role and proximity, and the laying on of hands. To answer these questions, Pentecostal literary scholars agree that the healing accounts found in the Gospels and Acts leave readers with plenty of gaps. Having said this, how is it that Pentecostal scholars find in Luke-Acts good reason for diverse healing practices to be taught and experienced, yet say so little of handkerchiefs?[33] In my search for answers, I return to Pentecostal stories and storytellers, and find only more questions.

First, if the end of the twentieth century marks a highpoint for literary analysis, the new century brings an array of new interpreters. Among the recent invitees to the methodological guild are feminist, cultural, social-scientific, post-colonial, and global/glocal readers. But what about the Pentecostal "interpreters" represented by the testimonies and reports cited above? Since many of the more recent interpreters represent formerly-muted voices, could it be that the Pentecostals represented by testimonies and sermons remain muted because they speak and write outside the methodologies that rule the day?[34]

Second, I call attention to Pentecostal scholars, a specific extension of the larger academy, for they pay little attention to the kind of (Canadian) Pentecostal interpreters represented in the aforementioned testimonies.[35] If Pentecostal newsletter editors saw fit to record even the occasional use of anointed cloths for healing, do they (and other Pentecostal communities) not deserve the tag of an interpretative community as much as concurrent historical critics? Is it judicious to relegate *testifiers* not recognized as "professional, scientific, objective, scholarly, and critical" to the status of inferior interpreters? Are uneducated, eccentric, and marginalized voices unable to produce valid readings and application? Also, what about the unspoken yet inherent

---

32. See Alexander, *Pentecostal Healing*.

33. Some scholars have suggested possible parallels to the woman healed by touching the hem of Jesus's garment (Luke 8:44) or the sick brought to cross the path of Peter's shadow (Acts 5:15). See Thomas, "Anointed Cloths"; Tipei, *Laying on of Hands*, 145–47. Concerning the accounts among modern Pentecostals, gaps prove even more difficult. How does this practice gain traction? Where did believers find common interest in the practice? How did they interpret the Scripture? What about opponents to the practice? Due to space to limitations, I must leave such questions for further study.

34. See Sawyer, "Role of Reception Theory," his go-to essay to promote reception history and the Blackwell series.

35. For Pentecostal models of effective history, see Archer, "I was in the Spirit," 68–118; Green, *Lord's Supper*, 74–181.

elitism concerning the uneducated? Must legitimate interpreters have formal education and theological training to gain an audience in the academy?[36]

Third, if Acts commentators and hermeneutics professors—including many Pentecostal scholars—find little reason to pause on Acts 19:11–12, reception historians will not resist the opportunity to scour our one-hundred-year history on the *nachleben* of any text too often ignored. I certainly recognize the methodological boundaries on display in commentaries and retain my ongoing concern for disciplined interpreters and sound preachers (believe me!), but is it not time to listen more carefully to our received story? Is it truly impartial for scholars to employ the impact of patristic, medieval, Reformation, and other period-/tradition-based interpretations for their contributions to doctrine and practice, yet ignore insiders of the Pentecostal tradition? Indeed, why do scholars fail to recognize or acknowledge that contemporary go-to commentators and hermeneuticians are themselves products of post-Bible interpretative communities? In other words, how is it that *modern* interpreters engage in twentieth-century "criticism" (think scholars), a legion of diversity, yet ignore our Pentecostal voices? At the very least, I suggest that our accounts deserve a place in the *nachleben* of Acts 19:11–12.

Fourth, I suspect some Pentecostal scholars, myself included, prefer to disregard certain voices because of disappointment over theological misinterpretation and abusive practices within our tribe. Do we distance ourselves out of shame? Are these accounts concerning handkerchiefs better ignored among those of us who seek to promote a Pentecostalism that has come of age? I suspect the waning use of handkerchiefs among certain Pentecostals reflects the commercialized and abusive shenanigans of prosperity preachers, but I feel little such concern over the stories cited earlier. Though most accounts show little context, they demonstrate no signs of commercialization. Moreover, testimonies typically refer to the efficacy of a praying community; those who employ anointed handkerchiefs do not identify them with specific individuals or ministries.[37]

---

36. Having said this, some of these newsletters undoubtedly derive under editors with theological education, and concerning those who send in their stories and reports, we know little of their educational backgrounds.

37. Hornik and Parsons, *Acts*, traces the long history of such concern. For example, while the Council of Trent (December 1563) affirms authentic healings proclaimed as "'extraordinary deeds' of God and not to the efficacy of the cloth or even the saint," John Calvin cautions "as if Paul sent his handkerchiefs that men might worship them and kiss them in honour of them. . . . Yea, rather, he did choose most simple things, lest any superstition arise by reason of the price or pomp" (Hornik and Parsons, *Acts*, 204). Similarly, the sarcastic disdain of English deist Peter Annet: "how long these aprons or handkerchiefs must have been with the holy Paul, to be thus impregnated with this healing quality: and if they resisted sweat, or could stand a lather" (Hornik and Parsons, *Acts*, 204). And the recent concern of Justo González: "The reference to Paul's handkerchiefs and aprons has provided some supposed evangelists with an opportunity to make money by selling handkerchiefs and other items they have blessed" (Hornik and Parsons, *Acts*, 206).

Hornik and Parsons could have easily cited similar concerns regarding the rise of mid-twentieth-century North American prosperity preachers. A. A. Allen (Miracle Valley, AZ) distributes pamphlets

Finally, I may be among the last to call for reclamation of handkerchief practices, but I find myself humbled by the passion and courage of others in my tradition. In the spirit of Canadian philosopher Charles Taylor, I wonder if reception historians might demonstrate that anxiety over exegesis and safety from abusive practices may also come under the larger umbrella of a diminishing enchanted worldview.[38] Is it possible that stories of anointed cloths sound too much like magic? Stated in Lukan language, if Pentecostals have long concluded that too many non-Pentecostal readers and interpreters of Luke-Acts undervalue "all that Jesus began to do and teach" (Acts 1:1), is it conceivable that some among us may require a dose of our own medicine? A look back at our stories serves as a reminder not to forget what had once "seemed good to the Holy Spirit and us" (Acts 15:28). If these favorite verses serve as more than anecdotal commentary on our reading of Luke-Acts, I submit that passages like Acts 19:11–12 must not function simply as finished texts for review, but as living texts filled with potential and waiting to be performed.[39]

---

such as "God will Heal You," through his miniature handkerchief, and "A Prosperity Blest Cloth for You: From God's Man of Faith and Power," where he discloses new possibilities: "The cloth has no power to bring wealth. It should be used as a point of contact by which you can bring YOUR faith in unison with MY faith. This united action against the demons of poverty will set you free to receive POWER TO GET WEALTH in your life. Receive this cloth in faith—believing God said to you, 'It is he that giveth thee power to get wealth' (Deut 8:18). Place the cloth in your billfold, purse, or bankbook." Years later, W. V. Grant turns from subtlety to boldness; in a personal letter with a prayer cloth to a woman—not yet a regular prayer partner (!), Grant explains how to use the handkerchief: "Believe in Him as you enclose an offering of at least $5.00. . . . As a PROVE GOD gift to help guarantee His blessing in your life and home" (Grant, "April 28, 1989").

38. For a superior application of Taylor, see Smith, *How (Not) To Be Secular*. Space limitations do not allow for conversation concerning Pentecostal convergence of an enchanted and sacramental worldview. On sacramental possibilities for Acts 19:11–12, see Thomas, "Anointed Cloths," 111; Alexander, *Pentecostal Healing*, 84.

39. Thiselton, "Holy Spirit," 214.

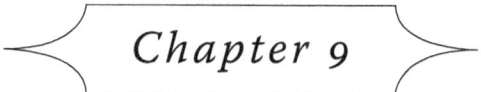

# St. Luke's Text and Postmodern Pentecostal Hermeneutics

BRADLEY TRUMAN NOEL[1]

The way how Pentecostals have read and used the Lukan texts has changed over the years. This chapter will trace the journey of Pentecostal hermeneutics from the Bible Reading method, through the embracing of the historical-grammatical method, to recent and distinctively Pentecostal contributions to hermeneutics that demonstrate an awareness of Postmodern influences and possibilities. We will conclude with an examination of the contributions of Pentecostal hermeneutics to our present reading of the Lukan material.[2]

## Pentecostal Hermeneutics

Early Pentecostalism, it may be said, did not have a carefully structured hermeneutic—or at least one of which they were aware. With the passing of the old "common sense" consensus, Protestants moved in one of two directions: Modernists or Liberals argued that the Bible's authority did not rest upon historical or scientific claims;

---

1. I consider it as a great privilege to pen this chapter in honor of Roger Stronstad. I did not have the pleasure of being his student, but I did discover his work early in my graduate studies. As a Pentecostal, studying at a Baptist institution, my professors took great care to ensure that I was thoroughly familiar with my own tradition. When the discussion turned to a topic for my thesis, my supervisor proposed that I examine the contribution of Gordon Fee to Pentecostal hermeneutics. This crucial suggestion initiated a life-long interest in Pentecostal theology in general, and our hermeneutics in particular. Not long into my research, I became aware of Stronstad's prescient work, *The Charismatic Theology of St. Luke*, one of the first to answer directly Fee's challenge concerning the importance of authorial intent in determining normative Pentecostal theology. In so doing, Stronstad made an early and inestimable contribution to Pentecostal understandings of Scripture.

2. This chapter draws directly and without constant referencing from Noel, *Pentecostal and Postmodern Hermeneutics*. Published by permission.

rather, authenticity was found in personal experience. In the opposite direction, the "academically informed Fundamentalists" continued to reaffirm the veracity and authority of Scripture by appealing to the older scientific Baconian Common Sense model.[3] It has been argued that Pentecostals and Wesleyan Holiness believers forged a third route, affirming both the objective nature of Scripture and the importance of personal experience as a means to reaffirm the inspiration of Scripture. Their concern ran deeper than simply proving facts from the Bible treated as a scientific textbook; Pentecostals sought to authenticate their Christianity via religious experience. "The Pentecostals said yes to both the authority of Scripture and the authority of experience. . . . Pentecostalism's lived experience was coloring their understanding of Scripture and Scripture was shaping their lived experience."[4]

Archer made a significant contribution with his detailed analysis of the interpretive process used by first-generation Pentecostals: "The Bible Reading Method was an inductive and deductive commonsensical method, which required all of the 'biblical data' on a particular topic to be gathered and then harmonized. Once this was accomplished, it could be formatted into a cohesive synthesis from a restorative revivalistic perspective."[5] Frank Ewart's historiography of Pentecostalism notes: "Their adopted method was to select a subject, find all the references on it, and present . . . a scriptural summary of what the Bible had to say about the theme."[6] The oft-quoted account of Charles Fox Parham suggests the same:

> Having heard so many different religious bodies claim different proofs as evidence of their having a Pentecostal baptism, I set the students at work studying out diligently what was the Bible evidence of the Baptism of the Holy Ghost, that we might go before the world with something that was indisputable because it tallied absolutely with the Word.[7]

As Parham's sister later confirmed, his students had no text but the Bible, and no method but to observe everything the Word had to say on a particular subject, and from there, with the help of the Holy Spirit, determine truth.[8] Again, this approach testifies to the widespread use of the *Bible Reading Method* among the earliest Pentecostals.

---

3. Archer, *Pentecostal Hermeneutic*, 40.
4. Archer, *Pentecostal Hermeneutic*, 63–64.
5. Archer, *Pentecostal Hermeneutic*, 91.
6. Archer, *Pentecostal Hermeneutic*, 75, quoting Ewart, *Phenomenon of Pentecost*, 60.
7. Parham, *Life of Charles F. Parham*, 52.
8. Parham, "Earnestly Contend for the Faith," 82.

## The Modernization of Pentecostal Hermeneutics

As Pentecostals established training institutions and interacted with scholars of other Christian backgrounds, a shift occurred. Whether it was motivated by a desire for increased acceptance among the larger evangelical community or influenced by the training the new Pentecostal educators had received at the hands of their professors from the wider University and Seminary world, Pentecostalism began to shed its reliance upon the Bible Reading Method. As Pentecostals were trained academically, increasing numbers "accepted the basic principles of Historical Criticism while rejecting the naturalistic worldview of Modernity . . . the historical-grammatical method became the primary method used by many Pentecostals. . . . The Pentecostals moved from the margins into mainstream, from the Paramodern into the Modern."[9]

By 1994, for example, in an article on Pentecostal hermeneutics, Gordon Anderson observes that there is indeed a place for "an identifiable, unique, and legitimate Pentecostal hermeneutic."[10] He notes, however, that, "Careful Pentecostal interpreters agree with other mainline evangelicals that the best way to interpret the Bible is to work to uncover the intended meaning of the text through the use of historical-grammatical methods."[11]

A decade earlier, Gordon Fee's popular *New Testament Exegesis* observes that "exegesis is primarily concerned with intentionality: What did the author *intend* his original readers to understand?"[12] Elsewhere Fee outlines three specific principles regarding hermeneutics and historical narrative. (1) Authorial intent is the chief factor in determining normative values from narratives. (2) That which is incidental to the primary intent of a narrative cannot have the same didactic value as the intended teaching, though it may provide insight into the author's theology. (3) For historical precedent to have normative value, it must be demonstrated that such was the specific intent of the author. If the author intended to establish precedent, then such should be regarded as normative.[13] As anyone familiar with Pentecostal hermeneutics and theology will quickly realize, the preceding "guidelines" challenged the Pentecostal position on Subsequence and Initial Evidence, each based on the assumption that Luke intentionally taught those doctrines from the related narratives in Acts. Further, the guidelines are grounded in the standard starting point of Evangelical hermeneutics: the search for authorial intent.

---

9. Archer, *Pentecostal Hermeneutic*, 131.
10. Anderson, *Pentecostal Hermeneutics*, 3.
11. Anderson, *Pentecostal Hermeneutics*, 5.
12. Fee, *New Testament Exegesis*, 27.
13. Fee, *Gospel and Spirit*, 92.

Three scholars, in particular, provided appropriate responses: William Menzies,[14] Roger Stronstad,[15] and Robert P. Menzies.[16] The reader will quickly observe that these scholars do not debate the merits of presupposing authorial intent as the foundation of the argument or appeal to experience as a qualified verifier of Pentecostal experience. Rather, those involved play by the rules set out by Fee, and work to demonstrate Luke's charismatic intent. In this discussion of Pentecostal theology, the embracing of "Evangelical hermeneutics" was well in hand.[17]

Several Pentecostal scholars view this new assimilation into Evangelicalism as negative and destructive to Pentecostal identity and doctrine. Mark McLean is representative:

> A strict adherence to traditional evangelical/fundamentalist hermeneutic principles leads to a position which, in its most positive forms, suggests the distinctives of the twentieth-century Pentecostal movement are perhaps nice but not necessary; important but not vital to the life of the Church in the twentieth century. In its more negative forms, it leads to a total rejection of Pentecostal phenomena.[18]

As a result, within the past 20 years, a variety of Pentecostal academics have proposed a Pentecostal hermeneutic that (1) takes seriously the strides made in biblical exegesis via historical and grammatical criticism; (2) places high priority upon the distinctive elements of the Pentecostal worldview, and (3) seeks to interact with trends in culture affected by postmodern thought—a subject we must now explore briefly.

## Basic Tenets of Postmodernism

At its essence, Postmodernism[19] is a worldview consisting of anti-foundationalism,[20] disbelief in pure objectivity, and deconstruction of "certain" knowledge, primarily characterized by a reaction to the prevailing worldview of Modernism. There are many facets of Postmodern thought; for the purposes of this chapter, I will provide a cursory look at four common themes.[21]

---

14. Menzies, "Methodology of Pentecostal Theology."
15. Stronstad, "Biblical Precedent for Historical Precedent."
16. Menzies, *Empowered for Witness*.
17. For a summary of this debate, see Noel, "Gordon Fee and the Challenge."
18. McLean, "Toward a Pentecostal Hermeneutic," 37.
19. For a sample of sources attempting to define Postmodernity, see Finger, "Modernity," 353–68; Gitlin, "Postmodern Predicament," 67–76; Percesepe, "Unbearable Lightness of Being Postmodern," 118–35; Van Gelder, "Postmodernism as an Emerging Worldview," 412–17; Kelly, *Understanding Postmodernism*.
20. "Foundationalism" may be defined as "Philosophical or theological approaches affirming specific truths as bases and criteria for all other truths" (McKim, *Westminster Dictionary*).
21. We are indebted in part for the breakdown of categories to Jaichandran and Madhav,

## Anti-Foundationalism

In the Postmodern mind, knowledge is uncertain. It, therefore, abandons foundationalism[22]—the idea that knowledge can be built upon the basis of irrefutable first principles and basic truths which lead ultimately to God, and upon which rational thought and progress can be based.[23] Postmoderns discard the Enlightenment assumption that truth is certain and therefore entirely rational.[24] Grenz observes, "The postmodern mind refuses to limit truth to its rational dimension and thus dethrones the human intellect as the arbiter of truth. There are other valid paths to knowledge besides reason, say the Postmoderns, including the emotions, experience, and the intuition."[25]

## Deconstruction

Jaichandran and Madhav note, "This is the essence of Deconstructionism—the knocking down of would-be big stories (worldviews with universalistic pretensions), often through listening to the local understandings of truth of minority communities."[26] Overarching universal narratives that connect with all of humankind (such as the biblical story of creation) are discarded out of hand. All meaning is created by the individual; the reality of one is as authentic as the reality of another, for we create our own realities. Though rejecting the universal stories of humanity, many Postmoderns accentuate the place of oral traditions, narratives, and stories within the community as essential.[27]

---

"Pentecostal Spirituality," 45–49.

22. Carl F. H. Henry considered anti-foundationalism "the one epistemic premise shared by all postmodernists" (Henry, "Postmodernism," 42).

23. See Erickson, *Truth and Consequences*, 252–72, for an excellent discussion on foundationalism, Postmodernity, and Christianity. Also, Depaul, *Resurrecting Old-Fashioned Foundationalism*.

24. Wallace asserts, "Concerning reason, postmodernists shun modernist views which inflate reason to the status of an entirely dependent, neutral, unbiased and objective instrument with which truth can and will be found" (Wallace, "Real Issue," 8).

25. Grenz, *Primer*, 7.

26. Jaichandran and Madhav, "Pentecostal Spirituality," 46. Grenz states: "The community of participation is crucial to identity formation. A sense of personal identity develops through the telling of a personal narrative, which is always embedded in the story of the communities in which we participate" (Grenz, *Primer*, 168).

27. Erickson, *Truth and Consequence*, 202. Another author suggests that "postmodernism [is] not a rejection of metanarrative itself, but [is] *a transitional phase rejecting the metanarratives of an integrated Western worldview for the emergence of new integrations in the global/local culture*" (Grigg, "Spirit of Church," 7).

## Denial of Absolute Truth and Importance of Experience

In the Modern mind, absolute truth is objective and available for discovery by the persistent truth-seeker. For the Postmodern, truth does not exist outside of subjective experience; therefore, no version of the truth is more significant than any other. Postmodernism is inherently pluralistic—some postmodernists believe absolute truth does not exist. The Postmodern mind rejects the Enlightenment notion that knowledge is objective.[28]

## Decimation of Individuality / Promotion of Community

For Richard Rorty, in particular, the self is created by external forces such as cultural and social factors, to the extent that searching for one's inner self is pointless—it does not exist. Postmoderns have decreased the prominence of the individual in favor of the importance of community. Rorty's strong emphasis on community and society denies humanity its traditional place within Modernism as the center of the universe. Grenz notes that in many cases,

> the postmodern worldview . . . affirms that whatever we accept as truth and even the way we envision truth are dependent on the community in which we participate. Further, and far more radically, the postmodern worldview affirms that this relativity extends beyond our *perceptions* of truth to its essence: there is no absolute truth; rather truth is relative to the community in which we participate.[29]

# Pentecostal Contributions to Hermeneutics

I join with those who believe that Pentecostalism was weakened considerably when it moved to an uncritical acceptance of a hermeneutic more in line with accepted Evangelical practices.[30] Further, reflecting upon the inroads postmodern thought is making in culture, we have called for a distinctively Pentecostal hermeneutic.

Kenneth Archer, for example, feels that if Pentecostalism is to remain the relevant missionary force that it has been, elements of Postmodernism are essential.[31] He notes with approval the efforts of some scholars to bring their Pentecostal spirituality and pneumatology to bear in their hermeneutical work.[32] Archer would blend the postmodern emphasis on the interpreter's context with classical Pentecostal spirituality.

---

28. Grenz, *Primer*, 7.
29. Grenz, *Primer*, 8.
30. Noel, *Pentecostal and Postmodern Hermeneutics*, esp. 96–121.
31. See, for example, Archer, "Pentecostal Hermeneutics." This line of thinking is found throughout Archer's work.
32. For example, Thomas, "Women, Pentecostals, and the Bible," 41–56. Thomas's work will be

> Today some Pentecostals attempt to express themselves with a purely modernistic hermeneutic (the historical-critical method), yet if Pentecostalism desires to continue in its missionary objective while keeping in tune with its classical ethos, then Pentecostalism must have a Postmodern accent; an accent which is both a protest against modernity as well as a proclamation to move beyond modernity; or better, after the modern.[33]

Although continuing to focus on authorial intent, Stronstad proposed hermeneutical guidelines, more in keeping with the early traditions and experience of Pentecostalism. On the role of experience within hermeneutics, for example, he has recommended that it must enter the process at the beginning, rather than the end as suggested by other Pentecostals scholars.[34]

> Stronstad contends that a Pentecostal hermeneutic will have a variety of cognitive (Protestant grammatico-historico exegesis) and experiential elements (salvation and charismatic experience). Stronstad recognizes that charismatic experience in itself will not enable one to become "an infallible interpreter" of Scripture; yet charismatic experience provides an important pre-understanding to the Scripture.[35]

Stronstad has challenged those who claim that Pentecostals often create theology from their shared experiences. By promoting the importance of experience at the beginning of the hermeneutical process, Stronstad has taken the first steps towards a truly Pentecostal hermeneutic.

Harlyn Purdy's 2015 effort endeavors to bring balance between those who would insist on maintaining Pentecostal allegiance to the historical-grammatical interpretation of Scripture, and those who would abandon it in favor of more reader-centered approaches. Acknowledging the Pentecostal debt to evangelicalism, Purdy holds that that this form of hermeneutics provides a bulwark against some of the more creative readings now advocated. He is, however, opposed to solely using the historical-grammatical approach, and insists that a distinctive Pentecostal hermeneutic is needed, with an eye towards postmodern thought, and open to a variety of critical methods including narrative, canonical, and rhetorical criticism. His contribution includes a quadratic approach that embraces scripture, the Spirit, the community, and interestingly, trained leadership. Although his use of Spirit-scripture-community mirrors proposals found elsewhere, the inclusion of trained leadership (to which Purdy devotes only ten pages, unfortunately), is a contribution to Pentecostal hermeneutics worth pursuing more deeply.[36]

---

explored in greater detail below.

33. Archer, "Pentecostal Hermeneutics," 80.

34. See MacDonald, "Classical Viewpoint," 58–75; Menzies, "Methodology," 1–14.

35. Archer, *Pentecostal Hermeneutic*, 143. See Stronstad, "Pentecostal Experience and Hermeneutics," 16–26.

36. Purdy, *Distinct*.

PART II—READING ST. LUKE'S TEXT: HERMENEUTICAL CONSIDERATIONS

In *Spirit Hermeneutics*, Craig Keener surveys the manner in which believers read Scripture "in the Spirit," and offers suggestions for improvement. He sets out to articulate what it means to interpret scripture in light of Pentecost when the Holy Spirit was poured out on the Church. Keener proposes a hermeneutic that takes experience seriously, but not without criteria that help keep it grounded. He wishes, therefore, to emphasize the importance of authorial intent, and the horizon of both original author and reader, but is determined to bring a Spirit-filled epistemology to bear that allows the reader to discern the pneumatic reading of texts.[37]

Eschewing the contribution of a particular hermeneutical method, Chris Green instead proposes "suggested practices in hopes of provoking the imaginative and affective sensitivities needed to read Scripture sanctifyingly."[38] Rather than beginning with the usual questions about Scripture's usefulness in revealing God and doctrine, Green instead begins with reader-focused concerns: how does the experience of reading Scripture contribute to our own sanctification? The answer comes in part via our own struggle with the difficulties of the biblical text. "The complexity and impenetrability of the language of the Scriptures, therefore, afford us sanctifying diversity. . . . The Scriptures teach us endurance not so much by providing us with examples of patience as by requiring us to persevere in the work of interpretation."[39] Through suggested practices such as "(Re) Reading in the Spirit, (Re) Reading with Community, (Re) Reading for Christ, and (Re) Reading from the Heart," Green desires to "construct an authentically Pentecostal hermeneutics [sic] and theology of Scripture that holds together in the tightest interplay the Spirit's work in prophecy and scriptural interpretation. . . . We have to read Scripture so that we are made wise with God's own wisdom, transformed as Christ's co-sanctified co-sanctifiers, meditators with him of God's divine-human beauty."[40] Green argues that his Pentecostal and charismatic readers need to shift from epistemological to soteriological conceptions of Scripture, and admirably succeeds in leading the way.

William Oliverio's recent monograph provides the reader with a useful survey of five types of Pentecostal hermeneutics since Azusa Street. (1) The original Pentecostal hermeneutic used by Parham, Seymour, Mason, and Haywood; (2) the "early evangelical-Pentecostal hermeneutic" availed of by stalwarts such as P. C. Nelson and Myer Pearlman; (3) the contemporary "evangelical-Pentecostal hermeneutic" observed above to be the choice of Fee, R. Menzies, and Stronstad; (4) the contextual-Pentecostal hermeneutic recently employed by Amos Yong, Chris Thomas, Jamie Smith and Ken Archer; and (5) what Oliverio describes as "the ecumenical-Pentecostal" hermeneutic favored by Mel Robeck, Frank Macchia, and Simon Chan.[41]

37. Keener, *Spirit Hermeneutics*.
38. Green, *Sanctifying Interpretation*, 142.
39. Green, *Sanctifying Interpretation*, 136.
40. Green, *Sanctifying Interpretation*, 119, 124.
41. Oliverio Jr., *Theological Hermeneutics*.

Focusing on both #3 and #4, above, Oliverio notes that the contemporary evangelical-Pentecostal hermeneutic stayed true to Hirsch's insistence on authorial intent, while the contextual-Pentecostal hermeneutic followed more in line with Gadamer's focus on mediating the reader's conceptual horizon with that of the text. In Oliverio's estimation, the latter phase commenced a distinctively Pentecostal approach to theology. Following Smith's "creational-pneumatic" model,[42] Oliverio proposes a hermeneutic that emerges not from human fallenness, but from God's blessing pronounced in Eden. Hermeneutics, therefore, proceed out of God's blessing on our creaturehood, flowing out of God's creational goodness.[43] As such, Oliverio concludes that "the best way forward for Pentecostal theology [is] a hermeneutical realism which allows for multiple productive hermeneutics to emerge that can faithfully account for the reality of the faith [including] new beliefs and practices that will surely emerge as a result of the continuing growth of Pentecostalism."[44]

## Contributions of Pentecostal Hermeneutics to Readings of Luke-Acts

Having explored the trajectory of Pentecostal hermeneutics, noting recent offerings in light of basic Postmodern thought, I will now conclude by exploring how the hermeneutics of Pentecostalism may contribute to a reading of Lukan texts. I will comment briefly on two areas, before unpacking a third in greater detail.

### The Pentecostal Story

Much has been made about the importance of both the metanarrative and personal stories within Pentecostalism, and rightly so. "What distinguished the early Pentecostal Bible Reading Method from the holiness folk was not a different interpretive method, but a *'distinct narrative.'* . . . The Pentecostal hermeneutical strategy at the foundational interpretive level was a unique story."[45] Faupel's work on Pentecostalism[46] is an important step in determining the Pentecostal story; indeed, he has demonstrated that the Latter Rain movement provides the "primary organizational structure for the Pentecostal narrative tradition."[47] This motif provided Pentecostals a framework by which they could interpret Scripture and determine their place within the narrative

---

42. Smith, *Fall of Interpretation*.
43. See Rice, "Bill Oliverio."
44. Oliverio Jr., *Theological Hermeneutics*, 361. Readers may also wish to consult Yong, *Spirit-Word-Community*; *Hermeneutical Spirit*; Noel, *Pentecostal and Postmodern Hermeneutics*; Archer and Oliverio Jr., *Constructive Pneumatological Hermeneutics*.
45. Archer, *Pentecostal Hermeneutic*, 94.
46. Faupel, *Everlasting Gospel*, esp. 19–43.
47. Archer, *Pentecostal Hermeneutic*, 100.

of Scripture. "The Pentecostal hermeneutical strategy at the foundational interpretive level was a unique story."[48]

For Pentecostals in particular, the postmodern emphasis on the value of narratives rings true with what has historically been a Pentecostal focus. As Erickson notes, a majority of the world's cultures still prefer oral, rather than written communication and find it easier to remember key pieces of information in story form, rather than rational, well-argued discourse.[49] Having gleaned the "distinctive doctrines" of Subsequence and Initial Evidence from the narratives of Acts, Pentecostals as a whole embraced the importance of the story long before the recent Postmodern focus. This alone has contributed significantly to our reading of Luke's theology, shared intentionally via narratives.

## The Miraculous Work of the Holy Spirit

Early Pentecostals strongly believed that they were the restoration of the New Testament church, the most precise expression of that which God intended the church to be since the days of the Apostles. As proof, Pentecostals often looked to the manifestation of miracles within their ranks. In their view, signs and wonders had been a regular occurrence during the days of the Apostles, but as one would expect, had ceased during the apostate reign of the Roman Catholic Church. God had withdrawn the working of miracles not permanently, as taught by Cessationists, but temporarily to show his displeasure with the lack of faith and unbelief of the church. Once the "true church" was again formed on the earth, miracles would again flow from the hand of the Almighty. For these earliest Pentecostals, their manner and method of scriptural interpretation was not only correct, but it was also consistently witnessed by God himself as the "signs followed" the correct preaching of His Word. One need not wonder whether Pentecostals had correctly interpreted their place in Christendom as recipients of the greater "Latter Rain" outpouring of the Holy Spirit; one need only witness the many miracles occurring within Pentecostalism to recognize the Divine stamp of approval on this "Full Gospel" message.

Recent offerings from Pentecostal scholars continue this focus on preserving the miraculous within a Pentecostal reading of Scripture. Almost to a person, those who bring a Pentecostal dish to the hermeneutical feast wish to preserve the early Pentecostal ethos that viewed the Spirit's working via the miraculous with the utmost appreciation. The application of this focus to readers of the Lukan text is quite apparent. From the many miracles of Jesus recorded in Luke, to the manner in which the Holy Spirit led the early Church through a variety of supernatural acts, the Pentecostal concern with reading Luke-Acts through eyes appreciative of the miraculous has never been more relevant. My own work has argued that for the sake of younger

---

48. Archer, "Pentecostal Story," 154.
49. Erickson, *Truth or Consequences*, 202.

generations in particular, receiving now the full impact of Postmodern influence and openness to the supernatural via human experience, Pentecostals must actively resist any reading of Scripture that fails fully to appreciate the miraculous.[50] Any tendency towards a hermeneutic, be it historical-grammatical or otherwise, that diminishes our focus on the early Pentecostal ethos of supernaturalism, imperils our discipleship and evangelistic efforts among our own sons and daughters.

## Pentecostal Hermeneutics and the Importance of Experience

For the Pentecostal, Scripture must primarily speak to the modern reader; simply focusing on what the text may have originally meant is not enough. Archer notes: "A hermeneutic that focuses only upon what the original inspired author meant . . . will not completely satisfy the requirements of a Pentecostal hermeneutic. The essence of Pentecostalism asserts that 'the spiritual and extraordinary supernatural experiences of the biblical characters are possible for contemporary believers.'"[51] French Arrington observes: "The real issue in Pentecostalism has become hermeneutics, that is, the distinctive nature and function of Scripture and the roles of the Holy Spirit, the Christian community, grammatical-historical research, and *personal experience in the interpretive process.*"[52] The Holy Spirit enables the reader to bridge the gap between the ancient authors of Scripture and the present interpreter.[53] Pentecostals contribute most substantially to hermeneutics in the area of experience and verification; some argue that Pentecostals and Charismatics, therefore, enjoy an edge in their reading of Scripture. Readers may be surprised to discover how many Pentecostal scholars have written in support of such a notion; a sampling will suffice.

### *John McKay*

McKay is highly critical of the tendency towards critical/analytical methods of scriptural study often found within academia, which does little to impart the truth of God to the student of the Scriptures.[54] Instead, he argues that charismatic readers must not let their involvement with the academy negatively impact their own interpretation of Scripture. McKay's personal experience with the baptism in the Holy Spirit changed his view of Scripture significantly, to the point that instead of embracing both "rational" and "spiritual" insight into Scripture as complementary, he chooses the more radical approach of suggesting the latter is superior to the former.

---

50. Noel, *Pentecostal and Postmodern Hermeneutics*; *Pentecostalism*, esp. 176–82.
51. Archer, "Pentecostal Hermeneutics," 75.
52. Arrington, "Use of the Bible," 101 (emphasis added).
53. Arrington, "Use of the Bible," 105.
54. McKay, "When the Veil is Taken Away."

It is not that charismatics cease to think theologically; quite the contrary. However, their theological perspective has changed, and changed so radically that they find their views no longer fit with those of the majority of today's biblical theologians, and furthermore that they fail to find much satisfaction from participating in their debates. It is my convinced opinion that a charismatic's view of the Bible must be different from everyone else's, be they fundamentalists, conservatives, liberals, radicals, or whatever.[55]

## William W. Menzies

William Menzies suggests three levels of a Pentecostal hermeneutic. The first is the *inductive* level, which is comprised of three varieties of inductive listening. The second is the *deductive* level, observing that after one has availed of inductive hermeneutics, certain patterns or theological motifs begin to emerge. Finally, he describes the *verification* level; if a biblical truth is to be promulgated, then it certainly ought to be verifiable and demonstrable in life. While others chide Pentecostals for their dangerous practice of "exegeting" out of the experience, Menzies argues that it is dangerous to develop theology and hermeneutics from *non-experience*.[56]

## Howard M. Ervin

Ervin suggests a *pneumatic* hermeneutic, "with a phenomenology that meets the criteria of empirically verifiable sensory experience (healing, miracles, etc.) and does not violate the coherence of rational categories."[57] A pneumatic epistemology also "provides a resolution of (a) the dichotomy between faith and reason that existentialism consciously seeks to bridge, though at the expense of the pneumatic; (b) the antidote to a destructive rationalism that often accompanies a critical-historical exegesis; and (c) a rational accountability for the mysticism by a piety grounded in *sola fidei*."[58] Because Pentecostals allow the experiential immediacy of the Holy Spirit to inform their epistemology, this contact with the *pneumatic* enlightens their hermeneutics in a way that may be considered beyond the traditional view of illumination. Ervin writes:

> Pentecostal experience with the Holy Spirit gives existential awareness of the miraculous in the biblical worldview. These events as recorded are no longer "mythological," but "objectively" real. Contemporary experience of divine healing, prophecy, miracles, tongues, and exorcism are empirical evidence of the impingement of a sphere of non-material reality upon our time-space existence with which one can and does have immediate contact. Awareness of,

---

55. McKay, "When the Veil is Taken Away," 38–39.
56. Menzies, "Methodology of Pentecostal Theology," 1–14.
57. Ervin, "Hermeneutics," 23.
58. Ervin, "Hermeneutics," 23–24.

and interaction with the presence of this spiritual continuum is axiomatic in a Pentecostal epistemology that affects decisively its hermeneutic.[59]

## John Christopher Thomas

Thomas seeks to develop a Pentecostal hermeneutic from the Acts 15 record of the Jerusalem Council, noting this passage records an example of hermeneutics based on the collective experience of the community, the Scriptures, and the primary role of the Holy Spirit in mediating these Scriptures to the context of the believers.[60] Contrary to the typical use of the historical-critical method, which regards authorial intent as a deciding factor in determining scriptural truth, he suggests that the tridactic method used in Acts 15 might better satisfy Pentecostals in their search for suitable hermeneutical principles.[61] Thomas's efforts clearly seek to present " hermeneutical approach that attempts to be consistent with early Pentecostal ethos and resists the complete adoption of an Evangelical and modernistic Historical Critical method."[62]

Regarding the role of context and community, Thomas notes that "the methodology revealed in Acts 15 is far removed from the historical-critical or historical-grammatical approach where one moves from text to context. On this occasion, the interpreters moved from their context to the biblical text."[63] Participants in the Jerusalem Conference first related their various *experiences* as God demonstrated his desired inclusion of the Gentiles in the plan of salvation. Only after these testimonies did the Apostles refer to Scripture; with the guidance of the Holy Spirit, passages were then chosen which supported the testimonies relating God's activity within the community. Indeed, the reference to the Holy Spirit in verse 28 indicates a stronger link to the Spirit's role in the interpretive process than many conservatives (or Pentecostals) are willing to admit.

## Roger Stronstad

I conclude by examining the work of our honoree. Stronstad believes there are five components to a Pentecostal hermeneutic: charismatic experiential presuppositions, the pneumatic, genres, exegesis, and experiential verification.[64] This is a clear wedding together of Pentecostal concerns with traditional Evangelical hermeneutics. If the five components are examined clearly, only the first and fifth are observed to be at all distinctive.[65]

59. Ervin, "Hermeneutics," 35.
60. Thomas, "Women, Pentecostals, and the Bible," 50.
61. Thomas, "Women, Pentecostals, and the Bible," 54–55.
62. Archer, *Pentecostal Hermeneutic*, 146.
63. Archer, *Pentecostal Hermeneutic*, 50.
64. See Stronstad, "Pentecostal Experience and Hermeneutics," 28–29.
65. In his recent work, Stronstad again lists five interdependent aspects of interpretation:

Stronsad is convinced that Pentecostals have much to offer traditional hermeneutics in the areas of pre-understanding and experiential verification: "The charismatic experience of the Pentecostal—ministering in the power of the Holy Spirit, speaking in other tongues as the Spirit gives utterance, being led by the Spirit—enables him to understand Luke's record of the activity of the Holy Spirit in Acts better than the non-Pentecostal."[66] Clark Pinnock writes, "We cannot consider Pentecostalism to be a kind of aberration born of experiential excesses but a twentieth-century revival of New Testament theology and religion. It has not only restored joy and power to the church but a clearer reading to the Bible as well."[67] Stronsad interprets this further:

> Charismatic experience in particular and spiritual experience in general give the interpreter of relevant biblical texts an experiential presupposition which transcends the rational or cognitive presuppositions of scientific exegesis. In other words, [the Pentecostals'] charismatic experience is an experiential presupposition which enables them to understand the charismatic life of the Apostolic Church, as Luke reports it, better than those contemporary Christians who lack this experience.[68]

## Conclusion

Recent Pentecostal hermeneutics, penned with an eye towards Postmodern realities, have much to contribute to a modern reading of the Lukan texts. While the excessive subjectivism often prevalent in the reader-response model of hermeneutics is not desirable within Pentecostalism, neither is the frequently detached and sometimes esoteric objectivity found within the historical-critical method. I believe Pentecostal hermeneutics ought to move towards the center of this debate, acknowledging and relying upon the historical-critical method with its objectivity on one hand, while remaining open to the more subjective verification of Pentecostal experience on the other. Does this openness to the role of experience leave the Pentecostals in a dangerous position as they read Luke-Acts? Hardly. William MacDonald declares: "Does this holy experience result in an experience-centered theology? Hardly. The better way to label it is this: Christ-centered, experience-certified theology."[69]

---

translation, exegesis, consideration of contexts, formation of biblical theology from exegesis, and applying the relevant application to the reader's life. We observe the charismatic dimension of hermeneutics is more muted. See Stronsad, "Some Aspects of Hermeneutics," 32.

66. Stronsad, "Some Aspects of Hermeneutics," 15. Badcock, *Light of Truth*, 139–44, agrees.

67. Pinnock in Stronsad, *Charismatic Theology*, viii.

68. Stronsad, "Pentecostal Experience and Hermeneutics," 17. This concept is not new. Indeed, some scholars believe that the reference to "private spirits" in the Westminster Confession of Faith refers to charismata in terms of interpretive help. See Curtis, "Charismata," 1–20.

69. MacDonald, "Classical Viewpoint," 64.

## PART III

# Reading St. Luke's Theology: Pneumatological Ambiences

"Pentecostals and Charismatics must remember that the gift of the Spirit is not just a spiritual blessing; it is a responsibility. Its meaning extends beyond the prayer room and the worship service to a world which needs to hear a prophetic voice in concert with the demonstration of the power of the Spirit."

—ROGER STRONSTAD, *THE CHARISMATIC THEOLOGY OF ST. LUKE*, 83.

# Chapter 10

## The Charismatic Ecclesiology of St. Luke
*Biblical and Systematic Theology in Tandem*

DAVID COUREY[1]

As a novice Pentecostal pastor, I was transfixed as I perused a brand new book by a teacher at Western Pentecostal Bible College. In my ministerial formation, I had read, with profit, Leslie Holdcroft's *The Holy Spirit: A Pentecostal Interpretation* but here was doctrine in a different key.[2] Roger Stronstad's *The Charismatic Theology of St. Luke* created a theological revolution for many a young Pentecostal in 1984.[3] In the wake of James Dunn's *Baptism in the Spirit* and Frederick Dale Bruner's *A Theology of the Holy Spirit*, both published in 1970, not much had come along in 14 years to buoy hopes that there was a way around or through Dunn's biblical and Bruner's theological impasse.[4]

Then along came Stronstad to redefine the whole game. The genius of Stronstad's work is that it articulated biblical arguments with strong theological corollaries that made a wholistic Pentecostal theology possible, and defensible. For me, as a searching young pastor, with the passion of a convert, Pentecostalism had nurtured the affective dimension of my being, but having encountered evangelical theology was destabilizing. Stronstad came at just the right time to assuage the cognitive dissonance, integrating for my intellect and affection. In 1999 he pushed the contours of his thought further with *The Prophethood of All Believers*, where, consistent with his

---

1. I have known Roger Stronstad through his writings since 1984. I was thrilled finally to meet him in 2012 at the Society for Pentecostal Studies. His humility, selflessness, and transparency were impressive for a scholar whose ministry has shaped so many pastors and has contributed so meaningfully to Pentecostal thought. I have long envied those who have known him personally, but I am honored to participate in this *festschrift*.
2. Holdcroft, *Holy Spirit*.
3. Stronstad, *Charismatic Theology*.
4. Dunn, *Baptism in the Holy Spirit*; Bruner, *Theology of the Holy Spirit*.

portrayal of Jesus as the eschatological Prophet, he demonstrated Luke's intention to cast the church as the eschatological and prophetic successor of Jesus.[5] In so doing, he created an eschatological and pneumatological ecclesiology gravid with theological potentials.

In this essay, I desire to explore "the charismatic ecclesiology of St. Luke" in the context of the interface between biblical and systematic theologies. In particular, I will show that Luke's ecclesiology is the consequence of his pneumatology and his eschatology and that this relationship tells us something about the interdependency between biblical theology and the loci of systematic theology. At least, in this case, biblical theology seems in need of systematic categories to make itself understood, and, in turn, relevant systematic contemplation can best be done nourished by biblical reflection.

## Tensions between Biblical and Systematic Theology

I will step into the troubled waters of this frothy debate, only long enough to establish the focus of the present paper.[6] Since Johan Philipp Gabler's inaugural lecture at the University of Altdorf in 1787, the relationship between biblical theology and systematic theology has been, to say the least, complicated. Gabler's point was that biblical theology is essentially a historical discipline, divorced from the dogmatic work of systematics, and therefore, occupied with grasping the authorial or cultural horizons of the text. As venerable an evangelical authority as J. I. Packer reminds the interpreter that "*iblical texts must be understood in their human context.*"[7] But, one the one hand, Gabler's approach without a countervailing emphasis on the unity of Scripture, atomizes the text, promoting the diversity of biblical testimony, and reducing its value for normative theology. On the other hand, evangelicalism has generally endorsed methodologies that emphasize the timeless unity of Spirit-inspired revelation, sometimes collapsing legitimate distinctions in search of its transcendent message.

The problem in the emergence of Pentecostal theology has been between these two fronts. Either the text of Scripture is so reduced to an ancient source, for historico-cultural exegesis that it does not lead to useful theologizing; or the appropriation of biblical data within a larger theological project has been more ideologically than textually driven. The former is endemic to the historical-critical project. As Ellen T. Charry has alleged, such approaches are ultimately "emotionally inaccessible to believers and academically unacceptable to the wider academy."[8] Jon Ruthven catalogs the latter problem. He noted in the mid-nineties that evangelicals could only, with

---

5. Stronstad, *Prophethood of All Believers*.

6. For sustained discussion see Green and Turner, *Between Two Horizons*; Klink III and Lockett, *Understanding Biblical Theology*; Reynolds et al., *Reconsidering the Relationship*.

7. Packer, "In Quest of Canonical Interpretation," 50.

8. Charry cited in Treier, "Biblical Theology," 22.

difficulty, imagine that the domains of biblical theology and charismatic theology could find any meaningful overlap. On the one hand, through content analysis, Ruthven demonstrated that evangelical theological categories drawn largely from systematics, obscured the charismatic emphases of the text. On the other hand, by applying the same categories as an objective means of doing biblical theology, doctrinal loci such as pneumatology and soteriology and subcategories like "faith" and "the kingdom of God" yielded profoundly charismatic profiles.[9]

The real challenge is not the objective reading of the text shorn of any tradition, but the awareness of traditional presuppositions within the larger Christian story. Of course, Pentecostalism can also bring its own ideological lens to bear upon the text. John Christopher Thomas mentions the theological paradigm of the five-fold gospel and the role of experience and narrative in the charismatic worldview, among distinctives of a Pentecostal hermeneutic which condition interpretation.[10] Such interpretation, nourished by the reflection of the charismatic community, and judiciously applied in conversation with the broader tradition can add polyphonic tone and depth to the contemporary discussion, rather than impede theological development. Jürgen Moltmann is one theologian who has discerned the way forward here.[11]

The impasse between systematic and biblical theology has led to lengthy discussion and acrimonious dissension. Reformed scholar, Richard B. Gaffin suggested the dismissal of the term "systematic theology" in favor of the more objective "biblical theology." Gaffin concurred with John Murray's charge that an unbalanced systematics demonstrates a "tendency to abstraction." In keeping with Murray's concern for theological overgeneralization, Gaffin suggested that "iblical theology is indispensable to systematic theology because biblical theology is regulative of exegesis" since it roots revelation in the redemptive history of God.[12] This view makes systematics the product or logical consequence of biblical theology. As late as 2000, D. A. Carson pronounced that "in terms of authority status there needs to be an outward-tracing line from Scripture through exegesis towards biblical theology to systematic theology."[13]

But Kevin Vanhoozer, representing the emerging movement toward theological interpretation of the Scriptures, claims that "systematic theology is not simply a second step that follows biblical theology; rather, it is a partner in the exegetical process itself."[14] This observation goes further than calling into question the possibility of an objective, value-free hermeneutic, or, suggesting, as Carson allows, theological

---

9. Ruthven, "Charismatic Theology and Biblical Emphases," 217–36.

10. Thomas, "Reading the Bible," 108–111.

11. Follow Moltmann's trajectory in conversation with the Pentecostal tradition in these three works: *The Church in the Power of the Spirit* (1977); *The Spirit of Life* (1992); and *The Source of Life* (1997).

12. Gaffin Jr., "Systematic Theology and Biblical Theology," 291, 293.

13. Carson, "Systematic Theology and Biblical Theology," 102.

14. Vanhoozer, "Is the Theology of the New Testament One or Many?" 38.

"back-loops" that inform the interpretive process.[15] Vanhoozer asserts that it enables contemporary believers to "express . . . the same judgments about what is fit for followers of Jesus to say and do—via different language and concepts, in situations far removed from the original context."[16] The very categories by which such interpretation is mediated are unapologetically the loci of systematic theology. As A. A. Hodge indicated years earlier, "there are several special departments classed under the general head of Exegetical Theology, which involve in some degree that arrangement and combination of Scripture testimonies under topics or subjects, which is the distinctive characteristic of Systematic Theology."[17] Rather than the terminus of a linear process, systematic theology may be seen as a partner along with biblical theology in the interpretive process that yields the useable gains of exegesis.

A considerable amount of Pentecostal reflection has taken place in the interstices between exegesis, biblical theology and this kind of theological interpretation. A forceful example arises from a pivotal claim in Stronstad's work, that "Luke is found to have a charismatic rather than a soteriological theology of the Holy Spirit."[18] This profoundly theological conclusion derived from Lukan biblical theology has provoked one of the defining debates in Pentecostal theology.[19] Here the systematic loci become fundamental to the argument, as Stronstad argues that confusing the vocational (prophetic) function of the Spirit with the soteriological dimension highlighted in Paul and John is a "serious methodological error and leads to a gross distortion of Luke's very clear and explicit pneumatology."[20]

In the spirit of Stronstad's work, and along with the contributors to *Reconsidering the Relationship Between Biblical and Systematic Theology in the New Testament*, this paper is an experiment in theological interpretation of the Lukan corpus. It demonstrates Stronstad's method of combining pneumatological and eschatological observations in the formation of a charismatic ecclesiology and closes by offering an example of how this can lead to fruitful theologizing.

---

15. It is not my intention to enter the debate surrounding theological interpretation of the Scriptures, which goes much farther than my modest proposal here. For a short but serviceable survey see Charlie Trimm, "Evangelicals, Theology, and Biblical Interpretation," 311–30.

16. Vonhoozer, "Is the Theology of the New Testament One or Many? 38.

17. Hodge, *Outlines of Theology*, 21.

18. Stronstad, *Charismatic Theology*, 14. The centrality of this affirmation is demonstrated by the fact that it is developed further in Stronstad, *Spirit, Scripture, and Theology*, which reproduces a 1987 lectureship at Assemblies of God Theological Seminary, along with other papers.

19. Stronstad frames his position squarely in opposition to Dunn. See Stronstad, *Charismatic Theology*, 73. For an extended discussion, see Turner, *Power from on High*; *Holy Spirit and Spiritual Gifts*, esp. 47–56; Menzies and Menzies, *Spirit and Power*; and, most recently, Atkinson, *Baptism in the Spirit*.

20. Stronstad, *Prophethood of All Believers*, 122.

## The Foundations of Lukan Ecclesiology

Concluding *The Prophethood of All Believers*, Stronstad points to the church. "The prophetic community and the Spirit-filled and Spirit-ful prophets who make it are the heirs and successors to Jesus, the eschatological anointed prophet who was himself powerful in works and word."[21] The culmination of Stronstad's charismatic theology of Luke is his charismatic ecclesiology. This is consistent with the theological reflections of other charismatic and Pentecostal thinkers. Catholic Ralph del Colle declared that "the church exists in the outpouring of the spirit [*sic*]."[22] Frank Macchia takes it as axiomatic that "*aptism in the Spirit is baptism into an ecclesial dynamic, the ecclesial Spirit.*"[23] That is, Spirit baptism is constitutive of Lukan ecclesiology. This is the import of the command to the disciples to wait in Jerusalem till they had been endued with power; the journey of Peter and John to Samaria to confer and witness Spirit reception; the explanation to the Jerusalem church of the baptism of the Gentile household of Cornelius; and the inclusion of the Baptist's disciples at Ephesus.

## The Theological Components of Luke's Spirit-Baptism

But what is this baptism in the Spirit? I have argued elsewhere that this Pentecostal baptism is, in fact, the nexus at which two significant theological trajectories within the Lukan narrative meet.[24] The Luke-Acts corpus narrates the downward movement of the Spirit as he comes upon the Virgin at the Annunciation, then again upon the Messiah at his baptism, then as he leads Jesus into the wilderness and ultimately to the cross. This account is repeated with the messianic community, from its Spirit-baptism through its persecutions and martyrdoms, and its *ethne*-transforming, empire-defying witness.[25] I have called this a *pneumatologia crucis*. But this dynamic is coupled with an eschatological dynamic that transfigures the Spirit-baptized community. The promise was that the disciples would be baptized with the Spirit and fire. The Old Testament resonances of apocalyptic judgment are clear, particularly when Peter's explanation of Pentecost places it within the eschatological context of Joel's prophecy. Such a notion of Spirit-baptism sees it as the means by which a here-and-now pilgrim people locked in the peril of the Christian mission are released into the liberty of the eschaton.[26] This *eschatologia crucis*, mediating the powers and hope of the age to come, is what nourishes the courageous witness of the charismatic community.

---

21. Stronstad, *Prophethood of All Believers*, 116.
22. Del Colle, "Outpouring of the Holy Spirit," 247–65.
23. Macchia, *Baptized in the Spirit*, 167 (emphasis added).
24. Courey, *What Has Wittenberg to Do with Azusa?*, 196, 198.
25. Courey, *What Has Wittenberg to Do with Azusa?*, 202–4.
26. Courey, *What Has Wittenberg to Do with Azusa?*, 196–97.

PART III—READING ST. LUKE'S THEOLOGY: PNEUMATOLOGICAL AMBIENCES

The above account betrays the theological paradigm that has informed my interpretation of the biblical data. I read the Luke-Acts corpus through the lens of Luther's theology of the cross, which I find to be an appropriate model for overcoming the triumphalism which has infected the popular Pentecostal reading of the text. But if this is an adequate account of Spirit-baptism, *per se*, what does it bring to an evaluation of Lukan ecclesiology? If Spirit-baptism is indeed constitutive of Luke's idea of the church, then it is best conceptualized by its component theological emphases.

Luke's ecclesiology does not appear as an independent locus of his thought, rather it arises as a result of his pneumatology and eschatology. Luke's carefully constructed narrative demonstrates an emerging ecclesiology among the early followers of Jesus. As a clear demarcation between Judaism and Christianity slowly develops, eschatology and pneumatology appear to be the fault lines of this separation, and Luke's ecclesiology becomes defined in these terms. I wish to demonstrate the close ties between theological loci and the biblical themes that undergird them. The emergence of the new community in Luke-Acts involves a close appreciation of the relation between Israel and the Gentiles; kingdom and power; and eschatological hope and pneumatological mission.

## Luke's Eschatological Ecclesiology

Spirit-baptism from the start discloses its eschatological significance from the fiery language of the Baptist in the Gospel, to the apocalyptic imagery of Joel at Pentecost. It collapses together OT metaphors of judgment and power, deliverance and vindication—all of which look to the final liberation and triumph of Israel, and the accomplishment of God's purposes in the earth. Also somehow, this includes the Gentiles—for God's Spirit will not be hoarded for Israel alone, but will be poured out on all flesh in the last days![27]

Darrell Bock, in assessing Luke's ecclesiology, notes that the church bridges old covenant and new covenant realities.[28] This is to follow N. T. Wright and Jacob Jervell. Wright claims, "Jesus did not intend to found a church *because there already was one*, namely the people of Israel itself. Jesus's intention was therefore to *reform* Israel, not to found a different community altogether."[29] Jervell sees the church in Luke-Acts as primarily a Jewish entity, a restored Israel, whose admission of Gentiles and experience of the Spirit are eschatological signs of the end of the age.[30] Indeed, the kingdom talk in Luke cannot be dissociated from Israel and its eschatological restoration.

---

27. Del Colle affirms that "the outpouring" and "the gift of the Holy Spirit is an eschatological sign of what is to come, even as it manifests itself in the present" (Del Colle, "Outpouring of the Holy Spirit," 262).

28. Bock, *Theology of Luke and Acts*, 371–72.

29. Wright, *Jesus and the Victory of God*, 275.

30. Jervell, *Theology of Acts of the Apostles*, 16, 40, 109.

This is precisely the burden of Pentecostal texts in Acts 1 and 2, where the relations of Israel, the kingdom, the church, and Spirit-baptism are so clearly in view.[31] The witness of the apostolic church contributes to the eschatological goal of Israel: drawing the nations under the reign of the Davidic King.[32] Stronstad demonstrates how Jesus follows the Davidic motif. He, too, receives the Spirit, but must await the fulfillment of his royal destiny. He, too, lives as anointed-but-not-yet king![33] But, says Stronstad, "the voice from heaven—specifically the quotation of Isa 42:1—turns the reader away from royal sonship to a new, radically different understanding of Jesus's ministry. . . . Jesus ministers exclusively, from first to last, as the anointed prophet."[34]

The charismatic community is also called to prophetic function as it seeks to span between the ages of Luke's inaugurated eschatology. The church also serves as anointed-but-not-yet-king. It follows the model of Jesus, whom God anointed with the Holy Spirit and power and who "went about doing good and healing all who were oppressed by the devil, for God was with him" (Acts 10:38).[35] Yet, like her Lord, the church faces rejection, persecution, and for some, martyrdom.[36]

The foregoing places the Lukan church and its mission firmly within an eschatological context. It presupposes continuities between OT promises and NT trajectories that strengthen the warrant of applying the eschatological category of systematic theology to plumb these biblical resonances for their contemporary ecclesial application. This is what Stronstad does as he picks up on the Royal motif and its turn to the Prophetic. Stronstad tells us, based on Luke 24:19, "that works empowered by the Spirit and words inspired by the Spirit are the complementary components of a *prophetic* ministry, both for Jesus and the disciples."[37] The inauguration of the last days is linked to the outpouring of this Spirit of prophecy, beginning with its incipient eruption surrounding the infancy narratives; the baptism of Jesus, and his programmatic declaration in Luke 4; but pre-eminently with the events of Pentecost. The eschaton finds further embodiment in the emergence of the charismatic community, which is marked by the Spirit of prophecy. In this regard, the prophetic daily pattern of "the church in the power of the Spirit" is its proleptic experience of the kingdom. In his description of "the prophetic way of life," Luke Timothy Johnson, sharpens the eschatological priorities for contemporary ecclesial practice: "being led by the spirit [sic], sharing possessions, engaging in an itinerant mission, exercising servant leadership,

---

31. Blumhofer summarizes Luke's basic hermeneutic as follows: "The belief that God's eschatological restoration of Israel has begun in the community gathered by Jesus Christ and that the effects of that restoration extend to the nations" (Blumhofer, "Luke's Alteration of Joel 3:1–5," 501).

32. Butticaz, *L'identité de l'Église*, 77–78; Blumhofer, "Luke's Alteration of Joel 3:1–5," 513–14.

33. Stronstad, *Prophethood of All Believers*, 44.

34. Stronstad, *Prophethood of All Believers*, 43.

35. Biblical references are taken from the ESV.

36. Twelftree offers an excellent perspective on parallels between Jesus and the church in Twelftree, *Luke-Acts People of the Spirit*, 30–44.

37. Stronstad, *Prophethood of All Believers*, 38.

bearing powerful witness before religious and state authorities."[38] A church-oriented in this way demonstrates a counter-cultural character identifying its locus of value in the eschaton.

## Luke's Pneumatological Ecclesiology

While Luke's ecclesiology has clear eschatological resonances, there can be little question that these are inseparable from the pneumatic dimension. Spirit baptism is constitutive of the church, but has as its goal something other than the church.[39] This is suggested by the global scope of the baptism's call to the ends of the earth; the "all-flesh" nature of its reach, the multicultural dimension of that day's xenolalia and the promise with which Peter closes his Day of Pentecost sermon: "for you and for your children and for all who are far off, everyone whom the Lord our God calls to himself" (Acts 2:39).[40] This spatial/temporal inclusiveness of the promise mediates the kingdom to us in the here and now, and beyond. What is staggering when contemplating the pneumatological aspect of the church is the breadth of the Spirit's grasp and mobilization of the anointed community toward the eschatological goal of the restoration of all things.[41] Thus, the pneumatological dimension of Luke's ecclesiology is largely missional.[42]

Stronstad makes this clear from the start of his *Charismatic Theology* all the way through *Prophethood of All Believers*, and throughout his corpus. Axiomatic to Stronstad's project is a highly theological construction of the distinction between a soteriological pneumatology in Paul and a charismatic, or vocational, or prophetic pneumatology in Luke.[43] This move on Stronstad's part creates an exegetical and biblical space in the Lukan writings for the development of theological concepts essential to Pentecostal theology; particularly for a pneumatically-driven missional ecclesiology.

---

38. Johnson, *Prophetic Jesus, Prophetic Church*, 4. Johnson, a proponent of theological interpretation of the Scriptures, sees the process of interpreting the prophetic (theological) significance as mediated through its canonical normativity as discerned by the gathered community. See Johnson, *Prophetic Jesus, Prophetic Church*, 5–7.

39. "The church is not incidental to Spirit baptism but is rather its integral outcome. Also, Spirit baptism is not a *super-additum* but is essential to the life of the church" (Macchia, "Spirit-Baptised Church," 206). See also Macchia, *Baptized in the Spirit*, 156.

40. Macchia, *Baptized in the Spirit*, 257–58.

41. Yong, *Missiological Spirit*, 13–50.

42. Significant contributions to Pentecostal ecclesiology which build on this missional dimension include Lord, *Spirit-Shaped Mission*; *Network Church*; Clifton, *Pentecostal Churches in Transition*.

43. In his collection of essays, Stronstad adds a Johannine perspective to the mix "Whereas Luke has but one dimension of the activity of the Spirit in his pneumatology, namely, service, and John has two, service and salvation, Paul has three dimensions: service, which he shares with both Luke and John; salvation, which he shares with John alone; and sanctification, which is his exclusive emphasis" (Stronstad, *Spirit, Scripture, and Theology*, 155). See especially chapter 6 (115–36) and the newly included chapter 7 (137–58).

Thus, Stronstad claims, "for Luke the gift of the Holy Spirit is charismatic; that is, it is given to God's people to empower them for effective service in His kingdom . . . the gift of the Spirit always results in mission."[44] He portrays this in the ministries of charismatic prophets (such as Peter, Stephen, and Paul), and of the community of charismatic prophets, all of whom extended the reach of the kingdom following the Acts 1:8 paradigm.

Considerable discussion in ecclesiology pits idealized renderings of the church against concrete descriptions of particularized congregations.[45] But the missional aspect of the church provides a dynamic, and pragmatic dimension to the proper theological discussion of the church, that delivers it from simple, static idealizations. While the pneumatic model of Lukan ecclesiology does not completely resolve the tension between these approaches, it opens a space so needed in the contemporary situation, for theological reflection on pragmatic church strategy.[46] There is room within the pneumatological imagination to elaborate Lukan motifs within current contexts. Yong suggests this may represent an application of Vanhoozer's notion of Spirit-directed speech-act interpretation within the contemporary "Acts 29" theo-drama of ecclesial practice.[47] Thus, Stronstad warns the church of wrong approaches to charismatic ecclesiology, that is, dramas which transgress the prophetic imagination. On the one hand, are those churches who stagnate setting aside *charismatic* ministry, for a more didactic model, on the other, he laments, are those churches who neglect prophetic service, seeking charismatic experience at the expense of the Spirit's missional dynamic.[48]

## Ecclesial Implications of Stronstad's Reading of Luke-Acts

In my effort to show the reciprocal relationship between systematics and biblical studies in Roger Stronstad's work, I have proposed that he may be understood as an unconscious exponent of theological interpretation of the Scriptures (TIS). I find this useful in developing my thesis that Stronstad proposes a distinctively charismatic ecclesiology through the implications of Luke's missional pneumatology and kingdom-driven eschatology. The claim that Stronstad applies TIS may seem a curious proposition to some. He certainly makes no pretension to such a designation, nor does he consciously write as a part of that community. But a simple comparison of his

---

44. Stronstad, *Spirit, Scripture, and Theology*, 155.

45. Healy complains that modern ecclesiology has become too abstract and normatively conditioned to attend to "the living, rather messy, confused and confusing body that the church actually is. It displays a preference for describing the church's theoretical and essential identity rather than its concrete and historical identity" (Healy, *Church, World, and the Christian Life*, 3).

46. Ormerod, "Structure of a Systematic Ecclesiology," 3–30.

47. Yong, *Hospitality and the Other*, 55–56.

48. Stronstad, *Prophethood of All Believers*, 120–22.

work, with the concerns of the movement, stated in Kevin Vanhoozer's introduction to the *Dictionary of Theological Interpretation of the Bible* makes Stronstad's *oeuvre* a good fit.

## Stronstad as Theological Interpreter of Luke-Acts

Vanhoozer tells us what TIS is *not*, and then gives a sense of what it *is*. First, it is not the imposition of a confessional grid on the text. Noting Stronstad's (even strict) application of an intensely literary and narrative methodology, it would be disingenuous to accuse him of reading the text through an expressly Pentecostal grid, though in a moment we will say in agreement with another definitional claim, that he does read it firmly ensconced in the Pentecostal community. Secondly, Vanhoozer claims TIS is not simply the result of a general reading hermeneutic such as one would apply to any book. Indeed, one sees this clearly in Stronstad through his careful ear to OT motifs, and particularly Septuagintal resonances. Thirdly, Vanhoozer asserts that TIS is not captive to methodology, but attends to the divine, a point he makes more forcefully later. Clearly, reading Stronstad makes evident his interest in the divine/human connection, and while he applies a coherent methodology, he is always aware of the divine dimension.

In affirming what TIS *is*, Vanhoozer maintains that all biblical interpretation within a faith context carries theological presuppositions. "Biblical scholars must have recourse to theology in order to make sense of the text's claims."[49] Stronstad constantly resorts to pneumatological and eschatological language in order to formulate his Lukan ecclesiology. The foregoing seems a pedestrian observation, yet the implications of arriving at a theologically value-free interpretation of Luke-Acts reduce the work to an artifact within a history-of-religions framework. This displaces Vanhoozer's next affirmation regarding TIS, which he claims is "characterized by a governing interest in God, [and] the word and works of God."[50] Certainly, the heart of Stronstad's ecclesial project is to attend to the divine Word and to take seriously the prophetic community "powerful in words and works." Finally, Vanhoozer proposes, in some sense not fully agreed upon, that Scripture has an ecclesial voice. Some may emphasize the divine authorship "behind" the text, while others find authority in inhabiting the symbolic world of the final form of the text. Still, others find meaning in the interpretive community itself. In this regard, Stronstad's work meets all three criteria to a greater or lesser extent. As already shown, there is little question that he is attentive to the divine action behind the text. Also, as evidenced by the intensely narrative treatment in *A Pentecostal Biblical Theology*, Stronstad receives the biblical account in its canonical unity tracing the turning points of the divine plot across history.[51] His supernatu-

---

49. Vanhoozer, "Introduction," 21.
50. Vanhoozer, "Introduction," 22.
51. Stronstad, *Pentecostal Biblical Theology*.

ralist account of Luke's charismatic theology demonstrates how fully he inhabits the thought-world of Scripture. On the third criterion regarding the interpretive community, however, it is unclear how to assess Stronstad. He clearly writes from within the Pentecostal family, but without imagining that this context conditions the reception of the text, as Vanhoozer suggests. Rather, Stronstad, I suspect, would argue that the objective reception of the text is formative of the charismatic community.

Stronstad practices an active theological engagement as he consciously lays the groundwork for Pentecostal theologizing. An oblique example is both interesting and illuminating. In discussing Gordon Fee's assessment of the biblical foundation of Pentecostalism, Stronstad calls him an iconoclast, "tearing down the hermeneutical pillars on which the structure of Pentecostal doctrine is built," claiming that his hermeneutic is "no longer Pentecostal in any normative sense of the word, for he has positioned Spirit baptism within conversion rather than with vocation."[52] If one's adherence to Vanhoozer's defining criteria for TIS, would mark a scholar as a proponent, it appears that Stronstad qualifies, and this hermeneutic influences his particular approach to a Lukan ecclesiology formed by pneumatology and eschatology.

## Power in the Charismatic Church of the Cross

If biblical studies and systematic theology must stand in a reciprocal relation, then one should never collapse into the other. Stronstad is careful to nuance his work clearly within the context of NT theology. But his interaction with systematic categories makes his work highly suggestive for theologians. In what follows, I would like to suggest one potential path that interacts with my own construal of Pentecostal theology through the lens of Luther's theology of the cross.

One dimension of Luke's missional pneumatology is the promise of power after the Spirit comes upon the church. Both Luke 24:49 and Acts 1:8 stipulate that this a specific kind of power: the power to be witnesses, like Paul, of all that we have seen and heard (Acts 21:15). This implies what Stronstad has already said, we have seen and heard because we have experienced the charismatic community mighty in words and works. And, oh what Pentecostalism has made of this power from the Wesleyan wells from which we drank, to the charismatic rivers which sprang up from us! B. H. Irwin's Fire-Baptized Holiness Association expected progressive baptisms of dynamite (from the Greek *dunamis*), selenite and oxynite, while the African American W. E. Fuller praised God for "the blood that cleans up, the Holy Ghost that burns up and the dynamite that blows up."[53] But even in more recent times, we are challenged to experience God in power encounters, power healings, and power evangelism. As a charismatic teacher, Joyce Meyers tells us, this power is available to assist each one.

52. Stronstad, *Spirit, Scripture, and Theology*, 11.

53. Fuller cited in Robins, *A. J. Tomlinson*, 44. "It was powerful enough to blow sin back to hell," Robins adds, perhaps tongue in cheek.

> The Holy Spirit is the third Person of the Trinity; He is the power of God. His multiple roles as Comforter, Counselor, Helper, Intercessor, Advocate, Strengthener and Standby can be summarized by saying that His purpose is to come into us with His abiding Presence and power and help us do things with ease that would otherwise be hard or even impossible.[54]

One might be excused for gaining a triumphalistic notion of Pentecostal power, were it not for the plainly kenotic trajectory of the Spirit in Luke-Acts.

Far from ever victorious, one might argue that the movement of the Spirit in Luke-Acts is downward. Luke's pneumatology of the cross Spirit moves from heaven to earth, from Jesus's baptism to the cross, and from the church's Pentecost to persecution and martyrdom. Along the way, both Jesus and the church serve their world with proclamation, healing, and modelling the radical love of the charismatic community. Supernatural empowerment as an expression of the kingdom, however, arises from Luke's *eschatologia crucis*. Power means persuasive words and acts; wisdom and faith; and guidance through prophecy and visions (Acts 2:41; 4:31; 6:3, 5; 10:17; 11:24; 16:9).[55] Together, these twin perspectives imply that the charismatic church offers its witness through Spirit-empowered acts of selfless service. Power is demonstrated in serving others, as the kenotic motif implies, and yet in that extended love, one might anticipate the miraculous, as the eschatology of the cross suggests.

In the North American context, the charismatic church of the cross poses an interesting challenge. While languishing in prison, Dietrich Bonhoeffer speculated about how the church could survive in "a world come of age." He may not have anticipated the charismatic dimension, but he captures the essence of the church that such a world will need.

> The church is church only when it is there for others. . . . The church must participate in the worldly tasks of life in the community—not dominating but helping and serving. . . . It will have to see that it does not underestimate the significance of the human "example." . . . The church's word gains weight and power not through concepts but by example.[56]

This kind of church, whether with signs and wonders or not, will still need a superhuman source of power, and its effectiveness will be measured, as it always should be, by how well it exemplifies its Lord. One wonders how Yong's imaginative pneumatology might evaluate the church we currently experience against the church Bonhoeffer imagined.

Stronstad's biblical work, then tempered by theological interpretation, offers highly suggestive access points for theological reflection on the praxis and nature of the church. Following the model of Spirit baptism as occurring at the nexus of

---

54. Meyer, *Filled with the Spirit*, 7–8.
55. Stronstad, *Charismatic Theology*, 51–52, 55, 72. See Mittelstadt, *Spirit and Suffering*, 24.
56. Bonhoeffer, *Letters and Papers*, 503–4.

eschatology and pneumatology, the notion that the charismatic community comes into being in precisely the same way presents a certain theological symmetry. When these insights are reflected upon theologically through Luther's *theologia crucis*, they propose a model of a charismatic church of the cross which could be powerfully effective in this "world come of age."

# Chapter 11

# Prayer for the Spirit in Luke 11:1–13

## Craig S. Keener[1]

Although the Lord's Prayer has often been discussed in connection with the *Sitz im Leben Jesu* and its setting in Matthew's Sermon on the Mount, less has been made of the function of this pericope in its Lukan context. In Luke 11:1–13, this prayer serves as a model prayer for receiving the Holy Spirit necessary for bold proclamation of the prophetic word of Jesus.[2] It also fits a pattern of prayer before several corporate outpourings of the Spirit in Luke-Acts (Acts 1:14; 4:31; 8:15; cf. 6:6; 9:11; 10:9, 30; 19:6), encouraging us as we pray for God to pour out the Spirit afresh today.

## Introductory Issues

It is often observed that it was customary for teachers to teach their disciples specific prayers,[3] as when R. Tarfon's disciples want him to teach them the appropriate blessing for a particular setting.[4] This verisimilitude suggests that Luke 11:1 transmits at least one of the original settings in which Jesus taught this prayer.[5]

---

1. It is a privilege to dedicate a redactional study regarding Lukan pneumatology to Roger Stronstad, whose redactional work on Lukan pneumatology has influenced a generation of us younger scholars. I wrote the original version of this study in 1989, planning to contribute it someday to an appropriate *festschrift*, of which none could be more appropriate than this one.

2. The notion of the Lord's Prayer as a prayer for the Spirit is not original with me. I originally learned it from my professor Ben Aker, to whom I am grateful. I am also grateful to my doctoral student Esteban Hidalgo for retyping my older, manually-typed paper into a Word program.

3. White, *Biblical Doctrine of Initiation*, 77; Jeremias, *New Testament Theology*, 170; Leaney, "Lukan Text," 110.

4. T. Berakhot 4:16–18, quoted in Smith, *Tannaitic Parallels*, 129.

5. The parallel passage in Matthew belongs to a topical arrangement on prayer (Matt 6:5–15).

Because prayer addressed the king of the universe, it was too crucial to be interrupted, even to return a king's greeting[6] or to save one's life.[7] This may explain why Luke adds an explanatory clause *hōs epausato* to the preceding temporal note in 11:1, if it is not simply a mark of the disciple's respect for Jesus.

Although fixed prayers were known in this period, they were often meant to be adapted.[8] One may therefore presume that Jesus's prayer here, given to the disciples, was meant to be adapted by them but taken very seriously, and this could help account for the two recensions of the prayer found in our extant Gospels.

M. D. Goulder argued that Matthew derived the material for the prayer from Jesus's teaching on prayer in Mark, adapting it to the Kaddish, and that Luke abbreviated Matthew's form.[9] Despite Matthew's freedom in midrashic adaptation, however, the Prayer is intrusive enough into the structure of its present Matthean context to suggest that Matthew would have been drawing on prior tradition rather than freely composing, and Goulder presupposes that Luke used Matthew rather than, as most scholars contend, both drawing on a common source. The parallels with the Gethsemane tradition that Goulder envisions as sources for the Prayer may simply attest to the cohesiveness of Jesus's teaching on prayer.

Van Tilborg adapted this thesis to argue that the Markan Gethsemane tradition used for the prayer in Q evoked the Kaddish prayer because of the language of "God's will."[10] It is unlikely, however, that Q should draw on the Kaddish, yet depend on Mark who explains, perhaps with some imprecision, Jewish customs for a Gentile audience (Mark 7:3); "God's will" is also noticeably absent from the Lukan recension of the prayer. Some plausibly suggest, though sometimes on questionable evidence,[11] that the Lord's Prayer in some form was known to Western Christianity by the time that Matthew wrote his Gospel in the East.

Later scribes assimilated the shorter Lukan reading of the prayer to the longer Matthean reading;[12] a majority of scholars view the shorter Lukan text as antecedent to the more developed one in Matthew.[13] In both forms, as in the Decalogue, matters

---

6. Exod. Rab. 9:3 ("We have learnt," appealing to b. Ber. 30a).

7. B. Ber. 32b–33a, bar. (a baraita was supposed to be earlier, Tannaitic tradition). On the greatness and efficacy of prayer, see Montefiore and Loewe, *Rabbinic Anthology*, 342–81.

8. M. Aboth 2:13 (Danby, *Mishnah*, 449). R. Simeon was a disciple of R. Joḥanan ben Zakkai. For warnings against fixed prayer, see m. Ber. 4:4 and other references cited by Sandmel, *Judaism*, 152, 438n40; Moore, *Judaism*, 2:220; Abrahams, *Studies*, 84.

9. Goulder, "Composition," 32–45. This view is adapted somewhat in Goulder, *Midrash*.

10. Tilborg, "Form-Criticism," 94–105. For the Kaddish's reference to God's will, see, e.g., Tilborg, "Form-Criticism," 105.

11. E.g., Botha, "Recent Research," 43, cites the ROTAS-SATOR square at Pompeii, but this may not suggest "Our Father" (Hofmann, "Sator Square").

12. See Bandstra, "Original Form," 25–30; Metzger, *Text*, 121.

13. See, e.g., Dibelius, *Jesus*, 120; Bandstra, "Original Form," 36. Though most liturgical prayers were in Hebrew, some (including the Aramaic Kaddish) were Aramaic, and some reconstruct the Lord's Prayer in Aramaic (Jeremias, *New Testament Theology*, 188–89; *Prayers*, 92–94; Dalman,

dealing directly with God precede material dealing more with interpersonal human affairs.[14]

It cannot be ruled out, of course, that both recensions go back directly to Jesus; he could have given the same basic prayer to his disciples more than once and adapted the words himself.[15] Some variants in what most scholars call the Q tradition are probably to be explained in this manner,[16] but this argument should not be overused. The Matthean context is almost certainly redactional, part of a larger Matthean structure,[17] and we know from narratives that almost certainly occurred only once and occur at a specific place in the tradition (such as the healing of the centurion's servant) that many of the traditions were reworked by both evangelists. We may also contrast the repetition of much material shared by these evangelists with the Fourth Gospel. This suggests that, while variant memories (from different disciples or traditions) and conflations no doubt occurred,[18] many variations owe their origin to the Evangelists.

Scholars often contend that Jesus's prayer was shaped in part by the Kaddish, an ancient synagogue prayer that originally may have run like this:

> Exalted and hallowed be his great name
>
> in the world which he created according to his will.
>
> May he let his kingdom rule
>
> in your lifetime and in your days and in the lifetime of the whole house of Israel,
>
> speedily and soon.
>
> And to this say: amen.[19]

It is entirely reasonable, though not provable, that Luke has accurately preserved the original life-setting as well as the earlier form of the prayer, if, as seems likely (but again cannot be proven) both recensions go back to a common original.

---

*Jesus-Jeshua*, 18–21).

14. Plummer, *Exegetical Commentary*, 96.

15. Botha, "Recent Research," 46.

16. See, e.g., Dunn, *Oral Gospel Tradition*, esp. 80–108.

17. Keener, *Gospel of Matthew*, 206, 210.

18. For conflation in cultural memory, see Vansina, *Oral Tradition*, 171; in biographies, see Derrenbacker, *Ancient Compositional Practices*, 94, 100–13; Licona, *Why Are There Differences*, 20, 48, 52, 56, 67, 91, 95, 109.

19. Jeremias, *Prayers*, 98. See Jeremias, *New Testament Theology*, 21–22; Moore, *Judaism*, 2:213; Smith, *Tannaitic Parallels*, 136; Vermes, *Jesus and Judaism*, 43; Gundry, *Matthew*, 104; Bonsirven, *Palestinian Judaism*, 133. Wilson, "Evangelical Perspective," 16; Guelich, *Sermon*, 285, also note parallels to the Amida. Similarities were not quickly obscured; a poor eighth-century translation of the Lord's Prayer from Latin to Hebrew uses some working from the Kaddish (Lapide, *Hebrew*, 8). Jewish prayers seem to have been commonly incorporated into Christian worship (cf. Did. 9.2–3 with the Kiddush blessing).

## "Our Father"

Greek prayers normally begin with the name of the deity; there is a heavy emphasis on finding the right name.[20] The next element in Greek prayers is often a localization of the god; "An attempt is . . . made to define the sphere of the god spatially by naming his favoured dwelling place or . . . places from which he is to come."[21] This could explain the use of "who is in heaven" in the Matthean form of this prayer, although, as will be observed below, this had become a fairly common spatial attribute in Jewish prayers. But in Greek prayers, it is the name and not a familial relationship that secures the answer to the prayers; one's relationship must be further defined to procure favor:

> This is followed by a justification for calling on the god, in which earlier proofs of friendship are invoked by way of precedent: if ever the god has come to the aid of the suppliant, or if the suppliant has performed works pleasing to the god, has burned sacrifices and built temples, then this should now hold good.[22]

It was now a commonplace of Hellenistic philosophy that God was father of the world by creation or of rational men by virtue of their reason.[23] Greeks also could address a chief deity as "father" in prayer.[24]

That Luke is aware of possible nuances that God's Fatherhood could have in a Greco-Roman context is certain; he appeals to it in Acts 17:28. But his normal usage is far more Jewish, and this may be said even of God's Fatherhood to Jesus. The problem with most suggested Hellenistic and Jewish "parallels" to the category of Jesus's Sonship is that they represent "sons," but not *the* Son in any special sense.[25] The Messianic use is more convincing, although it depends on Old Testament Messianic

---

20. Burkert, *Greek Religion*, 74. For piling up of names and endeavors to get the right one, including that of the Jewish God, often associated with magic, see *CIJ* 1:485, §673; 1:517, §717; 1:523, §724; 2:62–65, §819; 2:90, §849; 2:92, §851; 2:217, §1168; Isbell, "Incantation Bowls," 13; Nock, *Conversion*, 62–63; MacMullen, *Order*, 103; Knox, *St. Paul and the Church of the Gentiles*, 41–42; Tiede, *Charismatic Figure*, 170; Wilson, *Gnostic Problem*, 201; Koester, *Introduction*, 1:380. For other gods or heroes, see Reitzenstein, *Hellenistic Mystery-Religions*, 31–33; Guthrie, *Orpheus*, 39; Angus, *Mystery-Religions*, 51. For use in exorcisms see b. Giṭ. 68ab; Num. Rab. 11:3, 16:24; Deissmann, *Light*, 261; Tarn, *Hellenistic Civilisation*, 353; Bietenhard, "*Onoma*," 269–70; Scholem, *Jewish Gnosticism*, 32–33, 45.

21. Burkert, *Greek Religion*, 74.

22. Burkert, *Greek Religion*, 74–75.

23. Orphic Hymns 4:1; 15:7; 19:1 (cf. 12:6); Epictetus, *Disc.* 1.3.1; 1.6.40; 1.9.4–7; 1.13.3–4; 1.19.9, 12; 3.22.82; Musonius Rufus 18a (cited in Van der Horst, "Musonius," 309); Diogenes Laertius 7.147; Seneca, *Dial.* 1.1.5; cf. Martial, *Epig.* 10.28 (Janus). For Jewish view of Greeks, see Josephus, *Against Apion* 2.241 (Zeus as *patera tō logo*, but in reality a tyrant).

24. See, e.g., Homer, *Iliad* 3.276, 320, 350, 365; 7.179, 202, 446; 8.236; 12.164; 13.631; 15.372; 17.19, 645; 19.270; 21.273; 24.308; *Odyssey* 12.371; 20.98, 112, 201; 21.200; 24.351; Sophocles, *Oed. tyr.* 202; Aristophanes, *Acharn.* 223–25; Menander, *Dysk.* 192; Pindar, *Nem.* 8.35; 9.53; 10.29; *Isthm.* 6.42; Apollonius Rhodius, *Argonautica* 4.1673; Aratus, *Phaen.* 151–56 (esp. 51); Dio Chrysostom, *Or.* 36.36; Silius Italicus 10.432.

25. Hengel, *Son*, 24.

language that, apart from 4Q Florilegium, was not commonly reapplied in the New Testament period.[26]

God's Fatherhood as an expression of covenant relation had often been stressed in the Hebrew Scriptures, sometimes even in prayer.[27] The title also became common in Jewish prayers from the earliest strata of rabbinic tradition.[28] Such passages most often call God, "the Father in heaven," rather than simply, "our Father," although this is not true without exception. R. Phinehas ben Jair, for example, in the context of the Temple's destruction, cried, "On whom can we stay ourselves? On our Father in heaven."[29] "Father in heaven" was the liturgical title that came to dominate in later rabbinic Judaism.[30] Corporate Jewish and Christian prayers to God as Father are nearly identical.[31]

Jeremias suggests that the designation became much more common through the preference of R. Johanan ben Zakkai in the early post-70 period, so influencing the Matthean redaction of the Lord's Prayer and a number of other passages.[32] We do not *have* much Rabbinic tradition before ben Zakkai, however, and Matthew could add "heavenly" due to circles shared with sages rather than due to his date (cf. Luke and John).

Especially in the Judaism of the Diaspora, the Greek emphasis on God's Fatherhood seemed to suggest a universal fatherhood of God as creator. This appears

---

26. 4 Ezra 7:28–29 (Latin, Syriac, and Arabic 1) probably represents a later Christian interpolation. But for Old Testament language (besides 2 Sam 7; Ps 2; 89; 132; Isa 9), see Longenecker, *Christology*, 94–98; Hengel, *Son*, 21–23, 44; Conzelmann, *Outline of the Theology*, 76–77; Jeremias, *Parables*, 73n86; Montefiore, *Synoptic Gospels*, 1:85. Exod. Rab. 29:5 is probably Judean Amoraic polemic against Christian teaching (R. Abbahu).

27. See the listing in Jeremias, *Prayers*, 12, who is less impressed with the results. For intertestamental literature, see Jeremias, *Prayers*, 15–16. He also regards it as rare at Qumran (Jeremias, *Prayers*, 15–16; *Central Message*, 14).

28. Cf. Marmorstein, *Names*, 56–59; Moore, *Judaism*, 2:202–9. Contrast Bultmann, *Primitive Christianity*, 77.

29. M. Sotah 9:15 (Danby, *Mishnah*, 306). Cf. b. Ber. 30a, bar.; Lev. Rab. 1:3; 7:1–2; 35:10. See examples in McNamara, *Targum*, 116–18.

30. E.g., m. Sot. 9:15; tos. Ber. 3:14; B. K. 7:6; Hag 2:1; Pe'ah 4:21; Sipra Qed. pq. 9.207.2.13; Behuq. pq. 8.269.2.15; Sipre Deut. 352.1.2; b. Ber. 30a, bar.; 30b; 32b; 35b; 57a; Shab. 116a; 131b; Pes. 85b; 112a; R. H. 29a; Yoma 76a; Suk. 45b; Meg. 13a; 14a; Sot. 10a; 12a; 38b; B.B. 10a; Sanh. 94a; 101b; 102a; 102b; A. Z. 16b; Zeb. 22b; p. Sanh. 10:2, §8; Pesiq. Rab Kah. 24:9; Lev. Rab. 1:3; 7:1; 35:10; Song Rab. 7:11, §1; Tg. Neof. 1 on Deut 33:24; Tg. Ps.-J. on Exod 1:19 (with note in trans. 163n38). The phraseology must predate later rabbinic sources (cf. Mark 11:25; Luke 11:13), but in the NT appears especially in Matthew, the source closest to rabbinic usage (Matt 5:16, 45, 48; 6:1, 9, 14 [Mark 11:25], 26, 32; 7:11 [Luke 11:13], 21; 10:32–33; 12:50; 15:13; 16:17; 18:10, 14, 19, 35; 23:9).

31. Goshen-Gottstein, "God the Father" (excepting Jesus's special sonship).

32. Jeremias, *Prayers*, 16–17.

especially in Philo,[33] but also in various strands of the Sibylline Oracles.[34] Although there are, as noted above, some traces of this concept in Lukan theology (Acts 17:28), it is not the dominant form of God's Fatherhood expressed there.[35]

Usually Israel appears as God's son or sons, because they are his covenant people. This is fairly common in early Jewish sources.[36] Some individuals could also appear as sons of God in these texts, although usually within the context of the covenant.[37] But despite the "growing tendency to introduce the title 'Father' for God into the sayings of Jesus,"[38] it seems to have marked the teaching of Jesus, in a form that is more common than one expects in rabbinic texts. Indeed, as Jeremias points out, "To his disciples it must have been something quite extraordinary that Jesus addressed God as 'my Father.' Moreover not only do the four Gospels attest that Jesus used this address, but they repeat unanimously that he did so in all his prayer."[39]

"My Father" does not appear as a common personal address to God in Judean sources.[40] Jeremias suggests that Jesus avoided the more usual liturgical form *abinu* ("our Father") for the more familiar Aramaic address *abba*, which appears in the little Aramaic evidence we have for Jesus's wording (Mark 14:36). Charismatic Rabbis may have spoken of God as an *abba* in some contexts,[41] but the evidence does not appear in prayers and it is rare and late. Moreover, as Klausner noted, the rest of Judaism used it nowhere near as often (proportionately) as Jesus did, nor with the extreme emphasis he gave it.[42]

---

33. Philo, *Conf.* 170 (cf. the *logos* in 41); *Mos.* 2.238; *Decal.* 32, 51, 105; *Spec.* 1.14, 22 (though Loeb translates *patēr* as "ruler" here), 32, 41, 96; 2.6, 165; 3.178, 189; *Virt.* 64, 77, 218; *Praem.* 24; *Contempl.* 90; *Aet.* 13; *Leg.* 115, 293; cf. *QG* 2.60.

34. Sib. Or. 3.604 (maybe Egypt, second century BCE), 726 (*theon genetēra*, maybe second century BCE); 5.284, 328, 360, 406 (*genetēra theon pantōn*), 498, 500; cf. Theophilus, *Autolycus* 1.4; Athenagoras, *Plea* 13; 27. T. Ab. speaks of *tou aoratou patros* (16A) and of *tou theou kai patros* (20A), but the objects of his Fatherhood are not clearly defined.

35. Montefiore, "Father," 31–46, argues against the current usual denial of God's universal Fatherhood in the NT. Jeremias, *Prayers*, 43n70, critiques his position.

36. See, e.g., Jub. 1:25, 28; 2:20; 19:29; Ps. Sol. 17:28–30; b. Shab. 31a, 128a; Exod. Rab. 46:4–5; Num. Rab. 5:3, 10:2; Deut. Rab. 1:6; 3:15; Lam. Rab. Proem 23; cf. Bonsirven, *Palestinian Judaism*, 48–49; Hengel, *Son*, 51. Note esp. rabbinic parables, e.g., b. Yoma 76a; Exod. Rab. 15:30; Lev. Rab. 10:3; Num. Rab. 16:7; Deut. Rab. 2:25; 10:4; Lam. Rab. Proem 2; Lam. Rab. 1:17, §52; 3:20, §7; Song Rab. 2:16, §1; Pesiq. Rab. 15:17. Parables naturally tend to concentrate in haggadic collections.

37. Wis 2:18; 5:5; Philo, *Sobr.* 55–56; T. Ab. 12 A; b. Ber. 7a, 19a; Suk. 45b (the last transmitted in the name of R. Simeon ben Yoḥai but the traditionaries are quite late).

38. Jeremias, *Prayers*, 30. See Jeremias, *Prayers*, 29–31, 54.

39. Jeremias, *Central Message*, 17.

40. Jeremias, *Prayers*, 57, with documentation. On *abba*, see Jeremias, *Prayers*, 60. See also Martin, *Worship*, 34–35; Bruce, *Time*, 21–22; Gundry, *Matthew*, 105. For liturgy, see Jeremias, *Prayers*, 64–65.

41. Vermes, *Jesus and Judaism*, 42, cites some evidence and rightly notes that evidence on charismatic rabbis is so scarce in our extant literature that there could have been some parallels to Jesus's usage there. This is, however, partly an argument from silence.

42. Klausner, *Jesus of Nazareth*, 378. He cites Lev. Rab. as an example of the use of *abba*, but see Jeremias, *Prayers*, 109–110, on this passage.

It cannot, of course, be proven that every example of Jesus's "Father" must reflect an Aramaic *abba*, including in the Lord's Prayer. While the early Christians, even in a non-Aramaic milieu, may have felt that Jesus taught them to pray, "Abba, Father" (Rom 8:15; Gal 4:6), the practice need not derive from this prayer. It is even possible that Jesus prayed, "Our Father in heaven," which Luke shortened to simply "Father" for a broader audience unfamiliar with the longer phrase. But given the likelihood that Luke's shorter phrase is original, and that a prayer taught by Jesus would have continued to have been a model for prayer in the early Christian communities, it is not at all unreasonable to think that *abba* could have been the original word behind Luke's "Father," since that is its standard Greek translation in each New Testament text that uses it (Mark 14:36; Rom 8:15; Gal 4:6).

What might be most significant about the title "Father" in Luke's context is the inclusio that it forms with Luke 11:13, the climax to the argument of 11:11–13. There it is argued that God, as Father, will give us the Holy Spirit when we ask for that. The relationship with a loving Father is the basis for Christian prayer in Luke; and the gift of the Holy Spirit, as the climax shows, the most essential object of prayer. This will have implications for understanding the rest of the prayer in 11:2–4.

## "Thou" Petitions

Although Luke lacks Matthew's balance of three "You" petitions[43] and three to four "we" petitions; the first two petitions in Luke emphatically seek God's kingdom first, each one climaxes in *sou* ("your"). The Sanctification of God's name, a motif that occurs elsewhere in the New Testament,[44] was an important motif in early Judaism. The third benediction of the Amida', praising the holiness of God's name, is known as "the sanctification of the name,"[45] and a Samaritan daily prayer of uncertain date declares: "O God, the God of the Spirits of all the Flesh, His great Name is to be hallowed every evening and morning."[46]

In later rabbis, the sanctification of the name involved Israel's righteous behavior or the glory of God's just judgment. R. Samuel bar Naḥman, a third generation Judean Amora, claimed that Abraham would not intercede for his descendants after their sin,

---

43. Goppelt, *Theology*, 1:70, notes that "the first three petitions" (in Matthew) "explain each other. God's reign comes when he is recognized as God and when his gracious will is accomplished."

44. Some have drawn connections between Matt 6:9–13 and John 17 partly on this basis, though they may simply have a mutual connection with Jewish doctrine. See Walker, "Lord's Prayer," 237–56. Carson, *Farewell Discourse*, 174, suggests the same author of both prayers, but notes that the prayers, themselves, are different.

45. Rosh Hashanah (Mishnah tractate) quoted in Sandmel, *Judaism*, 148.

46. Bowman, *Samaritan Documents*, 328, 330n3.

but cried, "Let them be wiped out for the sanctification of Thy Name."[47] When Israel merits it, God acts for Israel; when she does not, he acts on behalf of his name.[48]

Righteous deeds hallowed God's name: in one late document, people fixed their eyes on Nahshon, the first to step into the Red Sea, and said, "This man has hallowed the name of the Holy One, blessed be He;"[49] in the same document, the tribe of Levi "devoted their lives to the sanctification of the name of the Holy One, blessed be He."[50] The *Kiddush Hashem*, the sanctifying of the name, "became a leading principle in deciding problems of relations towards Gentiles."[51]

In the same way, one could profane the name through evil deeds. Though some traditions stress sanctifying the name more than avoiding profaning it,[52] more prominent is the opinion which in one form is attributed to R. Il'ai the Elder, against some of his colleagues, that if one is about to succumb to the *yetzer hara'*, one ought to go somewhere and sin in secret so that the name might not be profaned publicly.[53] Hypocrites should be exposed to prevent profanation of the name.[54] All bad behavior could profane God's name,[55] but especially it could hurt Judaism's witness to the Gentile community.[56]

The name was especially sanctified in times of persecution, in acts of martyrdom.[57] Thus, in late tradition, even Abraham sanctified God's name in the fiery furnace he faced for repudiating idolatry.[58]

Earlier sources emphasize the eschatological hallowing of God's name. Just as the prophets had promised (e.g., Ezek 36:23; 38:23; 39:7, 27), God's name would be sanctified and no longer profaned in the final day, when he restored the fortunes of his scattered people, and he ruled all the earth in perfect justice. As the Qumran War Scroll proclaims, after the final battle, God would be "sanctified before the eyes of the

---

47. B. Shab. 89b.

48. Ruth Rab. 2:11. In 2 Bar. 1:4, God scattered Judah "that they may do good to the nations," i.e., make God known.

49. Num. Rab. 12:21.

50. Num. Rab. 15:12.

51. Urbach, "Self-Isolation," 283–84. On sanctifying the Name behaviorally, see further Moore, *Judaism*, 2:101–5; Patte, *Early Jewish Hermeneutic*, 105.

52. Num. Rab. 8:4.

53. B. Ḳid. 40a; Ḥag. 16a. See also Montefiore and Loewe, *Rabbinic Anthology*, 305, 499.

54. B. Yoma 86b.

55. E.g., in Montefiore and Loewe, *Rabbinic Anthology*, 397, citing Yoma 86a; Moore, *Judaism*, 2:105, citing Mek. Shir. 3.

56. See, e.g., Gen Rab. 39:7; Urbach, *Sages*, 1:359; CD 12.6–8; T. Levi 14:1 (during 70 weeks, 16:1). See Rom 2:24; Isa 52:5 LXX behind it (cf. Käsemann, *Commentary on Romans*, 71).

57. Cf. b. Pes. 53b; Song Rab. 2:7, §1; Urbach, *Sages*, 1:444; Siegel, "Meaning," 107; Montefiore, "Spirit of Judaism," 63–64.

58. Ruth Rab. Proem 7.

remnant of the nations."[59] In similar ways, God had sanctified himself through his many acts of judgment and vindication throughout human history.[60]

But his glory, both in the future and in the present, was primarily expressed through the obedience of his covenant people.[61] One of the most common blessings, in a variety of forms, continually repeats the idea that God had first sanctified, or set apart, his people, by giving them his commandments.[62] God sanctified his Law as well as his people,[63] and sanctified Israel that they might sanctify him.[64]

God's "name" was so holy[65] that uttering it could lead to permanent exclusion from the Dead Sea community, regardless of the reason.[66] The Tannaim required full punishment for blasphemy, only if the name had been pronounced.[67] "The Name" was sometimes used as a periphrasis for God,[68] so that, for example, hearing God's name could be equivalent to hearing him.[69]

Thus a prayer for the hallowing of God's name could be a prayer for the consummation, but was also a prayer for God's empowerment that the righteous might live in a way that would glorify him. In the context of Luke-Acts, it would also be a prayer for the Gentile mission, that God would be glorified among the heathen (Acts 13:47; 15:16–18; 26:17–18).

Related to this is the prayer for the coming of God's kingdom, a *marana tha* prayer (cf. 1 Cor 16:22). Despite some dissent,[70] most scholars concur that God's kingdom is especially his "reign," or sovereign exercise of power.[71] What has been more in dispute is the temporal orientation of that kingdom.

59. 1QM 11.15; cf. 1 En. 9:4: God's name is forever holy.

60. 1QM 17.2; Num. Rab. 4:5–8; cf. 1QM 11.3: David prevailed over the Philistines *beshem kodeshecah*, "by Your holy Name" (name of your holiness).

61. Haenchen, *John*, 2:155, sees "sanctify" as technical sacrificial language, which in John means that Jesus's disciples "must live exclusively in the service of God."

62. E.g., b. Ber. 11b, 51a, 60b; Shab. 137b; Pes. 7b; Pesiq. Rab. 3:2. For sanctifying in Jubilees, see 2:19 (people); 4:26 (earth, eschatological); 15:27 (the people, through circumcision); 22:29 (the people).

63. E.g., b. Ber. 33b; Deut. Rab. 11:6; cf. John 17:17.

64. Exod. Rab. 15:24.

65. See Let. Aris. 98; Josephus, *Ant.* 2.276 (though not *onoma*); b. Shab. 115b, bar.; Eccl. Rab. 3:11, §3; Song Rab. 5:7, §1; 8:5, §1; Pesiq. Rab. 22:7; etc. For Greek transcriptions, see Deissmann, *Bible Studies*, 321–36. Marmorstein, *Names*, 39; Urbach, *Sages*, 1:124–34, for more information; for mystic power, see Pesiq. Rab. 21:7 (use in creation).

66. 1QS 6.27–7.1.

67. M. Sanh. 7:5; cf. b. Sanh. 60a.

68. Jeremias, *New Testament Theology*, 10. It might be implied in the name of the fallen angel Semyaza in 1 Enoch 6:3, if it means "he sees the Name" (see Knibb's note, 67–68). See Longenecker, *Christology*, 43; Bietenhard, ὄνομα, 268–69.

69. Sib. Or. 3.17–19.

70. Cf. Aalen, "Reign," 215–40.

71. E.g., Dibelius, *Jesus*, 64; Dodd, *Parables*, 34; Taylor, *Gospel According to St. Mark*, 114; Betz, *What Do We Know about Jesus?*, 33; Perrin, *Kingdom*, 24; Ladd, *Theology*, 60–67.

It is clear that there is a special sense in which, in early Jewish sources, God will manifest his Kingship in the time of the end. In the end, "everyone will know that I am the God of Israel and the father of all the children of Jacob and king upon Mount Zion forever and ever. And Zion and Jerusalem will be holy."[72]

God will reign over all the earth when his sanctuary is restored.[73] It is to this future aspect of God's reign that Jewish prayers, such as the *Shemoneh Esreh* (the *Amida'*) and the Kaddish, look.[74] This pattern of Jewish prayer for the future kingdom reinforces the future orientation of Jesus's prayer for His disciples.

But God's rule was also very much a present reality in Judaism. Israel's faith in God's oneness and consequent fidelity to his Torah was submission to the yoke of his Kingdom.[75] This same tension between God's present rule over his creation and a future consummation of that rule may be felt by observing different passages from the Hebrew Scriptures:

> All Your works will thank You, Lord,
>
> And Your godly ones bless You.
>
> They will speak of the glory of Your Kingdom,
>
> And talk of your power . . .
>
> Your Kingdom is an everlasting kingdom,
>
> And Your dominion endures through all generations (Ps 145:10–13).

But while Psalm 145:10–13 contextually speaks of God's present kingship, many of the Messianic expectations are clearly future:

> There will be no end to the increase of his government or of peace,
>
> On the throne of David and over his kingdom,
>
> To establish it and to uphold it with justice and righteousness
>
> From then on and forever (Isa 9:7)
>
> And to him was given dominion,
>
> Glory and a kingdom . . .
>
> His dominion is an everlasting dominion
>
> Which will not pass away (Dan 7:14)

This same idea is present in early Christian literature, including Luke-Acts, where the Kingdom is particularly a present proclamation of the good news about Jesus (particularly in Acts), and a future hope of the pious (Luke 22:18; 23:42, 51). It

---

72. Jub. 1:28.

73. Mekilta Shirata 10:42–44 (in 2:79–80).

74. See Bonsirven, *Palestinian Judaism*, 176–77; Bultmann, *Primitive Christianity*, 80–86.

75. See Exod. Rab. 42:1; Moore, *Judaism*, 1:465–66 (especially citing m. Ber. 2:2); Bonsirven, *Palestinian Judaism*, 176. In Jewish mysticism, see Scholem, *Major Trends*, 54–55.

## PART III—READING ST. LUKE'S THEOLOGY: PNEUMATOLOGICAL AMBIENCES

is the Christocentric emphasis which distinguishes early Christian eschatology from the standard early Jewish expectations of that time.[76]

The expectation of a future consummation of the Kingdom has implications for one's submission to God's yoke in the present. As Tannehill observes: "The petition for the coming of God's reign (11:2) prepares for the eschatological instruction in 12:35–48, which also concerns a crucial future coming, that of the Son of Man (12:40)."[77]

Although the variant reading about the Spirit in this connection[78] may be later, it seems certain that, for Luke, the rule of God is actualized in the lives of Jesus's followers by the gift of the Spirit.[79] Some believed that the prophetic, divine Spirit had been quenched and/or would be restored eschatologically,[80] although the evidence is not as exclusive on the whole as has sometimes been thought.[81] Isaiah, Ezekiel, and Joel[82] clearly expected an outpouring of the Spirit associated with Israel's eschatological restoration, and at least Isaiah and Joel associated this with prophetic witness.[83]

Thus in Acts 1:4–8, it is not difficult to understand why, when promised the Spirit, the disciples expect the coming of the kingdom.[84] Peter's pesher reading of Joel as "in the last days" (Acts 2:17) is likewise accurate in the context of Joel and prophetic use of that phrase.[85] But for Luke, as for the rest of the New Testament, it

---

76. See Hamilton, *Holy Spirit and Eschatology*, 23.

77. Tannehill, *Gospel According to Luke*, 1:240.

78. On the reading, see Leaney, "Lukan Text," 104–5.

79. Talbert, *Reading Luke*, 131.

80. See, e.g., Josephus, *Apion* 1.8; t. Sot. 12:5; 13:3; 14:3; b. Sanh. 11a, bar.; Yoma 9b; Soṭ. 48b, bar.; Ḥul. 137b; Gen. Rab. 37:7 (attributed to R. Simeon b. Gamaliel); Num. Rab. 15:10; Song Rab. 8:9, §3; cf. Urbach, *Sages*, 1:306, 564–66; Rivkin, *Hidden Revolution*, 86; Freedman, "Prophecy," 23; Barrett, *Holy Spirit*, 123; Morris, *Apocalyptic*, 26; Grudem, *Gift of Prophecy*, 21–23 (24–33 rightly gives the other side, except for his emphasis on the difference between this and OT prophecy, which probably was not true in all circles); Davies, *Paul*, 208–215; Jeremias, *Parables*, 117, 126; Jeremias, *New Testament Theology*, 80–81 (noting exceptions at Qumran); Parker, "Concept of Apokatastasis," 56. Dunn, "Spirit and Kingdom," emphasizes the NT connection.

81. Some circles also continued to value prophecy (if not always "prophets"), especially outside the elite's "orthodoxy." See Josephus, *J.W.* 1.68, 78–80; 2.159; *Ant.* 13.299; 15.373; 17.346. See also Sandmel, *Judaism*, 174; Brinsmead, *Galatians*, 100; Sanders, *Jesus and Judaism*, 271; Knox, *St. Paul and the Church of Jerusalem*, 36; Abrahams, *Studies*, 126–28.

82. Isa 42:1; 44:3; 59:20–21; 61:1; 63:10–14 (in light of new exodus of which Isaiah also speaks); Ezek 36:26–27; 37:14; 39:29; Joel 2:28–29 (MT 3:1).

83. Isa 42:1, 6; 43:10–12; 44:8; 49:6; 52:7; 59:21; 61:1; Joel 2:28–29.

84. See further Baum, *Jews and the Gospels*, 167; Jervell, "Israel."

85. "Last days" in the prophets usually means the time of the end; this fits Joel's restoration context and Peter inserts the words for the more ambiguous "afterward." "Last days/times" is used in later literature as well—e.g., T. Iss. 6:1; Zeb. 8:2 (cf. 9:5); Dan 1:1 (here a person's last days); 2 Bar. 76:5; 1 En. 27:3; 108:1. See Johnson, *Literary Function*, 44; Cullmann, *Christ and Time*, 156. For textual modification in pesher, see Silberman, "Riddle"; Roth, "Subject Matter," 64–65. For comparison of pesher with allegory, see Brownlee, "Comparison with Sects," 68. For comparison with later Karaite exegesis, see Wieder, "Dead Sea Scrolls" 77. For the view that pesher is used here, see, e.g., Tiede, *Prophecy*, 89; Longenecker, *Biblical Exegesis*, 100.

is clear that the coming of the Spirit precedes the consummation of the kingdom, as a sort of "firstfruits" (Rom 8:23) or "downpayment" (2 Cor 1:22, 5:5; cf. Eph 1:13–14), to borrow Paul's language.

In Acts, the prophetic "word of the Lord" becomes, virtually without exception, the proclamation of the good news of Jesus; the Spirit's coming is to anoint believers to proclaim this message of the kingdom to all peoples (Acts 1:8), and the point of speaking in tongues in Acts 2 seems to be as evidence that the Spirit of prophecy has been made available[86] (especially for witness to the nations).[87]

Thus, the prayer for the coming of the kingdom is a prayer for future consummation, but also implies the fulfillment of the prerequisite of that kingdom, namely, the proclamation of the good news to all the nations through a church empowered by the Holy Spirit.

## "We" Petitions

Whereas the "you petitions" for God's kingdom are primarily eschatological, the "we petitions" address the needs of God's people in the present age. Since the hallowing of God's name and the coming of His kingdom have eschatological ramifications, it is sometimes held that the "we petitions" are likewise eschatological.[88] Thus *epiousios*, as applied to bread, is sometimes seen as "bread for the coming day," perhaps the eschatological Sabbath (cf. Exod 16:22–23),[89] especially on the basis of the Aramaic *mahar* Jerome found in the Gospel of the Nazarenes.[90]

Yet, "bread for the coming day" is not most naturally read as eschatological; if prayed in the morning or the evening, it prays for what the new day (reckoned from sundown) will bring.[91] The papyrus identifying the sense of *epiousios* as "daily rations"[92] has been lost and the reading may have been inaccurate;[93] but the idea of bread as daily rations is a common enough one in ancient Near Eastern literature.[94] Jesus emphasized God's provision of daily sustenance (in both Matthew and Luke following not long after the Prayer; Matt 6:25–34; Luke 12:22–34); nor was he alone

---

86. "This is that" (Acts 2:16) responds to, "What means this?" (2:12) just as, "It is too early" (2:15) responds to, "These people are drunk" (2:13). See, e.g., arguments in Lampe, "Grievous Wolves," 256; Zehnle, *Peter's Pentecost Discourse*, 27–28; Lindars, *New Testament Apologetic*, 36; Ladd, *Theology*, 380; Haenchen, *Acts*, 179; Parker, "Concept of Apokatastasis," 57.

87. E.g., Keener, "Why Does Luke Use Tongues," 177–78, 180–81; "Holy Spirit," 171.

88. E.g., Meier, *Matthew*, 62. Goppelt, *Theology*, 1:70, envisions a connection but in a different way.

89. Fenton, *Saint Matthew*, 101. See also Hoskyns, *Fourth Gospel*, 294. For Luke's change of the Eucharistic, eschatological intent, see Meier, *Matthew*, 61.

90. Jeremias, *Prayers*, 100; Leaney, *Commentary*, 185.

91. Botha, "Recent Research," 48; Filson, *Commentary*, 96; Gundry, *Matthew*, 107.

92. Cited as evidence by, e.g., Bruce, *Books*, 69.

93. Metzger, "How Many Times Does 'Epiousios,'" 52–54. See Manson, *Sayings*, 169.

94. See Yamauchi, "'Daily Bread' Motif," 145–56, esp. 148–53.

among Jewish teachers in emphasizing this.[95] The daily bread is probably primarily a prayer for God's provision in a society more conscious of its dependence of God's blessings to the land than most of modern Western society is.

But, perhaps like the first temptation in the temptation narrative (Luke 4:2–4),[96] the "daily bread" is also an allusion to the provision of manna in the present age of testing. Manna sometimes symbolized the Torah,[97] but was usually viewed as heavenly food,[98] and was sometimes expected to be renewed in the time to come.[99]

Both Jewish believers and gentiles who understood the biblical and Jewish foundation of their faith would have read God's provision of daily bread in terms of a new exodus analogy. The new exodus motif was common enough in the prophets[100] and continued in contemporary Judaism.[101] Thus, some see eschatological implications. Luke's later passage on provision (12:22–34) is in the context of watchfulness for the future consummation; breaking of bread in Acts 2:42, 46 may have also implied the eschatological connections of the Lord's supper (Luke 22:18) as well as provision of needs.[102]

These associations do not rule out the most basic implications of the context; however, bread seems to symbolize all read needs with which believers approach the Father (11:5; 11:11–12 omits "bread" [cf. Matt. 7:9–10]), and the emphasis is on daily dependence on God for one's needs.

---

95. See m. Ḳid. 4:14 (Danby, *Mishnah*, 329); b. Yeb. 63b, citing "Ben Sira"; Gen. Rab. 20:9. See also Abrahams, *Studies*, 106.

96. See Barrett, *Holy Spirit*, 51–52.

97. Philo *Det.* 118 (*tōn ontōn logon theion*); Gen. Rab. 43:6 (Samuel b. Naḥman); 54:1 (bread); 70:5 (bread); Lev. Rab. 30:1 (bread); Glasson, *Moses*, 47; Smith, *Tannaitic Parallels*, 158. Of course, given the commonness of bread for sustenance, bread would naturally be used figuratively as well. For bread symbolism in Judaism, paganism, and Christianity, see Goodenough, *Jewish Symbols*, 5:62–95. Later rabbis had a wide variety of manna traditions; they often linked manna with the merit of Moses (cf. b. Ta'an. 9a; Num. Rab. 1:2, 13:20; contrast Gen. Rab. 48:12). It could discriminate between the righteous and the wicked (b. Yoma 75a). An early Tanna reportedly said that it tasted different to each Israelite, according to his needs (Exod. Rab. 5:9; cf. 25:3). R. Eleazar of Modiim (a contemporary of Tarfon and Ishmael) said that manna came down 60 cubits high (b. Yoma 76a). The tradition in b. Pes. 54a says that ten things were created at twilight on the eve of the first Sabbath, including manna and the well.

98. Cf. b. Yoma 75b: R. Akiba called it angels' food, but R. Ishmael replied that angels do not eat food (though cf. Ps 78:25!); *Her.* 191 (*ouranion trophēn*, distributed by *theios logos*). See references in Odeberg, *Fourth Gospel*, 240–45.

99. Mekilta Vayassaʿ 3:42 (Lauterbach, 2:110); 5:63–65 (2:119). Later, Num. Rab. 11:2; Ruth Rab. 5:6; Eccl. Rab. 1:9, §1.

100. E.g., Isa 11:16; 40:3; Jer 16:14–15; 23:7–8; Hos 2:14–15; 11:11. See further Glasson, *Moses*, 15–19; Daube, *Exodus Pattern*, esp. 11–12.

101. Cf. probably Israel's "first salvation" in *CD* 5.19 (though contrast 7.21). See the commentary on Ps 37 in Gaster, *Dead Sea Scriptures*, 327–28; b. Ber. 12b; Lev. Rab. 27:4; Exod. Rab. 2:6; Pesiq. Rab. 31:10; Bonsirven, *Palestinian Judaism*, 202.

102. See 1QS 6.4–5, 20–21, and, less clear, Gen. Apoc. 21.20–22. Schiffman, *Sectarian Law*, 191–210, regards the meal as Messianic and eschatological at Qumran, but not sacral (all meals included a blessing).

The petition for forgiveness[103] may resemble the sixth of the Eighteen Benedictions: "Forgive us, our Father, for we have sinned against thee; Wash away our transgressions from before thine eyes; Blessed art thou, O Lord, who dost abundantly forgive."[104]

Matthew's wording, "debts," could be more original than Luke's more generic "sins"; *opheilēma* was sometimes used as "sin" in Aramaic (*hobha*)[105] and sometimes sins appear as debts in rabbinic parables[106] (cf. also Matt 18:23–35). God's forgiveness was not limited to the future day of judgment in Judaism, as the sacrificial system and especially the day of atonement testify.

The thought of God's forgiveness depending on human forgiveness would not have been unfamiliar in Jewish circles.[107] Thus, there is thus no need for Jeremias's retroversion into Aramaic to make God's forgiveness first;[108] the Evangelists saw no problem in the Greek words they used. The question about the priority for forgiveness, however, misses the point;[109] this is not a once-for-all prayer for forgiveness, so much as a continuing prayer for a continuing relationship. The initiation of that relationship may already be assumed in the address, "Father," and the meaning in the Gospel context is further explicated by parables such as, Luke 18:9–14 and Matthew 18:23–35.

The Prayer emphasizes not only forgiveness for past sin but also protection from future offenses. The final petition in the Lukan form of the Prayer[110] involves *peirasmos*. *Peiradzein* can bear the sense either of "testing" as trial (suffering, persecution, martyrdom, etc.) or "seduction toward sin,"[111] the former usage being far more typical of pre-Christian, non-Jewish Greek.[112] As in the Dead Sea Scrolls, it is sometimes "difficult to draw a line between testing and temptation."[113] Suffering often had a purifying, atoning, or meritorious value in Judaism,[114] so "testing" could be positive if one did not fail the test and fall into sin.

---

103. Cf. Matt 6:12; Did. 8.2; Polycarp, *Phil.* 6.2.

104. As cited in Grant, *Ancient Judaism*, 46.

105. Jeremias, *New Testament Theology*, 6n15, 196; Black, *Aramaic*, 140. See Gundry, *Matthew*, 108; Meier, *Matthew*, 62; McNamara, *Targum*, 120.

106. E.g., Pesiq. Rab. 51:8 (Judean Amora); Derrett, *Law*, 46; Marmorstein, *Names*, 63–64.

107. Montefiore, *Synoptic Gospels*, 2:103; cf. Sir 28:2; Polycarp, *Phil.* 2.3. Fensham, "Legal Background," 1–2, sees credit-slavery as the object of the forgiveness clause, but this is certainly too narrow. Lachs, "On Matthew 6:12," 6–8, could be closer in seeing a challenge to the *prosbul*.

108. Jeremias, *New Testament Theology*, 201.

109. Particularly in Luke, where the supplicants' forgiveness is continuous, unless this reads too much into the present indicative tense here.

110. See Polycarp, *Phil.* 7.2 (cf. Matt 6:13; 26:41).

111. Manson, *Sayings*, 170; Best, *Temptation*, 59.

112. Moule, "Unsolved Problem," 69–70.

113. Best, *Temptation*, 49–50.

114. See 2 Bar. 13:10; 1QS 8.4 (if concept is based on Isa 40, it is worthy of note that 8.14 cites

Before one can decide the specific nuances of *peirasmos* in this text, one must consider the meaning of "do not lead us" and the various allusions that have been proposed as informing the meaning of *peirasmos* here.

Jeremias and others find in *peirasmos* here a reference to the final time of testing by the powers of Antichrist.[115] Some Jewish people may have prayed to escape that period.[116] It is difficult, nevertheless, to suppose that those expecting an imminent end would have seen much difference between the sufferings of the present and the sufferings immediately preceding the end, an observation which seems to gain support from the Dead Sea Scrolls.[117]

Many scholars point to the absence of the definite article as speaking against the eschatological interpretation of *peirasmos* here;[118] an appeal to a different Semitic construction would not weaken this objection in Greek. Further, "testing" has a very common framework in Jewish thought without an appeal to eschatology:

> My child, when you come to serve the Lord, prepare yourself for testing. Set your heart right and be steadfast, and do not be impetuous in time of calamity. Cling to him and do not depart, so that your last days may be prosperous. Accept whatever befalls you, and in times of humiliation be patient. For gold is tested in the fire, and those found acceptable, in the furnace of humiliation. Trust in him, and he will help you; make your ways straight, and hope in him.[119]

Although testing is sometimes the work of Satan,[120] it can also be the work of God[121] (e.g., Gen 22:1; Deut 13:13), who is sovereign even in distress. Distress (*tsarati*,

---

something else from that context, perhaps suggesting a midrashic tradition on that text); 1QpHab 8.1–3; Mek. Baḥodesh 6:136ff (in Lauterbach 2:247); b. Ber. 5ab (Tanna with R. Joḥanan), 17a, 63a; Shab. 30b; B. Ḳ. 50a; Ta'an. 8a; Gen. Rab. 62:2 (Tanna), 96:5 (Judah ha-Nasi); Exod. Rab. 30:13; Lev. Rab. 9:1; 27:1 (citing Akiba); 32:1 (citing Judah ha-Nasi); Num. Rab. 9:24; Ruth Rab. Proem 7; Lam. Rab. 1:5, §31; 3:3, §1; 3:18, §6; 4:22, §25; Song Rab. 4:6, §1; Midr. Ps. 90:11; Pesiq. Rab. 22:5. See Urbach, *Sages*, 1:445; Bonsirven, *Palestinian Judaism*, 29, 81, 111; Davies, *Paul*, 263. For the comparable Greek conception, cf. Hengel, *Atonement*, 28.

115. Jeremias, *Prayers*, 105–6; cf. George, "Ne nous soumets pas à la tentation tentation," 74–79; Brown, "Scrolls," 4; Meier, *Matthew*, 62; Albright and Mann, *Matthew*, 76–77; with less certainty, Tasker, *Gospel According to St. Matthew*, 74.

116. B. Pes. 118a (interpreting Ps 115:1 in the Hallel).

117. Perrin, *Kingdom*, 197–98, following Kuhn. Gundry, *Matthew*, 109, thinks that Matthew shifted the original future to a present emphasis.

118. Schweizer, *Good News*, 156; Marshall, *Gospel of Luke*, 461; *Kept*, 68; Moule, "Unsolved Problem," 66–67. See Driver, *Jesus's Scrolls*, 532–33, on the Qumran texts.

119. Sir 2:1–6, NRSV; cf. 4:17.

120. See Jub. 17:15–18 (cf. Charles, *Jubilees*, lxxxv); Gen. Rab. 70:8. Abrahams, *Studies*, 101, connects *tou ponērou* in the Lord's Prayer with the *evil yetzer*. In early Christianity, however, the phrase normally refers Satan.

121. E.g., Philo, *Op.* 149 (God *apepeirato* Abraham); Gen. Rab. 55:2; Num. Rab. 17:2 (Abraham). In at least some sense, God was sovereign even in human sin, as certain biblical texts (e.g., Isa 63:17) could imply.

"my distress") could lead to stumbling through sinfulness of the flesh;[122] delays in answers to prayer could similarly be a trial of faith.[123] The test was an opportunity to hallow God's name.[124]

Jeremias cites an ancient Jewish evening prayer:

> Lead my foot not into the power of sin,
>
> And bring me not into the power of iniquity,
>
> And not into the power of temptation,
>
> And not into the power of anything shameful.[125]

Thus, Jeremias takes the causative in a permissive sense, which he applies also to the Lord's Prayer, with the sense, "Do not let us succumb to the Test."[126] Moule finds Jeremias's argument unconvincing here,[127] but concludes by adopting a sense not far removed: when we come to the test, deliver us from the evil one.[128]

One may compare texts in Jubilees. Abraham prayed that God would save him "from the straying of the sons of men" (11:17); God had tested him with tests such as famine, wealth, and circumcision (17:17). The angels tested him to see if he would exercise self-control when Sarah died (19:3); if one sinned against God, he would hide his face "and deliver you into the power of your sin" (21:22). God would keep Jacob both from destruction and the ways of error (22:23). The point seems to be that God grants protection from apostasy, and from tests that are too great at a given point for his servants to endure (cf. 1 Cor 10:13); those who were arrogant, he could hand over to their sin (cf. Rom 1:18, 24, 26, 28; 2 Thess 2:10–12; Rev 17:17), but those who called out to him would be delivered.[129]

Some have found in this test an allusion to Exodus, which might have come to many of the reader's minds.[130] One form of this view suggests that it means, "Keep us from testing you" (rather than us being tested), as at Massah in the wilderness.[131]

---

122. 1QS 11.13 in the context of 11.9–22.

123. Sir 7:10, cited in Moore, *Judaism*, 2:232.

124. Moore, *Judaism*, 2:105–7.

125. Jeremias, *Prayers*, 105; *Theology*, 202.

126. Jeremias, *Prayers*, 105; see Jeremias, *New Testament Theology*, 202; Montefiore, *Synoptic Gospels*, 2:103; on the Jewish prayer, and on the meaning, see Willis, "Lead Us Not into Temptation," 281–88; Gundry, *Matthew*, 109. See also Dahms, "Lead Us Not into Temptation," 223–30.

127. Moule, "Unsolved Problem," 72–73.

128. Moule, "Unsolved Problem," 74–75.

129. See b. Sanh. 64a: some Amoraim pray that the Tempter of Sin might be delivered into their hands, and he is. Patte, *Gospel According to Matthew*, 105, observes that the Tempter wished to prevent the disciples for whom this prayer was given from sanctifying God's name.

130. Walker, "Temptation," 287; Houk, "*Peirasmos*," 223.

131. Houk, "*Peirasmos*," 223. Less certain, Lewis, "Wilderness Controversy and Peirasmos," 43, who in the article rightly notes exodus parallels with the Lord's Prayer. James 1:13 may mean that God ought not to be tested. See Davids, "Meaning of *APEIRASTOS*," 386–92. On God not tempting in James, see the parallels cited by Mayor, *Epistle of St. James*, cxxvi; Ropes, *Critical and Exegetical*

This allusion seems unlikely, because even though it could find some support in the Synoptic tradition (Matt 4:7; Luke 4:12; cf. Acts 5:9), it is less common than the testing of people by Satan, above whom ultimately stands the sovereign God. The idea that God's people *receive* testing may *also* be located in the wilderness accounts and is more emphasized in early Christian literature.

Tannehill emphasizes the connection between this final clause in the Lukan form of the Prayer and related Lukan motifs:

> ... in summary statements about their past ministries, Jesus speaks of his "trials (*peirasmoi*)" which the apostles have shared (Luke 22:28), and Paul speaks of the "trials (*peirasmoi*)" which he has suffered "by the plots of the Jews" (Acts 20:19). Jesus prepares his disciples for such trials in Luke 12:4–12, which ends with the promise of the Spirit's assistance. Thus, a major part of the answer to the petition concerning temptation or testing may be the Father's gift of the Holy Spirit, promised in 11:13 and 12:11–12.[132]

Indeed, as Tannehill points out, all the themes introduced in this prayer, with the exception of forgiveness, are developed in chapter 12. Whether Luke has preserved the internal coherence of the original context of the material in the life of Jesus or has created connections by his arrangement of the material (and probably change of "good gifts" to "the Holy Spirit" in 11:13; see below), there are clear connections in the context that suggest a broader reading of the Prayer.

## The Friend at Midnight

Not least for safety considerations, night travel, and consequently midnight arrival, were rare in Judea and Galilee.[133] No shops would be open at night,[134] but in a small village it would commonly be known which homes still had bread.[135] Feeding the guest would have been obligatory for the sake of the village's honor as a hospitable place,[136] and the opening of the parable, "Who of you has a friend [who would not get up and supply bread in such a situation]," is worded so as to expect a definite reply of, "No one!" (Luke 11:11/Matt 7:9; Luke 12:25/Matt 6:27; Luke 14:5, 8; 15:4; 17:7).[137] The

---

*Commentary*, 154–55.

132. Tannehill, *Gospel According to Luke*, 1:239–40. On the question of Matthew's doxology as a later addition, see Bandstra, "Original Form," 18–25. For liturgical addition, see 1QM 18.13. For the antiquity of this one, see Did. 8.2 (since Did. 9–10 also have doxologies, they may be prior to the addition to Matthew; cf. esp. 9.4); Smith, *Tannaitic Parallels*, 137; Bonsirven, *Palestinian Judaism*, 134; Jeremias, *Prayers*, 106.

133. Bailey, *Poet*, 121.

134. Jeremias, *Parables*, 157–58.

135. Bailey, *Poet*, 122. On Greco-Roman bakeries in general, see Cary and Haarhoff, *Life*, 95.

136. Jeremias, *Parables*, 157–58; Bailey, *Poet*, 122; Derrett, *Jesus's Audience*, 39.

137. Jeremias, *Parables*, 158; Johnson, "Assurance," 124.

deliberate exaggeration appears humorous: the man inside protests that his rising will awaken his children, while the man outside, banging on the door, is just as certain to awaken them, as is the inside man's curt reply. The situation conceived is intended to be understood as ludicrous, as an assurance of the certainty of answered prayer.

But what sort of prayer does Jesus advocate here? The continued knocking might indicate persistent asking, given the contextual proximity of 11:9–10. This could explain how the key to the outside of man's answer, someone's *anaideia*, came to be translated "importunity."[138] Bold importunity, *chutzpah*, might be disapproved by some rabbis, but was respected as an effective means of addressing God for charismatic sages such as Ḥoni the Circle-drawer.[139]

There is, however, no early evidence for this interpretation of this word; with the possible exception of one instance in the Septuagint, it always means "shamelessness."[140] It would then appeal to the honor of the village which each member was liable to uphold by showing hospitality. Bailey, followed by others, argues from the grammatical structure and the sequence of pronouns that the text refers to the "shamelessness" of the person inside.[141] If it does refer to the person outside, it could imply his willingness to awaken his friend for the sake of the village's honor. Either way (though admittedly, especially on Bailey's reading), the text stresses the assurance of answered prayer, especially because God is involved in the honor of his people and the upholding or sanctifying of his name. Again, the significance of the believer's *relationship* with the Father is central, as well as the sanctifying of the Name.

The rhythmic[142] lines that follow emphasize the importance of asking and seeking, and the image of knocking[143] is naturally especially appropriate after this parable. The language, like that of the parable that precedes, is intentionally shocking,[144] meant to suggest that what is inconceivable with people is *qal vaomer*, "how much more," inconceivable with God.[145] (This approach is much more likely than the idea that the

---

138. Leaney thinks the parable refers to perseverance in prayer, as in Luke 18, though he admits that the Greek word is literally "shamelessness." If, of course, one takes the "shamelessness" as that of the knocker, it could be expressed in persistent knocking and have this point. See, Leaney, *Commentary*, 188,

139. See Vermes, *Jesus and Judaism*, 49.

140. See especially Johnson, "Assurance," 125–28. See also Talbert, *Reading Luke*, 132; cf. the use of *anaideiēn* in Sib. Or. 1.175, and *anaidea* in 3.466.

141. Bailey, *Poet*, 126–28. See Johnson, "Assurance," 129; Huffard, "Parable," 154–60.

142. See Tannehill, *Sword*, 46–47.

143. Bultmann, *History of the Synoptic Tradition*, 107; Guelich, *Sermon*, 357, follow Billerbeck's parallels for prayer expressed as knocking here.

144. Tannehill, *Sword*, 133.

145. On *qal vaomer* here, see Longenecker, *Biblical Exegesis*, 68; Bultmann, *History of the Synoptic Tradition*, 185. In general, see, e.g., Mek. Pisha 1:38; 2:36f; 7:48, 61; 9:45; 13:105; 16:119, 126; Beshallah 1:54; 2:73; 7:128; Baḥodesh 5:90 (less); 11:64, 109; Nezikin 1:101; 2:17; 3:43, 69, 128; 10:47, 67; 12:5; 16:92; 18:79, 80, 83, 97; Kaspa 2:26; 5:51, 80, 103; Shabbata 1:14; 2:41; b. Ber. 62b; B. M. 2b–3b; Shab. 143b; Ḥag. 27a; Tem. 16a; Gen. Rab. 60:7; 73:5; 81:4; 82:14; 92:7; 100:6; Lev. Rab. 25:6; 31:2; etc. See

fathers might simply confuse the Judean fish barbut with a serpent or the small round peasant bread with a stone,[146] a suggestion which empties the images of their force.)

The climax comes in the "how much more" argument of verse 13, where God is much more willing to give the Holy Spirit than earthly fathers would give bread (omitted by Luke), a fish, or an egg. Matthew's *ta agatha* is probably original,[147] given the specifically Lukan language of Luke 11:13,[148] and could refer to agricultural blessings[149] or simply good things in general.[150]

The gift of the Spirit is particularly the gift of prophecy in early Judaism,[151] and seems to function that way often also in Luke-Acts, where it is specifically empowerment for mission.[152] This is especially clear in Acts 2:16–18, where Peter's sermon defines the gift of the Spirit in terms of Joel's prophecy about God's people becoming his prophets in the last days.[153] This prophetic anointing is inseparably linked with

---

Strack, *Introduction*, 94, for general definition.

146. Meier, *Matthew*, 70. On the commonness of fish and bread in the diet, see Neusner, *Judaism in the Beginning*, 23.

147. Against Gundry, *Matthew*, 124. Gundry follows Rodd, "Spirit or Finger," in thinking Matt's "Spirit" (Matt 12:28) may be original, but not only is "finger" attested with regard to Hellenistic adjurations (Deissmann, *Light*, 306), it is more Hebraic (Exod 8:19). Luke has a strong interest in the Spirit, and Matthew is doing midrash on Isa 42 in the context, so that the Spirit marks Jesus out as the fulfillment of the passage (which, by rewording it, Matthew has also connected with Jesus's reception of the Spirit at his baptism). See also Schweizer, *Good News According to Matthew*, 287.

148. See Lindars, *New Testament Apologetic*, 57.

149. See Luke 1:53; 12:19; T. Iss. 3:7–8; Sib. Or. 3.659–60, 750.

150. Luke 10:42; T. Jos. 2:7.

151. In the Dead Sea Scrolls, the Spirit is also the purifier from sin. See 1QS 3.7; 4.21; *CD* 5.11; 7.3–4; Bruce, "Holy Spirit," 52–54; cf. Jub. 1:21, 23; 5:8; T. Sim. 4:4; T. Benj. 8:2; T. Ash. 1:9. But the Spirit was especially the Spirit of prophecy (Josephus, *Ant.* 6.166; Philo, *Fug.* 186; Jub. 31:12; 1 En. 91:1; 4 Ezra 14:22 [see remarks by editor Knibb, 278]; 1QS 8.16; *CD* 2.12; 1QH 9.32 [cf. Bruce, "Holy Spirit," 51]; T. Ab. 4 A; Theoph., *Autolycus* 2.33; 3.17; Martyr, *Dial.* 32–34; 1 Apol. 31, 44, 47, 63), and particularly in rabbinic texts (e.g., Mek. Pisha 1:150ff; b. Ber. 31b; Exod. Rab. 5:20; Lev. Rab. 1:3; Num. Rab. 13:20; 18:8; Ruth Rab. 4:3. See also Moore, *Judaism*, 1:237; McNamara, *Targum*, 113; Jeremias, *New Testament Theology*, 78; Marmorstein, *Names*, 99–100), though the Spirit also granted related functions, such as supernatural sight (Lev. Rab. 9:9; Deut. Rab. 5:15, later haggadah on R. Meir; Eccl. Rab. 10:8, §1, on R. Simeon ben Yohai). For the (very different) associations of the Spirit in Greek thought, see Long, *Hellenistic Philosophy*, 155–58; Nock, *Early Gentile Christianity*, 51. The Spirit's most noticeable role as the Spirit of prophecy was naturally as inspirer of Scripture. See 4 Ezra 14:22; 1QS 8.16; Martyr, *Dial.* 25; b. Ber. 4b; Pes. 117a; Meg. 7a; Gen. Rab. 63:14; 80:8; 91:5; 92:9; 93:7; 97, NV; Exod. Rab. 8:1; 27:9; 33:5; 48:6; Lev. Rab. 3:6; 4:1; Num. Rab. 10:2; 11:1; 19:15; 20:18; Lam. Rab. 2:20, §23; 3:58–60, §9; Eccl. Rab. 1:1, §1; 3:16, §1; Song Rab. 1:1, §§5–6, 9–10; 2:1, §3; 7:12, §1; Pesiq. Rab. 10:2; 11:2; 20:1; 30:1; 33:2–3; 34:1; 35:1; 37:1; 50:1, 4. Although Tannaim are sometimes cited, the distribution may suggest a later redactional tendency; but there is enough evidence to suggest that this view originated long before its amplification.

152. See, e.g., Stronstad, *Charismatic Theology*; *Prophethood of All Believers*, esp. 121–22; Menzies, *Empowered*; Haya-Prats, *Empowered Believers*, 31, 34, 192.

153. Some scholars also cite later rabbinic tradition that all Israel would be prophets (Davies, *Paul*, 216; Zehnle, *Discourse*, 29–30; Lake and Cadbury, *English Translation and Commentary*, 22). The antiquity and wide use of this tradition cannot be demonstrated, but it is a natural conclusion from Joel.

the Lukan church's commission to witness to the ends of the earth in the language of Isaiah (Acts 1:8).

It is here that the reader is most fully confronted with the Lukan interpretation of the Lord's Prayer. The demonstration of God's reign and the hallowing of his Name are actualized in the present by the power of the Holy Spirit, perhaps for purity of life but especially for prophetic witness. Perseverance may be linked with the coming of the Spirit; a link with the petition on forgiveness is less clear, unless it is that the Spirit renews the believers' ability to forgive. Had Luke not omitted "bread" when he includes "fish" and (against Matthew) "egg," the reader might naturally think that the petition for bread was also a petition for the Holy Spirit; but it is probably just a petition for daily sustenance, something that Luke 12 suggests God will supply. Still, the image of seeking loaves in 11:5 is suggestive.

The Lord's Prayer, then, includes a prayer for the coming of the Holy Spirit. Although this would include the initial "baptism in the Holy Spirit" as later described in the Book of Acts, the relevance of the prayer here cannot be limited to a single initiatory experience. Luke says that disciples should pray thus "when you pray" (11:2), and this suggests a daily confession of continued dependence on the Holy Spirit in prayer. This would include such experiences as, in Pauline terms, being "led" by the Spirit, "walking" by the Spirit, and certainly being continually filled with the Spirit (cf. Eph 5:18).

Acts illustrates that God often poured out his Spirit after his people's prayers (Acts 1:14; 4:29–31; 8:15; cf. 9:11, 17; 10:30, 44), just as the Spirit descended on Jesus while he was *praying* during his baptism (only in Luke 3:21). Although this is not an invariable connection—Acts illustrates God's sovereignty in adjusting such patterns—it fits Jesus's promise of the Father in Luke 11:13 (cf. Acts 1:4; 2:33). (Although I am certainly not the first commentator to notice the connection between prayer and the coming of the Spirit in Acts, it was perhaps the most spiritually important insight in my four-volume Acts commentary.)[154]

## Conclusion

In general, Luke's form of the Prayer is probably earlier than Matthew's, but some wording, such as "the Holy Spirit" (v. 13), appears distinctly Lukan. The parable is connected with the following traditional admonition to "knock" (11:9) by its image of the suppliant at the door; Luke may have connected the two, but the connection could also go back to Jesus directly.

The passage as a whole relates, in its wider context as part of Luke-Acts, to power to live out a Christian witness in a world of testing, with the assurance that God,

---

154. Given the character of the dedicatee and of this volume, it may be appropriate for me to note that on March 30, 2015, while I was ministering in Indonesia, I realized in a dream that this was the most important insight I had on Acts.

whose honor is at stake in his name, will help his people with the power of his Spirit. This he grants because of his relationship with those who call to him, when, by and for the Spirit, they desperately cry, "Abba!" So by praying for the power to fulfill their prophetic call, his children also look toward the consummation of Lukan eschatology, and so are crying also, "Marana tha!"

# Chapter 12

## Tracing St. Luke's Pneumatology
### *A Theological Study of Bezae's Textual Readings*

BOB WELCH[1]

Throughout the Bezan text (D05)[2] of Luke and Acts, there is a consistent presentation of statement and affirmation in contrast to Vaticanus (B03). This is shown in Luke with a number of doublets that serve to confirm the initial statement.[3] Categorical representations of this are presented here; one to show the immediate confirmation of fulfilling the command and the other to show prophetical affirmation of not only Jesus's words, but also implying the problem of misunderstanding the plan to the Gentiles.

The continued promise of affirmation is seen in Acts with the promise in Acts 2:38–39; 5:28 (obedience to God) and the affirmation of the plan to reach the Gentiles in Acts 10–11; 15. This is culminated in Acts 19 as the emphasis in receiving the Spirit with the affirmation of speaking in tongues.

Together, for affirmation, D05 consistently depicts the necessity of "speaking" and "doing." This means the pneumatology in the Bezan text reveals the Spirit as participating in fulfilling the completion of the initial proclamation contingent upon a synergistic action involving human interaction.

First, analysis of the initial doublet in Luke includes the "command" and then the "affirmation" by the Spirit, i.e., the naming of John is the command and when obeyed

---

1. It is with admiration and thankfulness to Roger Stronstad for his initial "ground-breaking work" on specific Lukan pneumatology that I have worked in this research. Stronstad's insights, when applied to textual criticism of the Lukan text, help to illuminate the intentional readings in the Bezae texts and their purposeful pneumatology. Bravo Dr. Stronstad!

2. Codex Bezae Cantabrigiensis, D05, is a Greek-Latin manuscript dated around 390 CE and basically includes the four Gospels, Acts, and parts of John's epistles. It was first obtained by Theodore Beza from the Monastery of Irenaeus of Lyons and presented to the University of Cambridge in 1581.

3. Welch, "Repetitive Prophetical and Interpretative Formulations." See also Welch, "Acts of the Holy Spirit."

by Zechariah, immediately his tongue is loosed, and he begins to speak and prophesy. This immediate ability to speak is the exact sign of the movement of the Spirit.

## Luke 1:13, 60, 63

| | | | |
|---|---|---|---|
| 1:13 D05: | and you will call his name | | John[4] |
| 1:60 D05: | but will be called | *his name*[5] | John |
| 1:63 D05: | John is | *(the)* his name | |

In the comparison of D05 and B03, the differences do not detract from the main point of the naming of John. The Bezan reading, however, of τὸ ὄνομα αὐτοῦ[6] (his name) at 1:60 replicates to a higher degree the exact words of the angel. There are parallels for the phrase in the LXX, κληθήσεται τὸ ὄνομα αὐτοῦ (his name will be called). Examples are Gen 17:5 for Abram's new name as well as the twice repeated formula for the renaming of Jacob to Israel in Gen 32:29 and 35:10.[7] This repeated text of τὸ ὄνομα αὐτοῦ emphasizes the fulfillment of the angel's words, and this is a reflection of instances of prophetic naming, e.g., Sara to Sarah (Gen 17:15), Isaac (Gen 17:19; 21:3), and children of Jacob (Gen 29:32–35; 30:6–24). Elizabeth states that her son is to be named John and this is repeated by Zechariah at 1:63 with the article (unmarked—a known name) in D05: Ἰωάννης ἐστὶν τὸ ὄνομα αὐτοῦ (B03 omits τὸ). D05's readings support the concept that John is the fulfillment of the words of the angel and, thus, parallel the 1 Samuel account concerning the naming of Samuel.

The word order in D05 text at 1:63 indicates that upon the statement by Zacharias, immediately there was an effect, "and immediately [παραχρῆμα] his tongue was loosed." The B03 text indicates that the people were surprised at the naming, and *then* "his mouth was opened." Luke 1:67 records in D05 that Zacharias was filled with the Spirit and then, εἶπεν, "said," and not B03 text's reading, ἐπροφήτευσεν λέγων, (prophesied saying). Accentuating the act of speaking God's word and affirming it by its fulfillment is seen in Luke 1:76. Zacharias "speaks" prophetically where he says about John, "and your child will be called *prophet* of the most high," and its fulfillment (D05 text reading) at Luke 7:28, "no one greater among those born of women than the *prophet* of John the Baptist."[8] B03 omits calling John a prophet in 7:28. Therefore, from D05's perspective, Jesus proclaims John as a prophet that is the fulfillment of

---

4. English translations from D05 are mine throughout the chapter.

5. Text in italics indicates the D05's additions, unique, or exegetically noticeable wording.

6. In this chapter, Greek alphabets are used rather than transliteration due to textual critical nature of the chapter.

7. Gen 16:11, 15; 21:3.

8. Emphasis added. The D05 readings support a positive position of John as prophet and yet cause a direct comparison of Jesus and John by saying "a younger than him in the kingdom of God is greater than him."

Zacharias's saying in 1:76. This is irrespective of any linguistic evidence emphasizing John's prophetic role apart from a priestly one, e.g., John "speaks" to the crowd at Jordan (Luke 3:7) telling them to "do" (or bear fruit to) repentance and they respond, "what shall we do to be saved? (D05)" (Luke 3:10, 12, 14).

## Luke 1:28 and 1:42[9]

| | |
|---|---|
| 1:28 D05: | As he entered *the angel* said to her, "Greetings you who are highly favored, the Lord is with you! *Blessed are you among women!*" |
| 1:42 D05: | and she exclaimed in a *loud* voice and said, "Blessed are you among women, and blessed is the fruit of your womb!" |

The phrase "blessed are you among women" is repeated by Elizabeth in v. 42. D05 shows the kind of pattern at the following locations in the Lukan Gospel: (1) 19:38 records Εὐλογημένος ὁ ἐρχόμενος, ἐν ὀνόματι κύριου εὐλογημένος. ὁ βασιλεύς εἰρήνη ἐν οὐρανῷ noting the twice occurrence of "blessed." (2) 7:48 and 7:50 concerning the woman, i.e., Ἀφέωνταί σου αἱ ἁμαρτίαι, (your sins are forgiven) and ἡ πίστις σου σέσωκέν σε, (your faith has saved you); (3) the two questions by Satan at the temptation: Εἰ υἱός εἶ τοῦ θεοῦ, (if you are the Son of God) at 4:3 and 4:9; (4) Ἀμὴν ἀμὴν λέγω ὑμῖν, (amen, amen I say to you) at 4:24.

The statement "blessed are you among women" is made apparent by Elizabeth's reaction to the greeting by Mary in Luke 1:42, i.e., specifically the D05 wording "she cried out with a *loud* voice" (φωνῇ μεγάλῃ). The reaction to Mary's appearance in this way is prefaced (1:41) with the reading that Elizabeth was "filled with Holy Spirit," thus signaling by the narrator that Elizabeth's reaction was important. The B03 text uses κραυγῇ, instead of φωνῇ, which refers to "shouting, or crying."[10] Although this has been suggested to support a thematic development of the Son of God being carried in the symbolic "Ark of the Covenant,"[11] i.e., Mary, it may also serve to confirm the messianic portrayal of Jesus, the divine presence amongst men.

The relationship between prophecy and the need for fulfillment, or confirmation, is evident in these two readings of 1:28 and 1:42. Therefore, not only does the repetition of "blessed are you among women" serve to establish the reliability of Mary and Elizabeth, but also that the connection between them was due to obedience to the law. They serve to interpret to the reader (Theophilus) that the conception of Jesus was not only a result of OT Scripture, but also to be interpreted as legitimizing his beginning. In addition, in Luke's statement in 1:70, "through the mouth of his holy prophets," Luke

---

9. The D05 reading is supported by most of the texts and indicates a wider historical distribution as opposed to the B03 text.

10. The words ἀνεφώνησεν φωνῇ appear together in 2 Chr 5:13 in the LXX at the conveyance of the ark to the Temple, whereas κραυγῆς (83 times in the LXX) only appears in 2 Sam 6:15 in connection with the Ark, but not with the word ἀνεφωνεῖν.

11. Laurentin, *Structure et Théologie*, 66–75, 160–61.

PART III—READING ST. LUKE'S THEOLOGY: PNEUMATOLOGICAL AMBIENCES

is stressing not so much a "proof-from-prophecy," but rather a "proclamation from prophecy," which would not emphasize an apologetic, but rather a "declaration."[12] The conclusion that D05 Luke 1:28 and 1:42 are connected prophetically, and not simply due to interpolation, is supported by the rhetorical use of repetition.[13] Thus, repetition accentuates a theological aim which, in this case, was the confirmation to Elizabeth that Mary was indeed the bearer of the Son of God. This confirmation of the original statement by the angel at 1:28 was fulfilled by the interpretation by Elizabeth that commended Mary's obedience.

## Luke 3:4–14

Importantly, the "prophetical/affirmation" signature continues in the orientation of Luke's presentation of "repentance" with the "gift of the Spirit." The D05 text lends more semantic weight to the importance of "repentance," which effects "salvation." The quotation in Luke 3:4 from Isaiah 40:3–5 reveals a reading that seems to increase the emphasis upon individual ethical repentance. This has been changed from "his" to "your," giving a more emphatic point to the application of repentance and reinforces John's ministry. This call to prepare a way for the Lord in the desert would normally require response from the hearers and, thus, moral preparedness is emphasized by the six-time repetition of [to do] in verses 8–12 and 14.

| | |
|---|---|
| 3:10 D05: | And the crowds asked him saying, "what should we do *in order that we might be saved*?" |
| 3:12 D05: | What should we do *in order that we might be saved*? |
| 3:14 D05: | Those serving as soldiers also asked . . . What should we do *in order that we might be saved*? |

It is important to note here that these readings by D05 directly connect salvation with a change in behavior. The B03 text, which omits these readings, lessens the connection of repentance to salvation. The "how" and "why" of these differences between D05 and B03 may not be fully understood here, but it could be posited that John the Baptist's ministry is clearly strengthened by the D05 text.

D05's emphasis of "salvation" as the result of changes of behavior, i.e., repentance, apart from the "Spirit" suggests the Johannine conversional baptism experience as *not* incomplete on the basis of forgiveness of sins. Apollos's instructional example of knowing only the baptism of John (Acts 18:25) did not invalidate his salvation experience, and this, despite having been instructed in the word of the Lord. This may imply that he had not received the "laying of hands" for the imposition of the Spirit by the apostles, or that he even had been in the apostles' presence.

---

12. Bock, *Proclamation*, 72.

13. "The Prophets and the Law," (Matt 11:13; "law . . . prophets" 5:17; 7:12; 22:40); "the lost sheep of the house of Israel," (Matt 10:6; 15:24); "Let him who has ears listen," (Matt 11:15; 13:9, 43; Luke 8:18; 14:35).

## Luke 3:16–17

The key text here of the comparison of the baptisms shows the theme of repentance changing to the reception of the Spirit, e.g., comparing/contrasting John and Jesus's ministry as foundational work of salvific repentance and Spirit-baptism "gathering" and "judging." Bezae emphasized "repentance" with the express terms used.

3:16 D05:     [He] *perceiving their thoughts said*, "I baptize *you* (pl.) with water *with reference to repentance* but one is coming (himself) stronger than me, whom I am not able to loose the strap of the *sandal*. He will baptize you (pl.) with the Holy Spirit and fire.

3:17 D05:     who has his winnowing fork in his hand *and* he will cleanse his threshing floor and *on the one hand* he will gather the wheat into a barn but on the other hand the chaff he will burn with fire unquenchable."

Verses 15–17 form an interdiction that is emphasizing the judgment of the fire. Verse 18 continues with another (μεν) which subordinates to the lengthened introduction of Herod in v. 19. This analysis shows that this section is not a section contrasting John's salvation by repentance message versus Christ's salvation via the cleansing of the Holy Spirit. Rather, the context is of the continuation of the "preaching" of salvation by Jesus with the added dimension that real judgment would be inaugurated by Christ. This clarifies the "command" and "affirmation."

## Luke 22:34, 61

22:34 D05 Until you have denied me three times     that *you do not know me*
22:61 D05 Three times you will deny me     that *you do not know me*

The duplicated you "do not know me" (μὴ εἰδέναι με) in D05 has the effect of reinforcing the fact of Peter's denial. Yet its more profound effect is that it serves as the fulfillment of Jesus's earlier words to Peter. This "fulfillment" in the Lukan text bears similarities to the Matthean and Markan texts, but includes the reading of Jesus looking at Peter when the rooster crowed. This gives evidence for two emphases as follows: (1) Jesus saw the struggle with Peter and "prophesied" both of his failure as well as his obedience (confirmed by Peter "remembering the word of the Lord"); and, (2) the important concept of "repentance" (ἐπιστρέφω—turn around) is highlighted by both the command (22:34) and Peter's weeping (22:62). D05 Acts 11:2 narrates Peter as fulfilling Luke 22:32, "Turn and strengthen your brethren," in his travel from Caesarea to Jerusalem, "strengthening the brethren." Therefore, Peter's weeping at the "cockcrowing" in his denial was not the "return" prophesied by Jesus. This requirement of action to confirm the real "return" is paralleled by the Levitical method for repentance in sacrifice and confession.[14] In this case, it is a "turn" that manifests the fulfillment of Jesus's statement.

Therefore, the larger question is how this repetition here of "you do not know me" proleptically reiterates the greater act of command and fulfillment. Since the context of Jesus's statements at Luke 22 involve the activity of "serving," and the example of serving Gentiles, it can be seen that the command to "turn" was to be completed much later in the story of Cornelius. Emphatically, the text at 22:34 and 22:61, "you do not know me," definitively links the two verses as a prophetic word and fulfillment. When this is coupled with the imperative ἐπίστρεψον (Turn!) at 22:32, and the fulfillment at Acts 11:2 (D05), one can see that the command by Jesus to "turn" may have formed the basis of incentive for Peter, as he comprehended Jesus's statement. Therefore, the connection between "spoken command" and the "doing" is explicit. We will now look at texts in Acts to examine the continued depiction of the Spirit involved in affirmation.

## Acts 2:38–39

The sense of confirmation and affirmation continues in Acts in D05 by a more direct view of seeing the purpose for receiving the Spirit, i.e., Acts 2:38–39; 3:19; 5:32. As attested in Bezae's readings, the strong Jewish purpose of the action of the Holy Spirit is affirmed. In 2:38–39, "repentance," or rather, the command to change was made and shows emphasis to the Jewish audience and not Gentiles:

> 2:38–39 D05 and Peter says to them, "Repent and be baptized, each one of you, in the name of the *Lord* Jesus Christ for (unto) the forgiveness of sins and you will receive the gift of the Holy Spirit; for the promise is to *us* and to *our* children and to all of those who are far away, as many as whom the Lord our God will call."

Furthermore, the procedural steps leading to the reception of the Spirit are delineated in a comparison of Acts 2:38–39 and 3:19. Is Peter indeed simply rephrasing 2:38? Repentance, turning from sin and receiving forgiveness, and the phrase, "times of refreshing," bear a distinct resemblance to 2:38. We may be able to understand the conjunction καὶ (and) used in Acts 2:38c through exploring Acts 3:19, which reads the following in D05: "Repent (μετανοεῖν) therefore, and turn again (ἐπιστρέφειν), (with the result) that your sins may be blotted out, *in order that* times of refreshing may come from the presence of the Lord."

The difference between μετανοεῖν and ἐπιστρέφειν is that the former signifies turning away from evil and the latter, a turning towards good. The result is the forgiveness of sins. The conjunction, ὅπως (in order that), is clearly used as a "purpose conjunction" and not a "result" conjunction. Furthermore, the "times of refreshing"

---

14. Boda, "Renewal in Heart," 13–14.

and its connection, with the reception of the Spirit, can be seen from an examination of Isaiah 32:15 in the Septuagint, which says, "until the Spirit from high comes upon you, and the wilderness becomes a fruitful field, and the fruitful field is reckoned a forest" and the Symmachus version that says, "until the refreshing from high comes upon you."[15]

Even though the translation of Isaiah 32:15 is always "until the Spirit is 'poured out' upon us from on high, " yet this word, ערה (to be poured out)—lay bare by removing contents, to empty, in the LXX is translated as ἐπέλθῃ, from ἐπέρχομαι and means to "to move to or upon—come upon (from above)" as in inspiration. Since the Symmachus version supports the idea of equating the "Spirit" with "refreshing," we can surmise that Acts 3:19 is referring to the Spirit. This is significant because of the fact that since Luke 24:49 is established as the "Spirit from on high," one can judge from this that Acts 3:19–20's "times of refreshing," is referring to the Holy Spirit of Acts 1:8; 2. This strongly suggests that Acts 2:38–39 can be equated with Acts 3:19. We can, therefore, say that the "and you will receive" in 2:38 does not indicate a sequential action—result function in an automatic fashion, but rather expresses the ultimate "purpose" for the reception of the Spirit without limiting the Spirit's timing.

In tying the connection between Acts 2:38 and 3:19, we also focus on the following: εἰς τo in 3:19, "with the result," shows the personal affect of repentance and ὅπως ἂν, "in order that," the wider cosmic-historical consequence. This significance of the relation of 2:38 and 3:19 is further enhanced by D05's change in 2:39 to "us" and "our children" from "you" and "your children." Many have observed that D05 consistently discriminates between Israelites and "others far off" (universal) in an application. This phrase "everyone whom the Lord our God calls" is from Joel 2:32d. Yet, the significant part excised is the previous part, Joel 2:32c, that directly concerns Zion and Jerusalem, and this is replaced with πᾳςῖν τοῖς εἰς μακπάν, "for all who are far away." Instead of a referral to the Jews, the phrase is added, and it stands in apposition to the phrase taken from Joel 2:32d. This transforms the understanding of the Joel passage to that of a universal sense, i.e., "everyone" and "all." It is suggested here that D05's use of "us" and "our children" as opposed to the usual "you" and "your children" reflect the otherwise omission of Zion and Jerusalem.

Therefore, Acts 2:38 and 3:19 show emphasis on Jews as the underlying assumption of the audience—not Gentiles. Yet the Spirit is emphasized as the substantive evidence of God's approval. In this, the continued interaction of Peter with the command to "turn" may also be seen in D05's persistent contrast between God's plan and Peter's in the argument with the Sanhedrin in Acts 5:28. D05 reads: saying, "Did we not command you an order not to teach in this name, and yet here you have filled Jerusalem with your teaching, and you intend to bring upon us *that* man's blood? *It is necessary to obey God more than men.*"[16]

---

15. Pao, *Acts*, 132–33.
16. Also Codex Floriensis; Perpinianus; Syrian Peshitto. See, Clark, *Acts of the Apostles*, 31.

This text in D05 is significantly different from the other witnesses: The statement, "It is necessary to obey God more than men" is ascribed to the high priest and not to Peter in D05. This difference in D05 here from B03 may be a sign that the displacement was not simply a copyist's error. In addition, the anaphoric reference to Peter, i.e., the omission of the article, is justified by 5:15, where he is singled out from the apostles. At this point, it would be safe to remember Acts 4:7–8 where the high priest questioned the apostles, "by what power or by what name did you do this?" The specific point of "authority" is the key. Peter's response forces the key issue of the reception of the Spirit to illustrate the completion of the command to "obey and you will receive." Acts 5:32 D05 reads, "And we are witnesses to these things, and so is the Holy Spirit, whom God has given to those who are obeying him."

Because the Sanhedrin actually focused the question on obedience to God—"obey God rather than man"—Peter's answer is to insist on the evidence of their obedience—the reception of the Holy Spirit. Obedience is a recognition of the authority of God. The point is that a confirmatory signal of divine acceptance is established by the expression of the presence of the Spirit. Thus, Peter argued for this as the evidence of acceptance by God. In Acts 8, Simon desires this authority, but misunderstands that it is God and His authority—not an authority originating in man. The obedience stressed here must be the condition and not the result, because evidence must be shown of prior obedience before the reception. The fact that this is a present state in no way detracts from the explicit answer to the priest. The proof of their present obedience to God is the fact that they have received the Holy Spirit—which must be the "Spirit of Prophecy." This is an affirmatory purpose in concluding that the Spirit witnesses as the respondent and fulfiller of God.

## Acts 11:1–2, 17; 15:1–2, 4, 7–9

In the continued depiction of the activity of the Spirit in Acts, in the sense of affirmation, the Cornelius event (Acts 10:44–46) is "explained" by Peter in Acts 11. This indicates both the fulfillment of "strengthen the brethren" as well as serving to impart information in the continued understanding of Peter in the interaction with the Spirit.

> 11:2 D05[17] Peter, *therefore, for a considerable time wished to travel* to Jerusalem; *and having called to him the brethren and having strengthened them, making much word through-out the country [and] teaching them; who also met them and reported to them the grace of God.* But the brethren of the circumcision disputed with him.

As can be seen, D05's reading is significantly longer than ℵ01/B03. One view put forward to explain this is that this was necessary to explain Peter's absence from the council in Jerusalem. The shorter version, however, can be seen as an abridgment of

---

17. Attestation: Syriac Philoxeniana; Clark, *Acts of the Apostles*, 66.

the longer text that explained the circumstances leading up to the greater dispute with the "party of the circumcision." But for the purposes of seeing the affirmative action here, D05's reading completes the text of Luke 22:32, as stated earlier. Furthermore, the dynamics of doctrinal and administerial control begin to reveal the great debate of what constitutes inclusion into the family of God in the reception of the Holy Spirit.

> 11:17 D05: If therefore God gave to them the same gift as even us who believed upon the Lord Jesus Christ, was I able to prevent God *to not give to them the Holy Spirit who believed upon Him*?[18]

In this verse, God "gave" (ἔδωκεν) the Holy Spirit, but the participle that is repeated in D05 cannot be a simultaneous event. The πιστεύσασιν (who believed) must have occurred previously, although one cannot be more specific.

The pivotal statement here from the D05 text reveals that "believing" was the *prerequisite* in order to receive the Holy Spirit. The "to prevent God" or "to hinder God" stands as the ultimate defense in the search for the "authority" to grant the Holy Spirit, from where Peter rhetorically asks: "Who was I?" Peter did not have the authority to question the validity of the Gentiles' experience and, in effect, God himself authorized their sincerity of heart experience by giving them the same gift of the Holy Spirit. It was the common understanding that only those obeying the Mosaic law, which included circumcision, could even begin to satisfy the requirements for inclusion into the community of God. The concluding agreement of the members of the council at Jerusalem (Acts 11:18) was that God had granted "repentance that leads to life." Yet this issue was not fully accepted as can be seen sometime later at the Council in Acts 15.

> 15:2 D05: And when Paul and Barnabas had no small dissension and debate with them, *because Paul spoke firmly maintaining (them) to remain thus just as when they believed; but those who had come from Jerusalem ordered them,*[19] Paul and Barnabas and certain others, to go up to Jerusalem to the apostles and elders *that they might be judged before them* about this question.

The particularly sharp detail as evidenced in D05 reveals the central administrative control and authority that resided within the council in Jerusalem.[20] It was the seat of judgment for the church, especially in doctrinal matters. The difference between D05 and the other manuscripts is especially keen concerning how Paul and Barnabas were "ordered" to appear in Jerusalem and defend Gentile inclusion into the Kingdom of God, apart from the observance of the Mosaic law. Yet D05's treatment of the texts

---

18. Also it[(ar)]; Syriac Harclensis; cop[meg]; Augustine; UBS4 451.

19. Text in italic reads in Greek D05: ἔλεγεν γάρ ὁ Παῦλος μένειν οὕτως καθὼς ἐπίστευσαν διϊσχυριζόμενος οἱ δὲ ἐληλυθότες ἀπὸ ἱερουσαλὴμ παρήγγειλαν αὐτοῖς; Also, Codex Thomas; Ephraemus

20. Two different spellings of Jerusalem are noticed in Codex Bezae, Ἰερουσαλήμ, a Semiticism distinguishing the Hebrew context of Jerusalem being the religious center of Judaism, and ἱεροσόλυμα, the Hellenistic derivation. Luke-Acts uses the Hebrew spelling generally, whereas Matthew, Mark, and John prefer the Hellenistic. See Read-Heimerdinger, *Bezan*, 311–44; Rius-Camps, "Spelling," 84–94.

shows the importance of the reception of the Spirit as validator as thus in 15:7 D05: ... ἀνεστέσεν ἐν πνεύματι²¹ Πέτρος καὶ εἶπεν πρὸς αὐτούς; ... *then Peter stood up in the Spirit and said to them.*

D05 gives a more dramatic sense of the monumental event by stating that Peter was "in the Spirit," which was tantamount to confirmation of God's judgment. This explicitly goes to the heart of the debate, which is "what is the intent of God in the bestowal of this gift of the Spirit upon uncircumcised Gentile believers?"

D05 is consistent in using "the Holy Spirit *upon* them," always following the OT in focusing attention on the locative sphere of action of the Spirit. This leads to the interpretation as the "Spirit of Prophecy," as opposed to the inward action of a purifying/cleansing mode. Of particular importance is the phrase, "confirmed them" or "bore witness to them," because this was in fact "evidence" in the defense of the apostles' argument. Since it has already been established that a repented heart was necessary before the Spirit reception was possible, it follows that an outward and physical sign, as opposed to inward and non-physical, was understood as the confirmation from God.

The major problem is the cause of "distinction" between Jewish and Gentile believers. The outward perceivable evidence of acceptance by God was through visible obedience of the laws as such and this was the basis of distinctions between the Jews, Gentile proselytes, and the "nations." Upon examination, it is seen that Luke always attributes forgiveness (ἄφεσις), which is granted in response to faith/repentance, to Jesus and never to the Spirit.[22]

Rabbinic thought shows that repentance was the prerequisite before restoration of the Spirit was seen. In this case, we find a general understanding of the Spirit departing from Israel because of sin, though the Spirit would return at a future time,[23] e.g., Isa 44:13 (Deut Rab 6:14).[24] The inclusion of the Gentiles was not normally seen in this fashion, i.e., with reception of the Spirit of Prophecy, but was to be confirmation of fulfillment of the Targum of Zechariah 14, dealing with inclusion of the nations in worship, and the Targum of Isaiah 24:16, concerning "joy from the sanctuary to all inhabitants of the earth." This is attested also in Targum Jonathan, Tobit, and Jubilees.[25] This expectation of global worship in the Temple may indeed have served as the eschatological hope that was fulfilled by the Spirit reception in this way. Therefore, the transition from dependence upon repentance as confirmation to dependence on

---

21. Also Codex Thomas; Tertullian; Cassiodorus; Ephraemus; Rius-Camps, "Spelling," 93.

22. See Acts 2:38; 5:31; 13:38; 26:18; Luke 1:77; 3:3; 4:18; 24:47. See also, Menzies, *Spirit and Power*, 80.

23. Menzies, *Spirit and Power*, 101.

24. "And because I will cause my Divine Presence to rest upon you, all of you will merit the Torah and you will dwell in peace in the world" (Deut. Rab. 131).

25. Chilton, "Aramaic," 389–90.

receipt of the Spirit as the salvific confirmatory sign was in motion. This is confirmed for the disciples in Acts 19:1–6:

19:1 D05: And Paul, *desiring on his own decision to travel to Jerusalem, the Spirit said to him to return to Asia,* and he having passed through the upper parts arrived into Ephesus.[26]

19:2 D05: and finding certain disciples, he said to them, "Did you receive the Holy Spirit after you had believed?" But they said "We have not heard *of those who are receiving*[27] the Holy Spirit."

There is a radical difference between D05/P38 and ℵ01/B03 readings. The previous verse indicated that Paul was directly led by the Spirit to these "disciples." But questioning whether or not the Holy Spirit exists and/or whether or not people were receiving the Holy Spirit are different thoughts. The singular reference to "disciples" means they are new in this story and this forms a narrative function of the section. The "knowing the Baptism of John" is important because people who had received John's baptism might have been expected to know the Old Testament expression "Holy Spirit" (cf. Ps 51[LXX50]:11) and to be aware of John's words about the mightier one than himself who would baptize ἐν πνεύματι ἁγίῳ.[28] Therefore, these disciples were indeed no different than the twelve apostles had been, with the exception of incomplete knowledge of John the Baptist's fulfilled words about Christ or the Spirit. Furthermore, "Did you receive the Spirit?" is not in an initiating or soteriological context.

19:5 D05: But hearing *this,* they were baptized into the name of the Lord Jesus Christ *for pardon from sin.*[29]

Nothing is said about the connection between baptism and the Holy Spirit. The expression, "pardon from sin," indeed serves to separate water baptism and the reception of the Spirit. The Holy Spirit is given after repentance and faith in Christ and validates the experience.

19:6 D05: and when Paul had laid his hands on them, *immediately*[30] the Holy Spirit came upon them and they were speaking in tongues and prophesying.

The correlation between "laying on of hands" and the conferral of the Holy Spirit has been examined, but without enough conclusive evidence (cf. Acts 5:12). The word "immediately" distinctly reinforces a causal link of laying on of hands, thereby

26. Attestation: P38; Codex Thomas; Ephraemus; Clark, *Acts of the Apostles*, 121.
27. Also P38; P41; syr$^{hmg}$.
28. Bruce, *Acts of the Apostles*, 406.
29. Also Minuscule 614; Syriac Philoxeniana; Minuscule 2147; Minuscule 2412.
30. Singular reading. ℵ01/B03 have a different word order for χεῖρας.

decreasing soteriological symbolism. Of interest, however, is the usage of "the Holy Spirit came *upon* them," which is so common in Luke-Acts. D05 displays regularity in preferring ἐν for location within a place and εἰς for movement towards a place with no ambiguity, except at three places, 11:25; 18:21, 27.[31] The action of the Holy Spirit was similar to a mantle being draped over them and coincided with the Old Testament understanding of the Holy Spirit's work in empowering an individual. As in previous texts, invasive glossolalia was manifested upon reception of the Holy Spirit, not at repentance. Whether this was free vocalization or *xenolalia*—speaking in an unlearned foreign language[32]—we can only say that unlike Acts 2, these "tongues" did not have the consequence of the evangelism of unbelievers. Rather, the context indicates a lesson on a particular "norm" for depicting Christian experience in eschatological terms. The importance for confirmation by reception of the Spirit is thereby clarified.

## Conclusion

Recognition of the parallels of (1) Zechariah's speaking at the fulfillment of the naming, (2) the "blessed are you among women" phrase by Elizabeth by the unction of the Spirit, (3) the immediacy of reception of the Spirit in Acts 11, and (4) the reception of the Spirit in Acts 19, all affirm the Spirit's filling in the sign of speaking. In this manner, the texts examined here in D05 suggest that a consistent pattern of affirmation is connected with the Spirit with the purpose of (1) confirming acts of obedience to the spoken will of God, (2) establishing prophesied truths, (3) distinguishing between the act of repentance and the purpose of Spirit reception, and (4) establishes the effect of belief and the confirmation of the gift of the Spirit to those without the law.

The connection between these points is that before "command" and "obedience," the affirmation is the function of the Spirit in the act of causing the physical aspect of speaking, but without human assistance. Ultimately, D05's pneumatology suggests the primary activity of the Spirit continues similarly in the OT and NT time periods, i.e., the "confirmatory stamp" or seal to establish affirmation of prophetical statements and signaling the completion of faithful obedience.

---

31. Read-Heimerdinger, *Bezan Text of Acts*, 196.
32. Hovenden, *Speaking in Tongues*, 3.

## Chapter 13

# Charismatic Ministries in St. Luke's Theology

JOHN W. WYCKOFF[1]

In 1984, when Hendrickson Publishers first published Roger Stronstad's, *The Charismatic Theology of St. Luke*, no one, including the author himself,[2] foresaw the impact it would have upon Lukan studies. Now it is widely recognized, by both those who agree and those who disagree with Stronstad's conclusions; from that time forward, the landscape for Lukan studies has forever been changed. In his relatively small volume of a little over 100 pages, Stronstad remarkably delivers, among other things, three momentous achievements in Lukan studies: he shows the didactical nature of Luke's historical narrative; he re-establishes the theological independence of Luke's teaching; and, he substantiates the charismatic and vocational purpose of Luke's works.

Obviously, an accomplishment of this magnitude work creates new interest in the subject area and generates related scholarly works. Among other projects, *The Charismatic Theology of St. Luke* has resulted in various kinds of comparisons/contrasts analyses of the Lukan writings and the Pauline epistles. One example is the implications in Acts that "glossolalia is the essential evidence for the baptism in the Holy Spirit,"[3] contrasted with Paul's apparent silence on the matter. Another example

---

1. Having similar backgrounds and interests in theology and biblical studies, Roger Stronstad and I met through the Society for Pentecostal Studies, and soon became great friends. As Church Ministries and Biblical Studies Department Chairperson at Southwestern Assemblies of God University in Waxahachie, TX, at that time, I arranged for Roger to come to our campus for a week-long seminar related to his first edition of *The Charismatic Theology of St. Luke*. This was, of course, a great blessing to our students and faculty. His second edition continues to be one of our textbooks. Though our relationship is now limited to email communications, Roger continues to be a great friend and wonderful inspiration to me!

2. Roger Stronstad told me this in a personal phone conversation in March 2018. One exception to this may be Clark H. Pinnock, who wrote the foreword to Stronstad's first edition of *The Charismatic Theology of St. Luke*. Pinnock anticipates the significance and impact of this work.

3. Stronstad, *Charismatic Theology*, 2.

is the nature and purpose of tongues-speech according to Luke, compared to the same according to Paul.

## Charismatic Ministries in Luke's Writings

### Objectives and Approach

Another similar comparative analysis, I argue, is fruitful when studying St. Luke's theology of charismatic gifts/ministries, the topic which we are about to look at in this essay. This approach is also meaningful because popular opinion is that there is a dichotomy between Luke and Paul, suggesting that Luke's emphasis is more on "the *power* of the Spirit" whereas, Paul's emphasis is more on "the *gifts* of the Spirit." Therefore, below I present a comparison of the teachings and emphases of Luke and Paul on the charismatic ministries of the Spirit.

Admittedly, at first look we could possibly get the impression that Luke does not teach much, if anything, similar to the Pauline concept of "the gifts of the Spirit." Then, therefore, perhaps he does not have much emphasis on charismatic ministries. In fact, Luke does not at all use the particular phrase, "the gifts of the Spirit." Possibly Luke's emphasis is most noticeably upon the "power of the Spirit."

I believe, however, there is no dichotomy between Luke and Paul regarding their emphases and teachings on the charismatic ministries of the Spirit. The notions that Luke emphasizes "the power of the Spirit" more than Paul, and Paul emphasizes "the gifts of the Spirit" more than Luke, are both only misleading impressions. These false impressions are a result of the Pentecostal/Charismatic Movement's considerable focus on Luke's statements about the power of the Spirit; and, the presupposition that Paul's impressive discussion of Spiritual [gifts] in 1 Cor 12–14 means he emphasizes the gifts of the Spirit more than Luke. This essay seeks to show that there is no dichotomy between Luke and Paul in this area of their teachings.

Ideally, this comparison could include a comprehensive analysis of the pneumatology of both Luke and Paul. Such a massive project is obviously beyond the limits of this essay, and I believe, unnecessary. Thus, this essay proceeds on the belief that the basic issues of this comparison can be addressed with a more narrow focus. In particular, this essay addresses three questions. One, to what extent does Luke teach on and emphasize the charismatic ministries of the Spirit in Luke-Acts? Two, does Paul emphasize the concept of "the gifts of the Spirit" more than Luke? Three, does Luke emphasize the concept of "the power of the Spirit" more than Paul?

Two approaches are used in this comparison. One is to analyze Luke-Acts to reveal Luke's pervasive emphasis on "charismatic" activities in both Luke and Acts. By "charismatic," I mean the Spirit anointing, empowering and/or inspiring believers and the ministry results of these activities of the Spirit.[4] The second approach is similar

---

4. My definition of "charismatic" may be technically a little different than Stronstad's; but,

to Stronstad's method of comparing Luke's emphasis on the Spirit to the emphases on the Spirit in Matthew's Gospel and in Mark's Gospel.[5] A very simple counting reveals that Luke references the Spirit eighteen times, as many times as Matthew and Mark combined.[6] Obviously, Luke emphasizes the Spirit considerably more than both Matthew and Mark.

In the analysis at hand, however, Luke and Paul use very different terminologies when discussing the ministries and workings of the Spirit. This makes our task much more difficult. Also, this task includes a brief comparative analysis of Luke's and Paul's emphasis on the power of the Spirit. Therefore, this comparison will require considerably more elaboration than Stronstad's comparison of Luke's emphasis on the Spirit with that of Matthew and Mark.

In order to show this, the next main two sections show the pervasiveness and significance of Luke's teachings on the *charismatic ministries* of the Spirit; first, in his Gospel; and, second, in the Book of Acts. The third section provides a comparison of the emphases of Luke and Paul, specifically in the areas of "the works/gifts of the Spirit" and "the power of the Spirit." Finally, the Conclusion briefly summarizes and re-states the results of this analysis.

## Luke's Teaching Intent and Purpose

As a writer, Luke certainly is a historian. So, his literary genre is narrative historiography. As Stronstad most ably shows, however, Luke's purpose for writing history is far beyond providing "a simple description of events."[7] Rather, Luke is a writer of historical theology—he is a "Historical Theologian." He writes with the purposeful intent of teaching theological truth.[8] His technique is historiography, his purpose is didactic and his subject is theology.

Realizing Luke has a purposeful intent raises an obvious and important question. What is Luke's special purpose? Among other things, it likely includes something related to his notable emphasis on the Spirit. Yes, indeed, it does! In Luke-Acts, Luke's purpose is to concentrate a unique teaching focus upon something *no other* New Testament writer has provided—an emphasis on the role of the Holy Spirit in both the origin and the spread of the gospel.

---

practically, I think we are basically talking about the same thing. See Stronstad, *Charismatic Theology*, 16.

5. Stronstad, *Charismatic Theology*, 39.

6. In counting references to the Spirit in Luke's Gospel, Stronstad does not count Luke 4:18, which must be included. Also, obviously, Luke 24:49 is a reference to the Spirit, though the term "Spirit" is not in the text.

7. Stronstad, *Charismatic Theology*, 10.

8. Some scholars contend that Luke, in his historical narratives, does not intend to teach doctrine and theology. For a full discussion of this position see Hoekema, *Holy Spirit Baptism*; Stott, *Baptism and Fullness*; Fee, *Gospel and Spirit*.

PART III—READING ST. LUKE'S THEOLOGY: PNEUMATOLOGICAL AMBIENCES

# Charismatic Emphasis in Jesus's Life and Ministry: The Gospel According to Luke

## Gospel with a More Detailed Charismatic Focus

For the reason mentioned above, Luke envisions and carries through a strategy designed to accomplish his unique purpose. But why does he need to compose yet another gospel besides the two that already existed? Why doesn't he just take up the story where Matthew and Mark leave off? Because neither Matthew nor Mark provides an adequate background for Luke's unique purposes. Luke needs a background that provides a more detailed account of the Spirit's work from Jesus's birth, throughout his ministry, until his crucifixion and ascension. That is, he needs a gospel account with a special charismatic emphasis.

Furthermore, neither of the two earlier evangelists even elude to the outpouring of the Holy Spirit on the Day of Pentecost that launches the Church into its mission. In Acts, Luke will highlight the fact that Jesus's followers need the power of the Spirit to take the gospel from Jerusalem to the rest of the world. The need for this account is obvious. Therefore, besides giving new emphasis on the charismatic character of Jesus's life and ministry, Luke also needs to provide an account of the momentous Day of Pentecost events.

Accordingly, in his first volume, Luke shapes his historical narrative in such a way that it brings this singular charismatic focus upon the whole Christ Event.[9] This focus begins immediately. Of Luke's eighteen references to the Spirit in his Gospel, thirteen are located in his first four chapters. The first seven, concentrated in chapters 1 and 2, are called infancy narratives, because they occur around the time of Jesus's birth. The next six, concentrated in chapters 3 and 4, are called inauguration narratives, because they pertain to the beginning of Jesus's public ministry. Luke's next four references to the Spirit come later, in chapters 10, 11, and 12. His last such reference in his Gospel is in the final chapter.

## Charismatic Beginning of Jesus's Life

Luke's first reference to the Spirit is in his account of the angel *prophetically* telling Zacharias that his son, John, will be "filled with the Holy Spirit while yet in his mother's womb" (Luke 1:15). The next two are in direct relationship to Jesus's birth. The angel *prophetically* tells Mary that she will bear a child conceived by the Holy Spirit (Luke 1:35). Then, when Mary visits Elizabeth, Luke notes that Elizabeth is filled with the Spirit and, "with a loud voice," cries out a *prophetic* utterance about Mary (Luke 1:41).

---

9. Jesus Christ's birth, ministry, suffering and crucifixion, resurrection, post-resurrection appearances, and ascension.

Finally, at the time of John's birth, Zacharias, "filled with the Holy Spirit," *prophesies* about salvation to come through Jesus (Luke 1:67–79).

In chapter two, the remainder of Luke's references to the Holy Spirit in the infancy narratives provide further emphasis upon the Spirit's activity following, but still near Jesus's birth. When Jesus is 40 days old, according to the Old Testament custom, Mary and Joseph bring their firstborn son to the Temple for His dedication (Luke 2:21–24), as prescribed by the Law (Lev 12:1–8). That same day, a devout man named Simeon is led by "the Spirit into the Temple," because "it had been revealed to him by the Holy Spirit that he would not see death before he had seen the Lord's Christ" (Luke 2:25–26). When he takes the Child into his arms, inspired by the Spirit, Simeon *prophesies* about the salvation coming for all through the Christ Child (Luke 2:27–32). He also *prophesies* about the suffering the Child and Mary must endure (Luke 2:33–35). At the same time, a "prophetess" named Anna is likewise in the Temple. When she sees the infant Jesus, she, too, *prophesies* concerning the Christ Child (Luke 2:36–38). The pattern is obvious. Luke's focus in the infancy narratives is the charismatic gift of *prophecy*.

## Charismatic Launching of Jesus's Ministry

Luke's next six references to the Spirit make up the inauguration narratives (Luke 3:15–4:30). Whereas in the infancy narratives, Luke's emphasis is upon the charismatic gift of prophecy about the Child Jesus, his emphasis in the inauguration narratives is upon the charismatic character of Jesus and his ministry.

In Luke 3:16, John declares the Christ would baptize in the Holy Spirit. Then, later, when John baptizes Jesus in water, the Spirit descends "upon Him in bodily form like a dove" (Luke 3:21–22). Thereby, Jesus is empowered by the Spirit and is ready to begin his charismatic ministry. There is one more part in this inauguration event, however, before Jesus actually begins his ministry. He must face the enemy, Satan, and be victorious over him. Jesus, "full of the Holy Spirit" (Luke 4:1a), is "led around by the Spirit in the wilderness" (Luke 4:1b), where he is tempted by Satan. The implication is clear—precisely because "Jesus [is] full of the Holy Spirit" (Luke 4:1), he is able to overcome the temptations of Satan.

At this point, Luke extends his emphasis upon the charismatic activity of the Spirit yet further beyond that of both Matthew and Mark. He does so by providing significant additional narrative details about the beginning of Jesus's ministry. Specifically, even though Matthew (4:12) and Mark (1:14) both tell about Jesus going to Galilee after his temptation, only Luke makes the charismatic point that he does so, "in the power of the Spirit" (Luke 4:14). Further, only Luke provides an account of Jesus going into the synagogue of Nazareth (Luke 4:17–19), where, he reads from Isa 61:1–2a: "The Spirit of the Lord God is upon me, because the Lord has anointed me."

Especially by including this dramatic scene in the synagogue, Luke makes it clear, his main point in the inauguration narratives is that Jesus's ministry is charismatic. That is, *what Jesus does, he does, not simply because he is the Son of God; but, rather because he is the Son of Man, empowered by the Spirit.* Accordingly, everything Jesus does after "the Holy Spirit descended upon Him" (Luke 3:21–22), he does in the "authority and power" of the Spirit (Luke 4:36), because he is "full of the Holy Spirit" (Luke 4:1).

## Examples of Jesus's Charismatic Teachings

Luke's next four references to the Spirit do not come until chapters 10, 11 and 12. Here Luke records Jesus, himself, teaching about the Spirit. In chapter 10, Luke tells the story of Jesus sending out seventy of His followers to minister in various cities. When they return and report to Jesus, Luke notes Jesus "rejoice[s] greatly in the Holy Spirit" (Luke 10:21). In Luke 11:11–13, Jesus teaches His followers about the heavenly Father's willingness to give them the gift of the Holy Spirit. In chapter 12, verse 4, Jesus warns his followers concerning the danger of blaspheming against the Holy Spirit. Then, in verses 11–12, Luke records Jesus telling his followers when they face persecution, "the Holy Spirit will teach you . . . what you ought to say." Following these four references, Luke records more of Jesus's teachings and miracles right up to the time of his crucifixion (Luke 22:49–51).

## Charismatic Emphasis in Luke's Closing

Luke provides three narrative elements, which he uses to link his two volumes together. The first one is in the introduction of both volumes where he addresses them both to Theophilus. The other two elements are found in the closing section of his Gospel account (Luke 24:44–53). Luke will refer back to these in his introduction to the Book of Acts. One of these is Luke's final reference to the Spirit in his Gospel. He records Jesus telling his followers: "And behold, I am sending forth [the Holy Spirit,] the promise of the Father, upon you" (Luke 24:49). Jesus is, of course, referring to the charismatic power of the Spirit, which is essential to the spread of the Gospel. Thus, this particular linking narrative element is especially important because it points to the central event of Luke's charismatic emphasis in Luke-Acts—the outpouring of the Spirit on the Day of Pentecost. Finally, the third narrative element that links the two volumes is Luke's account of Jesus's ascension back to his heavenly Father (Luke 24:50–53).

## Charismatic Ministries of the Church: The Book of Acts

As noted above, for the sake of linking his two works together, in the introduction of his second volume, the Acts of the Apostles, Luke briefly refers Theophilus back to the first volume. Luke notes that there he had written about "all that Jesus began to do and teach, until the day He was taken up *to heaven*" (Acts 1:1–2). Next, in his second linking element, he supplies further details of Jesus giving his followers instructions concerning the empowering experience he wants them to receive (Acts 1:8). Luke, then provides more details of Jesus's ascension (Acts 1:9–10). He thus uses his three especially designed narrative elements to link his two volumes together, historical and theological.

### Charismatic Beginning of the Church

Now, to move on in giving his account of how the Gospel supernaturally spreads from Jerusalem through Judea, Samaria and beyond, Luke needs only to provide that otherwise missing account of the giving of the Spirit to the Church on the Day of Pentecost. The importance of this part of his narrative is seen in the realization that Luke's Day of Pentecost account is the center of his story. Historically and theologically, as well as locationally in Luke's narration, this event comes in the middle, between his account of the Christ Event, on the one hand; and, his account of the spread of the gospel throughout the Roman Empire, on the other.

Luke reports that, as instructed, Jesus's followers return to Jerusalem, where 120 of them, "all with one mind, were continually devoting themselves to prayer" (Acts 1:14). They continue this until the day comes to celebrate the annual Feast of Pentecost. On that day, Jesus does what he promised he would do: "I am sending forth the promise of My Father upon you" (Luke 24:49). Luke reports: "They were all filled with the Holy Spirit and began speaking with other tongues, as the Spirit was giving them the utterance" (Acts 2:4). The followers of Jesus now have the power of the Spirit they need to accomplish what he has called them to do.

### Charismatic Ministries of Jesus's Followers

In providing this essential Day of Pentecost account, Luke now has everything he needs to follow through with his unique purpose—emphasizing the role of the Spirit and the charismatic ministry of Jesus's followers in advancing the Gospel from Jerusalem to the rest of world. Luke begins by reporting the response of the large crowd of people gathered in Jerusalem from all over the Roman Empire for the Day of Pentecost. They are amazed and perplexed when they hear the 120 speaking in tongues. How can these Galilean followers of Jesus be praising God in the crowd's many different languages? Peter, responding to their inquiry, "raised his voice and declared"

(Acts 2:14), explaining to them the meaning and significance of what they had just witnessed (Acts 2:5–13).

F. F. Bruce suggests the Greek term for "declared" may indicate Peter spoke by divine inspiration.[10] Indeed, this is the case. The language here is similar to the language Luke uses to describe Elizabeth's prophetic blessing upon Mary in Luke 1:42, where "she cried with a loud voice." Thus, we have the record of the first two charismatic works of the Spirit following the giving of the Holy Spirit to the Church—speaking in tongues and prophesying. This is also our first introduction to a member of "the charismatic Prophethood of all believers"—the Apostle Peter.[11] But, Peter is only the first. The heavenly Father wants *all* of Jesus's followers to accept his gift of the Spirit and become charismatic prophets after the likeness of Jesus himself and the Apostle Peter.

Flowing directly from the miracle of Pentecost, Luke's narration in the Book of Acts provides a portfolio of miraculous events in which it is clear that *the Spirit is doing his works through the followers of Jesus, just as he did earlier, through Jesus himself*. After being "filled with Holy Spirit" (Acts 2:4), like Jesus himself, everything Jesus's followers do, they do in the power and authority of the Spirit. Thus, on the one hand, in his first volume, Luke's emphasis is upon the "charismatic" ministry of Jesus. On the other hand, in his second volume, Luke's focus is upon the "charismatic" ministry of his followers.

In his second volume, Luke references the Spirit over fifty times. From the beginning of Acts to its end, Luke records multiple incidents in which the Spirit enables believers to speak in other tongues, prophesy, manifest special faith, heal the sick, manifest unusual boldness, speak words of supernatural knowledge, performs miracles, manifest uncommon benevolence, receive supernatural deliverance, speak words of unusual wisdom, endure severe persecution, be transported supernaturally, raise the dead, see visions, receive divine direction, cast out demons and perform other miraculous works of the Spirit. Luke's point is clear! The power given to Jesus's followers who are baptized in the Spirit, is given to them for the purpose of performing charismatic ministries and, thereby, advance God's kingdom.

So, with every example, Luke teaches his readers about the Spirit anointing, empowering and inspiring Jesus's followers for the divine service to which he has called them. Apostles, including Peter, James and John, the sons of Zebedee, Barnabas, James the brother of Jesus, and Paul, are the most prominent. Accordingly, we have the book's traditional title: "The Acts of the Apostles." Luke continues his focus upon the involvement of the Spirit, however, not only through the Apostles, but also through many other believers. This makes the book worthy of the title: "The Charismatic Ministries of the Followers of Jesus." Thus, Luke hereby *teaches* us that all of Jesus's followers are to be "charismatic prophets" through whom the Spirit works to advance the gospel.

---

10. Bruce, *Book of Acts*, 60
11. See Stronstad, *Prophethood of All Believers*.

# Comparing the Charismatic Emphases of Luke and Paul

Having analyzed Luke-Acts in order to ascertain Luke's emphasis on the ministries and workings of the Spirit, we are now ready to compare Luke's and Paul's emphases on charismatic ministries. At the beginning of this essay, we identified two common suggestions concerning a supposed dichotomy between Luke and Paul in this area. One suggestion is, Luke's emphasizes is more on "the power of the Spirit" and little, if any, on "the gifts of the Spirit." The second suggestion is, Paul's emphasis is more on "the gifts of the Spirit" and less on "the power of the Spirit." The following comparison responds to these suggestions by using the above analysis to answering the three questions posed at the beginning:

1. To what extent does Luke teach on and emphasize the charismatic ministries of the Spirit in Luke-Acts?

2. Does Paul, indeed, emphasize the concept of "the gifts of the Spirit" more than Luke?

3. Does Luke, indeed, emphasize the concept of "the power of the Spirit" more than Paul?

## Emphases on Charismatic Ministries

Comparing two biblical authors on any given topic is somewhat like the proverbial "comparing apples to oranges." This is certainly the case in attempting to compare the teachings and emphases of Luke and Paul on "the works/gifts of the Spirit." Luke and Paul use much different terminology to discuss what may be essentially the same topic: the ministries and workings of the Spirit. On the one hand, Luke does not use the uniquely Pauline terminology, "gifts of the Spirit." He simply has no interest in discussing the specific concept of "the Spirit distributing gifts" among believers, as Paul does in 1 Cor 12:4–11 and Rom 12:6–8. Correspondingly, on the other hand, Paul does not use some of Luke's terminology, such as the Spirit "descending upon" (Luke 3:22), "coming upon" (Luke 1:35; Acts 1:8; 19:16) or "falling upon" (Acts 10:44; 11:15) believers. He simply has no interesting in discussing this specific Lukan concept.

Also, interestingly, Paul himself never uses the actual phrase "the gifts of the Spirit." This phrase is appropriate, however, because it is logically derived from Paul's discussion of "Spiritual [gifts]" in 1 Cor 12–14. In a similar fashion, while Luke never uses the phrase, "the works of the Spirit," such a phrase can be logically derived from and applied to the miracles of Jesus in the Gospel of Luke, as well as the miracles of Jesus's followers, in the Book of Acts. The reason for this observation will become evident later.

Admittedly, these differences in Lukan and Pauline terminologies, are significant. In view of this, on the one hand, one might conclude there simply is no ground common between Luke and Paul upon which we can make this comparison. That is, perhaps the differences are more than just terminology and Luke simply does not discuss anything similar to this topic. On the other hand, however, Luke and Paul may be using different terminology to discuss essentially the same topic. If so, to make this comparison, we will need to identify such terminology in Luke-Acts.

Possibly the closest idea to Paul's concept of the Spirit "distributing gifts" to be found in Luke-Acts, is Luke's concept of the Spirit "descending," "coming," or "falling" upon believers. As noted above, however, Paul does not use this particular Lukan terminology.

Regardless of these substantially different terminologies, nevertheless, are not both writers actually talking about the same thing? That is, whether one thinks in terms of "the Spirit gifting believers"; or, if one thinks in terms of "the Spirit descending, coming or falling upon believers," either way, both authors, are teaching about essentially the same thing—*how the Spirit equips believers*, enabling them to be cooperative partners in the ministries and workings of the Spirit. Thus, "the gifts of Spirit" is Paul's conception of *how and what the Spirit does*. Also, "the works of the Spirit" is a similar conception in Luke's discussion of the same. Hence, a combination of these two phrases, "the works/gifts of the Spirit," (which I have used occasionally already), becomes the common ground upon which to move forward with this comparison.

Obviously, this suggestion is very significant. If valid, this means that wherever Luke discusses "the works of the Spirit," he is teaching and emphasizing operations of Spirit which are similar (and therefore comparable) to those of Paul, when he discusses "the gifts of the Spirit."

Now, consider Luke's pervasive emphasis upon the activity of the Spirit in Luke-Acts, as shown by our analysis above. Clearly, by numerous examples of Jesus's charismatic ministry in his Gospel and the charismatic ministry of Jesus's followers in Acts, Luke provides extensive teaching on the works of the Spirit. With only two or three exceptions, Luke discusses all of the "gifts" listed by Paul in his Epistles (Rom 12:6–8; 1 Cor 12:8–10, 28; Eph 3:7; 4:11). In fact, in Luke-Acts, these references are too numerous to be identified and listed here. Further, Luke discusses additional "works/gifts" found only in Luke-Acts. Further yet, and more significantly, by discussing multiple examples, Luke provides an important additional understanding of these works of the Spirit. Therefore, rather than lacking in emphasis on charismatic ministries, Luke's teaching in this area is substantial.

## Emphases on Charismatic Power

The second related idea to be addressed in this comparison, is the notion that Luke emphasizes "the power of the Spirit" more than Paul. On this topic, Luke and Paul use similar terminology. Thus, this aspect of the task lends itself well to the straightforward approach of counting the number of times each author refers to the "power of the Spirit" and comparing these. Hence, this aspect of our task is much shorter than the one above comparing Luke and Paul regarding "the works/gifts of the Spirit."

To begin with, both Luke and Paul always use the same Greek word, *dunamis*, for "power" when writing about this topic. Interestingly, whereas Luke uses the actual phrase "the power of the Spirit" only once (Luke 4:14), Paul uses this exact phrase twice (Rom 15:13, 19). Perhaps this is our first clue that Luke may not emphasize "the power of the Spirit" any more than Paul.

Further, however, there are other references in both Luke-Acts and in the Pauline Epistles where it is logical to think that the idea of the power of the Spirit is being referenced, even though the full phrase, "the power of the Spirit," is not used. More precisely, in these particular references, the context indicates that "the power of" part of this phrase, though not included, is implied. For example, this is the case for Luke in Acts 13:9. The suggestion is, the verse would read: "Saul, who was also *known as* Paul, filled with [the power of] the Holy Spirit, fixed his gaze on him" (NASB). In the Pauline Epistles, Gal 5:25 is a good example. In this instance, the verse would read: "If we live by [the power of] the Spirit, let us also walk by [the power of] the Spirit."

If all of these kinds of references are included in our analysis, in Luke-Acts, Luke references the power of the Spirit a total of about 14 times. For Paul, this total is about 21 times. Thus, in this analysis, as surprising as it may be, Paul references and discusses the power of the Spirit half again more times than Luke!

## Conclusion

I believe, there is no real dichotomy between Luke and Paul regarding their teachings and emphases on either "the works/gifts of the Spirit" or "the power of the Spirit." This conclusion will be substantiated by using the findings of the analysis above to answer the three questions proposed in our Introduction.

The first question is, to what extent does Luke teach on and emphasize the ministries and workings of the Spirit? Again, obviously, this analysis clearly demonstrates that the answer to this question is: Luke's presentations of the charismatic activities of the Spirit are pervasive throughout both his Gospel and the Book of Acts. This is exactly what we expected to find. Why? Because, as noted early in this essay, a significant part of Luke's purpose in Luke-Acts is to provide a unique emphasis on the role of the Holy Spirit in both the origin and the spread of the gospel. Luke accomplishes this special purpose. Thus, his teachings and emphases on charismatic ministries, are as much or more extensive than any other New Testament writer, including the Apostle Paul.

The second question is, does Paul emphasize the concept of "the gifts of the Spirit" more than Luke? As shown above, if we look strictly for where Luke specifically teaches on the idea of "giftedness" and the concept of the Spirit "distributing gifts," the answer is, Luke does not teach anything on this. Hence, if we remain this strict in our analysis, for this part of our comparison, there is nothing in Luke to compare with Paul.

We have proposed that, while Luke's terminology is different than Paul's, however, Luke's concept of the Spirit "descending," "coming" or "falling" upon believers, is comparable to Paul's concept of the Spirit "distributing gifts" among believers. That is, though their terminologies are different, both of these authors are talking about basically the same thing—*how the Spirit works in relationship to believers* to advance God's Kingdom. Also, as just noted, Luke's narrative presentations of the ministries and workings of the Spirit are extensive and pervasive throughout his Gospel and Acts.

Thus, if these differences in Luke's and Paul's use of terminology are taken into account, and if this method of comparing these is acknowledged to be valid, then Luke actually teaches more on this topic than Paul. Therefore, at least in this way of comparing these, the notion that Paul emphasizes "the works/gifts of the Spirit" more than Luke, is false. Incidentally, whether or not this particular conclusion is received as valid, the conclusion above that Luke emphasizes charismatic ministries as much or more than any other New Testament writer, remains solidly true.

The third question is, does Luke emphasize the concept of "the power of the Spirit" more than Paul? This idea seems to be an illusion that has arisen due to the Pentecostal/Charismatic Movement's hyperfocus upon Luke's obviously strong emphasis on "the power of the Spirit." When all references where Luke and Paul use *dunamis* to refer to the power of the Spirit are taken into consideration, however, a different view emerges. In fact, in this analysis, we discover that Paul discusses this concept at least half again more than Luke. Therefore, the suggestion that Luke emphasizes "the power of the Spirit" more than Paul, is likewise a false notion.

Finally, Luke's contribution to our understanding of the charismatic ministries of Jesus and the New Testament Church is unmeasurable! Without the Gospel of St. Luke we would not have his special focus on the role of the Spirit in the life of Jesus and His charismatic ministry. Without Acts we would not have an official record of the charismatic ministry of the first-century followers of Jesus and how the gospel spread throughout the then known world. Without Luke-Acts we would be lacking background information that is essential to our understanding of Paul's ministry and his Epistles. Luke's focus on charismatic ministries and the overall function of Luke-Acts in the New Testament corpus are indispensable.

# Chapter 14

## Sin, Science, and the Spirit
### *A Pentecostal Reading of St. Luke*

AMOS YONG[1]

The following attempt is to demonstrate a distinctively Pentecostal perspective on sin that is in dialogue with science.[2] To my knowledge, there has been little to no critical reflection on the Christian teaching about sin from the Pentecostal academy, which begs further the question of how to extend such a non-existent enterprise into the theology-and-science arena. Obviously, the plausibility of this exercise can only be discerned at the end of the discussion, but two preliminary comments are in order. First, it's not that Pentecostal theologians have not considered hamartiology at all, but that the various forays into this arena have traversed well-worn tracks carved out by the evangelical tradition, rather than being guided by specifically Pentecostal perspectives. The following thus seeks to press more deeply into the achievements of the emerging Pentecostal theological academia in order to reconsider sin from such a more particular horizon, and yet simultaneously envision how the unfolding efforts might also further explorations in the interdisciplinary domain where theology and the sciences continue in cross-fertilization.

---

1. I am grateful to be included herein knowing Professor Roger Stronstad's own theological inclinations are different, perhaps contrasting, to my own—at least if his review of *Who is the Holy Spirit* is any indication. But my *Who is the Holy Spirit*, as well as the overall arc of my work, is really an attempt by a systematician to do within his discipline what Professor Stronstad as a biblical scholar has achieved in this field, that is to read St. Luke on his own terms, rather than being dismissed as mere historian (for me) or subordinated to other scriptural voices (for Professor Stronstad). Even if we might differ on the details of the trajectory I have charted, this essay is humbly submitted as at least aspiring to follow, if not being consistent with, Professor Stronstad's path-breaking scholarship on Luke-Acts.

2. This essay was initially presented at the Faith & Science Conference, Evangel University, Springfield, Missouri, September 23, 2016, and its full version is "The Social-Psychology of Sin: A Pentecostal Perspective" published in Yong, *Hermeneutical Spirit*, 141–61. Thanks to Riku Tuppurainen, who took the lead in shortening it for inclusion in this book. Published by permission.

Second, although barely underway, there is every indication that the Pentecostal theology and science interface, even in its very short term, has been generative of insights and debate, both indicators of the fertility of the conversation so far and inviting of further inquiry.[3] This essay seeks to press further into this node via attentiveness to the doctrine of sin, not only to see how scientific viewpoints might be informative also, but to forge distinctive Pentecostal reflection that may have broader ecumenical purchase. More precisely, following the paths charted so far from the intersection where Pentecostal theology and science have converged, we will inquire more specifically into hamartiology from a specifically pneumatological perspective, one that begins with Christian understandings of the person and work of the Holy Spirit.

We will proceed first to map discussions in theology and science on the topic or theme of sin, and then, second, suggest how Pentecostal vantage points might fare amidst that discussion. I will urge that the Day of Pentecost narrative in Acts chapter 2 provides springboards toward what might be considered a pneumatological theology of sin. Our goal, given the present state of the discussion, cannot be a fully developed Pentecostal theology of sin.

## Sin: Interdisciplinary Formulations

Here our goal is to overview contemporary understandings of the notion of sin, particularly as such have been informed by a scientific worldview.[4] I hold that theology can be illuminated by advances in other spheres of human knowledge (the sciences included), even as the goal is never to revise orthodox understandings for the sake of novelty or to "keep up with the times," so to speak. Instead, truth will prevail no matter where such may be found, and, from a faith-seeking-understanding posture, Christian theologians can proceed interactively with other branches of knowledge, drawing from them, but also speaking from their own stance as appropriate. When talking about sin, then—which is first and foremost a *theological* notion of homo sapiens not being aligned with the will and glory of God—the question is how twenty-first-century understandings can be helpfully illuminated from scientific outlooks. We begin here with the literature on sin assessed in empirical and scientific perspective and then relate such with the current state of Pentecostal understandings of sin.

---

3. Besides my own monograph (Yong, *Spirit of Creation*), I have edited a collection of articles in one of the foremost scholarly journals devoted to the theology-and-science dialogue and two other books in this area. The former is introduced by Yong, "Pentecostalism, Science, and Creation." The two edited volumes are Yong, *Spirit Renews the Face of the Earth*; Smith and Yong, *Science and the Spirit*.

4. For arguments for such an enterprise see Yong, *Renewing Christian Theology*, 279–92; "Pentecostalism and Science."

## Sin in Empirical Perspective

Although from two generations ago, Reinhold Niebuhr's claim, "the doctrine of original sin is the only empirically verifiable doctrine of the Christian faith,"[5] remains with us today. Even if Niebuhr meant no more than the truism that sin is easily observable all around us, the recent interface between theology and the sciences has generated unexpected empirical perspectives extending the discussion. My awareness of the nascent literature at this intersection where sin and science meet suggests that we can grasp the convergences at least at three interrelated levels: the genetic-sociobiological, the neuro-psychological, and the socio-cultural.

At the *genetic* level, if Augustinian notions of original sin and hereditary guilt have been predominant in the Latin or Western theological tradition, recent proposals may, intended or not, instigate a retrieval and restatement of the bishop of Hippo's ideas, albeit in conversation with the evolutionary sciences.[6] In its most basic form, scientists and theologians working amidst the foundations of the discussion presume the evolutionary history of the world and the concomitant set of ideas about random mutation at the genetic level and natural selection of the fittest traits at the level of organic populations. Although the author of the notion of the "selfish gene" has been particularly hostile to theism and its religious matrices,[7] that fundamental idea has been quite productive at the science and theology intersection, urging formulations such as *original selfishness*, the notion that the genetic drives toward replication generate self-preservational instincts, tendencies, and behaviors in living organisms at every level of the evolutionary chain, including that of homo sapiens.[8]

The *sociobiological* perspective deepens the analysis of what happens at the level of organisms. Here, reductive egocentrism, as opposed to reciprocating behaviors, actually is maladaptive for the organism within its population group in the long run. Hence, altruistic relations emerge selectively first among kin as adaptive strategies competing over and against out-groups.[9] The "fittest" groups survive and reproduce on the basis of their cooperative behaviors, albeit not without struggle and competition internally and vis-à-vis outsiders.

*Neuroscientific* perspectives shed further light on the sinful dispositions and behaviors of homo sapiens. Proper functionality of the mammalian brain nurtures trust, even as a healthy limbic system facilitates memory and fosters meaning-making. The neocortex organizes thinking and funds inquiry, while the frontal lobes and forebrain cultivate intentionality and provide orientation and direction (teleology). From this vantage point, one way to understand sin is in terms of the brain's functions "'falling

---

5. Niebuhr, *Man's Nature and His Communities*, 24.
6. Peters, *Sin*, 320–27, for example, asks if original sin is now understandable as "hereditary sin."
7. Dawkins, *Selfish Gene*.
8. Domning and Hellwig, *Original Selfishness*.
9. Williams, *Doing without Adam and Eve*.

short' of potentialities and demands,"¹⁰ in that its various parts or systems work improperly (malfunction) or do not provide the needed checks (defenses) and balances (for safety) for defining in binary terms what is helpful and what is harmful essential for harmonious relationship of human persons within their wider social environment.

From this, correlations can be specified between the genetic, biological, and neurological domains and the psychological profiles of sinful dispositions and behaviors. Psychologist and neuroscientist Matthew Stanford, for instance, argues that rage (so-called *intermittent explosive disorder*) is undergirded by a dysfunctional prefrontal cortex that fails to restrain an over-activated amygdala; that irresponsible sexual behaviors are driven by dysfunctional or neurochemically misfiring attraction and attachment systems; that impulsive, aggressive, and even criminal behaviors (stealing for example) are often the result of personality disorders, including *borderline personality disorder*, impairing the regulation of social and interpersonal relations; and that addictions derive from *reward deficiency syndrome* that require greater and greater stimulants in order to restore organismic equanimity or equilibrium.¹¹ What needs to be emphasized is that such underlying neurological factors are understood, not deterministically, but dispositionally, preserving the psychological dimension of human moral decision-making, albeit as operating within its neuro-genetic constraints.

Last (for our purposes), but not least, is the *sociocultural* level. Here human interactions work in, through, and with the genetic, neurological, and physiological "hardware" of the human body, whether initially through nurturing by parents and caregivers or later through culture-making activities, with the result that some dispositional pathways are perpetuated and opened up and others marginalized or neutralized through social learning and practices.¹² One route of inquiry observes how biologically rooted experiences of anxiety, pride, and concupiscence generate distrust, scapegoating, and cruelty in relationship to others—not in any one-to-one causal sense but through the webs of interpersonal and social exchange—such that we talk about a spectrum of sin and evil from and between the human soul and the social sphere.¹³

Another perspective, going back to Niebuhr himself during the time between the two world wars, emphasizes that personal human virtuousness is undermined by societal relations and dynamics.¹⁴ Human persons and their self-understandings are themselves constituted by society even as their behaviors are shaped into conformity with social roles and conventions, so that in this framework we would need to talk about *social sins*, like slavery or racism, that is "rooted, embodied, and perpetuated in

10. Ashbrook and Albright, *Humanizing Brain*, 157.
11. Stanford, *Biology of Sin*.
12. van den Toren, "Human Evolution," 16–17. See also Wilcox, "Proposed Model."
13. This is the argument of Peters, *Sin*, although his discussion is less linear than I have characterized here.
14. Famously argued in Niebuhr, *Moral Man and Immoral Society*.

social institutions."[15] Recognition and critical analysis of such societal sinfulness requires an inter-subjective "structural epistemology" that identifies the interwovenness of the personal (in all its bio-physiological, cognitive, and psychological complexity) and the social.[16]

## Traditional Pentecostal Views of Sin

If the broader theology-and-science conversation's ruminations on the topic have focused on the doctrine of original sin more specifically, such emphases are also consistent with heretofore Pentecostal forays in this area. Traditional Pentecostal perspectives foreground analysis of the origins, nature, universality, transmission, and consequences of sin.[17] The origins of sin, whether through Adam or the serpent in the Garden (representing Satan), is related to original sin, which elucidates the mysterious but yet all encompassing nature of sin that binds all persons into sinful solidarity with each other and inclines all toward sinful acts and behaviors. The consequences of sin–its results and effects–are destruction (personal, social, cosmic), suffering, and death, ultimately alienation from God, which perpetuates the suffering due to sin in the present life to eternity.

Parallel treatments can be found among charismatic theologians, that is those informed by the neopentecostal movement within the mainline Protestant denominations since the 1960s. One account, unfolded from out of a three-volume *Systematic Theology from a Charismatic Perspective* frame of reference, situates the hamartiology in the first volume amidst the broader discussion of the doctrine of creation. Two chapters totaling over 50 pages also expound on the origins, nature, and consequences of sin,[18] including further elaboration in the last part on the guilt and punishment demanded by sin alongside the separation, estrangement, and bondage sin initiates and effects. This work, developed from out of a Presbyterian or Reformed perspective, is also careful to specify how a sovereign God can, nevertheless, create a world with freedoms that allow for sin's tarnishment, which is minimized in another, more baptistic approach. The latter discussion of the nature and consequences of sin transitions also between theological anthropology (the *what* that needs saving) and Christology (the *who* that brings salvation),[19] while discussing the fall, Adam and original and inherited sin, the nature and universality of sin, and the results of sin.

---

15. O'Keefe, *What Are They Saying?*, 3.

16. See Arokiasamy, "Sinful Structures," 91.

17. For a Church of God (Cleveland, Tennessee) perspective, see part 2 in vol. 2 of Arrington, *Christian Doctrine*; and for an Assemblies of God perspective, see Marino, "Origin, Nature, and Consequences," 255–90, a one chapter version of what Arrington covers in 40 pages. Both are denominationally authorized theological textbooks.

18. See Williams, *Renewal Theology*, 1:221–73, on sin and the effects of sin, respectively.

19. Hart, *Truth Aflame*, 249–76, on sin.

Two summations are in order. First, if the science-and-theology conversation (above) has by and large focused on understanding the nature of original sin, Pentecostal spirituality appears to spotlight the personal character of sin, how the fall has resulted in sinful inclinations within each and every person.[20] There is a sense in which this is expected: if Pentecostal spirituality lifts up the saving work of Jesus Christ through the person and work of the Holy Spirit, then it also makes sense that its general understanding of sin revolves around what is wrong in the world, such that the intervention of the triune God is redemptive. Second, following their evangelical counterparts, much of Pentecostal hamartiology is shaped by the received dogmatic tradition, especially as mediated through conservative Protestant streams. Within this venue, if science appears at all in the discussion, it would be in the chapter on the doctrine of creation, and in that context, the focus is usually on (or against) the theory of evolution and its (disastrous) implications for Christian theology of creation.[21]

While evangelical—and hence Pentecostal—engagements with science ought not to be confronted frontally, given the historical suspicions and polemics,[22] I think it is possible to make some headway if explorations were grounded within ecclesially defined traditions, in this case according to Pentecostal spirituality and its sensibilities. The following thus seeks to delineate first steps toward such a hamartiology from specifically Pentecostal starting points.

## Sin: A Pentecostal Intervention

I think a productive way forward is to press more deeply into the Day of Pentecost message in the book of Acts that has been generative for modern Pentecostal piety and practice and has thus operated loosely as a canon-within-the-canon for theologizing within the Pentecostal movement.[23] The following thus gestures toward a preliminary hamartiology from out of the Pentecost account, situates such within the broader Lukan theological framework, and then attempts to reconnect to the preceding scientifically elaborated notions of sin. Our goal is to outline a distinctively Pentecostal, but no less ecumenical platform for a theology of sin for a scientific world, one that views sin

---

20. Warrington, *Pentecostal Theology*, 35.

21. Williams, *Renewal Theology*, 1:112–13, is against the evolution of species, hinging his position on the Genesis narrative's indication regarding creatures being formed according to their own *kinds*, but Hart, *Truth Aflame*, 168–78, is more of a progressive creationist, albeit one open to arguments from a theistic evolutionary point of view. Munyon, also, rejects macroevolutionary ideas, but does say that "the Scriptures simply do not speak in support of [any creationist] models with the degree of specificity [we] would like" (Munyon, "Creation of the Universe," 235). See also Munyon, "Creation of the Universe," 222–35.

22. Some of which is charted by Elbert and Yong, "Christianity, Pentecostalism."

23. Professor Stronstad's books have led the way in this regard for Pentecostal biblical scholars and theologians like me; consultation of the indices to my various books will confirm that I have repeatedly cited his work as laying the Lukan foundations for Pentecostal theological reflection.

## Sin—In, Through, and After Pentecost

An initial pause might be to address the concern that Acts 2, whatever else it might discuss, is not intended to develop a theology of sin.[24] Yet we begin here, since the second chapter of Acts provides the basic arc for understanding the promised Spirit-empowered witness "to the ends of the earth"[25] (Acts 1:8), culminating in the arrival of the gospel to Rome in the final chapter, even as those from Rome were already found gathered in Jerusalem and recipients of the Spirit's outpouring at Pentecost (2:10).[26] Hence every endeavor to think theologically in dialogue with this book will be forged in light of its Pentecostal witness to the good news of Jesus Christ. Our approach, therefore, asks a twofold set of questions from this Day of Pentecost starting point: first, what is it that the Spirit does in the Day of Pentecost outpouring, and second, how might such activities of the Spirit provide insight into what is wrong with human beings and their world? Conceptualizing the latter will provide a springboard, I will argue, for outlining a Pentecostal theology, of at least the effects of sin.

We begin by noticing that the Spirit descends on human "flesh" (Acts 2:17a). This summarizes what the author describes earlier in 2:2–4. Note here that there is a carnal dimension to the Spirit's coming: human ears resound, human bodies are perceptive, human heads are touched, and human tongues are activated. The Spirit's arrival registers itself across the full human sensorium. Thus, one might ask what is it about human embodiment that is targeted by the Spirit's gift and giftings?[27] Might it be that human perceptibility, epistemology, and renewal are being accomplished in the Spirit's redemptive work?

Next, the author wants us to understand that "there were devout Jews from every nation under heaven living in Jerusalem" (2:5), and that these include alongside local Galileans other representative groups from around the Mediterranean world (2:7–11). As important, amidst the bewilderment, amazement, astonishment, and perplexity (2:6, 7, 12a) of the multitude of tongues and languages unleash at the event, there is an unfathomable intelligibility: the exclamation that, "in our own languages

---

24. Sin appears only once in that chapter, namely in Acts 2:38. This call to repentance resulting in the expiation of sin is repeated in the next chapter (Acts 3:19), even as it is consistent with the passing references to *sin* in the rest of Acts (5:31; 10:43; 13:38–39; 26:18). The only other reference is to Stephen not holding the sin of his murderers against them (7:60). For broader perspective on the Lukan notion of forgiveness of sins see Moessner, "'Script' of the Scriptures in Acts."

25. The Scripture citations are taken from the NRSV.

26. For argument regarding Acts 2 as central to any theology of Acts, much less a Pentecostal theological reading of the book, see Yong, *Spirit Poured Out*, 167–202.

27. I develop these ideas further in my Pentecostal (Acts 2) theology of diverse (dis)abilities. See Yong, *Bible, Disability, and the Church*, 82–117.

we hear them speaking about God's deeds of power" (2:11b) proceeds alongside and simultaneous with the cacophonous, "What does this mean?" (2:12b). Many others have commented on what is here obscurely understood: that whatever else Pentecost means, it somehow reunifies what the Tower of Babel dispersed, but achieves such results not by silencing but by harmonizing in pneumatological key the many tongues and languages of the world.[28] Thus, one might ask how such divine redemption is responsive to the plight of human sociocultural and transnational alienation, not least the demarcation between Jew and Samaritan, much less Jew and Gentile, both segregations clearly reconciled in the rest of Acts. Could the Pentecostal miracle, in other words, be addressing the sin of human ethnocentrism, the biased preferences for the in-group over and against all other (out) groups?

Peter's exposition in response to the wonderment of the crowd provides additional clues to the problems at which Pentecost might be directed. Here, Luke records Peter appealing to the book of Joel, effectively providing an authoritative (scriptural) explanation of the pentecostal outpouring as justifying egalitarian prophesying from out of the mouths of women, youth, and slaves (2:17–18), groups of persons traditionally not viewed as recipients of divine favor or authorization. Yet another way to read Peter's (and Luke's) use of sacred writings is to inspire the overcoming of hierarchical divisions or other chasms—between male and female, young and old, slave and free—prevalent in the ancient world, but no longer relevant in the community of the redeemed. It might even be further speculated from the apocalyptic themes in the Joel text preserved here in Acts 2 that the division between the human-cultural world and its/their natural environments (2:19–20) is also minimized. That the witness of the gospel comes through those on the margins and through cosmic signs and wonders suggests that it is the work of the Spirit to eliminate the hierarchies of being, both those conventionally erected and those presumed to be natural to the created order, not in order to instantiate anarchism but to renew human community and relationality in its various domains.

Yet central to the Pentecostal message proclaimed by Peter is Jesus's resurrection from the dead (2:24), understood also through the witness of ancient Israel's scriptures (2:25–28, 31). If David, the prophet of resurrection, remains dead and buried (2:29–30), then Jesus shows himself to be Messiah through his exaltation to the right hand of the Father (2:33–36). Death and bodily corruption, in other words, are part of the Pentecostal witness of the Spirit, consistent in this regard with the broader apostolic claim that Jesus "was declared to be [the] Son of God with power according to the spirit of holiness by resurrection from the dead" (Rom 1:4). So, if elsewhere the evangelists witness to death being the crucible from out of which life flows (e.g., John

---

28. From a Pentecostal perspective, Macchia best represents the basic thrust upon which this essay proceeds. See Macchia, "Babel and the Tongues of Pentecost."

12:24),²⁹ it is worthwhile asking here about what kind of death the Pentecostal arrival of the Spirit overcomes.

Finally, Acts 2 concludes with the instantiation of the Pentecostal community, one characterized by mutuality and gratuitous reciprocity (2:42–47). Herein is epitomized pneumatic koinonia and sharing, made possible through an economy of grace dispersed through the Spirit's residing upon carnal human bodies and transforming their self-centeredness and greed into communal flourishing.³⁰ Thus, the Pentecost chronicle convincingly registers the counter-effects of the Spirit vis-à-vis human behaviors of hoarding, greed, or self-preservation.³¹

## An Implicit Lukan Theology of Sin

I now want briefly to situate the present discussion against the broader Lukan message, especially as portrayed in his gospel account. Again, one would be hard pressed to insist that the Third Gospel includes within it a developed theology of sin.³² Yet it will be clear that there is no denying the presence of a Lukan ethical vision that provides orientation to what the evangelist considered as plaguing the human condition,³³ even as there are major thematic threads connecting the two books he wrote that I suggest sustain the incipient hamartiology distilled above. Four lines on inquiry provide cues for a Lukan understanding of sin relative to our quest.

First, if Acts 1:8 provides the outline for that book and Acts 2 frames its overarching horizons, then Jesus's Nazareth message provides orientation for his ministry and message in the Third Gospel. Here, the Isaianic text serves as the blueprint:

> The Spirit of the Lord is upon me,
>
> because he has anointed me

---

29. This would be central to an evolutionary universe. See my discussion in Yong, *Renewing Christian Theology*, 255–92.

30. Which explains why the economic sins of Ananias and Saphira in Acts 5:1–10 were judged so harshly. See Kuecker, "Spirit and the 'Other.'"

31. See my monograph, Yong, *Spirit of Love*.

32. The word *sin* appears in Luke's Gospel much more often than in his sequel, but again, is associated with the good news of forgiveness made available through or proclaimed by and in relationship to Jesus (mostly although not exclusively): Luke 1:77; 3:3; 5:20–24; 11:4; 17:3–4; 24:47. The few other references include confessions of sinfulness (5:8; 18:13), comparisons between perceived sinner and the presumed just (6:32–34), Galileans who were political martyrs (13:2), the story of the sinner who kissed and washed Jesus's feet with her hair (7:36–50), the parables of the lost sheep, coin, and son (15:7, 10, 18, 21), and Jesus being put to death at the hands of sinners (24:7). For our purposes, the repeated observation of Jesus eating with sinners (5:30–32; 7:34; 15:2; 19:7) is suggestive and will be commented on further, momentarily.

33. Thus, Conzelmann writes: "The conception of sin [in Luke], compared with Paul's has a strong ethical colouring, and the same is true also of deliverance from sin" (Conzelmann, *Theology of St. Luke*, 228). Other than passing statements, such as this one, and with one exception, I have not otherwise been able to locate any substantive or focused treatment of the doctrine of sin in the Lukan writings. Thus, we proceed cautiously.

> to bring good news to the poor.
>
> He has sent me to proclaim release to the captives
>
> and recovery of sight to the blind,
>
> to let the oppressed go free,
>
> to proclaim the year of the Lord's favour
>
> (Luke 4:18–19; cf. Isa 61:1–2a).

Clearly, the gospel according to the Third Evangelist is concerned with the poor and, even more so, for those marginalized and oppressed in general, and Jesus's consistent teaching in the rest of the gospel is that people should put their trust not in their wealth but be open to giving to others by following the heart of the Father God.[34] That Jesus intends to inaugurate the "year of the Lord's favour" also hearkens back to the Jubilee message of the First Testament and is consistent with the community of sharing and mutuality formed through the Pentecost outpouring of the Spirit.[35] The correspondence between this primary feature of Jesus's mission and what was instantiated, however short lived, in the early followers of the messianic message, supports a social understanding of sin that divides oppressor from oppressed, the affluent from those in poverty, the political elite from those in the margins of society.[36] A Pentecostal perspective emphasizes the central role of the Spirit, who accomplishes this delivering work through the anointing of Jesus in the Gospel and then within the egalitarian community in Acts.[37] For our hamartiological purposes, then, we can observe that the missions of the Triune God, in the incarnation of the Son and in the Pentecostal gift of the Spirit, counters the structural and systemic sinfulness of socioeconomic oppression pervasive in a fallen world.

Second, note that the unveiling of Jesus's public ministry passes through his Spirit-enabled wilderness sojourn where he is tempted, and even attacked, by the devil (Luke 4:1–13). Recognition that this is surely a spiritual encounter does not mean denying its materially constituted, politically charged, and environmentally situated character. The point is that if the Joel passage defines the Pentecostal outpouring as having apocalyptic and cosmic dimensions (see above), then nothing less would be anticipated from Jesus's own mission in the Spirit. The brokenness of humanity's

---

34. The themes of poverty and wealth are palpable throughout the Third Gospel: e.g., 4:16–18; 16:1–15; 18:9–11; 19:1–10, 11–27; 20:9–26; 21:1–4. See Pilgrim, *Good News to the Poor*; Johnson, *Sharing Possessions*; Gillman, *Possessions and the Life of Faith*; Phillips, *Reading Issues of Wealth and Poverty*.

35. See Ringe, *Jesus, Liberation*. Note also in this connection both Sanders, "Sins, Debts, and Jubilee Release"; Sri, "Release from the Debt of Sin," which are arguably the only sustained discussions of the Lukan notion of sin, albeit framed vis-à-vis the good news of the cancellation of debt that foregrounds the poverty-wealth ways of categorizing the issues in the Third Gospel.

36. See further the discussion of Jesus's "social stance" in Cassidy, *Jesus, Politics, and Society*, 20–33.

37. Argued by Wenk, *Community Forming Power*. Relative to liberation theology's famous "preferential option for the poor," see also the recognition of "God's special love for the poor and marginalized" by Pentecostal theologian, Rodriguez, *Liberating Mission of Jesus*, 125–38.

social world here finds its symbolic counterpart in the barrenness of the wilderness, and in its hostility toward full human flourishing.

Third, and consistent with the initial point, Luke also identifies one of the major features of the gospel as what might be called an *upside-down world*. I get this from the reputation the apostles earned as those who were "turning the world upside down have" (Acts 17:6), but this is the Acts rendition of what John York describes in the Third Gospel as the "rhetoric of reversal" that begins with Mary's Magnificat, the humbling of the exalted and vice versa (Luke 14:11; 18:14), and Jesus's teaching that, "some are last who will be first, and some are first who will be last" (13:30).[38] The point is that the perspective of the coming reign of God, heralded in Jesus's life and teachings contrasts with the conventions of the world that are hierarchically organized (sinful) and that privilege certain groups, while subordinating others. If, as indicated earlier, the Joel text undergirding the significance of the Day of Pentecost event overturns the anti-gospel hierarchies of the world, then the Third Evangelist's theology of reversal suggests the dismantling of socially structured systems that disempower the masses. The implications for a Lukan hamartiology are further extrapolatable: that the contributions, voices, and perspectives of those otherwise socially excluded and sin-against are restored and redeemed, especially, but not only the women, beginning with Mary and continuing with prophesying young women. Thus, sinful realities in a fallen world are those forces that perpetuate the conditions of those socially marginalized by authoritarian powers and those on the underside of history. The coming of the Spirit confronts, unmasks, and subverts these destructive schemes and arrangements.

Last, but not least, for our purposes, the "to the ends of the earth" motif structuring Acts is clearly anticipated in the universalistic arch of Luke's Gospel. The crucial role of the later portions of Isaiah already seen re-emerge along this front, now in the form of Deutero Isaiah's universalistic message of Israel as "light to the nations" (Isa 42:6; 49:6) that is cited, not only in Acts (13:47), but also as part of Simeon's announcement regarding the arrival of Jesus:

> my eyes have seen your salvation,
>
> which you have prepared in the presence of all peoples,
>
> a light for revelation to the Gentiles
>
> and for glory to your people Israel (Luke 2:30–32).

The universality of Jesus's significance is reiterated at the end of the Third Gospel in Jesus's commissioning the disciples—"that repentance and forgiveness of sins is to be proclaimed in his name to all nations, beginning from Jerusalem" (24:47)— even such is symbolized in the genealogy that traces his lineage, not through David to Abraham as in Matthew, but back to "Adam, son of God" (3:38), and is promoted

---

38. See York, *Last Shall Be First*, 39–93. See also Mary's song (Luke 1), esp. Luke 1:52–53.

through inclusion of Jesus's intentional journeying through Samaria (9:52).[39] The point is unmistakable: the good news of Jesus is not just for the Jews but also for all humanity, for the nations to the ends of the earth, in Lukan parlance.[40] Thus, the gospel account provides a ramp toward the Pentecostal baptism of all flesh, those from every tongue, tribe, and nation, by the Spirit. For hamartiological purposes, the saving purposes of God in Christ overcomes the ethnocentrism dividing people groups from one another via the pneumatological visitation starting in Jesus's mission in Judea and intending, from the beginning, the inclusion of the Gentiles.

## Toward a Pentecostal and Scientific Theology of Sin

The goal of this essay is to initiate discussion about the possibility of a Pentecostal theology of sin engaged with, and perhaps even informed by, the sciences. Our investigation, forged in dialogue with St. Luke's Pentecostal theology, intimates a view of sin that resists the Pentecostal work of the Spirit, inclinations and behaviors that are oppressive rather than liberative, selfish rather than other-concerned, xenophobic rather than hospitable to and embracing outsiders, etc. To be sure, we are still far from any final word on this topic, so our concluding remarks ought to precipitate further inquiry. One theological and one methodological comment are intended to provide the impetus.

Theologically, we must begin as Pentecostals, even as Christians, with our theological commitments. Hence, if at the center is Pentecostal spirituality as normed by the Day of Pentecost story, then it is not just generic theistic questions that emerge but specific pneumatological, soteriological, and eschatological concerns. Starting with the Spirit of Pentecost thus ensures that the Christian dialogue with the sciences is never theologically neglectful and also not ignorant of the sinful realities that the gift of the Spirit is designed to correct and redeem. More pointedly, a pneumatological perspective in conversation with the sciences shifts our gaze from the primordial past, with its obsessiveness on origins, to the eschatological future and its concerns about how the coming reign of God can be grasped given what science anticipates about how a fallen and finite cosmos will come to an end.[41] What emerges might be an eschatological theology of sin, not one that talks about sin's evolution—although there is a sense in which the emergence of higher and higher levels of complexity involves intensification of sinful propensities over deep time—but one that recognizes how the alien intrusiveness of sin in a good creation is being perpetually countered by a triune

---

39. Other distinctive Lukan references to the Samaritans are 10:25–37; 17:11, which in turn anticipate the apostolic witness into Samaria in Acts (1:8; 8:2–25). See also Yong, *Who is the Holy Spirit*, 81–90 (on Samaria).

40. The contours of which are superbly portrayed in Mittelstadt, *Reading Luke-Acts*, 138–42.

41. I argue for this shift of perspective in Yong, *Spirit of Creation*, esp. 72–132.

God seeking reconciliation with all creation.[42] Obviously, this is not meant to bar the path to inquiry about the cosmic past, but it is to say that a Pentecostal orientation will ask other, equally important, but yet heretofore neglected, questions in dialogue with the sciences, and do so in ways that are consistent with its theological ideals, and even guided and normed by them.

Methodologically, thus far our observations suggest that any Pentecostal theology of sin that springs off the heart of the Pentecostal experience grounded in the Day of Pentecost narrative is ill-equipped to take on the major questions related to evolution and human origins that Pentecostal scholars (parallel to their evangelical counterparts) have focused on at the theology-and-science interface. While these matters are not unimportant, I suggest they are not the initial site from which Pentecostal engagement with the sciences ought ensue. Rather, if we attended to the working of the Spirit launched at the Day of Pentecost and regarding which modern Pentecostal believers are most keen to experience and participate in, it is discovered that the Spirit's redemptive activity is explicable in anthropological, cultural, sociological, and environmental terms, and that this, therefore, invites, I urge, consideration of scientific perspectives in these domains.[43] Christians can thereby understand what science has to contribute at these levels first, and what its limitations are therein—particularly as impeded by the effects of sin, which is after all our primary topic—and then, perhaps later, they can devote effort to comprehending the issues about which others have been concerned. Hence, the anthropological and biological sciences can help us understand the effects of sin, even the biological death that is intertwined with biblical claims, and may, hence, even enable our cooperation with the redemptive work of the Spirit in and through the suffering of our personal lives and also death of our bodies.[44] The social sciences can illuminate how human individualism and self-centeredness and our group predilections, behaviors, and structures have all been defaced by sin, and perhaps, thereby inspire human repentance and concomitantly corrective attitudes and behaviors in the social sphere.[45] Then, the natural sciences can clarify how fallen human relations impact and are shaped by their environmental situatedness, not only on our planet but also within our solar system and beyond, and could even facilitate our reorientation from paths of self-destruction toward activities that herald the coming reign of God.[46] How these scientific perspectives can illuminate human

---

42. See here Bradnick, "Pentecostal Perspective on Entropy."

43. That the effects of sin are multidimensional corresponds with the way in which I developed a Lukan soteriology in an earlier work. See Yong, *Spirit Poured Out*, 81–120.

44. The essay by biologist Mitchell, "Let There Be Life!," is instructive with regard to understanding death in both scientific (biological) and theological (Pentecostal) terms.

45. The Godly Love research project focused on studying altruism among Pentecostal-charismatic exemplars from social scientific perspectives carves out venues for such explorations. See Lee and Yong, *Science and Theology of Godly Love*.

46. I have attempted to outline a pneumatological theology of the environment in dialogue with the sciences (and in dialogue with other faith traditions) in Yong, *Cosmic Breath*, 177–241.

creaturely and sinful realities at their proper levels without undermining theological (and pneumatological, soteriological, and eschatological) perspectives will need to be a matter of ongoing research and reflection. None of this is to say that science becomes salvific—far from it. Instead, science can be a helpful handmaid within a broader theological quest, perhaps even guided by the Spirit.

The result thus far is not any scientific theology of sin that trumps other perspectives, but the much more modest proposal about the possibility of pneumatological and scientific perspectives converging toward a hamartiology that, in turn, complements the dogmatic tradition in this regard, particularly proposals that have sought to formulate and develop sin in interpersonal and social terms. I hope other Pentecostal theologians can build on these insights, and that such discussions would benefit even the broader ecumenical conversation. Does this exercise generate optimism regarding how an apostolic, Pentecostal, and pneumatological approach could push the discussion forward? I submit such to be one promising venue in quest of a theology of sin in a scientific age.

# Chapter 15

# Towards Pentecostal Missional Pneumatology
## *An Affirmation and an Assessment*
### VELI-MATTI KÄRKKÄINEN[1]

## A Sketch of a Pentecostal Mission "Ethos"

Scholarly consensus holds that whatever other reasons may help us understand the centrality of mission for Pentecostalism, it has everything to do with the two formative factors underlying the whole Pentecostal spirituality: eschatological fervor and the crucial role of the Holy Spirit.[2] These two factors are integrally related to each other. Pentecostals believe that they have been called by God in the "last days" (Acts 2:17) to be Christlike witnesses in the power of the Spirit. The hope in the imminent coming of the Lord has energized Pentecostal churches and movements in their worldwide missionary enthusiasm and activity. Pentecostals have consistently taught that the church must be ready for the coming of the Lord by means of faithful witness and holy living.[3]

When attempting a more specific list of factors behind Pentecostal missions ethos, the American missiologist Gary McClung's intuitions seem to be right on target. He mentions seven such characteristics of Pentecostal missions:[4]

---

1. As soon as Roger Stronstad's study on Luke's charismatic theology was translated in Finnish, I read it with great interest. It was a testimony to the fact that a Pentecostal exegete's voice was heard in the wider academia and that the Pentecostal reading of the biblical text was as valid as any. What a groundbreaking discovery!

2. This essay is a slightly edited excerpt from Kärkkäinen, "Mission and Salvation," presented at the Annual Reformed-Pentecostal International Dialogue in Antalya, Turkey, on December 2–6, 2015. It draws directly (and without constant referencing) from my two recent essays, namely, Kärkkäinen, "Pentecostal Mission and Encounter with Religions," 294–312; "Pentecostal Mission," 28–49. It also repeats materials from other recent essays of mine, particularly Kärkkäinen, "Pentecostal Understanding of Mission," 26–44.

3. See further Kärkkäinen, "Mission, Spirit, and Eschatology," 73–94.

4. McClung Jr., "Pentecostal/Charismatic Perspectives," 11–21.

- experiential and relational
- expressly biblical with a high view of inspiration of Scripture[5]
- extremely urgent in nature
- "focused, yet diversified," prioritizing evangelization, but not to the exclusion of social concern
- aggressive and bold in its approach
- interdependent (both among various Pentecostal/Charismatic groups and in relation to older churches and their mission endeavors)
- unpredictable as to the future

Similar kinds of characterizations have been posed by other Pentecostal missiologists who have spoken of naïve Biblicism, eschatology, individualism, total commitment, pragmatism, flexibility, a place for emotions, personal testimonies, establishment of indigenous churches as a goal of missions, demonstration of the power of the Spirit, and participation of all believers.[6]

In case this analysis is even nearly accurate, it begs the question: What, then, might be the role of the Holy Spirit in Pentecostal mission and emerging missiology? This is the focal point of the current essay. It seeks to provide a sketch of what might be called "Pentecostal missional pneumatology." The essay begins with a brief look at the emerging Pentecostal missiology from the perspective of pneumatology and thereafter delves into an analysis and sympathetic-critical assessment of the status of a Pentecostal missional pneumatology.

## The Development of Pentecostal Missional Pneumatology

Without in any way disparaging earlier attempts by some Pentecostal leaders and teachers to reflect on the theological basis of Pentecostal mission, including the first missiological treatise by Melvin L. Hodges, *The Indigenous Church* (1953) and the sequel about two decades later, *Theology of the Church and Its Mission*,[7] it was not until 1991, when the major compendium of Pentecostal missiology titled *Called and Empowered: Global Mission in Pentecostal Perspective*[8] was published. It was put together by a younger generation of Pentecostal academics and practitioners. The book contains biblical, theological, strategic, cultural, and religious viewpoints on the global Pentecostal mission. It still is a landmark work worthy to be consulted.

---

5. For a useful discussion, see Burgess, "Nigerian Pentecostal Theology," 29–63.
6. See further, Kärkkäinen, "Missiology, Pentecostal and Charismatic," 877–85.
7. Hodges, *Indigenous Church*; *Theology of the Church*. For an evaluation, see McGee, *This Gospel Shall Be Preached*, 2:157–58.
8. Dempster et al., *Called and Empowered*, 1991.

An important impetus towards a Pentecostal missional pneumatology comes from the guild of some exegetes who have done serious work in the area of New Testament pneumatology, especially in Luke-Acts.[9] That work has a lot of missiological potentials. The Pacific Rim missionary Robert Menzies has written on distinctive features of Lukan pneumatology with a view to mission. In his *Empowered for Witness*,[10] Menzies argues that the church, by virtue of its reception of the Pentecostal gift, is a prophetic community of empowerment for missionary service. His line of thought is developed and specifically focused on mission by Australian J. M. Penney in his *The Missionary Emphasis of Lukan Pneumatology*.[11] Penney contends that the reason why Luke-Acts has been so dear to Pentecostals is that Pentecostalism—from inception a missionary movement—saw in the Spirit-baptism of Acts 2 a normative paradigm for the empowerment of every Christian to preach the gospel. "Acts is more than history for the Pentecostal: it is a missionary manual, an open-ended account of the missionary work of the Holy Spirit in the church, concluding, not with ch. 28, but with the ongoing Spirit-empowered and Spirit-directed gospel preaching of today."[12]

A major recent contribution to Pentecostal missiology comes from the Korean couple Julie and Wonsuk Ma, long-term missionaries to the Philippines, who also have a long experience in academic teaching and research in Pentecostal missiology. In 2010 published *Mission in the Spirit: Towards a Pentecostal/Charismatic Missiology*[13] makes a number of significant contributions with a great deal of relevance beyond Pentecostal and Charismatic movements. The book develops a robust and holistic account of the work of the Spirit of God, beginning from the Old Testament, in the work of the Spirit of Yahweh in creation. The turn to the Old Testament is a needed corrective to the one-sided focus on the New Testament. Hence, a pneumatological creation theology is developed first (ch. 2) and only then does the work of the charismatic Spirit of God come to play (ch. 3), including signs and wonders (ch. 5).[14] This kind of theology supports the care for the environment as an essential part of mission work and affirms the importance of theological anthropology as well. This Korean Pentecostal theology also pays close attention to the social context of mission, particularly the Asian cultures (ch. 6), and highlights the importance of tackling issues of oppression, poverty, and various forms of human abuse. An important part of the cultural task is to engage the diverse religious traditions of the continent (ch. 7). Along with careful tackling of biblical, theological, cultural, and other basic missiological issues,

---

9. Some missiological insights can be gleaned from Stronstad, *Charismatic Theology*, with its idea of the transference of the Spirit from Jesus to his followers.

10. See also R. Menzies earlier work, Menzies, *Development of Early Christian Pneumatology*.

11. Penney, *Missionary Emphasis*.

12. Penney, *Missionary Emphasis*, 12.

13. Ma and Ma, *Mission in the Spirit*.

14. The Canadian Pentecostal theologian Steve Studebaker has issued a similar call to appreciate the Spirit's role as the principle of life and creation in Studebaker, "Christian Mission and the Religions."

the Mas also offer a detailed consideration of the praxis of mission work, including church planting (ch. 8), church growth (ch. 9), women's role (ch. 13), and similar issues, as well as a look into the future.

The very latest contribution to emerging Pentecostal missional pneumatology has to do with the relation to other faith traditions.[15] In his important work titled, *The Spirit Poured Out on All Flesh: Pentecostalism and the Possibility of Global Theology*, the Asian-American Amos Yong issues a call to all Pentecostals to work towards a public theology by engaging Pentecostal pneumatology with interfaith dialogue. His thesis is that

> a pneumatologically driven theology is more conducive to engaging [interfaith issues] . . . in our time than previous approaches. . . . Religions are neither accidents of history nor encroachments on divine providence but are, in various ways, instruments of the Holy Spirit working out the divine purposes in the world and . . . the unevangelized, if saved at all, are saved through the work of Christ by the Spirit (even if mediated through the religious beliefs and practices available to them).[16]

A highly significant recent contribution comes from Bishop (Cleveland, TN) Tony Richie, whose monograph, *Speaking by the Spirit: A Pentecostal Model for Interreligious Dialogue* (2011), both considers carefully typical objections posed by Pentecostals against the engagement of interfaith issues and seeks to construct a viable approach to religions, building especially on the core Pentecostal practice of testimony. Richie considers it important to pursue this task in the matrix of Pentecostalism's "strong heritage of evangelism and missions, generally conservative ethical and theological history, and undeniable multicultural variety."[17] He also takes lessons from some Pentecostal pioneers in whose ethos Richie sees seeds of openness to religions, while at the same time faithfully representing tradition.[18]

Having outlined key recent developments in Pentecostal missiology, it is time to delve deeper into theological intuitions behind Pentecostal mission theology and Holy Spirit's role therein.

## Trinitarian and Holistic Pentecostal Missional Pneumatology

While the Holy Spirit is the key to Pentecostal mission work and mission theology, the Spirit never works alone. Wherever there is the Spirit, there is also the Savior Jesus

---

15. For recent collection of essays, several of them relevant to interfaith issues, by Pentecostal theologians representing widely global diversity, see Kärkkäinen, *Spirit in the World*; Yong and Clarke, *Global Renewal*.
16. Yong, *Spirit Poured Out*, 235–36. See also Yong, *Hospitality and the Other*.
17. Richie, *Speaking by the Spirit*, 3.
18. See also Richie, "Azusa-era Optimism," 247–60.

Christ and the Father who creates and cares. It is noteworthy that intuitively—most probably without any sustained theological reflection—the profile of a Pentecostal missional pneumatology is trinitarian. Without an attempt to oversimplify or "codify" theological intuitions behind the mission work of this enthusiastic movement, the following kind of sketch might be useful:

- Jesus Christ and the Full Gospel
- the Holy Spirit and Empowerment
- Salvation and the Vision of Holism
- Church and the Spirit of *Koinonia*

## Jesus Christ and the Full Gospel

Against the assumptions of uninformed outside observers, pneumatology does not necessarily represent the center of Pentecostal spirituality. Rather, Jesus Christ is the center, with the Holy Spirit in relation to Christ. At the heart of Pentecostal spirituality lies the idea of the "Full Gospel," the template of Jesus Christ in his fivefold role as Savior, Sanctifier, Baptizer with the Spirit, Healer, and Soon-Coming King.[19]

On this robust "Spirit-Christology," stands the Pentecostal missiological vision:

> Thus, the outpouring of the Spirit at Pentecost constituted the church as an eschatological community of universal mission in the power and demonstration of the Spirit. The tongues at Pentecost and Peter's subsequent sermon meant that the church in general and each Spirit-filled individual are to be and to give a witness to the mighty acts of God in saving humanity. This witness centers in Jesus Christ and must therefore be given in the power of the Spirit if it is to have continuity with his ministry and fulfill the promise of the Father through Christ. The "full gospel" of the Jesus who is Savior, Sanctifier, Healer, Baptizer in the Holy Spirit and coming King can and should be proclaimed in the fullness of the Spirit so that the kingdom will be manifested in the midst of the world in words and deeds.[20]

The term "Full Gospel" signaled to Pentecostals the desire to embrace "all" of Christ.[21] Observing the preaching and mission of other churches, Pentecostals

---

19. The classic study is Dayton, *Theological Roots of Pentecostalism*. It seems to me the "Full Gospel" template, with a robust "Spirit-Christology," is a valid interpretation even in light of the important and useful criticism coming from the Singaporean Pentecostalist Ling, *Pentecostal Theology*, 102–3, according to which a robust Christological and Trinitarian focus may be missing in Pentecostal theology.

20. Land, *Pentecostal Spirituality*, 60–61.

21. Materially, the Pentecostal term "Full Gospel" carries the same meaning as the ancient term of "catholicity," the idea of wholeness and completeness (literally: "no missing anything"). For a theological discussion, see Kärkkäinen, "Full Gospel."

wondered if older traditions were missing some crucial aspects of the Full Gospel.[22] The healing work of Christ is a case in point. Pentecostals were glad to hear Lutherans preach the gospel of justification by faith and Methodists/Holiness movements highlight the importance of sanctification. What they did not hear in the preaching of other churches and their missionaries was the dynamic New Testament testimonies to the healing power of Jesus, the One who is the same yesterday, today, and tomorrow (Heb 13:8).[23]

The prioritization of the Christ and his Full Gospel does not of course mean downplaying the work of the Holy Spirit. Rather, it is to put pneumatology in the proper perspective.

## The Holy Spirit and Empowerment

Whereas for most other Christians the presence of the Spirit is just that, *presence*; for Pentecostals the presence of the Spirit in their midst implies *empowerment*.[24] While this empowerment often manifests itself in spiritual gifts, such as speaking in tongues, prophesy, or healings, it is still felt and sought by Pentecostals, even when those manifestations are absent. The main function of the Pentecostal worship service is to provide a setting for an encounter with Jesus, the embodiment of the Full Gospel, to receive the (em)power(ment) of the Spirit.[25] As important as a sermon, hymns, and liturgy are, they all take second place to the "meeting with the Lord," as Pentecostals put it.

Part of the texture of enthusiastic missions ethos is a spirituality that incorporates the importance of visions, healing, dreams, dance, and other archetypal religious expressions. The Harvard theologian Harvey Cox rightly remarks that "the reemergence of this primal spirituality came—perhaps not surprisingly—at just the point in history when both the rationalistic assumptions of modernity and the strategies religions had used to oppose them (or to accommodate to them) were all coming unraveled."[26]

Gifts of the Spirit, such as prophesying, prayer for healing, and works of miracles are enthusiastically embraced and sought by Pentecostals. Belief in the capacity of

---

22. Of course, the early Pentecostals at times were guilty of an ideological use of the term "Full Gospel." They were not only sincerely concerned about the well-being of other churches, but also sometimes used the Full Gospel template as a way of criticizing, making pejorative comments, and even condemning their "dead" spiritual life. That human fallibility, unfortunately, is not limited to Pentecostals alone (!); however, misuse of the term is hardly a reason to ignore its positive contribution.

23. Rightly, the Korean Lee forges an integral connection between Christ, Full Gospel, and healing of the body, a central theme to Pentecostal spirituality. See Lee, *Grace and Power in Pentecostal*, 109–110. See further Purdy, "Divine Healing," 508–9.

24. In this distinction I am indebted to the Benedictine Catholic expert on Pentecostal-Charismatic movements, Fr. Kilian McDonnell, OSB, who was my mentor in post-doctoral studies.

25. See Albrecht, *Rites in the Spirit*.

26. Cox, *Fire from Heaven*, 81–82.

the Spirit to bring about healing, whether physical or emotional/mental, is one of the hallmarks of Pentecostalism. A related belief is the Spirit-given capacity to engage in "spiritual warfare"[27] and exorcise demonic spirits.[28]

## Salvation and the Holistic Vision

In their search for a holistic vision and experience of salvation that includes, not only the spiritual, but also physical, material, and socio-relational, Pentecostals seem to echo the postmodern insistence on a holistic understanding of the body-mind relationship, as has been noted by some scholars of Pentecostalism[29] and Pentecostal theologians.[30] The common features between the two movements include the principle of embodiment, search for holism, as well as the attention paid to "experientalism." Be that as it may, it seems that Pentecostalism "has succeeded because it has spoken to the spiritual emptiness of our time by reaching beyond the levels of creed and ceremony into the core of human religiousness. . . . Pentecostals have touched so many people because they have indeed restored something."[31] No doubt, in their yearning and search for a holistic account of the Full Gospel, Pentecostals came to embrace the notion of "holistic salvation," long before the term gained fame in some mainline theologies.[32]

In an important essay titled "Materiality of Salvation: An Investigation in the Soteriologies of Liberation and Pentecostal Theologies," the Yale theologian Miroslav Volf, who comes originally from the Pentecostal Church of Croatia, former Yugoslavia, has argued that with all their differences, these two Christian movements share a vision of salvation in this-worldly, physical, material, embodied terms.[33] While neither of the movements, of course, leaves behind the eschatological, future-oriented hope, relegating salvation merely to the future will not do either. True, liberationists focus their efforts on socio-political (including gender) liberation, while for Pentecostals it is more about the individual's release from sicknesses and ailments, physical or emotional—however, not to the exclusion of socio-political dimensions either.

From early on, Pentecostals invested money and energy for building schools, hospitals, orphanages. While giving priority to evangelism and individual conversion, Pentecostals were never oblivious to social concern, even though that myth exists

---

27. Kalu, "Preserving a Worldview," 122.
28. See further, Onyinah, "Deliverance," 181–202.
29. See especially Cox, *Fire from Heaven*, 299–301.
30. An important contribution here is Johns, "Pentecostalism and the Postmodern Worldview," 73–96. Lately, however, more modest and self-critical remarks have emerged, such as those found in Poirier and Lewis, "Pentecostal and Postmodernist Hermeneutics," 3–21.
31. Cox, *Fire from Heaven*, 81.
32. Yong, *Spirit Poured Out*, 82.
33. Volf, "Materiality of Salvation," 447–67.

among outside observers of Pentecostalism.[34] With all its problems with "other-worldliness," Pentecostalism is also characterized by a commitment to social justice, empowerment of the powerless, and a "preferential option for the marginalized" tracing back to its roots at Azusa Street as a kind of paradigm of marginalization—a revival in an abandoned stable, led by an African American preacher.[35]

At the same time, the idea of the materiality of salvation in the hands of too many Pentecostals and Charismatics has also turned into a gross materialistic search for financial and other benefits. Any visit to some Pentecostal churches, not only in the United States, but also all over in the Global South from Africa to Asia to Latin America paints a picture raising serious questions for any theologian and missiologist. Health and wealth are sometimes made the prime indicator of God's blessings, and spiritual techniques for reaching them are fine-tuned by ever new itinerant charismatic preachers. Pentecostalism also at times suffers from the same kind of "spiritualist" reductionism that Volf sees indicative of many traditional theologies, namely, prioritizing the salvation of the "souls" to the point where the wholeness of the human being as an embodied *imago Dei* is being missed. In Pentecostal preaching and witnessing, you can hear simultaneously both voices: seeking for the wholeness of salvation and emphasis on the salvation of the soul.

## Church and the Spirit of Koinonia

While only few Pentecostals have joined the vibrant ecumenical conversation about communion theology,[36] in their aggressive and creative church planting work, they have intuited the importance of communal dimensions and communities. Despite the lack of fully developed ecclesiology, a good case can be made for the claim that "Pentecostal soteriology and pneumatology point . . . unmistakably in the direction of an *ecclesiology of the fellowship of persons*."[37] Pentecostals speak of the church as a charismatic fellowship, a fellowship of persons, the body of Christ.[38]

In contrast, in a dynamic opposition to this communion orientation, much of Pentecostalism, especially in the Global North and as a result of missions work from the North, has tended to foster the hyper-individualism of the post-Enlightenment mentality.[39] That said, there is no denying the fact that a charismatically conceived communion theology, with an inclusive vision, has supported Pentecostal missions

---

34. See further Kärkkäinen, "Are Pentecostals Oblivious of Social Justice," 50–65.

35. See the important discussion by the Hispanic Pentecostal ethicist Villafañe, *Liberating Spirit*, 218.

36. See Kärkkäinen, "Church as the Fellowship of Persons," 1–15. An exciting collection of essays on Pentecostal ecclesiology focused on the Full Gospel template is Thomas, *Toward Pentecostal Ecclesiology*. See also Kärkkäinen, *Ecclesiology of the Pentecostal Churches*.

37. Kuzmic and Volf, "*Communio Sanctorum*," 2.

38. See further, Kärkkäinen, *Spiritus Ubi Vult Spirat*, 100–121.

39. See Macchia, *Baptized in the Spirit*, 203, 205.

efforts and led to mushrooming of communities that have experienced the multifaceted *koinonia* described in Acts 2:42–44, a dear passage to Pentecostals.[40]

## Concluding Remarks: Continuing Tasks and Challenges for Pentecostal Mission

The rapidly developing Pentecostal missiology and missional pneumatology faces significant and important challenges. There are a number of topics and themes to be tackled in order to mature. At the conclusion of this essay, let me highlight some of them with the hope that others might pick up them and develop them more fully.

In the midst of great numerical success in missions work, one of the impending tasks for Pentecostals has to do with the issue of suffering, a topic counterintuitive to much of the Pentecostal ethos of "overcoming" and victory.[41] Rightly, the Indian Pentecostal theologian, Gabriel Reuben Louis, laments that today's Pentecostalism is in danger of neglecting the "way of the cross" and, instead of looking for Christ's benefits, mainly look for the sake of this-worldly goods and enjoyment. While the theme of suffering, he continues, "may not be that relevant for a Pentecostal theology in a rich and prosperous West . . . [it is] in a poor and miserable Asia."[42] The omission or downplaying of the theme of suffering among Pentecostals is of course not limited to the Asian or Western contexts; similar kinds of charges have been leveled for example against African Pentecostalism.[43] Mindful of the importance of this theme, several Pentecostal theologians and missiologists have begun to address more intentionally the theme of suffering in human life and Christian experience. The Pentecostal biblical scholar and missiologist William W. Menzies, hence, suggests a theology of suffering for Pentecostals.[44] This task has been taken up by another Pentecostal biblical scholar, Martin William Mittelstadt, with his *The Spirit and Suffering in Luke-Acts*.[45] Focusing on the theme of suffering in the book of Acts is significant for more than one reason. First, Acts is by far the most popular book among Pentecostals and widely believed to be the *magna charta* of that movement's spirituality. Second, Acts is about mission; and third, the role of the Holy Spirit therein is profound and robust. Several

---

40. In the third phase of the Roman Catholic–Pentecostal International Dialogue, the theme of communion was studied in some detail, leading to an important ecumenical document, "Perspectives on Koinonia."

41. See Kärkkäinen, "Theology of the Cross," 150–63.

42. Louis, "Response to Wonsuk Ma." This is a response to Ma, "Toward an Asian Pentecostal Theology."

43. See further Asamoah-Gyadu, *African Charismatics*, 218, 228–32.

44. William Menzies, "Reflections on Suffering," 141–49. See also the important essay by Keith Warrington, the British Pentecostal biblical scholar who has written extensively on healing, in Warrington, "Healing and Suffering in the Bible," 154–64.

45. Mittelstadt, *Spirit and Suffering in Luke-Acts*.

other Pentecostals from various global contexts, including Puerto Rico[46] and Sudan,[47] have tackled the issues of suffering, poverty, injustice, and similar topics from a Pentecostal perspective.

Other noteworthy tasks for Pentecostal missiology include the relation of Pentecostal grassroots spirituality to the spiritualities of living faiths. Pentecostalism, particularly in the Global South, not unlike, say, Roman Catholicism, is to a large extent a folk religion, with deep footage in local cultures. What are the implications of that for the future of Pentecostal mission, on the one hand, and the relation to other local faiths, on the other?

Several other academic and practical tasks could be listed, crucial to the future of Pentecostal missions, including continuing reflection on the identity of Pentecostalism—"What makes Pentecostalism, Pentecostalism?"[48]—both in relation to "spiritual cousins," Charismatics within the existing churches, and neo-Charismatics, Pentecostal-type Christians among a bewildering number of independent movements in African Instituted Churches, in Chinese House Churches, and so forth. Does Pentecostalism, and her mission, represent a distinctively unique manifestation in Christian history or is it, rather, an offshoot from a wider religious revival?[49]

---

46. Solivan, *Spirit, Pathos, and Liberation*.
47. Dau, *Suffering and God*.
48. See Kärkkäinen, "Identity and Plurality," 500–504.
49. For some aspects, see Kärkkäinen, "Re-Turn of Religion," 469–96.

# PART IV

# Reading St. Luke's Pneumatology with other Texts

---

"In the history of the Protestant interpretation of Scripture there has always been a tendency to emphasize the unity of the message at the expense of diversity. Thus, whether we are speaking of the entire canon of Scripture, or of either the Old Testament or the New Testament, the unity and diversity is often reduced to mere uniformity. This uniformity is often the expression of some 'pet' center, a cannon within a canon, such as the Deuteronomic history for the Old Testament or the Pauline Epistles for the New Testament. This problem is particularly acute for the would-be interpreter of Luke-Acts."

ROGER STONSTAD, *SPIRIT, SCRIPTURE, AND THEOLOGY: A PENTECOSTAL PERSPECTIVE*, 170.

## Chapter 16

# The Charismatic Spirit in the Torah and Former Prophets

### LEE ROY MARTIN[1]

In his groundbreaking work, *The Charismatic Theology of St. Luke*, Roger Stronstad points out the Old Testament's influence upon Luke's charismatic theology. He finds parallels between the Old Testament and Luke–Acts both in terminology regarding the Spirit[2] and in the theological role of the Spirit. The impact of Stronstad's monograph, which remains in print today, can hardly be overstated.[3]

In this brief survey of the charismatic Spirit in the Old Testament, I will build upon Stronstad's work and focus attention upon the Spirit empowerment as it relates to the people of God. Although the Spirit's work in creating and sustaining the cosmos and the life that fills the cosmos is exceedingly important, this chapter will examine only those biblical texts that describe the Spirit's charismatic work. The charismatic work of the Spirit corresponds broadly to the New Testament concept of Spirit baptism, Spirit fullness, and the accompanying charismatic gifts. Charismatic gifts include any kind of divine enablement that either adds to a person's abilities or grants them new abilities.

---

1. I consider it a great privilege to contribute to this volume honoring Roger Stronstad. All of today's Pentecostal scholars are indebted to Roger, because at a time when Pentecostal theology was under attack by non-Pentecostal biblical scholars, he rose to the occasion and presented a resounding affirmation of Pentecostalism's charismatic foundations. Not only did Roger's work revolutionize the study of Luke–Acts, but also his faithful teaching ministry and his personal character of holiness have validated his scholarship. May the Lord reward him according to his works (Matt 16:27).

2. In its various contexts, the Hebrew *ruach* does not always refer to the Holy Spirit. At times it can be translated "wind" or "spirit." This chapter is limited to the study of those texts in which *ruach* signifies the Holy Spirit; therefore, I will use the upper case "Spirit."

3. Stronstad, *Charismatic Theology*. Baker Academic published a second edition in 2012. His section on the Old Testament was first published as Stronstad, "Influence of the Old Testament," 32–50.

Spirit empowerment in the Old Testament may be understood in terms of the community of faith. The Old Testament presents two forms of that community: the covenant community (Israel) and the eschatological community described by the prophets (fulfilled in the New Testament). In the Old Testament, Spirit empowerment almost always relates to the people of Israel. Balaam was the only non-Israelite to be given power by the Spirit of God, and the purpose of his endowment was that he might bless Israel.[4] The thesis of this chapter, therefore, is that Spirit empowerment is granted in the Old Testament to a small number of individuals in strategic situations to enable them to perform some activity that is of substantial benefit to the covenant community. Limitations of space require that this study examine only the charismatic Spirit in the Torah and the Former Prophets (the books of Genesis through Kings).

## The Charismatic Spirit in the Torah

### Joseph: Preservation of the Covenant

Joseph is the first person in the Old Testament who is said to have the Spirit of God. Through the Spirit, Joseph experienced his own dreams, along with their interpretations, and he was able to interpret the dreams of his fellow prisoners and of the Egyptian Pharaoh. In the ancient Near East, the ability to interpret dreams was considered a characteristic of the wise; therefore, the Pharaoh describes Joseph as "discerning and wise" (Gen 41:39).[5] Furthermore, the source of Joseph's wisdom is declared to be the "Spirit of God" (41:38).[6] Joseph's wisdom was confirmed when he quickly devised a plan to deal with the famine that Pharaoh had foreseen in his dreams. The influence of the charismatic Spirit in Joseph resulted in the preservation of the covenant family—the descendants of Abraham, Isaac, and Jacob.

### Bezalel and Oholiab: Preparations for Worship

The charismatic gift of wisdom is mentioned next in the book of Exodus. In the Old Testament, wisdom is also known as skill and creativity. It is the Spirit who enables artisans to construct the priestly garments (Exod 28:3) and the tabernacle (Exod 31:3; 35:31; 36:1–2). After giving directions for the construction of the tabernacle,

---

4. It might be argued that the "anointed" status of Cyrus signifies that he was empowered by the Spirit; but the Spirit is not mentioned in relation to Cyrus. Anointing was the sign of God's authorization of priests and rulers, but did not necessarily imply Spirit empowerment.

5. Quotations of Scripture are taken from the NASB unless noted otherwise.

6. My translation. Inasmuch as this declaration comes from the mouth of the Egyptian Pharaoh, most translations render *ruach* with the lower case "spirit" (NRSV). As pointed out by Neve, however, the Egyptians did not speak of the gods as "having a spirit" (Neve, *Spirit of God*, 1). Therefore, the text "reflects an Israelite rather than an Egyptian idea." For this reason Neve argues for upper case "Spirit" (Neve, *Spirit of God*, 28).

and all the items necessary for worship, the Lord appointed the builders whom he had chosen to accomplish the work. Bezalel was chosen to be the master builder, to superintend the entire work and to complete the artistic work. The Lord also chose Oholiab, who would assist Bezalel in designing intricate details and in teaching the other craftsmen. Bezalel was filled "with the Spirit of God, in wisdom, in understanding and in knowledge and in all craftsmanship" (Exod 35:31). Bezalel's charismatic gift enabled him to work in gold, silver, bronze, precious stones, wood, embroidery, and weaving. This "communication of an extraordinary and supernatural endowment and qualification"[7] did not preclude either natural capacity or skill. Ronald Clements suggests that these men were already recognized craftsmen with a natural aptitude.[8]

In addition to the gift of craftsmanship, the Lord gave to Bezalel and Oholiab the gift of teaching (Exod 35:34), inasmuch as they were to instruct the other workers who were engaged in their respective tasks. According to Rylaarsdam, God had chosen also these others for he had put in their minds the ability to do the work.[9]

Exactly what were these craftsmen empowered to do? Bezalel is given four qualities that uniquely equip him for his task: skill (*hokmah*), ability (*tebunah*), knowledge (*daʿat*), and craftsmanship (*melakah*). John Durham translates them as (1) "wisdom," the "gift to understand what is needed to fulfill Yahweh's instructions"; (2) "discernment," the "talent for solving the inevitable problems involved in the creation of so complex a series of objects and materials," and (3) "skill," the experienced hand needed to guide and accomplish the labor itself."[10] Bezalel is now "the ideal combination of theoretical knowledge, problem-solving practicality, and planning capability who can bring artistic ideals to life with his own hands."[11]

Brevard Childs argues that the significance these passages is that each "detail of the structure reflects the one divine will and nothing rests on the *ad hoc* decision of human builders."[12] Gispen, however, disagreeing with Childs, states that "verse 4a seems to warrant the conclusion that Bezalel could contribute his own ideas.... There was room for creativity."[13] In either case, it is clear that the charismatic Spirit is deeply involved in the preparations of the tabernacle, which will be the location of the Ark of the Covenant and the center of Israel's cultic life.

---

7. Keil, "Second Book of Moses," 217.

8. Clements, *Exodus*, 199. See also Gispen, *Exodus*, 289.

9. Rylaarsdam, "Exodus," 1085.

10. Durham understands *melakah* (workmanship) to be repetitious (Durham, *Exodus*, 410). The structure of the sentence, however, and the addition of the preposition indicate that all four terms are parallel.

11. Durham, *Exodus*, 410.

12. Childs, *Book of Exodus*, 540. See also Durham, *Exodus*, 410.

13. Gispen, *Exodus*, 289.

## Seventy Elders: Sharing the Burden of Leadership

In Numbers 11:17–29, God puts his Spirit upon seventy elders of Israel. On this occasion, the constant complaining of the people had caused Moses to feel overburdened by the heavy responsibilities that had been laid upon his shoulders. He responded to the people's complaints by crying out to God, saying that he would rather die than to endure the continual grumbling. Moses said, "I alone am not able to carry all this people, because it is too burdensome for me" (Num 11:14). As a solution to Moses's problem, God instructed him to gather seventy men, known to be elders and officers of the people, and bring them to the tabernacle. God said to Moses, "I will come down and speak with you there, and I will take of the Spirit who is upon you, and will put *Him* upon them" (Num 11:17). These seventy elders would help bear the responsibility of leading the people.[14]

Moses was to select seventy of the elders. These men were known to be elders and officers of the people (11:16). According to George B. Gray, these were established leaders, "leading men of the various families."[15] They were part of an existing organization. Gordon J. Wenham suggests that the duties of these elders were not administrative but were spiritual.[16] Rashi proposed that these elders were those who had been appointed as officers in Egypt in connection with the rigorous labors imposed upon them. They had taken pity on their fellow Hebrews and had been beaten (Exod 5:14). Just as they had suffered in distress, now they were to be made great.[17] Although there is disagreement over the exact nature of authority expressed here, these men evidently were already leaders, for God instructed Moses to choose men that he "knew" to be leaders. According to Martin Noth, this charismatic endowment of established leaders is a "remarkable combination of institution and charisma."[18]

In this passage, five different terms or combination of terms are used that relate to Spirit empowerment: (1) God will "take (*'atsal*) of the Spirit"; (2) The Spirit is "on" (*'al*) Moses; (3) God will "put (*sim*) the Spirit on (*'al*) them"; (4) He "put (*natan*) the Spirit on (*'al*) the seventy elders"; and (5) The Spirit "rested (*nuach*) on them." In addition to the evaluation of these terms, other pertinent questions must be addressed:

1. Did the Holy Spirit remain with them permanently?
2. Why did they prophesy, and what was the nature of their prophecy?

---

14. A preliminary question regarding this passage concerns the nature of the "spirit." Is this Moses's spirit or God's Spirit? The fact that it is called "the Spirit that is upon" Moses, may imply that it is Moses's spirit, but according to the text (Num 11:29), Moses certainly understood it to be God's Spirit. See Ashley, *Book of Numbers*, 211.

15. Gray, *Critical and Exegetical Commentary*, 109–110.

16. Wenham, *Numbers*, 108. Wenham states that the administrative duties of the elders had been established in Exod 18:13–26

17. Rosenbaum and Silbermann, *Numbers*, 55.

18. Noth, *Numbers*, 87.

3. Did they prophesy only once?

4. What can be learned from Eldad and Medad, who remained in the camp?

God proposed to "take" of the Spirit that was upon Moses and "put" it upon the elders. Depending on the context, several translation equivalents are available for the verb (*’atsal*). Holladay lists "take away" (Num 11:17, 25), "lay aside" (Gen 27:36), and "refuse" (Eccl 2:10).[19] The translation of *’atsal* as "take" is undoubtedly possible in Num 11:17, 25, but it is not the best translation. "To take from Moses" emphasizes removal, whereas *’atsal* seems to denote a separating or setting aside. This is a subtle distinction, but an important one.

It cannot be determined from the text whether the transfer of the Spirit was discernible to the senses. The most straightforward view of the text seems to indicate that the prophecy of the elders was the outward sign that demonstrated the presence of the Holy Spirit. Wenham points out that prophecy is a mark of God's Spirit in other parts of Scripture (1 Sam 10:6–13; 19:20–24; Joel 2:28; Acts 2:4; 1 Cor 12:10).[20] Keil and Delitzsch agree that the prophecy was "a convincing proof."[21] Noordtzij insists that the people would not have recognized the authority of these elders without the display of the Spirit. He says the important aspect of this prophecy is that it was a "visible demonstration" that the Holy Spirit controlled the elders.[22] Hotrum agrees, saying that prophecy was "evidence that [God] had equipped them to help lead the people."[23]

According to v. 25, the elders did not prophesy again, but the King James Version reads, "they continued to do so." The NIV gives this reading in the footnotes, presumably based on the alternate wording found in the Targums.[24] The Septuagint Rahlfs, Septuaginta correctly translate the[25] and supported by the Vulgate and Onkelos.[26] Thus, they did not prophesy any further.[27]

According to Ashley, the prophesying may have been temporary, but the presence of the Holy Spirit continued to be on them. Gray, however, insists that their reception of the Spirit caused a "prophetic frenzy," but had no permanent effect on them. If the Scripture text is to be taken seriously, then Ashley must be correct. The purpose of the Spirit's coming on the elders was that they might serve as Moses's helpers, bearing the burden of the people. That task was an ongoing assignment, just as it

---

19. Holladay, *Concise Hebrew and Aramaic Lexicon*, 26.

20. Wenham, *Numbers*, 109.

21. Keil and Delitzsch, "Fourth Book of Moses," 70.

22. Noordtzij, *Numbers*, 103.

23. Hotrum, "Inductive Study of the Old Testament," 31.

24. Isaiah, *Numbers*, 115; Grossfeld, *Targum Onqelos to Deuteronomy*, 33. Sanh.17a interprets Num 11:25 as "They prophesied, and continued to do so."

25. *Masoretic Text*.

26. Rosenbaum and Silbermann, *Numbers*, 55.

27. Keil and Delitzsch, "Fourth Book of Moses," 70. See also Ashley, *Numbers*, 214; Neve, *Spirit of God*, 17–18.

had been with Moses. The power of the Spirit, therefore, would rest upon the elders in a permanent fashion, just as it had rested upon Moses.[28] Ashley comments, therefore, that Numbers 11 is an important passage on shared leadership. Gray, offering a slightly different view, wrote that it illustrates the "free range of the spirit," that God does not restrict his gifts to "particular persons or class."[29]

Eldad and Medad did not follow the instructions given to them, and the Holy Spirit came upon them in the camp. This seems to indicate that God did not limit the work of Holy Spirit to particular places or times.[30] Eldad's and Medad's prophesying in the camp prompted Joshua to exclaim, "Moses, my lord, restrain them" (11:28). Moses, however, was delighted to learn of the Spirit's work, and replied, "Are you jealous for my sake? Would that all the Lord's people were prophets, and that the Lord would put His Spirit upon all of them" (Num 11:29).

Moses's desire seems to have been prophetic. He understood that every member of the community needed a personal relationship with God. If Moses's burden was so great that he needed to appoint seventy elders, then surely the burden would only increase as the years passed. Moses was echoing the desire of God, the desire for a people who would all be ministers, and a people who would all be prophets. Joel predicted the fulfillment of Moses's desire and Peter proclaimed it: "And it will come about after this that I will pour out My Spirit on all mankind; and your sons and daughters will prophesy" (Joel 2:28; Acts 2:17). The New Testament church is a prophetic church, empowered by the Holy Spirit. The gifts of the Spirit are promised to every believer (1 Cor 12:7), and the power of God should be evident in every Christian's life (Acts 1:8; 8:15–16; 19:2).

## Joshua: Wisdom for Leadership

The Holy Spirit worked in a variety of ways within the Old Testament community of faith, but the most frequently mentioned area is that of leadership. Leaders of any community originate through the social channels of heredity, status, and natural ability. These channels were also true of Israel; but, in addition, the Holy Spirit sometimes chose and equipped leaders for particular tasks. Sometimes these charismatic leaders were already serving in a position of authority, but at other times God chose persons who had no previous experience in leadership.

Near the end of the wilderness wanderings, when the Israelites approached Canaan, the Lord took Moses up to a mountain overlooking the promised land. Moses's

---

28. Ashley, *Numbers*, 214. See also Keil and Delitzsch, "Fourth Book of Moses," 70–71; Gray, *Numbers*, 113. Neve, *Spirit of God*, 16–17, observes that this is the first passage to link Moses with the Holy Spirit. Numbers 11 is valuable partly because only here is Moses's power directly attributed to the Holy Spirit's being upon him.

29. Ashley, *Numbers*, 211, 217; Gray, *Numbers*, 115. John Marsh agreed with Gray. See Marsh, "Numbers," 199; Noordtzij, *Numbers*, 103. This may speak to the elitist tendencies of some groups.

30. Neve, *Spirit of God*, 17–18.

time had come to an end. His last request was that God would appoint a leader over the community, a man to be their shepherd. The Lord appointed Joshua, and He instructed Moses to hold a commissioning ceremony before the entire congregation. He says to Moses, "Take Joshua the son of Nun, a man in whom is the Spirit, and lay your hand on him" (Num 27:18). At this commissioning service, Joshua was given a special anointing for the task at hand. Although he had worked very hard to earn the respect of his peers, and he had demonstrated his faithfulness to God, he needed a greater empowering of the Holy Spirit to enable him in leadership. The result of Joshua's inauguration was that Joshua "was filled with the spirit of wisdom, for Moses had laid his hands on him" (Deut 34:9). Wisdom was considered an important characteristic of anyone who served as a leader in Israel (Deut 1:13–15; 16:18–19; Prov 20:26).

At least four points can be deduced from the account in Num 27:18:

1. Joshua was divinely chosen; he was not elected.
2. His authority was given through Moses, the previous leader.
3. The laying on of hands signified the transfer of the Spirit.
4. His power was not as great as that of Moses (Joshua required the services of the priest when inquiring of the Lord, but Moses spoke to God face to face.)

Regardless of his previous experience and qualifications, Joshua required a special anointing for the task of leadership to which God appointed him. His accomplishments, no matter how great, were not so great that he could function effectively without the empowering gift of the Spirit.

As a concluding word to the Pentateuch, Deut 34:9 restates and expands Numbers 27:18. This passage adds four facts to the information about Joshua's Spirit enduement:

1. He was "full" of the Spirit. The Spirit had been "in" him already, but he was not "full" of the Spirit. This is the first time the word "full" is used in reference to the Holy Spirit.
2. The Spirit is the Spirit of "wisdom."
3. This text repeats the statement that Joshua's Spirit-fullness came "because" Moses laid his hands upon him.
4. The people followed Joshua because they recognized the presence of the Spirit upon his life.

It is interesting that of all the attributes that could be associated with the Holy Spirit, wisdom is the attribute that is given to Joshua. This is not the only passage in which wisdom is directly attributed to the influence of the Holy Spirit. Note the following: Exod 28:3; 31:3; 35:31; Isa 11:2; Dan 5:11, 14; Luke 2:40; Acts 6:3, 10; 1 Cor 12:8; Eph 1:17. At the time of Joshua, Israel was like an adolescent child, in need of guidance. Israel was a people in the making, learning the ways of God. Therefore,

Joshua is granted the gift of wisdom so that he could direct the newly-formed people of God.

Is not the same need apparent in every generation? The Church is a community of believers who are growing, learning, and developing. Only a man or woman of wisdom can guide the flock of God. We often covet gifts that bring power, prestige, and self-glory; but without wisdom, our churches will never be transformed into the image of Jesus Christ. Without wise leaders, Christians will continue to bicker, fight, and devour one another. Many leaders rise to power using worldly wisdom, but only spiritual wisdom can discern the needs of God's flock.[31]

## The Charismatic Spirit in the Former Prophets

### The Judges: Empowered for Acts of Salvation

The word "judge" (*shofet*) is used of many different persons in the Old Testament. Generally, it means "an official with authority to administer justice." The patriarchs were judges in their own families; communities used elders as judges; the kings were judges; and the priests sometimes functioned as judges. In the book of Judges, however, the judges were military leaders endowed by the grace of God to deliver and govern his people in time of oppression. These judges were not connected to the normal tribal or community governments, but they were divinely chosen and empowered by the Lord.

Robert Boling argued for an understanding of the judges as illustrating "office charisma," in disagreement with earlier views that saw the judges as charismatic leaders which were not institutionalized.[32] He may be correct that the judge was a recognized office, but candidates were not selected by heredity or by election; they were chosen by the Lord. The office of judge was not hereditary; it was independent of social status, age, or gender. Jephthah was the son of a prostitute; Gideon was the youngest of his family; Deborah was a woman. This pattern is also seen in King David, who was the last choice of Samuel.[33]

The role of the Spirit in the lives of the judges and kings is not altogether clear. Apparently, the Spirit was given to them, first, as a sign, authorization, or confirmation of their divine appointment that caused the people to follow their leadership. Secondly, the Spirit imparted courage and decisiveness (especially in regard to military affairs). Thirdly, the Spirit gave them the wisdom that was needed to rule. In the case of the judges, the text emphasizes their role as saviors; but it also indicates that

---

31. For a thorough study of the Spirit in Genesis-Deuteronomy, see Schumacher, "Spirit of God in the Torah."

32. Boling, *Judges*, 26.

33. Hoppe, *Joshua, Judges*, 215.

the judges ruled for many years in peace (Judg 3:11, 30; 5:31; 8:28; 12:7; 16:31), during which time they would serve the community and settle disputes (Judg 4:5).

The Holy Spirit was a powerful external force that came upon the judges, enabling them to perform mighty feats. The Spirit of the Lord, here, seems to be a particular gift with reference to military ability. It is again a free gift, given to them, not for their own benefit, but for the benefit of the chosen people.[34] The Spirit is said to "come upon" them (*hayah*), or to "leap upon" them (*tsalach*). In the case of Gideon, the Holy Spirit clothes him (*labash*) like a garment.

In any case, the Holy Spirit came upon the judges in a powerful way, enabling them to do mighty works in the battle for God's people. The work of the Holy Spirit in the lives of the judges is paralleled, to a degree, in the book of Acts. Although the Apostles were full of the Holy Spirit, there were times when they were invested with special temporary powers; e.g., Acts 4:8, 31; 13:9. Furthermore, many of the gifts of the Spirit are not in continuous operation, but the Holy Spirit comes upon a person enabling them for a particular task; and, like the judges, we are empowered by the Holy Spirit for the benefit of the community of faith, not for our own personal gain.[35]

The judges were often very common, humble persons, who would never have been chosen for leadership. Gideon was hiding from the Midianites, but the Angel of the Lord addressed him as a "valiant warrior" (Judg 6:12). The judges foreshadow the New Testament promise: "you will receive power when the Holy Spirit has come upon you" (Acts 1:8).

## Saul and David: Charismatic Kings

The first and second of the kings of Israel (Saul and David) were charismatic leaders who had the Spirit upon them. Both of them received the Spirit at their inauguration when they were anointed by the prophet Samuel. They were authorized and empowered by the Spirit, and at times they demonstrated great wisdom (although the text never states that Saul or David possessed wisdom). The stories of the judges, Saul, and David demonstrate that the Spirit enhances the human volition, but does not displace it. Gideon, Jephthah, Samson, Saul, and David committed grave errors and sins while the Spirit was upon them.

The king was expected to receive a divine empowerment. This expectation is illustrated in the action of anointing. Samuel poured the anointing oil upon both Saul and David. There is a fourfold theological significance to the anointing (*mashach*):

1. The anointing represented separation for service, which included both increased honor and increased responsibility (2 Sam 12:7).

34. Benson, *Spirit of God*, 72.

35. As works of the Holy Spirit, regeneration and sanctification are certainly for our benefit, but these inward works of the Holy Spirit are not part of this discussion. We are looking at charismatic endowments.

2. The anointing signifies God as the authorizing agent, and the anointing is inviolable, sacred (1 Sam 24:8–13).

3. The anointing symbolized divine enablement through the Holy Spirit (1 Sam 10:6–13; 16:13–23).

4. The anointing is prophetic of the Messiah, which means "anointed one" (Isa 9:1–7; 11:1–5; 61:1).

The description of Saul's anointing clearly states that one purpose of the gift of the Spirit is to give a sign to confirm or authenticate God's call to leadership. Samuel tells Saul that a sign will confirm that the Lord has "anointed you a ruler over His inheritance" (1 Sam 10:1). Actually, three signs will come to Saul: (1) at Rachel's tomb he will learn that the lost asses have been found, (2) at Bethel he will be given two loaves of bread, and (3) at Gibeah the Spirit of God will come upon him and he will prophesy (1 Sam 10:2–6).[36]

Gift of the Spirit of prophecy not only gives Saul the experiential confirmation or sign that God is with him (1 Sam 10:7), but also publicly demonstrates to the nation that Saul is the Lord's anointed.[37] For Saul, the gift of the Spirit of prophecy may function as but one sign among others, but this sign is also observable in several other narratives. As mentioned above, at the beginning of their new leadership responsibilities, the Spirit is placed upon the elders and they prophesy (Num 11). Moreover, the gift of the Spirit to David at his anointing is described in identical terms to the earlier gift to Saul, authenticating him as the chosen king of Israel, but no sign is reported when the Spirit comes upon David.[38]

In addition to the explicit sign function of the prophetic dimension of the gift of the Spirit, there is also a general association of the gift of the Spirit and prophecy. In Chronicles, for example, the texts follow an invariable pattern: the description of the gift of the Spirit is always followed by a report of direct speech. And so, whether the evidence comes from the experience of Saul, the seventy elders, the writings of the Chronicler or elsewhere, the prophetic gift of the Spirit always has an experiential and functional dimension; a dimension, which in some cases, at least, serves as an explicit sign to authenticate or confirm God's call to service.[39]

P. Kyle McCarter observes two differences between the Spirit's empowerment of Saul and that of David. First, there was a temporal interval between Saul's anointing and his Spirit empowerment, but the Spirit came upon David immediately following his anointing. Second, the Holy Spirit was permanently upon David, but Saul's experience was apparently temporary.[40] Ralph Klein agrees, stating that David's

---

36. Stronstad, "Influence of the Old Testament," 36.
37. Stronstad, "Influence of the Old Testament," 36–37.
38. Stronstad, "Influence of the Old Testament," 36–37.
39. Stronstad, "Influence of the Old Testament," 36–37.
40. McCarter, *1 Samuel*, 276.

Spirit endowment was superior to Saul's because it was permanent, while Saul's was "spasmodic."[41] Hans Hertzberg sees David's anointing also as temporary, equating it with that of the Judges and Saul.[42] McCarter, Klein, and Hertzberg, however, seem to be reading too much into the account. There is nothing in the text to indicate that Saul's Spirit empowerment was meant to be temporary; it became temporary because of Saul's disobedience. David's experience could have been the same; but, because the writer's vantage point is in the future, he knows that the Spirit remained upon David "from that day forward" (1 Sam 16:13).[43]

## Solomon: An Understanding Heart

In the case of the king Solomon, the text repeatedly emphasizes his great wisdom, but that wisdom is never attributed directly to the Spirit. In a dream, the Lord offers to give Solomon any request, and Solomon asks, "give Thy servant an understanding heart to judge Thy people to discern between good and evil" (1 Kgs 3:9). The Lord replies, "Because you have asked . . . for yourself discernment to understand justice, behold, I have done according to your words. Behold, I have given you a wise and discerning heart" (1 Kgs 3:11–12). Although the Spirit is not mentioned, the terminology of "gift" suggests that the wisdom given to Solomon was, in fact, a bestowal of the Spirit.

## Conclusion

I would like to conclude with a summary of implications drawn from the Old Testament examples of Spirit empowerment:

1. Spirit empowerment is granted in the Old Testament to a small number of individuals in strategic situations, to enable them to perform some activity that is of substantial benefit to the covenant community.

2. The power of the Holy Spirit is not given on account of experience or accomplishments.

3. Only a man or woman of wisdom can guide the flock of God. We often covet gifts that bring power, prestige, and self-glory; but without wisdom, our churches will never be transformed into the image of Jesus Christ.

4. Like the judges, we are empowered by the Holy Spirit for the benefit of the people of God, not for our own personal gain.

---

41. Klein, *1 Samuel*, 162. See also Smith, *Critical and Exegetical Commentary*, 147.
42. Wilhelm Hertzberg, *1 and 2 Samuel*, 139.
43. For a thorough theological reading of the Spirit texts in Joshua-2 Kings, see Wadholm Jr., *Theology of the Spirit*.

5. God is looking for humble servants, men and women after his own heart (1 Sam 13:14). God wants leaders who will serve, rather than be served.

6. The anointing represents separation for service, which includes both increased honor and increased responsibility (2 Sam 12:7).

7. The anointing signifies God as the authorizing agent, and our anointing is inviolable, sacred (1 Sam 24:8–13).

8. The Holy Spirit often gives signs that confirm his anointing. The elders (Num 11) and Saul (1 Sam 10) prophesied. The sign was temporary, but the anointing was intended to be lasting.

9. Sometimes the Holy Spirit grants permanent endowments for service (David, the elders), but at other times the power of God is of a temporary nature (the judges).

10. God does not limit the work of Holy Spirit to particular places or times. He often works outside the accepted channels of power.

11. Moses's desire that all the Lord's people were prophets, and that he would put his Spirit upon all of them (Num 11:28–29) is fulfilled in the New Testament church where every Christian is a prophet, priest, and king.

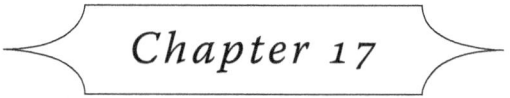

# Man Shall Not Live on Bread Alone
## *The Burden of Prophetic Leadership in Numbers 11*
### WILF HILDEBRANDT[1]

Much ink has been used to explain the episode in Numbers 11 where the Spirit upon Moses is shared with seventy elders, causing them to prophesy. Literally, Roger Stronstad has hand written his analysis of this text to clarify what happened several centuries before the Gospel of Luke describes similar prophetic activity. Roger's views have been very influential to a whole generation of Pentecostal scholars who often elucidate their experiences with Old Testament narratives.

## Theological Perspectives

Stronstad was on the fore-front of Pentecostal scholarship to feature the theological importance of Numbers 11 regarding Spirit and prophecy. He interprets this narrative as the foundational passage for the OT pattern of the Spirit transfer motif and sign-motif. In one of his summary statements he claims, "In this and subsequent examples, the transfer of the Spirit is the necessary complement to the transfer of the responsibility of leadership."[2] Furthermore, he states it is also a sign and vocational motif. "This gift of the Spirit to Israel's leaders often has an experiential dimension, such as the manifestation of prophecy, to serve as a sign to confirm God's call."[3] This thesis

---

1. This essay is written with much appreciation for Roger Stronstad's keen insights into the Scriptures that brought clarity to important theological developments in the study of pneumatology. Over the past 40 years Roger influenced and mentored many cohorts of students and I was fortunate to have been one of them. Not only did he teach, but also he inspired a generation of students to search diligently the Scriptures. Several went on to contribute their understanding in published theological materials.

2. Stronstad, *Charismatic Theology*, 21.

3. Stronstad, *Charismatic Theology*, 24.

is clarified in his other writings to highlight how Numbers 11:25–29 is the wellspring for the doctrine of the prophethood of all believers.[4] Another writer claims that this episode shows how an objective sign provides the seventy elders with the authentication for leadership roles.[5] Others emphasize the ecstatic nature of the prophesying claiming it to be similar to the expression of Saul (1 Sam 10–19) or "unintelligible ecstatic utterance" as in a few NT examples of *glossalalia*, and not intelligible prophetic language.[6] This characterization follows the conclusion of R. Wilson and B. Levine who claim the *hithpael* form of *nāb'* often implies ecstatic external behaviourisms when the spirit of God seizes a person.[7]

With these variations concerning the narrative of Numbers 11, my contribution is focused on the events of this chapter along with its core theological emphases. Numbers 11 has a paradigmatic role in the Torah concerning the role and function of prophetic leadership which God uses to lead and to feed his people with physical and spiritual sustenance. Furthermore, we will trace some thematic links from Numbers 11 as motifs in Luke's Gospel and Acts.

## Torah Context of Numbers 11

The book of Numbers chronicles an epic pilgrimage of Israel under the leadership of Moses, the greatest Old Testament prophet (Exod 34:29; Deut 18:15). In glowing terms, the Torah concludes: "Since then, no prophet has risen in Israel like Moses, whom the Lord knew face to face, who did all those signs and wonders the Lord sent him to do in Egypt" (Deut 34:10–12).[8] The crux of Numbers 11 has to do with the task of leadership, a primary theme in the Pentateuch succinctly summarized in Numbers 27:16–17: "May the Lord, the God who gives breath to all living things, appoint someone over this community to go out and come in before them, one who will lead them out and bring them in, so the Lord's people will not be like sheep without a shepherd." Numbers 11 begins with an issue of physical provision for a massive group of migrants, but then proceeds to the spiritual issue of managing the daily burden of people's needs. For this challenge of re-locating a nation from one country to another, Moses needs the miraculous intervention of Yahweh as well as human leadership assistance. For so many people to reach the covenant land promised by Yahweh, an immense amount of resources and stamina are required. This journey, as well as other great themes of Israel as a nation, are rooted in the Pentateuch which chronicles the liberation of Israel as a people from their oppression in Egypt. Before the journey can begin, the people must be released from the social oppressive reality of Pharaoh's

4. Stronstad. *Prophethood of All Believers*, 75. See also Hymes, "Numbers 11," 257–81.
5. Wonsuk Ma, "If It Is a Sign," 167.
6. Wenham, *Numbers*, 109.
7. Wilson, *Prophecy*, 87–88; Levine, *Numbers 1–20*, 340.
8. Quotations are from the NIV translation (2011).

Egypt and its imperial religion.[9] Such a formidable challenge requires the determination of a great prophet and Moses must rise to the challenge of confronting Pharaoh.

The pivotal event of the exodus occurs at Mount Sinai where Israel formalizes the covenant. Several times in Exodus Moses reminds them of the covenantal promises where God selected and delivered them from Egypt and vowed to bring them to their own land (Exod 6:7–8). When the nation leaves Sinai they are reminded by Moses that their heritage goes back to their covenantal father who also embarked on an epic journey from Ur at the command: "Go to the land I will show you" (Gen 12:1). To understand the narrative details and implications of Numbers 11 we must note the patriarchal connections and two principal themes that flow through the Pentateuch, namely, prophetic leadership and divine provision.

Long before Moses was called to lead Israel out of Egypt, Abram was summoned by God to depart from his home and lead a group of almost four hundred people to a distant land. Abraham successfully navigated his journey from the Mesopotamian city of Ur, through many challenges to the place God provided. Although a land of promise, it included threats, enemies, and pagan religion amidst Canaanite occupation. God enabled prophet Abraham (Gen 20:7) to pass several tests, accomplish impossible feats and realize a son for the divine purposes, through faith, trust and obedience. God foretold that his descendants would experience a 400-year exile where they would be tested, but eventually released (Gen 15:13–14). It would take dynamic leadership enabled by prophetic insight, power, and vision to accomplish all that God required. The patriarchal pattern includes a call, revelation, instruction, guidance and covenantal relationship. Abraham is the covenantal father of Israel who exhibits a remarkable faith in the promises of Yahweh.

A second theme in the Torah is the preservation of God's people in hostile environments. Although the covenantal promises included the gift of land—famine, drought and inhospitable neighbors force Israel to take refuge in Egypt. The episodes concerning their exile in Egypt will encompass twelve chapters in Genesis, which narrate the adventures of Jacob's son Joseph, who eventually becomes the vice-regent by virtue of his God-given skills. Joseph finds favor in Potiphar's household, which Yahweh blesses (Gen 39:5). All the episodes of Joseph's life are steeped in the providence of the God who gives Joseph the unique ability to interpret accurately dreams (Gen 40:8; 41:16). His God-given administrative strategy for the coming period of famine in the land (Gen 41:33–36) is recognized by Pharaoh and his officials who credit the Spirit of God in Joseph for this ability. He is elevated in the court to administer rations for the populace during the severe famine.[10] When people cried out to Pharaoh for bread, they were instructed to see Joseph who provided bread (Gen 41:55).

---

9. Brueggemann, *Prophetic Imagination*, 3–19.

10. Pharaoh asks, "Can we find anyone like this man, one in whom is the spirit of God?" (Gen 41:38). This pattern of dream, interpretation and exaltation to leadership is evident in the Joseph, Esther and Daniel narratives. See Collins, "Court Tales," 220–27.

Joseph attends to the food needs of Egypt and surrounding nations but more importantly, is used by God to preserve Israel—even to the extent of providing extravagant care in the land of Goshen (Gen 47:27). God was generous to Jacob's descendants, providing land and population growth to fulfill the patriarchal promises (Gen 48:4). In these narratives, food/bread [*lahem*] is a focal theme for without it, survival during the severe famine was improbable (Gen 37–50). This is Joseph's purpose: "God has sent me ahead of you to ensure your survival on earth, and to save your lives in an extraordinary deliverance" (Gen 45:7; cf. 50:21). There is a persistent development of the patriarchal covenantal promises whereby God blesses his chosen people—they multiply by impressive numbers and are established in the promised land (Gen 48:15–16). The blessing of Joseph's sons by Jacob features the faithfulness of the covenantal promises to the patriarchs by Yahweh. Not only for Israel, but Joseph's managerial skills are used to feed all those affected by famine who bought grain in Egypt (Gen 41:52).

A common denominator in the success of Abraham and Joseph is the mention of the Spirit. To be true, there is scant reference to *ruah* in the Pentateuch (18 references). The theological notion of the Spirit's role among humankind begins quietly, but with vital import as progressively revealed. In Numbers 11, with seven references, the power of God for leaders is elucidated. It will be much later in history when Isaiah provides a clear understanding of Moses's leadership empowerment through the Spirit (Isa 63).

## Moses's Leadership Burden

Many years later the situation of the Israelites in Egypt deteriorates to the place where the nation suffers in miserable slavery, but their cry for relief is heard by God who is concerned about their sufferings. The answer to the dilemma will involve another leader who is called, instructed and commissioned to serve. Here the issue initially is not food but relief from servitude to the Egyptian imperial dream. God's answer to the cries of the people includes the appointment of Moses to deliver and care for the nation of Israel. They are even more dependent on God for their survival in a wilderness that has limited provisions unless manna falls from heaven. Moses tries to avoid this call and can be characterized as a reluctant leader, but from his providential salvation as a child to his leadership appointment, Yahweh has plans for him.

Moses is called to prophetic leadership. This is not a secular form of leadership involving power and military force, but a subjugated obedience to the will of Yahweh. Moses must hear and lead according to God's instructions. Interestingly, the title "prophet" is not applied to Moses until the end of his forty years of service.[11] Not

---

11. Exodus 7 states that Aaron will be Moses's prophet while Moses will be like God to Pharaoh. God will use great acts of judgment to bring his intentions to bear. Moses declares that both Israel and Egypt will witness the miraculous exodus (Exod 14:13–18), with positive outcomes: "And when the

only is he lauded the greatest prophet but also he is the one to be emulated by all other prophets.[12] The characteristic phrase, "the Lord spoke to Moses," highlights the relational reality of God's presence with the redeemed people of Israel. This reality is expressed in a variety of phrases, which feature the truth that God is not silent. In fact, God communicates vociferously, and his audible speech can be frightening! The narratives in Numbers reflect the arrangement requested by the people and accepted by Yahweh whereby the selected mediator would share God's words, received in private, with the nation in public—God speaks through prophets and the people must listen (Exod 18–19; Deut 5:23–29; 18:15–17).[13] In the Book of Numbers alone there are about one hundred and fifty expressions of Yahweh communicating with Moses. This is a primary element in prophetic leadership.

But as great as Moses becomes in history, he will need helpers to accomplish the tasks God arranged for him. Key leaders include his brother Aaron and the elders [*zaqen*].[14] Even with the immense talents and roles that Moses exhibits, along with the privileges accorded to him on mount Sinai in the presence of God, he was just a man with all the limitations that entails. He got angry, tired, distraught and frustrated. He required help from Aaron with the communication functions that God called him to. In tandem with Aaron, Moses also depends on the elders of Israel to work with the Israelites (Exod 3:16, 18; 12:21). The seventy elders as a group are featured in Exodus 24 where they have special privilege to worship in the presence of God. These *zaqen* will accompany him to witness some of the awesome revelations of Yahweh. God instructs Moses to assemble the elders who are active representatives of the people when Moses begins his leadership role.

The prophetic role necessitates persuasion—Moses must convince not only Pharaoh but also Israel's elders that they should trust him as God's representative to lead them (Exod 3:11, 16). The elders have the closest connection to the people as tribal representatives and are integral for a positive response. They are to be assembled, instructed and involved in the confrontation with Pharaoh (Exod 3:16–20). Moses and

---

Israelites saw the mighty hand of the Lord displayed against the Egyptians, the people feared the Lord and put their trust in him and in Moses his servant" (Exod 14:31).

12. Deuteronomy 34:10 claims that since his lifespan of 120 years, "no prophet has risen in Israel like Moses whom the Lord knew face to face." The prophetic role for Israel is essential (Deut 18:18–19). Illustrating these texts, Numbers 11:17 shows how Yahweh related to Moses by speaking with him and empowering him by the Spirit. In addition to his prophetic role, Moses was a scribe, poet, priest, author, hero deliverer, lawgiver, miracle worker, intercessor and servant of the Lord.

13. God's speech may be evident in explicit instruction (Num 1 and 4), warning (Num 1:51–53; 4:17–20), explanation (Num 3:11–13), testing (Num 5), and blessing (Num 6:22–27). The favorite place of communication was Sinai but on a regular basis, the tent of meeting. "When Moses entered the tent of meeting to speak with the Lord, he heard the voice speaking to him from between the two cherubim above the atonement cover on the ark of the covenant law. In this way the Lord spoke to him" (Num 7:89).

14. The term *zaqen* refers to respected leaders within specific social groups and give tribal representation at meetings. They voice the concerns of their communities and exercise local jurisdiction for key decisions (Deut 21:1–9, 18–21; 25:5–10; Exod 24:1–9). See Hildebrandt, *Spirit of God*, 110–11.

Aaron work together with elders who are vital to bring about the desirable deliverance and compliance. Persuasion, however, comes with the help of miraculous signs, the glory cloud, as well as prophetic words (Exod 4:1–16; 19:9). The elders accept Mosaic leadership, they hear and believe (Exod 4:29–31; 19:7).[15] Elders become helpers and are often present for certain leadership events (Exod 18:12) where they share a meal in the presence of God with Moses, Jethro and Aaron. In Exodus 18, the task of making judicial rulings is observed by Jethro who discerns the heavy burden upon Moses, who explains: "When they have a dispute, it comes before me, and I decide between one person and another, and I make known the laws and teachings of God" (Exod 18:16). His role as judge demanded most of his attention until some of his judicial authority is eventually delegated to selected, trustworthy leaders who become officials to assist with dispute resolution. It is not clear whether the elders are some of these men, but the type of work they do in the nation will be comparable. Crucial themes are foreshadowed in the Exodus narratives, including, prophetic leadership with elders helping, communication, the burden of people care, and divine provisions.

## Numbers 11 and Prophetic Leadership

After a largely positive experience for Israel leading up to Numbers chapter 11, we come to events that vividly present the immense challenges faced in the wilderness. Chapter 11 records the first of several serious complaints made by people (cf. 12:1–2; 14:1–4; 17:6–7; 20:2–3; 21:5).[16] The text will fluctuate between food issues (11:4–13, 18–20, 31–34) and leadership matters (11:16–17, 24–30; 12:1–15), which feature crucial principles for Israel's future.[17] Furthermore, there are blended resolutions to the issues through the provisions of God and the work of Moses. This includes acts of judgment and correction by Yahweh. The departure from Egypt and pilgrimage to the promised land called for a disposition of faith, trust and cooperation but, characteristically, Israel was dismayed by the hardships. In Numbers 11 we witness two basic challenges of life in the wilderness, namely, how will the nation's physical needs be cared for and who will manage domestic issues that arise?

Numbers 11 is introduced with a crisis when Yahweh causes fire to strike the outskirts of Israel's camp (*mahineh*). The location of the judgment will become instructive and, as a reminder, it is named *Taberah* (burning). The divine reaction came as a response to the people's complaints so early in their journey. No doubt the wilderness privations were extensive, but Yahweh's deliverance and covenant provisions with

---

15. "Moses and Aaron brought together all the elders of the Israelites, and Aaron told them everything the Lord had said to Moses. He also performed the signs before the people, and they believed. And when they heard that the Lord was concerned about them and had seen their misery, they bowed down and worshiped" (Exod 4:29–31).

16. Milgrom, *Numbers*, 82.

17. Ashley, *Numbers*, 206–7.

promises of care were to be valued. The clamour intensifies when the people lament the loss of their Egyptian menu and covet meat (11:4–6). They quickly tired of the daily manna provisions that appear to be tasty, nutritious, and easy to prepare for a nomadic situation (11:7–9). Just as the people cried out for deliverance from Egypt and were heard by God (Exod 2:23–25), they now cry out to Moses for protection (11:2). But true to human nature they soon forget and continue in their characteristic complaining that not only angers Yahweh but also irritates Moses. Like a good prophet, Moses usually is quick to intercede on behalf of the people (Exod 17; 32:11–14), but the compounding of daily issues to deal with, takes its toll—Moses has a candid and aggressive tone:

> Why have you brought this trouble on your servant? What have I done to displease you that you put the burden of all these people on me? . . . I cannot carry all these people by myself; the burden is too heavy for me. If this is how you are going to treat me, please go ahead and kill me—if I have found favor in your eyes—and do not let me face my own ruin" (11:11–15).

Yahweh responds in a similar way as he did when Moses tried to evade his prophetic calling—he addresses Moses's primary problem of "the burden."[18] This burden involves communication and encompasses the provision of guidance, water/food, dealing with domestic issues that arise when people are in close community, health matters, birth and death—literally, the weight of a nation needing special care. When Moses claimed he could not speak properly as a prophet to Pharaoh, Yahweh provided Aaron to help with persuasion. Now to help with the daily burdens of the people, Yahweh calls for seventy elders who function as leaders and officials among the people. By sharing some of the power of the Spirit that is on Moses, these elders will be able to help with the "burden" of the people (11:16–17; 24–25).

Secondly, Yahweh attends to the food issue at hand—meat will be provided as craved.[19] But preparation for the feast is required and people must consecrate themselves before they receive the miraculous provision. As is often typical in prophetic leadership, the prophet is to announce what will come to pass. This reinforces Moses's role and verifies that Yahweh has heard and answered according to the prophetic word—they will be fed until they are sick of meat and realize their lack of trust in Yahweh. The feast will be another lesson to trust in the Lord who is able to provide and guide like a good shepherd. But even Moses has reduced his stately demeanor to that of complaint as well as mistrust in Yahweh's ability. The Lord's reply addresses both issues of leadership burden and food: "Is the Lord's arm too short? Now you will see whether or not what I say will come true for you" (Num 11:21–23).

The characteristic that makes Mosaic leadership so impressive over all prophets is his obedience. He communicates the words of the Lord and gathers the elders

---

18. *massaʾ* (burden) appears seven times in Num 11.
19. The emphasis on eating *ʾakal* occurs eight times in chapter 11:1, 4, 5, 12, 18 (2x), 19, 21.

around the tent of meeting according to Yahweh's instructions. Now the Lord acts according to what was promised. First, he appears at the tent of meeting in a cloud and speaks with Moses. Then he takes some of the Spirit (a withdrawal) that was on Moses and puts it on the elders, consequently causing the spontaneous expression of prophesying.[20] Not only do the elders prophesy at the Tent of Meeting, but also Eldad and Medad, who are in the camp, also prophesy (Num 11:27). The withdrawal signifies that some leadership authority will be shared with the elders. This gives credibility and authority with the people in the daily work and encouragement required for ministry. Secondly, the Lord sends a wind that drives quail from the sea to pile up around the camp. It is a miraculous, abundant provision, but it results in another illustration of judgment—those who craved other food, are struck with a plague.

Two elders named Eldad and Medad, who had not gone with the others to the tent, also experience the Spirit upon them and prophesy back in the camp [*mahineh*]. When Joshua hears about this he views it as a potential threat to Moses's leadership or impinging on his authority and wants them stopped. But Moses perceives a desirable development here as noted in his response: "Are you jealous for my sake? I wish that all the Lord's people were prophets and that the Lord would put his Spirit on them!" This episode usually gives rise to several views ranging from illegitimate prophecy to a threat of ambitious leadership. The location of their act of prophesying in the camp [*mahineh*], however, is accentuated four times in 11:27–30. This is the same locale of judgment described in Numbers 11:1 and noted three times in 11:31–32. Eldad and Medad remained in the camp with the people, so it is possible they were attending to the people who were in a state of fear due to Yahweh's judgment and witnessed the withdrawal of leaders to the Tent of Meeting. The incident shows that Yahweh recognizes them as "registered" leaders who are already positioned to assist Moses with his leadership burden. Moreover, it is Yahweh who puts his Spirit on them—they prophesy where the people witness God's authentication of their service. Moses applauds the activity because he sees it as the answer to the burden—people hear the prophetic word and can now have confidence that there are authorized elders who can help them with their social and domestic issues. The act of prophesying here emphasizes verbal expression. Levison considers it a visionary experience for the elders in a communal context, but it is impracticable to see how a communal vision would have any impact on the people. Unless a vision is communicated by a prophet in verbal terms, the vision is a personal experience—rarely a communal one. Prophecy is mainly a

---

20. For clues to the interpretation of "prophesying" in Numbers 11, many scholars have imposed concepts of ecstasy from narratives pertaining to Saul and a few other prophets. The ancient presentation of leadership in the nation, however, is rooted in Pentateuchal narratives. In his excellent article, Levison makes a legitimate case for verbal and thematic links to Exodus and dismisses that prophesying here describes an ecstatic state. Rather, "prophesying entailed a more ordered experience that served to assist Moses as he led Israel" (Levison, "Prophecy," 514).

verbal function to communicate and affirm the divine will, including the ability to speak judicial wisdom and comfort into situations that arise.[21]

The narrative returns to the opening theme concerning the people's desire for meat to eat. The provision is extraordinary but comes with a severe act of judgment. The Lord's anger "burns" and another place name is given as a reminder of this episode, *Kibroth Hattavah*—a grave for those who crave (11:31–35).

In summary, Numbers 11 is a classic narrative that describes Israel's wilderness adversities and the divine response through human leadership to meet needs. For Israel's epic migration to the land of promise, the difficulties were intense and required physical and spiritual stamina. Here we see a pattern of how God provides for Israel's needs with physical sustenance, guidance and instruction, from patriarchal to prophetic leadership positions—in Stronstad's terms it is programmatic and paradigmatic. From glimmers of the Spirit's work in Abraham and Joseph, Numbers 11 verifies the power/necessity of the Spirit in leaders. This narrative presents how an endowment of the Spirit on Moses (cf. Isa 63:11–14), is shared with elders for authorized leadership duties in the nation to lessen the "burden." An example of how this works is recorded in Numbers 9 where the people ask Moses and Aaron a procedural question for ceremonial application in keeping with the law—Moses takes the issue to the Lord for instruction (Num 9:8). This pattern occurs again in Numbers 15:32–36, 27:1–11; 36:1–12, with a concluding note that Yahweh gave his commands through Moses (36:13). In a similar fashion the authorized elders would function to provide instruction and application of the law to people's domestic/community disputes, thereby lessening Moses's burden. At the tent they have a remarkable spiritual experience, but then take this new authority into the camp where the daily needs of people are managed. The incident with Medad and Eldad serves as an example for people in the camp who witness the divine impartation—they hear and see that God will not always judge but will comfort and be among them.

The sharing of the Spirit on Moses with the elders does not abdicate his leadership responsibilities.[22] The passage suggests two levels of leadership; the macro level is for Moses and his successors, while a micro level is for elders. When Joshua reacts to this occurrence he is assured by Moses that this blessing of Yahweh's presence is intended for all his people—Spirit-reception, prophetic insight, plus an intimate relationship with Yahweh.[23] This will be affirmed when Joshua is appointed as the

---

21. Levison claims, "By the same token, Exodus 24 supplies what is implicit in the narrative of Numbers 11: prophesying consisted principally of a visionary experience within a controlled central setting, with an established social hierarchy and an appointed locus of revelation. The elders had been appointed earlier to bear Moses's burden with him, had gathered at a locus of revelation, on Mt. Sinai, and had participated in a communal visionary experience alongside Moses" (Levison, "Prophecy," 513).

22. Moses remains the paradigmatic prototype of a prophet who has face to face communications with Yahweh and unequaled power. "For no one has ever shown the mighty power or performed the awesome deeds that Moses did in the sight of Israel" (Deut 34:12).

23. Although Yahweh permitted the role of prophet as mediator in the nation, the divine ideal was

one who will succeed Moses. In Numbers 27:16–20 we have the thematic thesis for a paradigmatic leadership transfer in answer to Moses's prayer for God to provide authorized leadership. Joshua has the "spirit" of leadership and, as commissioned, will take Israel into the land of promise. This was not a sudden matter, however, as it took extensive time for Moses to mentor his protégé who was known to linger at the tent of meeting (Exod 33:11) and was among the elders who prophesied. Moses is instructed by Yahweh for the divine appointment: "Take Joshua son of Nun, a man in whom is the spirit of leadership, and lay your hand on him. Have him stand before Eleazar the priest and the entire assembly and commission him in their presence. Give him some of your authority so the whole Israelite community will obey him." In this provision, Israel would have leaders to guide, instruct and provide for their daily needs.

The pattern for leadership is essential for every generation, but OT evidence shows how prophetic leadership was rare and selective. Therefore, OT prophecy will look forward to a time when the pattern will be fulfilled in the anointed Messiah, his disciples and NT elders (Acts 6:1–6).

## Lukan Motifs: Prophetic Words and Provisions

Luke presents narratives that illustrate the renewal of several OT style prophetic functions, showing how God attends to his people who need liberation and care. Some of the narratives in Numbers have typological links to the NT occurrences.[24] This is observed in the outburst of the prophetic word and in the ministry of social care given by Jesus to the multitudes. The role of the Spirit in the description of prophetic activity is vital in the Lukan narratives, evidenced by about seventy references to the Spirit's activity! With the renewal of the Spirit's action, there is a dramatic increase of prophetic activity that had been lacking in Israel for some time.[25] Luke's Gospel begins with the renewal of prophetic activity, then proceeds to the Spirit endowed leadership of Jesus, featuring his teaching and miraculous acts of provision.

Luke uses the terminology of being "baptized" in the Holy Spirit (Luke 3:16; Acts 1:45; 11:15), to indicate consecration for service as an experience leading into ministry. This is illustrated in Jesus's baptism which inaugurates his ministry through the anointing by the Holy Spirit (Luke 4:18). Luke's most common phrase is to be "filled with the Holy Spirit" which identifies the prophetic ministry for which God's people are "baptized." John the Baptist's father has an extraordinary experience where

to foster a personal, individual, and intimate relationship with his people. Yahweh desired for all his people to know him and have access to him in the same way the prophets did.

24. It is difficult to verify linguistic references to Numbers by Luke, but the overwhelming thematic and typological parallels indicate an impressive theological consistency and application of examples/illustrations.

25. Credit is due to Dr. Stronstad for his careful analysis of texts that show the development of the Spirit's action from the OT into the NT. In many of his publications he catalogues and exposits the prophetic theme from the program initiated by John the Baptist to Jesus the Spirit baptizer.

he is informed that he will have a miraculously born son by the providence of God, who will be filled by the Spirit to function as a prophet (Luke 1:15–17). This opening episode in Luke's Gospel features inspired prophetic speech—God can give and take away the human ability to speak. He removes Zechariah's capacity to speak for nine months, but then returns his speech and inspires him with prophetic utterance. Zechariah's prophecy has extensive ramifications for Israel as a nation. Filled with the Spirit he prophesies giving glory to God for redemption. He acknowledges the role of the prophets, salvation from enemies and the covenant made to Abraham. Finally, he recognizes the role his son will make in the lineage of prophets who will prepare the way and present knowledge of salvation to a new generation (Luke 1:67–79). Luke also summarizes God's providential blessing on John with a connection to the wilderness theme: "And the child grew and became strong in spirit; and he lived in the wilderness until he appeared publicly to Israel" (Luke 1:80). The word of God comes to John where he is shaped and prepared in the wilderness for a prophetic ministry that will feature a message of repentance. John's prophetic work is focused, extensive and preparatory for the coming of the Messiah.

Luke continues to disclose Spirit inspired prophetic speech through Elizabeth and Mary (Luke 1:39–56). Similarly, this activity is evident with Simeon's prophetic outburst (Luke 2:25–35), and with Anna, who has prophetic standing and spiritual ministry in the temple (Luke 2:36–38). Luke then features themes in the life and experience of Jesus Christ that reflect motifs in Numbers. After his baptism, Jesus is led into the wilderness by the Spirit for his own period of testing. After forty days without food, he does not complain—nor will his hunger be satisfied by the devil's instigation to make bread. Jesus responds with the spiritual truth that there is more to life than food, "Man shall not live on bread alone" (Luke 4:4; Deut 8:3)! Whereas Israel put the Lord to various tests in the wilderness, Jesus dismisses the tempter's efforts (Luke 4:12; Deut 6:13). With a fresh victory over this period of testing, Jesus makes his prophetic ministry advent in Nazareth by reading and applying the prophetic word from Isaiah 61. With the Spirit upon him, he makes prophetic pronouncements concerning his ministry of deliverance, provision and proclamation of good news to a people who are amazed at his teaching. Further to the thematic development of wilderness testing to spiritual empowering, Jesus features the example of Elijah who also provided for the hungry during a period of severe famine. This example of prophetic interpretation brings anger and consternation, a typical response to prophets (Luke 4:24–30; cf. Num 14:1–4).

Luke advances these themes in chapter 6 beginning with the hunger of the disciples who harvest and eat grain on the Sabbath. Jesus gives a fresh interpretation of the law to permit his disciples' actions—the hungry will be satisfied. This example will be followed with Jesus's sermon with spiritual and moral teachings for disciples. Here Jesus focuses their attention to things "above," rather than conditions "below." "Blessed are you who hunger now, for you will be satisfied" (Luke 6:21). The spiritually hungry will be filled, but "woe to you who are well fed now, for you will go hungry" (Luke 6:25). In these narratives, Jesus trains the disciples for public ministry (Luke 6; 9), showing them that prophetic ministry entails prophetic speech as well as physical and spiritual provision. He even tells the disciples to feed the crowds (Luke 9:15). With overtones from the Mosaic provisions in the wilderness, Jesus teaches the disciples by feeding the multitudes in a miraculous display (Luke 9:1–17). When we take Jesus's teaching and numerous acts of provision together, there is an unmistakable juxtaposition between the temporal needs of disciples—"give us each day our daily bread" (Luke 11:3)—and the future reality when all need will be satisfied.

In Acts we see the prophetic words of Jesus fulfilled in the coming of the Spirit on the day of Pentecost. As John the Baptist proclaimed, Jesus baptizes the 120 disciples who wait for the Spirit to be poured out—similar to the seventy elders who gather at the Tent of Meeting and experience Spirit and prophecy.[26] The results of Pentecost are observed in the apostolic ministries where Spirit baptism describes, prophecy which can be observed in words of praise (Luke 1:68), in Spirit-inspired exegesis (Acts 2:17), words of witness to unbelievers (Acts 4:8) and in words of judgment (Acts 13). Furthermore, the phrase "Filled with the Holy Spirit" is a potentially repetitive experience where Peter and Paul will often be inspired to preach, witness and provide prophetic leadership (Acts 2:4; 4:8, 31; 9:17; 13:9, 52).

Another leadership characteristic is observed in the amazing generosity of the charismatic leaders and community. As in any growing fellowship there will be needs which include physical and spiritual elements. Needs will be met by those who are called to leadership, but priority must be given to the teaching of the word. This is expressly stated and illustrated in the early church community's activities (Acts 2:42–47). The believers were unified, they prayed together and broke bread in homes. They also shared their possessions as a spiritual response of generosity towards those in need. Some sold property and trusted the apostles to distribute as needed (Acts 4:32–35). Other challenges, however, arose as the group of believers included diverse traditions and ethnicities. In Numbers the diverse people were referred to as rabble. In Acts 6, cross cultural issues arise revealing favoritism as Greek speaking Hellenists complain against other Jews or Hebrews resulting in some widows being overlooked in daily servings of food. These Greek speaking Hellenists were converts to Christ but raised in Greek culture outside of Palestine and considered "foreigners." Faced with a challenge, the leaders address it by selecting Spirit filled men with wisdom to manage the conflict in food distribution (Acts 6:1–4).

In conclusion, it appears that the Lukan motifs describing prophetic leadership functions derive from the powerful trajectory of Torah narratives which show how the Spirit of God empowers leadership in Israel to meet the physical, domestic, and spiritual needs of people who cannot exist on bread alone.

---

26. Interestingly Luke 10:1, 17 refers to 72 disciples sent out for ministry (some manuscripts say 70). If Luke considers Numbers 11 here, it may include Eldad and Medad for a parallel reference.

## Chapter 18

# Restoring Righteousness to Creation
## *An Overview of Matthew's Theology of the Spirit*

BLAINE CHARETTE[1]

This paper seeks to present a brief yet reasonably comprehensive overview of Matthew's theology of the Spirit. The discussion essentially follows the order in which references to the Spirit appear in the Gospel and organizes Matthew's presentation in relation to the Spirit's role in the new creative work of God, in promoting righteousness through enabling obedience and overcoming that evil which works against God's will, and finally in the prophetic activity of God's people bearing witness to God justice.[2] The basic premise of the discussion is that in Matthew the activity of the Spirit relates closely to the establishment of that righteousness essential to God's rule for the benefit of the created order. The discussion of Matthew's theology of the Spirit will conclude with succinct observations on how Matthew's perspective relates to that of Luke.

### The Spirit and the New Beginning

The first mention of the Holy Spirit in Matthew is at 1:18 with reference to the birth of Jesus. What is especially noteworthy is that this birth is described as a "genesis" or "beginning" (*genesis*). More common terms related to birth (e.g., the verbs *tiktō* and

---

1. It is a delight for me to contribute this paper to a volume honoring Roger Stronstad. I first heard of Roger when as a young professor I was teaching in Canada. Years later we met and became friends through our involvement in SPS and on several occasions I have invited him to teach on Acts at Northwest University. Like so many others, I am grateful for Roger's scholarship and his faithful service over the years to the larger Pentecostal community.

2. I have chosen not to summarize or repeat what I have written elsewhere regarding the Spirit in Matthew but rather treat this as an opportunity to approach the topic in a fresh manner. Also, given the limits on the length of this discussion, I have also chosen not to interact with other secondary literature but simply present a personal statement on Matthew's theology of the Spirit.

*gennaō*) are found within the infancy account, so it is remarkable that Matthew would first announce the birth as a "genesis" effected by the Holy Spirit.[3] This use of *genesis* augments the earlier and only other use of the term by Matthew in the title of his Gospel at 1:1 where it is described as a "book of genesis." It would appear that Matthew intends his reader to understand his Gospel as an account of a new beginning by which God will accomplish his purposes for his creation and that this new beginning is realized through the birth of Jesus which is the consequence of Mary being with child from the Holy Spirit.

This language is evocative of OT descriptions of the Spirit's role in creation. Passages such as Gen 1:2; 2:7; Job 26:13; and Psalm 33:6 speak of God's *ruach* ("spirit," "wind" or "breath") as active in bringing life, order, and protection to creation. What Matthew is emphasizing by twice noting that the child born of Mary is from the Holy Spirit (1:18, 20) is that through this child, who is none other than Emmanuel or "God with us" (1:23), the creative or better re-creative activity of God is now at work to bring about the renewal of God's creation. This idea finds further expression later at 19:28 when Jesus speaks of a "regeneration" or "renewal" of creation (*palingenesia*) that occurs at the end of the age when the Son of Man, seated on his glorious throne, exercises judgment. This critical event most probably coincides with the passing away of heaven and earth, about which Jesus speaks at 5:18 and 24:35, to be replaced by an entirely new creative order.[4] The birth of Jesus marks a new beginning inasmuch God is now active in the present age, through his Spirit and his Son, to bring about restoration and transformation that will result in the full realization of his intentions for creation.

These notions of restoration and renewal closely relate to the kingdom theme that pervades Matthew's Gospel. Throughout the infancy account the kingship of the child is emphasized. The genealogy describes his royal descent from David, which is also intimated in the Isa 7:14 quotation at 1:23. The magi come to pay homage to the child born king of the Jews (2:2). Additionally, his kingship is set in sharp contrast to that of King Herod who typifies all that is wrong with the exercise of rule in the present age. Throughout his ministry Jesus, endowed with the Spirit, displays what divine rule looks like by bringing about wholeness through healing and forgiveness and by overcoming those powers that would seek to undermine the righteousness and goodness of creation. Jesus's ministry, which establishes a model for his disciples, marks the inbreaking of the new creative energy of God that will culminate in the ultimate realization of the kingdom when he returns at the end of the present age ushering in the renewal of creation.

---

3. The only other use of *genesis* in the NT with reference to birth is in the Lukan infancy account (1:14) when the angel announces the birth of John to Zechariah.

4. Note that at 5:18 the phrase "until heaven and earth pass away" finds its semantic complement in the phrase "until all is accomplished." Once Jesus, the Son of Man, accomplishes God's purposes the present age comes to an end and the new creation comes into its fullness.

## The Spirit and Righteousness

Following the infancy narrative Matthew next mentions the Holy Spirit in the context of the preaching of John the Baptist. John, recognizing the close proximity of God's rule, calls upon the people to repent (3:2). In addition, he speaks of the necessity of producing "fruit" appropriate to repentance (3:8), warning that those who do not produce such fruit will be cut down and thrown into the fire in keeping with the fate of fruitless trees.[5] Fruit, which is metaphorical of the essence and product of one's life, is an important motif in Matthew and functions as a close complement to the concept of righteousness which is central to Jesus's teaching. Jesus cautions his disciples that apart from proper righteousness they will not enter the kingdom (5:20) and bolsters this with the challenge to set as a priority the seeking of God's kingdom and righteousness (6:33). This teaching is restated later in the Gospel when Jesus speaks of the kingdom of God as ultimately given to those who produce the fruit of the kingdom (21:43). John can be described as "coming in the way of righteousness" at 21:32 since even prior to Jesus he also calls others to produce such fruit in view of the coming of the kingdom.

To support such righteousness John not only preaches repentance but also baptizes in water for that purpose (3:11). It is in the context of his baptizing activity that John speaks of a mightier one coming after him who will baptize in the Holy Spirit and fire.[6] What this baptism of the coming mighty one involves is not explicitly stated but the context, supported by the winnowing image appended to the declaration, suggests that it consists in both a redemptive event, closely related to the righteousness required for eschatological inclusion in the kingdom, but also a judgment on those who reject such righteousness. The mighty one will effect a baptism according to which the Spirit motivates the fruit essential to the kingdom yet with the obverse affect that those who refuse repentance and righteousness experience a judgment that condemns them to eschatological fire.[7] The mighty one through the nature of his mission will bring about a baptismal winnowing that results in the identification and ultimate separation of the righteous from the unrighteous.

Jesus, the mightier one, is himself the first to undergo this baptism in the Holy Spirit. When John seeks to dissuade him from his baptism, Jesus responds by noting that this action is proper in order "to fulfill all righteousness" (3:15). This is the first appearance of "righteousness" (*dikaiosunē*) in Matthew and its association with the baptism of Jesus indicates that this event is important for understanding the nature of righteousness in the Gospel. John relents and when Jesus is baptized the Spirit of God

---

5. Jesus will restate this principle at 7:19.

6. Whereas in Mark the coming one will baptize in the Holy Spirit, in Matthew and Luke he will baptize in the Holy Spirit and fire. It is clear from the context that fire signifies judgment.

7. Note that in Matthew eschatological judgment is often described in terms of fire (see Matt 5:22; 13:42, 50; 18:8–9; 25:41) which is suggested in the present context by the phrase "unquenchable fire."

descends upon him.⁸ The effect of the coming of the Spirit upon Jesus is not directly stated but the context provides important insights into what Jesus's experience of the Spirit of God involves. Directly following his baptism Jesus is led by the Spirit into the wilderness to be tempted by the devil (4:1). There he is tested at the level of his faithful obedience as the Son of God.⁹ Jesus demonstrates his commitment to God through trust, obedience, and devoted worship. That Jesus responds to all three temptations with statements drawn from Deut 6–8 reveals he is committed to a way of righteousness that Israel (also described as God's son in that section of Deuteronomy) had not adhered to in the past. The close association of the baptism and temptation accounts indicates that the Spirit who comes upon Jesus supports him in his obedience to God in the face of temptation.¹⁰ From this point forward Jesus continues to model obedience to the will of the Father and to teach others to follow him in the manner of righteousness.

Jesus makes it clear that he has come to fulfill the Torah and the Prophets (5:17), which is to say that he has come to uphold and reinforce the emphasis found throughout the Hebrew scriptures on living faithfully in covenant relationship with God. In his teaching he underscores and summarizes what it is that God wishes for his people (cf. 7:12; 22:40; 23:23) and protects the integrity of God's commandments against those religious teachers who, though making an outward show of righteousness, do actual harm to the commandments through their teaching and actions (cf. 15:1–9). Matthew presents a Jesus who, having received his messianic anointing when the Spirit comes upon him at his baptism, executes his Spirit anointing by living out and teaching others to follow in the righteousness and obedience that is characteristic of covenant faithfulness. Given this emphasis it is not surprising that when baptism is linked with the Holy Spirit later in the Gospel, in the context of the Great Commission, it is associated with obedience to Jesus's commandments.

Following his resurrection Jesus meets with his disciples on a mountain in Galilee where he announces to them that as the risen Lord he has been given all authority in heaven and on earth and directs them to make disciples of all nations (28:16–20). The task of making disciples embraces the two activities of first baptizing them "into the name of the Father, and of the Son, and of the Holy Spirit" and then "teaching them to keep all that I have commanded you." This statement expresses the fulfillment of the promise made by John at 3:11 concerning the coming powerful one who will

---

8. Matthew is alone among the Gospels in using the designation "Spirit of God" (3:16; 12:28). In Mark and John it is "the Spirit" who descends; in Luke it is "the Holy Spirit."

9. The baptism account ends with the declaration of the voice from heaven, "This is my Son" and the temptation account opens with the tempter's taunt, "Since you are the Son of God."

10. Mark also closely connects the temptation to the baptism but does not include the three temptations with their Deuteronomic associations. Luke includes the three temptations but separates the baptism from the temptation by inserting the genealogy of Jesus and thus diminishes the connection between the two narratives.

"baptize you in the Holy Spirit."[11] As the disciples of Jesus under his authority baptize others into the name of the triune God those who are thus baptized are now able to keep the commandments of Jesus and thus live out faithfully the covenant that has been established through his death.

All that Jesus commands includes the entirety of his teaching as presented in Matthew. As the messianic interpreter of Torah he affirms the commandments of God as he provides the definitive understanding of God's intention in giving the commandments. Jesus's position is expressed succinctly in his charge to the rich man, "If you wish to enter life, keep the commandments" (19:17).[12] Entrance into the kingdom, or full and final participation in the eschatological salvation Jesus brings about, is not possible apart from this righteousness to which Jesus calls his disciples. For Jesus to do the will of the Father is the *sine qua non* of redemption (cf. 7:21–23). There is no true discipleship apart from obedience to Jesus's commands just as there is no true participation in the messianic community without the fruit God requires of those who would be his people. Yet, this is not a demand without benefit of promise and gift. Jesus fulfills all righteousness by the enabling presence of the Spirit who comes upon him at his baptism and as the risen Lord he baptizes others in the same Spirit so they, too, might live out this righteousness.

## The Spirit and Overcoming Evil

When John announces the messianic figure who comes after him he observes that he will be more powerful (3:11; *ischuroteros*). Presumably it is when the Spirit of God comes upon Jesus at his baptism that he effectively becomes this mighty or powerful one. As the temptation narrative which closely follows demonstrates, the manner in which the power of Jesus is most evident is in his confrontation with evil. That the first action of the Spirit following the baptism is to lead Jesus into the wilderness for a contest with the devil indicates that the overcoming of evil is central to the messianic mission. Jesus is empowered by the Spirit to defeat the devil and to deliver people from the damaging influence of his rule.

In keeping with the emphasis on commandments and righteousness in Matthew, the nature of the temptations Jesus faces in the wilderness is significant. The tempter encourages Jesus to issue commands that would serve his own needs while ignoring the words God had spoken. The devil uses scripture itself in an attempt to undermine Jesus's obedience and trust. Ultimately, the devil reveals his true objective in seeking to corrupt Jesus and in this way receive his worship. This episode previews later

---

11. The trinitarian language of the Great Commission does not lessen the connection between these two passages especially since the baptismal narrative is itself remarkably trinitarian referring not only to the Spirit of God but also to the declaration of the Father identifying Jesus as the Son.

12. This assertion is characteristic of the bold approach of Jesus in Matthew to Torah and commandments. It is not surprising it is not found in the parallel accounts of Mark and Luke.

encounters Jesus has with religious leaders in which they also seek to tempt Jesus (cf. 16:1–4; 19:3–9; 22:15–21, 34–40).[13] It also anticipates that opposition to Jesus often results from misapprehensions or the misuse of God's commandments (cf. 12:1–8; 15:1–19; 19:3–9) and that the distortion of commandments can result in empty and false worship (15:1–9). Evil in Matthew is frequently depicted as setting itself in opposition to the correct understanding of God's word. The interpretation of the parable of the soils, for example, describes the situation of the person who hears the word of the kingdom, but without understanding; as a consequence, they become vulnerable to the evil one who comes and snatches away the word that was sown (13:19).[14] This is why Jesus's teaching that correctly interprets Torah is such an important concern to Matthew.

Jesus more forcefully confronts the power of evil through his exorcisms. The public ministry of Jesus is characterized by several episodes of Jesus casting out spirits or demons (e.g., 8:16, 28–34; 15:22–28; 17:14–18). Moreover, he authorizes his disciples to cast out demons as well (10:1, 8). Of particular interest are two occasions when Jesus casts a demon out of a man who was mute (9:32–34) and a man who was both blind and mute (12:22–24). On both occasions the Pharisees attribute the power of Jesus to cast out demons to the ruler of demons, Beelzebul. In the latter scene this denunciation provokes Jesus to question the soundness of their contention, since this would indicate that Satan is divided against himself, as well as to make the remarkable claim that since he casts out demons by "the Spirit of God" then the kingdom of God has come to them (12:28). His power over the demonic is in Matthew the clearest and strongest evidence for the presence of the kingdom.

Jesus not only counters the charge that his exorcisms are due to the power of Beelzebul but also asserts that he is much more powerful than Satan or the demonic. In the parable of the binding of the strong man Jesus describes a scenario in which one takes what a strong man possesses by entering his house and overpowering him (12:29). It is significant that Satan is depicted as a "strong man" (*ischuros*), which conspicuously echoes the description of Jesus at 3:11 as the "stronger" or "more powerful" one (*ischuroteros*). It is also noteworthy that it is "the Spirit of God" who comes upon Jesus at his baptism (3:16), the very same description of the Spirit used at 12:28 when describing the source of the power behind his exorcisms. Matthew is the only Gospel writer to employ the term "the Spirit of God" and uses it only in these two contexts.

---

13. The verb *peirazō* ("to tempt" or "to test") is used in both the temptation narrative as well as in these polemical scenes. With respect to the character of evil Matthew makes no distinction as to whether the challenge comes from a diabolical or human source. In 16:1–4 Jesus responds to the test of the Pharisees and Sadducees in requesting a sign by describing them as "an evil and adulterous generation." When Peter at 16:21–23 "tempts" Jesus by seeking to deter him from the way of suffering and death, Jesus forcefully responds, "Get behind me, Satan!"

14. Matthew uses the more ambiguous term "evil one" (cf. "Satan" in Mark and "the devil" in Luke), most probably because the adversary could be either diabolical or human. The woe of 23:13 condemns the scribes and Pharisees whose teaching prevents others from entering the kingdom.

Most probably this description denotes the divine power inherent in the Spirit which enables Jesus to carry out his messianic mission and in particular to exercise power over Satan in order to free those whom he has taken captive.

The exorcisms are forceful demonstrations of God's redemptive activity empowered by the Spirit and carried out through the agency of Jesus. In view of this situation, Jesus challenges his opponents to accept his exorcistic activity as the result of God's Spirit signaling that God is now at work establishing his redemptive rule. To reject what God is doing in their midst and even worse to continue to attribute this work of the Spirit of God to Satan is to speak against or to blaspheme the Holy Spirit (12:31–32). The consequence of holding this position, however, is to place oneself outside of the context of forgiveness since what they are rejecting is nothing other than the forgiving work of God. Their rejection and denunciation of God's redemption identifies them as bad trees producing evil fruit (12:33–37) and thus clearly those who have no place in the kingdom.

Jesus's severe rebuke of his opponents on this occasion is not unusual in Matthew. He frequently refers to them as "an evil and adulterous generation" (12:39; 16:4; at 17:17 he more broadly reproves his contemporaries as a "faithless and twisted generation"). The essential problem is that their hearts are far from God and, as a consequence, yield evil intentions (15:8, 19). They are unable to understand with their hearts in order to turn and be healed (13:15) but, rather in the face of the healing activity of Jesus, think evil in their hearts (9:2–7). In the interpretation of the parable of the weeds of the field (13:36–43), Jesus argues that the weeds which cause offense (*skandalon*) and promote lawlessness (*anomia*) and thus undermine the good work of God's kingdom represent the "children" (*huioi*) of the evil one. The focus of the parable is broader than Jesus's immediate opponents,[15] yet the assertion stands that they think evil and speak evil because they are the offspring of evil.[16] These weeds meet the same fate as trees that do not bear good fruit and are thrown into the fire. Since they are the offspring of the evil one it seems only fitting they are consigned to the eternal fire prepared for the devil and his angels (25:41). Opposition to the kingdom excludes one from participation in it its redemptive goals.

There is a terrible poignancy in this opposition towards Jesus's exorcisms since this aspect of his redemptive activity signifies the more profound reality of God removing the unclean spirit from this generation. At the conclusion of his interaction with the scribes and Pharisees, Jesus recounts the parable of the return of the unclean spirit (12:43–45).[17] An unclean spirit having gone out from a person seeks a place of

15. Note, however, that the scribes and Pharisees are described at 23:28 as "full of hypocrisy and lawlessness (*anomia*)."

16. Reiterating John's condemnation of the Pharisees and Sadducees (3:7), Jesus refers to his opponents as a "brood of vipers" at 12:34; 23:33.

17. It is possible that this parable alludes to the prophecy of Zech 13:2, which speaks of the future day when Yahweh will cut off the names of the idols from the land as well as remove from the land the prophets and the unclean spirit. This is the only place in the Hebrew Bible or Septuagint where the

rest but, finding none, returns to the person bringing seven other spirits eviler than itself. Jesus observes that the last state of the person is worse than the first and declares that this situation is analogous to that of his own generation. Through Jesus's liberating activity on behalf of the people God seeks to remove the unclean spirit. Yet most are closed to this truth and do nothing to receive or act upon this opportunity for renewal and restoration. It is for this reason that the people of Nineveh and the queen of the South will condemn this generation at the judgment (12:41–42). They responded positively in the past to God's activity but this generation rejects the deliverance of God which is of far greater importance than all that had happened before. Through the messianic activity of Jesus, the Spirit of God overcomes the demonic and seeks to remove the adverse influence of the unclean spirit. Yet many of this generation refuse to acknowledge or accept this and miss out on the redemptive purposes of God.

## The Spirit and Prophetic Discernment

Those who deny that Jesus is the redemptive agent of God empowered by the divine Spirit and who, as a consequence, refuse the benefits of the messianic mission often do so because they disregard the prophetic witness of the past. Matthew is careful to note that almost every aspect of Jesus life and work corresponds to what had been spoken though or written by the prophets. A continual refrain recurring throughout the Gospel is that significant incidents "fulfill what had been spoken" through various prophets (cf. 1:22; 2:5, 15, 17, 23; 4:14; 8:17; 12:17; 13:35; 21:4; 26:56). This correlation between prophetic expectation and messianic realization, along with Jesus's commitment to upholding righteousness, is key to the way in which Jesus fulfills both the Torah and the Prophets (5:17).[18] Many come to regard Jesus as a prophet (16:14; 21:11, 46) but very few recognize him as the one who fulfills the prophetic hopes expressed in the past. This is due in part to the hostility of people to the prophetic voice as evidenced in the pattern of persecuting and silencing the prophets.

An important theme in Matthew is that of the rejection and killing of the prophets. Jesus quotes the proverb, found in all the Gospels, that prophets are not without honor except among their own people (13:57). He rebukes the religious leaders for honoring the prophets and righteous who had been killed in the past and by this means seeking to absolve themselves from the sins of their fathers who had shed the blood of the prophets. But, as Jesus perceptively observes, in so doing they merely testify against themselves that they are the "sons" of those who killed the prophets

---

term "unclean spirit" appears. The passage refers to a cleansing of the land that will remove impediments to true faithfulness before God.

18. A distinctive feature of Matthew is that the prophet and the righteous person (*dikaios*) are presented at times as synonymous figures (10:41; 13:17; 23:29). For Matthew the prophet functions as a representative and advocate of covenantal righteousness. Therefore, those who practice lawlessness (*anomia*) cannot be considered true prophets (cf. 7:22–23).

(23:29–36). Their share in the sins of their fathers will become evident when Jesus sends them prophets, sages, and scribes whom they will kill, crucify, scourge, and persecute.[19] Jesus concludes his harsh censure of this generation with a lament over Jerusalem as a city that kills the prophets and stones those who are sent to her (23:37). That Jesus's contemporaries honor prophets of the past while killing prophets in the present indicates they lack the discernment to recognize those who are sent by God and to attend to what God speaks through them.

It is in the context of preparing his disciples for such persecution that Jesus makes a remarkable observation concerning the activity of the Spirit at such times which further highlights their role as prophets. They will be handed over to councils, scourged in synagogues, and brought before governors and kings (10:17–18).[20] At such times they are not to worry about how they are to speak or what they are to say, since what they are to say will be given to them in that hour. It will not be they who speak but "the Spirit of your Father" will speak through them (10:19–20).[21] Although not acknowledged as prophets by those who oppose them the disciples will, nonetheless, function as prophets speaking the words the Spirit of the Father gives them. They must discern what the Spirit wishes to speak through them and in this way provide a witness (*marturion*) to the Gentiles or nations (*ethnos*).[22] If, as is probable, their opponents refuse to listen and kill them, their witness further aligns them with the prophets of the past who spoke for God but were silenced.

Jesus's instruction to his disciples accords with what is intimated about his own mission in the Isaiah (42:1–4) quotation at 12:17–21. The context of the quotation is one in which opposition to Jesus takes a dramatic turn. It is immediately preceded by a sabbath controversy when Jesus heals a man with a withered hand. This motivates the Pharisees to conspire how they might destroy him (12:9–14). Following the quotation Jesus heals a blind and mute demoniac which prompts the Pharisees to charge that his exorcisms are the work of Satan (12:22–24). The quotation, from the first servant song of Isaiah, concerns the chosen servant of the Lord with whom he is pleased. The Lord declares that he will put "my Spirit" upon him with the result

---

19. The reversed time progression moving from killing to persecution may be for literary affect further connecting their actions not only to those of their fathers but even back to the blood of the righteous Abel (23:35). In the addendum to the final beatitude at 5:11, Jesus encourages persecuted disciples by noting that the prophets who came before them were also persecuted.

20. The description of persecution in 10:16–23 anticipates what is stated in 23:34 as well as matching the account of Jesus's own passion.

21. There are parallels to this statement at Mark 13:11, in the context of the eschatological discourse, and at Luke 12:11–12, where it is linked to the saying about blasphemy against the Holy Spirit (12:10). In those Gospels it is the "Holy Spirit" who speaks (Mark) or who teaches them what to say (Luke). Matthew is unique not only in the use of the phrase "the Spirit of God" but also in this reference to "the Spirit of the Father."

22. Compare the emphasis in Matthew's eschatological discourse where it is noted that even though the followers of Jesus will be handed over and put to death, nonetheless the good news of the kingdom will be proclaimed throughout the world as a witness to the nations (24:9–14).

that he will proclaim justice to the nations (*ethnos*). As a consequence of his work, justice will be victorious and in his name the nations will hope. Jesus carries forward his proclamation in the face of persecution speaking by the authority of the Father's Spirit.[23] His disciples similarly, in the face of persecution, speak under the direction of the Spirit of the Father. Additionally, as the servant of the Lord, Jesus fulfills Israel's vocation of bringing justice and hope to the nations. In a comparable manner the disciples, inspired by the Spirit, bear witness to the nations which now include Israel. This prophetic role of the disciples is most clearly represented at the close of Matthew's Gospel when they, having themselves been baptized in the name of the Father, Son, and Spirit, make disciples of all nations.

## Observations on Matthew's Perspective on the Spirit in Comparison with Luke

Although the prophetic element is developed to some extent in Matthew, Luke significantly expands this aspect of the Spirit's work. Whereas Matthew's infancy narrative places emphasis on the birth of Jesus as marking a new beginning, the opening of Luke largely focuses on the return of the prophetic Spirit to Israel. Luke's infancy account is distinguished by key individuals being filled with the Spirit and prophesying. It is perhaps significant that in Luke the term *genesis* is used only with reference to the birth of John the Baptist (1:14), presumably because he is a unique prophetic figure who is filled with the Holy Spirit before his birth as well as a transitional prophetic figure who marks the shift in the ages with the coming of the kingdom (cf. 7:28; 16:16).

The language of "filling" (*pimplēmi*) is essential to Luke's description of the prophetic Spirit. In the infancy account, and throughout Acts, people are typically filled with the Holy Spirit before speaking a prophetic word (cf. Luke 1:41–45, 67–79; Acts 2:4; 4:8–12, 31; 13:9–12). A common depiction in Acts of those who exemplify the various qualities produced by the Spirit is they are "full" (*plērēs*) of the Spirit along with those specific attributes whether they be wisdom, faith, generosity, etc. (cf. 6:3, 5, 8; 9:36; 11:24). This resonates with the description of Jesus who is "full" of the Spirit (4:1) following his baptism and just prior to his temptation. In Matthew Jesus's experience of the Spirit often serves to underscore the "fulfillment" (*plēroō*) of prophecy, while in Luke Jesus becomes the paradigm of what it means to be "full" of the Holy Spirit.

The connection between Spirit and power (*dunamis*) is also characteristic of Luke. Frequently Spirit and power are paired (Luke 1:17, 35; 4:14; Acts 1:8; 10:38) and, as in Matthew, the language of power is often suggestive of the Spirit (cf. Luke 4:36; 5:17; Acts 6:8). Luke, however, also closely associates power with the baptism in the Holy Spirit (Luke 24:49; Acts 1:8) which is not the case in Matthew. As noted above,

---

23. In view of the allusion to Isa 42:1 in the declaration of the Father when the Spirit comes upon Jesus at his baptism it is appropriate to understand "my Spirit" here as "the Spirit of the Father."

for Matthew baptism in the Holy Spirit is closely associated with the obedience and righteousness to which Jesus calls his disciples.

Both Matthew and Luke explain Jesus's experience of the Spirit with reference to the servant of Isaiah. Matthew at 12:17–21 presents Jesus as the servant upon whom the Lord places his Spirit in order to accomplish his justice for the sake of the nations. Luke, in the inaugural sermon at Nazareth, has Jesus declare the fulfillment of Isa 61:1–2 and thus identifies himself as the one anointed by the Spirit of the Lord to announce the good news of release to those who are oppressed (4:16–19).[24] The précis of Jesus's ministry at Acts 10:38 echoes the language of this prophecy in describing Jesus as one anointed by the Holy Spirit who went about doing good and healing all who were oppressed by the devil.

Matthew and Luke share much in common with respect to their understanding of the Spirit which is not surprising since they draw from much the same tradition. Different emphases obviously emerge relating to different interests and concerns. There is, however, a certain irony evident in their use of Isaiah's servant to describe Jesus's experience of the Spirit. Matthew portrays Jesus as the one given the Spirit in order to accomplish God's purposes for the Gentiles, which is a significant Lukan theme. Luke, on the other hand, portrays Jesus as the one anointed by the Spirit to bring about the restoration of Israel, a key interest of Matthew. This interconnecting of theological interests suggests that their perspectives on the role and activity of the Holy Spirit are not significantly different but rather serve to complement each other.

---

24. Isa 61:1–7 is typically not counted among the servant songs of Isaiah since the servant is not mentioned. However, in view of the importance of this passage to Luke's Christology and the fact that in the early chapters of Acts Jesus is often referred to as the "servant" (*pais*, the same term used in the LXX for Isaiah's servant; cf. Acts 3:13, 26; 4:25, 27, 30) it appears that Luke considers this passage as one of the servant songs.

## Chapter 19

# The Holy Spirit in Mark

### RIKK WATTS[1]

Mark is generally regarded as having little to say about the Holy Spirit.[2] Even allowing for his Gospel's being half the length of Luke or John, its six references to the (Holy) Spirit (1:8, 10, 12; 3:29; 12:31; 13:11) are significantly outweighed by their particular and famous emphases on the Spirit/Paraclete. Matthew, too, hardly matches Luke and John. But his two "birth narrative" references (1:18, 20) and unique account of Jesus as Isaiah 42:1–4's Spirit-anointed servant (12:17–21)[3] still constitute a significant expansion of the Spirit's role compared to Mark.

Nonetheless, of Mark's references, four—fully two thirds—closely associate the Spirit with Jesus. Significantly, three are concentrated in the context-setting prologue (1:8, 10, 12) with the final fourth appearing quite early, in Jesus's own words, and at the climax of the pivotal Beelzebul controversy (3:29). Three speak directly to Jesus's ministry (1:8, 12; 3:29), and one, principally, to his identity (1:10), though two others are highly suggestive (1:8; 3:29). Of these four, the first and last alone use the full expression "the Holy Spirit" which could suggest bracketing (see below). Strikingly,

---

1. Though I've met Roger Stronstad just the once and even then in passing, I first encountered his work during my seminary studies. Thank you, Roger, for setting an example to us younger Pentecostals of the profound necessity, for the well-being of our movement in particular and the kingdom in general, of engaging deeply, rigorously, and passionately, with Scripture. I offer this essay in honor of that legacy.

2. See, e.g., earlier Barrett, *Holy Spirit*, 140–43; then Hengel, *Charismatic*, 63; Best, *Story*, 77. The single major work of which I am aware is Mansfield, *"Spirit."* He proposes that Mark's redactional highlighting of the Spirit is to counter false prophets in his church who appealed, for their authority, to their signs and wonders as the work of the exalted Jesus. Reminding them of Christ's sufferings and cross-bearing discipleship, Mark validated his case by inserting material about, and in other places emphasizing, the Spirit's role in Jesus's earthly ministry (1:8; 3:29; 12:36; 13:11). Creating a unique genre, his Gospel's repristinated Jesus, himself baptized in the empowering and authoritative Spirit—whose presence can then be seen, or at least mostly implied throughout the work—provides a more balanced model for charismatic practice

3. See, e.g., Beaton, *Christ*, 122–91.

nothing more is explicitly said of Jesus's relationship to the Spirit in the remaining 85 percent of Mark.

The final two references, both now to the Holy Spirit and both also in Jesus's own words, occur in Mark's final "third," in Jerusalem (12:31; 13:11). In the first, he invokes the Holy Spirit to underscore the authority of David's declaration (Ps 110:1), thereby heightening its remarkable implications for his Messianic identity (Mark 12:31; cf. 1:3). In the second, he assures his disciples that the same authoritative Spirit will give them what to say when on trial during their proclamation of the gospel to all nations (13:10–11).

Concentrating on the Spirit's relationship to Jesus, this paper will argue that for Mark, John's promised overwhelming baptism in the Holy Spirit (Mark 1:8) is not merely a reference to a future event in Acts (1:5; 11:16; cf. 1 Cor 12:13). It is already powerfully apparent in Jesus's ministry (Mark 3:29).[4] Evident from the outset in Jesus's private Spirit-driven inaugural defeat of the "strong man" (1:12–13; cf. 3:27), the Holy Spirit's formidable presence is especially clear in Jesus's very public and awe-inspiring mastery of the unclean spirits (e.g., 1:27–28; 3:11; 5:1–20; hence 3:22). Second, to the extent the Holy Spirit is identified with the Lord himself (LXX Isa 63:8–11; Ps 139[138]:7), Mark's close identification of Jesus with the Holy Spirit (3:28–29) both confirms the Gospel's opening designation of Jesus as "Lord" (1:3), and affirms Jesus's implicit self-identification in citing the Holy Spirit-inspired David (12:31; Ps 110:1). Third, this identification demonstrates that in Jesus Isaiah's last great prayer for a new Exodus is now being fulfilled (Isa 49:24 in Mark 3:27; cf. 1:12–13). Fourth, and on the other hand, the descent of the Spirit in the form of a dove speaks to Jesus's identification with God's true Israel (1:10). For Mark, then, the presence of the Spirit testifies to Jesus first and most importantly as the "strong man"-binding Lord, but also as God's Spirit-indwelt true Israel-son. Fifth and finally, with all this in view it appears that for Mark the Holy Spirit-inspired testimony of the disciples before the nations should at least principally be a matter of testifying to, and embodying, the overwhelming power and authority of the Lord Jesus (cf. esp. Acts).

## Mark's Prologue: John's Message and Jesus's Baptism

Our first encounter with the Spirit in Mark's Gospel is in John the Baptist's preaching (1:8). Contextually, John is Malachi's Elijah (Mark 9:13; cf. 1:6; 6:16–29; Mal 4:5, ET). In various Jewish traditions, Elijah was expected to prepare the nation for the Lord's return to Israel at the end of days (Mal 4:5–6, ET).[5] This coheres with Mark's opening editorial citation of Isaiah (Mark 1:2–3). First, it locates his larger narrative horizons

---

4. This, I subsequently discovered, is also the position of Brown, *Miracles*, 300–310, citing the earlier broader study of Yates, *Spirit*, who emphasized "the sifting and judging" role of the Spirit.

5. E.g., Sir 48:9–10; *Tanḥ.* Exod 6:12; cf. 4 Ezra 6:26; 4Q521 2 III, 1; 4Q558 1 II, 4. See further Watts, "Mark," 118–20.

within the eschatological hopes predominantly of Isaiah—far and away the most popular prophet in this period—but also of Malachi, both of which are concerned with the coming not of the Messiah but of the Lord himself. Second, the specific mention of the messenger who is to prepare the Lord's way (Mark 1:3; Isa 40:3) is immediately realized in John (Mark 1:4–8) who appears as promised "in the wilderness" (v. 4a; 1:3a, NRSV).

The climax of Mark's introduction of John comes in 1:7–8 with a two-part declaration. As one might expect of a preparatory messenger, it concerns the one who comes after him. Already anticipating this to be the Lord (1:3b), Mark's John tells us, first, that the coming one is stronger and unimaginably more exalted than himself (v. 7), and, second, that he (i.e., the coming one) will "baptize you with the Holy Spirit" (v. 8). Several points can be made.

First, although frequent in later Jewish writings, the exact phrase "Holy Spirit" is surprisingly rare in Israel's Scriptures,[6] especially when compared to the more than one hundred references, *simpliciter*, to the "Spirit" (of God / of the Lord). It occurs once in a traditionally Davidic Psalm where David implores God to create in him a clean heart (51:10a, ET) and not to remove his "holy spirit" from him (51:11, ET).[7] The only other two occurrences, and the only ones in an eschatologically oriented text, are in the last great Isaianic lament (Isa 63:10–11).

Here, the prophet recalls the Lord's saving act of the Exodus, when through the angel of his presence he himself saved them (Isa 63:9).[8] But Israel grieved his holy spirit, who[9] according to Psalm 139 [138]:7 is equivalent to the Lord's presence, causing God to become their enemy (v. 10). After lamenting the absence of the one who set his holy spirit in "his" (Moses's or the people's)[10] midst, the prophet concludes with a plea that the Lord might, as he had in the past, again rend the heavens, come down, and perform fearful and amazing mighty deeds that caused his adversaries to tremble (64:1–3, ET; cf. LXX).

---

6. Whereas it is customary in NT scholarship to range across the full gamut of intertestamental and rabbinic literatures, since Israel's Scriptures appear to be Mark's only cited authoritative written source (e.g., 1:2; 7:6; 11:17; 14:27; cf. 1:11, 44; 2:25; 4:12; 7:6–7, 10; 10:19; etc.), we will focus mainly on them.

7. See LXX Dan 5:12; 6:4 which describe Daniel as having "a holy spirit in him."

8. Following the MT, which closely identifies the "angel of his presence/face" with the Lord himself; see Blenkinsopp, *Isaiah*, 252; apparently combining Exodus' promise of "angel" (Exod 33:2) with "my face/presence" (Exod 33:14). Reflecting a clearer syntactic structure, the LXX reads Exod 33:8b, 9a as one: it was no angel but the Lord himself who saved them. This apparently sees Exodus' offer (Exod 33:14) of God's own presence (33:18), instead of an "angel" (33:2), as Moses's preferred option. See further, e.g., Goldin, "Angel."

9. The personal pronoun is appropriate since only persons can be grieved.

10. The MT and Syriac have the singular, probably referring to Moses in the preceding v. 11a and following v. 12a. Alternatively, perhaps because of the plurals throughout, LXX and Tg. have the plural here, meaning the people.

What makes this latter text of particular interest is not only its eschatological perspective, but also its parallels with Mark's account of John's setting and preaching. Isaiah 63:7–14 is the only place in all of Israel's Scriptures where the presence of the Lord's "holy spirit" among his people, their passing through the waters (sea), and a reference to Israel's "desert" journey appear together. Given, too, the intimate identification of the Lord's presence with his holy spirit, one might expect that the Lord's longed-for descent through the rent heavens (64:1–3) would be similarly attended by the manifestation of his holy spirit.

It looks, then, as though both John's practice and his promise of a future baptism in the Holy Spirit have been shaped by Isaiah 63's unique Exodus memory.[11] If so, whereas John can recapitulate Israel's passing through the waters, he is well aware that he cannot baptise with the Holy Spirit. That prerogative belongs solely to God (e.g., Joel 3:1–2 [2:28–29, ET]; Isa 32:15; 44:3; Ezek 11:19; 36:26–27; 37:14; 39:29).[12] So, given the Isaiah 63–64 background, that prerogative's exercise is implicitly and intimately linked to the awesome intervention (64:3) of the avenging Yahweh-Warrior (see Isa 63:16; cf. vv. 1–6).[13]

This is exactly what Mark's opening Malachi 3:1 citation implies, and his Elijah John's call for repentance makes explicit: the coming of Yahweh's fearful presence and of his Holy Spirit presages severe judgment on his adversaries, including his faithless people. It had happened in the past when a rebellious Israel grieved the Lord's Holy Spirit in his first Exodus's coming (Isa 63:10, the Lord himself becoming their enemy). Also, Isaiah and Malachi had both warned it could happen again during his second Exodus coming (Isa 64:3; 65:1—66:6, 14b–16, 24b; Mal 3:5–6; 4:1, 3, 6b; cf. Isa 63:3–6).

This might explain John's strikingly original use of "to baptise" and "stronger than." The usual eschatological language is of the Spirit being "poured out" (e.g., Isa 44:3; Ezek 39:29; Joel 2:28, 29, ET; 4Q504 f1 2Rv:15).[14] Yet, if Mark's John is drawing on Isaiah 63's Exodus imagery, then his recapitulation of Israel's historic passing through the windswept sea (cf. 1 Cor 10:2; Mark 1:10; Isa 63:11), especially in light of the fate of Pharaoh's armies past, would warrant his striking use of "baptism/to baptise" which elsewhere frequently describes traumatic and final events, such as foundering ships overwhelmed by monstrous seas,[15] the catastrophic destruction of Jerusalem by

---

11. See Webb, *Baptizer*, 360–66, who similarly but more broadly suggests an exodus/new exodus background. Unsurprisingly, Israel's ancient Exodus and conquest traditions seem also to have shaped the proclamations of several other contemporary "prophets," especially Theudas (Josephus, *Ant.* 20.97–8), but also the Egyptian (Josephus, *J.W.* 2.261–63; *Ant.* 20.169–72). See also Josephus, *J.W.* 2.258–60; *Ant.* 20:167–8. Further, Horsley, "Types"; Barnett, "Sign."

12. Further, e.g., 1QS 4:20–21. T. Jud. 24:2–3; T. Levi 18:11, are sometimes cited as evidence of the Messiah pouring out the Spirit. But only the latter is specific, and both appear to be Christian interpolations.

13. On John's "coming one" being Yahweh, see Hughes, "Forerunner," and works cited therein.

14. For individuals who were "filled," see Exod 31:3; Mic 3:8, or, far more commonly, "upon" whom the spirit came, e.g., Num 11:25; 24:2; 27:18; Jud 3:10; 11:6; 1 Sam 16:13; etc. or would come, Isa 61:1.

15. Josephus, *Ant.* 9.212, the extreme threat to Jonah's vessel; Josephus, *J.W.* 3.368, 525.

the Romans,[16] personal disaster (by Jesus [Mark 10:38–39]), individuals drowning whether in an act of murder,[17] in naval warfare,[18] or, again, in mountainous seas,[19] the soul being overwhelmed by impetuous passions or drunkenness,[20] or a suicide burying his sword in his own bowels.[21] Such a sense would be more than appropriate in an already threatening context.

The equally striking comparative—the one who is "stronger than me"—similarly suggests overmastering judgment. The comparative is itself unknown as a description of an expected eschatological human agent. On the other hand, given that "strong/mighty" is a *topos* for Yahweh, the comparative "stronger" does occur in three places in relation to God's unyielding and irresistible judicial decision (1 Cor 10:22; Rab. Eccl. 6:9; Tg. Eccl. 6:10).[22] From this perspective, John knows that the Lord himself is coming in inescapable and devastating judgment and, as in the case of Jeremiah 15:1, it cannot be turned aside. Lest they be swept away with the rest of the Lord's adversaries, Israel's only hope is to repent. This seems to be the logic behind Jesus's questioning response to the Temple hierarchs' challenging of his authority (11:27): their Temple will be destroyed (Mark 11:17; 13) and the land cursed (11:1–14, 20; cf. Mal 4:6b) because they refused to submit to John's call for repentance.

When combined, these various elements suggest that, within Mark's Scriptural horizons, John's "baptism" in the "Holy Spirit" was mostly a matter of the Lord's overpowering eschatological judgment upon his adversaries and with it the overwhelming end of one age and the beginning of another. Of course, this is not to deny the very positive sense that was already, if rarely, in circulation by the time Mark writes (e.g., Acts 1:4–5; 11:15–16, the latter in parallel with "fell"). My point here is simply to note, in keeping with the Scripture's thorough-going blessing/curse duality, that the positive sense is not the only one. Indeed, given the implications of the "baptism/stronger one" language and John's call to repentance, it is likely not the one he foregrounded. This might be one reason why Mark does not say that Jesus himself was "baptized" in the Spirit during his baptism.

## Jesus's Baptism

In the context of John's preparing the way "of the Lord" (1:3) and his culminating announcement of the "Spirit-baptizing" "coming stronger one" (1:7–8), Mark's

---

16. Josephus, *J.W.* 4.137; cf. 2.556, a hopelessly lost city
17. Josephus, *Ant.* 15.55; *J.W.* 1.437.
18. Josephus, *J.W.* 3.525, 527.
19. Josephus, *J.W.* 3.423.
20. Philo, *Alleg. Interp.* 3.18; *Worse* 176; *Migr.* 204; *Contempl.* 46; *Prov.* 2.67.
21. Josephus, *J.W.* 2.476. Further, Taylor, *Immerser*, 49–52.
22. Watts, "Stronger," 6–12.

statement that Jesus "came" (1:9) most naturally identifies Jesus as the coming Lord (cf. 12:35–37; already in 1 Cor 8:6; 1 Thess 1:1; also Col 2:9).[23]

But as noted in the introduction, the voice from heaven subsequently also identifies Jesus as God's Isaianic servant, Davidic messianic king (Ps 2:7; Isa 42:1 in Mark 1:11), and, allowing the scene's Exodus-like setting, his true son Israel.[24] Just as Isaiah 63's Exodus memory recalled the Lord's putting his Holy Spirit among/in his "sons" as he brought them up out of the sea (vv. 8, 11), so also in Mark the Spirit descends on/into Jesus. Although much debated and unable to be argued here, since the dove is most frequently associated with Israel (Hos 7:9–11;[25] Ps 74:19; 4 Ezra 5:26; Mek. Exod 12:36; 14:13 [citing Cant. 2:14], 21, 24, 31; Tg. Ps 68:14; b. Ber. 53b), the voice and context strongly suggest an interpretation along this line.[26] According to the prophets, the indwelling eschatological Spirit would enable formerly "silly" dove-Israel (Hos 7:11) to "know" the Lord and follow his law (Isa 44:3; Ezek 11:17–21; 36:24–31; 39:25–29; Jer 8:7a). The dove-like Spirit's "descent" (1:10; cf. LXX Isa 63:14a) into Jesus (not "hovering over/upon" as numerous other alternatives require) speaks to the Spirit's role in Jesus's true son-like obedience to and dependence upon his father (cf. Isa 63:14, 16; "father," bis).

## Jesus's Confrontation with Satan in the Desert

In view of the above, we are not surprised to learn that the very first Spirit-related activity of Jesus, who will himself baptize in the Holy Spirit, was his being "driven/cast out" into a wilderness confrontation with Satan (1:12–13). Mark's use of the same word that elsewhere describes Jesus's driving out of unclean spirits (v. 12; cf. 1:34, 39; 3:15, 22–23; 6:13), and which characteristically occasioned the crowds' fearful and amazed response (e.g., 1:27–28; 5:17), continues the sense of the awesome encounter earlier implied by John's pairing of "baptism/stronger one."

Even so, that this is a "testing" indicates that the encounter was not about brute power. In keeping with the Spirit-dove symbolism, it was instead a question of Jesus's faithfulness and obedience to his immediately preceding and heaven-rending "commission." In this sense the temptation can be seen as integral to the baptism account (cf. v. 12's "and immediately" with its being used to link vv. 9 and 10).[27] If we allow that John's baptism is already a recapitulation of the "exodus," then the obvious parallels—between Israel's post-sea wilderness journey and Jesus's post-baptismal forty-day

---

23. On Mark's "Yahweh" Christology, see Watts, *New*, 86–88, 135–82. Perhaps unsurprising given Paul's earlier and already unproblematic inclusion of Jesus in the *Shema*. See Fee, *Christology*, 88–94.

24. For a recent survey and discussion, see Watts, "Mark," 122–29.

25. Noting it is Israel who is silly, whereas doves, in contrast to "my people who do not know the ordinance of the Lord," are exemplary (Jer 8:7).

26. Watts, "Stronger One," 12–17.

27. See Gibson, "Wilderness."

wilderness sojourn—confirm as much. Just as Israel's faithfulness and obedience was tested in the first exodus, so, too, Jesus in this fulfillment of Isaiah's hoped for new exodus.

But in all such cases the differences are at least as, if not more, significant. In the first Exodus, God tested Israel. But following the voice's resounding affirmation (Mark 1:11), and as we already know Jesus is both Lord (1:3) and the Spirit-baptising coming stronger one (1:7–8), such is hardly needed or even appropriate. Instead, it is Satan who tempts. Even though Mark's brevity borders on terse—a clear statement of the catastrophic consequences of Satan's failure will have to wait until the very public declaration in the Beelzebul controversy (3:22–27)—it is evident from the outset that the Lord's chief adversary has been bested. Not only do the angels come to minister—hardly likely if Jesus had betrayed his messianic servant sonship—but also his soon-to-follow first public appearance in a Synagogue is a stunning display of his awesome authority, expressed particularly in his effortless dismissal of a terrified and impotent unclean spirit (1:23–28).[28] This authority is apparently so impressive as to warrant special mention as a singular characteristic of his early ministry (1:34, 39; 3:11–12). Indeed, it is so notable as to become the focus of Jesus's first, and potentially lethal, encounter with the hostile authorities from Jerusalem (3:22).

Several observations can quickly be offered. First, in Mark, Jesus's defeat of Satan (cf. 3:27, see below) is predicated, not on brute spiritual power, but on his dove-like-Spirit-inspired faithfulness to God's call.[29] This might say something to Mark's audience as to the true nature of "spiritual warfare."[30] Second, although Jesus will continue to encounter Satan's demonic minions and even humans who act as his proxies, from this moment on, Satan himself is impressively absent. He never again personally confronts Jesus. This suggests that what transpired in the Temptation was significant enough to render Satan impotent of any future *direct personal* opposition to Jesus.[31] This would explain why every one of Jesus's subsequent demonic confrontations, including "Legion," was for all intents and purposes over before they began (beginning with 1:23–26, and classically, 5:6–10). When Jesus is present, Satan is simply incapable

---

28. We should not forget, however, that before being declared God's messianic servant son (Mark 1:11), Jesus is already Lord and stronger one (1:3, 8). Just as only God can baptize in his Spirit (1:8), only he can destroy unclean spirits (1:24). Reading Mark aright requires both identities to be affirmed together.

29. This correlation might explain the only occasion in which we hear of the disciples' failure to cast out an unclean spirit, 9:14–29. They had only recently rebuffed Jesus's embrace of the cross, 8:31–38; cf. 8:14–23.

30. Reflected, perhaps, in Galatians' description of true freedom being expressed in the fruit of the Spirit (Gal 5:13–26) and Ephesians' emphasis on maintaining the unity brought by the Spirit as a demonstration of Christ's victory over the powers (Eph 4:1—6:9) and as the basis for their collectively putting on the armor of God (Eph 6:10–20).

31. Luke alone speaks of Satan's departing until an opportune time (Luke 4:13) most commonly associated with the Passion (22:3, 31). But the first (22:3) is through a human agent, and the second (22:31) does not concern Jesus, but his disciples.

of offering any aid. Third, this defeat, however, is effective only for Jesus; it does not mean Satan's complete removal from the scene. Clearly, he and his agents are still active in the lives of others (e.g., 4:15).

## The Beelzebul Controversy

One point that cannot be denied here is that Jesus, in front of the crowds, his family, and for the first time, Jerusalem's scribes, is anything but reticent in identifying himself, and in particular his undeniable power over unclean spirits, with the presence and activity of the Holy Spirit (3:28–30).[32] Several features attest the account's pivotal and climactic role. As already noted, this is the first time we meet scribes from Jerusalem, specially arrived from the capital to offer their "authoritative" denunciation of Jesus's manifest authority over the unclean spirits (3:22). We first heard of scribes in general back in Jesus's inaugural synagogue-demonstration of his authority, compared to which they had none (1:22, 27). They later appear in person and on both occasions are unstintingly critical of Jesus's words and deeds (2:6, 16).

The Beelzebul controversy, then, essentially crystalizes the tension that began in the Capernaum synagogue, rapidly escalated due to Jesus's subsequently burgeoning reputation (1:21–45), and peaked in his increasingly outrageous words and deeds, such that some had already sought his death (2:1–3:6). Given Mark's emphasis on the crucifixion in Jerusalem, it is easy to miss his claim that attempts against Jesus's life began very early and in Galilee. The Jerusalem scribes' potentially lethal accusation is of one cloth with the Pharisees' and Herodians' plot (3:6). But in levelling that charge, a blasphemously unforgiveable line had been crossed (3:28–30). A rupture has opened up in Israel and from here on everyone, including Jesus's family, must now choose to be either insiders or outsiders (3:31–35; 4:1–34). The extent of the material (3:20–35) and its triple chiastic structure further emphasize the exchange's significance.[33]

In question is the source of Jesus's authority. After implicitly rebuking their foolishly slanderous "Beelzebul" by instead speaking of Satan (v. 23b; cf. Jude 9; 2 Pet 2:11), Jesus demonstrates the impossibility of their assertion with three counterfactual conditional clauses (vv. 24–26). The last is noteworthy. What initially looks like a past simple condition (v. 26a)—"If Satan was divided against himself, except that he is not divided"—has two unexpected present indicatives in its apodosis "but, nevertheless, he is in fact unable to stand and is at an end." If this is Mark's sense, then Jesus is

---

32. See Barrett, *Holy Spirit*, 158, for whom one reason for the relative paucity of (Holy) Spirit texts is that "direct emphasis upon the Spirit had to be avoided . . . because Jesus was keeping his Messianic secret." There is no such avoidance here.

33. As follows: (a) the crowds come to Jesus (Mark 3:20); (b) Jesus's family hear and take action, thinking he is beside himself (3:21); (c) the Jerusalem scribes make their accusation; (d) Jesus's response and counter accusation (3:23–29); (c1) the scribes' accusation restated (3:30); (b1) Jesus's family seek to take charge (3:31); (a1) the crowds who sit around Jesus are his new family (3:32–35). Initially, Watts, *New*, 145, and now "Mark," 145, and the literature cited therein.

affirming that Satan's rule is indeed at an end (cf. the panicked unclean spirit's question concerning "us," 1:24). But this is not because he is divided against himself (v. 26a). It is instead because Jesus has already bound the strong man and so can forthwith plunder his house (v. 27).

The only place this kind of language appears in Israel's Scriptures is Isaiah 49:24. There, God promises to deliver Israel from the apparently unassailable strong man Babylon (in fulfillment of Isa 40:1–11; noting also Mark's opening and horizon-establishing appeal to Isa 40:3). Jesus's allusion to this text implies that it finds its ultimate fulfillment in his prior ("first") personal binding (and hence defeat) of Yahweh's and therefore of Israel's ultimate adversary, Satan.[34] Hence, what might initially seem contradictory—how can Jesus argue first from the fact that Satan's kingdom is yet standing (Mark 3:24–25) and then declare that it is in fact ending (3:26–27)?[35]—is resolved by the earlier recognition that the temptation's defeat of Satan is localized around the person of Jesus, himself; I would argue, Mark's "mystery of the kingdom" (4:12). The "end" of Satan's kingdom, if we will, radiates out from faithful Jesus's authoritative personal presence.

Although hotly debated,[36] the only place in Mark's narrative where this "first" binding (3:27) could have happened—and how can one bind one's opponent without first defeating him?—was during the Temptation.[37] If so, then perhaps Mark's reason for his disconcerting brevity on the Temptation is that he wanted to delay, and wanted his readers to recognize it as a deliberate delay, any comment on the outcome and especially its significance until there was clear, public, and evidential warrant of Jesus's victory. Ironically, this is exactly what his most prominent opponents, the Jerusalem scribes, provide.

Given the controversy's pivotal role, it is likely significant, too, that (a) this is the last time Mark speaks of Jesus's relation to the Spirit, (b) it is the only time he does so using Jesus's own words, and (c) Jesus himself uses John's unusual "Holy Spirit." That this is Jesus's final word on the matter—from this point on there will be neither further clarification nor even comment—strongly suggests that Jesus is here giving his own climactic take on the true significance of his fulfillment of John's own earlier climactic declaration (1:8). What Mark's opening appeal to Malachi evoked, and John's arresting "baptism/stronger one" terminology implied, is now made clear. The Holy Spirit baptism of which John spoke means first and foremost the stronger Lord Jesus's overwhelming engulfing of his adversaries: Satan and his unclean spirits/demons.[38]

34. Again, Watts, *New*, 140–57; "Mark," 145–48.
35. E.g., Marcus, *Mark*, 1:282–83.
36. See, e.g., Twelftree, *Exorcist*, 111–17; Stein, *Mark*, 185.
37. Argued earlier by Best, *Passion*, esp. 12, 61; though admittedly with some unresolved issues, hopefully answered in Watts, "Cross."
38. See Pimental, "Unclean Spirits," 175, for whom Jesus understood his exorcisms to be "the beginning of the purification of the whole world into the kingdom of God."

In the context of this ultimate antithesis between the unclean and the holy, to identify Jesus's actions with Satan is inexcusably culpable, and doubly so for those leaders from Jerusalem who hold themselves expert in Scripture. It is nothing short of blaspheming the Holy Spirit. That Jesus is already the Lord, and the Spirit-baptizing stronger one, necessarily implies, as it did in Isaiah 63:9–12 and Psalm 139 [138]:7, his intimate identification of the Holy Spirit with himself.

Consequently, in the light of the clear centrality of Israel's Scriptures for Mark, it is probably not accidental that "the closest, and perhaps, the only . . . parallel" to blaspheming the Holy Spirit is in Isaiah 63:10.[39] If so, then from Mark's Jesus's perspective, just as Israel had grieved God's holy spirit thereby making God their enemy, so now in this new exodus. In rejecting such clear evidence of God's awesome and fearful intervention, the Jerusalem scribes place themselves in serious jeopardy of again making God their enemy. John's Holy Spirit-baptism by the coming stronger one means, for them, that Jesus's announcement of the Temple's coming destruction (11:12–22, 27–33; 12:1–9; 13) is already looming.

## David by the Holy Spirit Declared . . .

It is, therefore, probably not co-incidental that the next time the Holy Spirit is explicitly mentioned, and that after a very long absence, is in the final controversies in Jerusalem (12:13–37). Having silenced his opponents (12:34b), Jesus turns the tables by asking his own question to which, again, they have no answer (cf. 11:29–33). For the first time in public, Jesus challenges the view that the Messiah is merely David's son (12:35–37).

Although Jesus's messianic identity has always been present (1:11; 8:27–30; 9:7; cf. 3:11; 5:7; 10:47–48), it really only comes to the fore and in a flurry of texts beginning with his entry into Jerusalem (Ps 118:25–26 and 22–23 in 11:9–10 and 12:10–11 respectively; Ps 110:1 in 12:36 and 14:62; Ps 22:19, 8, 2 in 15:24, 29, 34 respectively).[40] Even so, Jesus's appeal to Psalm 110:1 is the first time he speaks publicly about the Messiah, whom he then, in the one breath, and in a uniquely explicit messianic interpretation, provocatively identifies as the Lord.

We cannot here explore the exegetical details,[41] but several observations can be made. As in the climax of the Galilee confrontations Jesus had invoked the Holy Spirit, so, too, here at the climax of their Jerusalem equivalents. And both speak to his identity. In the first, Jesus intimately connects his exorcisms with the Holy Spirit's *work*,

39. Barrett, *Holy Spirit*, 104–5.

40. Watts, "Psalms."

41. See further, Watts, "Mark," 220–23. Interestingly, Ps 110 is often understood as a new development of the promises in Ps 2. Both are cited twice in Mark, Ps 2 by the heavenly voice speaking to Jesus's identity (Mark 1:11; 9:7) and Ps 110, by Jesus, and again speaking to his identity (Mark 12:36; 14:62).

which in Mark's horizon signifies the Lord's presence. Here, the Holy Spirit's *word* now explicitly affirms Jesus as the Lord. Second, if denying the former blasphemed the Holy Spirit, then surely also denying that Jesus is Lord does the same. The scribes having made God their enemy, Jesus immediately goes on to denounce them (12:38–44), and leaving the Temple for the last time, announces its imminent destruction (Mark 13). Third, Jesus's Lord-son sequence (12:37) can be seen to echo Mark's prologue: Jesus is first "the Lord" (1:2–3; cf. 1:7–8) before he is declared "son" (1:11). Hence, the cluster of Davidic psalms notwithstanding, Jesus comes to the city first as its Lord. This might explain why the Spirit is hardly prominent in Mark. What really matters is Jesus's identity as Lord[42] and it is this to which the Holy Spirit primarily bears witness.

## Jesus's Promise to the Disciples

Here we must be brief. That the "Holy Spirit" appears first in John's testimony about Jesus, then Jesus's testimony about himself, and next in Jesus's appeal to David's testimony about him, strongly suggests that this final occurrence (13:11) also speaks to bearing testimony, but this time by the disciples. Nothing is said of what the Holy Spirit will give them to say, but if Mark's previous indications are any guide, we may expect at least two things. First, the disciples will bear witness to Jesus's identity (e.g., classically, the Holy Spirit-filled Peter, Acts 4:8–12, 33) as Lord and messianic son. Second, this bearing witness similarly implies eschatological division, which depending on how the hearers respond will result ultimately in life for some and being swept away for others (e.g., Acts 2:34–41).

## Conclusion

Although John's promise of a baptism in the Holy Spirit is traditionally seen as anticipating Pentecost, this paper has argued that for Mark this baptism had already begun in Jesus. Whereas outside the Gospels, Spirit "baptism" means being "filled with" or "receiving" the Spirit, for Mark this initial "baptism" was largely a matter of Satan's kingdom being overwhelmingly swept away in and through the overmastering person of Jesus, in whom the Lord himself was awesomely present, and to which fact the Holy Spirit bore witness. This reality is clearly registered by the utter discomfort of the unclean spirits, no matter how powerful, whose defeated and bound master had from the outset been rendered incapable of aiding them. This being so, as John warned, Israel's only hope was to repent. To reject this Lord, would mean suffering the same fate. At the same time, the Spirit also marks Jesus out as David's messianic son, and faithful servant Israel. As the disciples take this gospel to the nations, the same Spirit will enable them to bear witness to these same realities.

---

42. See Watts, *New*, 86–88, 135–82; Fee, *Christology*, 88–94.

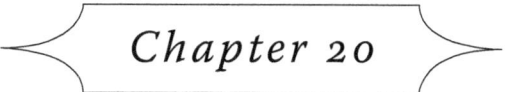

# Chapter 20

## The Paraclete

### *The Spirit of Prophecy in the Johannine Community*

BENNY AKER[1]

The Spirit as Paraclete in John is a mountain that many have assailed. Here is yet another attempt to ascend it. This essay will focus on the Paraclete in John's Gospel leaning upon the patronage system of the first century to explain its meaning and setting. Studies in social-scientific criticism are fleshing out the patronage background of the NT in the first century. Particularly within this social setting, Jesus is the broker (mediator) between God and humans.[2] In the farewell discourse of John, the Spirit is called the Paraclete and functions as broker acting as the attendant mediator[3] on behalf of the incarnate Jesus who is now absent. In this role he is a subordinate mediator,[4] for Jesus is the primary one. (Both Jesus and the Spirit retain the equal

---

1. Steve Hendrickson (Hendrickson Publisher's Inc.) and I worked together to form a publishing venture to give Pentecostal and Charismatic scholars and writers a venue for their voice. At the time, a dearth existed for venues like this, a place where more scholarly approaches, even different methods and viewpoints, could be aired. We sensed a great need of this nature to advance Pentecostalism and other spiritual awakenings. During the early stages of this startup, William (Bill) Menzies called to suggest that I look at a manuscript that another publisher in Springfield had turned down—It was Roger Stronstad's Master's Thesis. We agreed to publish it—we tried to take away some of the formal characteristics of a thesis to make it more presentable to the public. And as they say, the rest is history. It made quite a contribution to Pentecostalism and brought some recognition for Hendrickson. I speak not only for myself but also for Hendrickson Publishers when I express gratitude to Roger, not only for this first book, but for succeeding ones and for his influence over the years.

2. See deSilva, *Honor, Patronage, Kinship & Purity*; Brown, *Spirit in the Writings of John*; Danker, "Benefactor." The literature is quite plentiful on this topic. Brown contains an excellent discussion on just the concept of "broker. Other words for broker occur in the NT. With Jesus and the Spirit both perceived as brokers, it should be noted that exclusiveness is profoundly emphasized. In the first-century world, a great deal of competitiveness between brokers existed. John clearly presented Jesus and then the Spirit as the only way to God.

3. See further below.

4. The term belongs to Brown, *Spirit in the Writings of John*. By subordinate, I mean "according to

status with the Father as brokers do in the brokerage system. Only the functions differ.) Thus, Jesus sends another comforter who will mediate him and the Father in all things. Also, what has emerged in the last few years is that scholars are realizing that both Luke-Acts and John depended, especially, upon Isaiah 40–55 for their stories of Jesus and the Spirit. These accounts of Jesus and his messianic ministry are the narratives of the new exodus promised in the Hebrew Bible, especially in Isaiah, bringing redemption and cleansing to Israel's remnant.[5] Isaiah also laid out the plan for the salvation of the Gentiles incorporating them into the kingdom of God. The prophet promised judgment to the hardhearted people and salvation to the remnant, to those who waited for the promise of God (Isa 40). The conditions of an obdurate people in Isaiah's time endured into the first century.

## Issues in Interpreting Paraclete

The first, and perhaps the most important, issue we mention relates to the source for paraclete. The root of "paraclete" occurs in the verbal form (*parakaleō*)[6] with some frequency, the noun *paraklēsis* also appears often in a variety of places; but the noun "paraclete" occurs only four times—and all in Johannine literature.

The title "Paraclete" arises in part from God's promise of a new exodus to a people who lived in oppression because of their unfaithfulness. Isaiah 40:1–2 contains the significant text that sets forth the entire enterprise of new exodus deliverance in terms of "comfort" or "consolation" (LXX *paraklēsis*, paraclete). Among the other relevant verses 51:12 is quite significant: "I, I am he who comforts you." I AM is the One in John who fulfills this. In 52:9 (Hebrew only) "comfort" and "redeem" are parallel; also of note, Jerusalem is parallel here with "people" and is the recipient of this activity. "Comfort" (Heb., *naham*), used three times in 66:13, is directed to those in Jerusalem (Jerusalem is important for both John and Luke). Thus, "comfort" speaks to a downtrodden and persecuted people whose experience is opposed to God's historic and prophetic dialog with and promises to them. They (i.e., the remnant) long for the day of salvation and deliverance from their enemies.

---

function" not essence.

5. Other NT writers depended on Isaiah, too, but our interest here is in John and Luke. See, for example, Williams, *I am He*; Strauss, *Davidic Messiah in Luke-Acts*; Ball, '*I AM*' *in John's Gospel*; Moyise and Menken, *Isaiah in the New Testament*. Also, this contrasts to some who believe that the new exodus theme originated from Deuteronomy. See, for instance, Moessner, "Luke 9:1–50"; Moessner, *Lord of the Banquet*.

6. Brown does not consider important the lexical information in understanding "paraclete." She writes: "Still I take the title seriously and do not resort to explaining the noun παράχλητος [*paraklētos*] by using verbal or adjectival forms of the word" (Brown, *Spirit in the Writings of John*, 186). For the sake of space, I do not discuss other contexts in which the word occurs. See also, e.g., "*parakaleō*," "*paraklētos*," and other related words in Danker, *Greek-English Lexicon*.

Comfort/consolation is deeply embedded in John's Gospel as well as in Luke-Acts where it likewise contains a profound eschatological sense. As Strauss writes: "'Israel's consolation' (παράκλησις τοῦ Ἰσραηλ/paraklēsis tou Israēl) [Luke 2:25] which Simeon anxiously awaits . . . is a major theme of Isaiah 40–55 (Isa 40:1; 49:13; 51:3; 52:9; 57:18; 61:2)." He further notes that "In rabbinic tradition this terminology was used of the messianic hope and sometimes given the name of *Menahem [nāham]*, 'Consoler.'"[7] TWOT likewise notes:

> The second primary meaning of nāḥam is "to comfort" (Piel) or "to be comforted" (Niphal, Pual, and Hithpael). *This Hebrew word was well known to every pious Jew living in exile as he recalled the opening words of Isaiah's "Book of Consolation," naḥămû naḥămû ʿammî* "Comfort ye, comfort ye my people" (Isa 40:1). . . . It is God who comforts his people (Ps 71:21; 86:17; 119:82; Isa 12:1; 49:13; 52:9). God's "compassion (niḥûm, a derivative of nḥm) grows warm and tender" for Israel (Hos 11:8).[8]

The title, grounded in the arrival and teachings of Jesus, the OT promise of the Spirit, even the whole of salvation known as "comfort" in Isaiah, arose in the context of the conflict between Jesus/Church and the synagogue/Judaism. Jewish leaders, and the people they led, followed the same *Tanak* traditions (such as Isaiah), practices, and observed the same holy days, i.e., the Feast of Booths and Passover.[9] Tensions were in the air over Rome's dominance; some, such as the ones at Qumran, separated themselves from the Jerusalem temple center of power. Many looked for the deliverance promised especially by Isaiah—the Spirit of Truth witnessed to the True Deliverer.

Furthermore, John includes in his story of the Messiah instances of the divine name used in Isa 40–55. The occurrence of I am (in the absolute form) and its use with predicates indicate this. I am (Gr. *egō eimi*, Heb. *anu hu* of Isaiah) occurs in this way only in John's Gospel and is one of the rather strong indicators that John used Isaiah in his story of Jesus. Ball writes especially to this point:

> By the using the words ἐγώ εἰμί [*ego eimi*], Jesus takes upon himself a phrase that speaks of the fact that Yahweh, the one true creator God will come to his people and save them. As such the phrase is eschatological, expressing the time when the Lord [*sic*] will come to Zion and when the messenger will proclaim "The Lord reigns" (52:6, 7). This phrase is also soteriological, for the purpose of his coming is to save his people (52:7) [I might add: pneumatological as well]. However, most striking of all is the fact that Jesus takes on himself a phrase that is reserved for Yahweh alone and thus intimately identifies himself with God's acts of creation and salvation."[10]

---

7. Strauss, *Davidic Messiah*, 118n2.
8. Wilson, נָחַם (*TWOT* 2:571 [emphasis added]).
9. Especially as noted in John's Gospel.
10. Ball, "*I Am*," 203. Cf. larger context.

Another issue pertains to the Paraclete's place in the Gospel. Why does the term occur only in the farewell discourse and why not earlier? The answer lies in the process of salvation history. Jesus was the main broker between God and sinful humans. Before his ascension he was involved with effecting the requirements of the mediator between God and humans. It was not until the time of the completion of his work and that of his approaching earthly departure did he announce and elaborate upon the next stage.

Still, another issue pertains to the function of the Paraclete. Is it agency? Is it forensic, that is—does he act as advocate in a legal sense?[11] Or is it simply as a broker? I substantially agree with Brown who notes that the evidence can be explained better by using the broker model.[12] Broker will also include the meaning of mediator/intercessor for the Spirit, One who works on behalf of Jesus and the Father: the Paraclete's activity occurs both in individuals and among the community at large, manifesting himself in persons to provide such things as joy and peace, and among the community through prophecy to give guidance and to respond to other needs within. I now move to the farewell discourse to point out the brokerage elements in it.

## Spirit and Brokerage in the Farewell Discourse[13]

The farewell chapters are filled with brokerage concepts. I begin with a key text that we will appeal to several times: "And I will ask the Father, and he will give you another Helper, to be with you forever" (John 14:16).[14] "Asking" is the specific work of a broker/mediator. The word translated "helper" is the word *paraklēton* (παράκλητον), its first occurrence in the farewell discourse. "Paraclete" is the title John supplies for the Spirit-mediator/broker. The adjective "another" (*allon*) modifies paraclete in this verse and is usually translated as "another" and refers to Jesus as being a mediator. The Paraclete would continue being a mediator carrying on Jesus's presence and work. Some would disagree, however, and say that the verse should be punctuated differently, "*allon*" followed by a comma, making the translation—"he will give you another, a paraclete"—and not making Jesus a mediator. The most appropriate translation, "another paraclete," however, informs us that Jesus is the first mediator and, therefore, the one that administers the subordinate paraclete in the farewell discourse.

Several observations arise. First, Jesus, as mediator, is foundational—he is both patron and broker. For example, he fulfills the role of I Am (*egō eimi*) of Isaiah 40–55,

---

11. Brown, *Spirit in the Writings of John*, 180–86, gives a valuable discussion of theories and proponents. Too many theories exist to be discussed here. The legal sense seems to be more prevalent.

12. Brown, *Spirit in the Writings of John*, 186. While her use of social-scientific criticism greatly assists us, she falls short methodologically in properly assessing the topic. See Ball.

13. I choose to limit the parameters of the discourse to chapters 14–16.

14. The ESV will be used throughout.

as the suffering servant, and the one upon whom the Spirit dwells.[15] He effects the Isaianic new creation and new exodus.[16] In short, he performs all that God has established through prophecy and thus acts as mediator. Jesus is the "foundational" mediator because the Church is exhorted to pray in Jesus's name (16:23–24) and because the Paraclete will glorify Jesus (16:14). This is the significance of praying in Jesus's name—he is broker/mediator. Second, the Spirit as paraclete/mediator operates in a subordinate role supporting Jesus's (and the Father's) work. That role is to be with Jesus's body (i.e., group of followers) on earth, mediating Jesus to the saints. His work, while being like Jesus, is different in a sense because the Spirit is not the Son. Yet, his major purpose was to glorify Jesus. Jesus acted, instead of, but as the Father, on earth, creating (both first and new), redeeming, mediating and revealing the Father, as indicated by John's Gospel. The Father has committed all things into Jesus's hands.[17]

## Paraclete as Spirit of Truth

Two titles for the Spirit occur in the farewell discourse. They are *paraklētos* (Paraclete) and *to pneuma tēs alētheias* (the Spirit of Truth). The Spirit of Truth occurs only four times in the NT and all of them are in Johannine material: John 14:17; 15:26; 16:13; and 1 John 4:6. Of note is that this title occurs only in the farewell discourse and in 1 John, and when in the Gospel with the same material as that of the Paraclete. This name is placed in parallel with Paraclete in John 14:17; 15:26 and implied in 16:13. Why the paraclete is called the Spirit of Truth is important. This title can be analyzed with the following conclusions. Both nouns have the article attending them. The presence of these articles means that significance is spread between them. "Truth" is being equally emphasized and attached to the Spirit. Furthermore, the article (the) and noun (truth) in "of the truth" are in the genitive case which should be considered an objective genitive. That is, the truth receives the action of the Spirit—he will bear witness that Jesus is the true Messiah, the Son of God, i.e., the Truth (cf. 14:6; 1:17, 8:45–46, et al.). And the Paraclete will bear witness that Jesus is the true broker/paraclete (cf. 15:26) as opposed to others, such as angels, Moses, and Abraham.

---

15. In John this idea prevails as in Isaiah 11:2 the Spirit will *rest* upon the "root of Jesse"—implied also in other places in Isaiah.

16. I intend "new covenant" to be included with new creation and new exodus.

17. Importantly, Jesus had the authority to give the Spirit. Thus, when Jesus "baptizes with the Spirit" he would give the Spirit as God "with full rights."

PART IV—READING ST. LUKE'S PNEUMATOLOGY WITH OTHER TEXTS

# The Work of the Paraclete

## Mediation

The first occurrence of Paraclete is in 14:16 but the entire paragraph (15–24) provides the function of Paraclete.[18] The function of the Spirit is to be with them, forever. The empty void that Jesus's ascension leaves will be filled by the Paraclete and he will mediate the presence of Jesus and the Father. The role of the Spirit as mediator in the absence of Jesus on earth highlights the significance of the incarnation. The resurrected, human, Jesus is permanent, something quite different from what Gnostics believe, for example. (Even Judaism did not believe in the incarnation.) The Trinity forever is changed in a relational way—the Son of God remaining what he was became what he was not:[19] the incarnate One—Jesus is limited in respect to his humanity. This divine process also brought about a new manifestation of the Spirit, heretofore nonexistent and quite distinct, since it came about as a result of the person and work of Jesus. The Paraclete's new manifestation helps believers to understand the mutual indwelling of the Father, Son, the Spirit and believers.[20] It also clarifies the significance of the Spirit's permanency in the Spirit's descent upon Jesus in 1:32–33, and this dwelling crystalizes the significance of "unity" which John so emphasizes. The necessity of this change of an earthly mediatorship is indicated in 16:7: "I tell you the truth: it is to your advantage that I go away, for if I do not go away, the Helper will not come to you." The verb tenses in this verse and the action of Jesus suggest the giving of the Spirit in John 20:22. His going away (i.e., resurrection and ascension) precipitates the coming of the Spirit, and the Spirit would continue to be as Jesus in and among his church—indwelling his temple.

## The Paraclete and Godliness: Fruit of the Spirit

Another function of the Paraclete in his mediating role is that he will sustain and develop Christ's body in the world and extend his mission through his body to the world. The Paraclete's function/work will develop characteristics of godliness within

---

18. It would be helpful to exegete this at length, but that would take away from our task at hand. We make some observations.

19. Not to the divine essence but the effect that the humanity of Jesus related to divinity and gave expression to the plan of God to create a people for himself. This well-known saying is based upon Gregory of Nazianzus, *Oratio* 29:19. Cf. also St. Leo, *Sermon* xxi. The Spirit's attendant new manifestations likewise contributed to this marvelous manifestation.

20. John's description of this process is one of the greatest contributions that he makes to pneumatology. This surfaces a weakness of the *donum superadditum* theology—not the experience—of classical Pentecostalism. Brown and some others believe that this stresses more than anything the absolute distance between God and humans. This is surely true, but may not be what is explicitly intended. If so, this highlights even more so what God did to overcome the gap between him and humans with both Jesus and the Spirit. See Brown, *Spirit in the Writings of John*, 197.

each believer and within and among the community. His work will also be visible and audible through prophetic inspiration.[21]

We elaborate briefly upon the work of the Spirit in building godliness. Paul calls godliness the fruit of the Spirit. John likewise uses the same word—fruit—and with it connects his much-used word "love" in John 15 and beyond with Pauline usage. Similar circumstances exist in Pauline settings. For instance, in Rom 5:5 the Spirit pours love into the believers' hearts. The context is one where suffering seems to indicate that Christians are not justified. Paul responds by placing suffering into a larger context, saying that suffering builds hope. Paul strongly implies that during the times of suffering and character building that "God's love has been poured [and is being poured] into our hearts through the Holy Spirit who has been given to us." The subordinate participle translated "has been given" is aorist and indicates the gift of the Spirit as a one-time event—the giving is finished. Verse 1 indicates that God is the giver and the Spirit is the One in v. 5 who indicates that God has reconciled humans and the Divine. The Spirit, now given, is residual and continually pours out God's love. This continual action is indicated through the perfect tense verb "pour." The moment the Spirit arrived, it was a gift of love. Now that the Spirit lives in believers, he continually assures believers that they are all right and loved by God.

In similar manner, in John the Paraclete is given and dwells in the believer testifying to them of love and peace in the middle of turmoil. Love is interwoven in the farewell discourse and prominently fills out the most profound expression of the relationship indicated by the reciprocated and mutual dwelling of Jesus, the Father, and the Paraclete. Of all the NT, it is in John and his First Epistle that most emphasizes the concept of love. Of the 39 times love (both *philos* and *agapē*) appear in the Gospel, chapters 14–16 alone have 22 of them. In this discourse, love anchors the ethical dimension of God's nature and presence. Love is manifested in keeping Jesus's commandments, although they are not specifically given—they are to be understood—especially in the context of love and the Paraclete's dwelling.[22] Jesus's word (14:23), however, is parallel with commandments and loving is keeping Jesus's word (parallel with Jesus's teaching). Jesus's word is the Father's word. So, to love the Son is to love the Father and it is because Jesus loved his disciples for whom he left the Father and gave his life. Also, the disciples are to love one another while on this earth. It is this that indicates the presence of the Paraclete because he mediates love from the Son and the Father to believers. It is the Paraclete's dwelling and working in the community that produces the divine, ethical characteristics. Not to love one another, then, is not to love the Paraclete, the Son, or the Father. Other fruit, however, are displayed, also.

---

21. See footnote above. Others, focusing on the function of the Paraclete, somewhat similarly, see the Paraclete as some form of a prophet (spirit of): Boring, "Influence of Christian Prophecy" 113–23; preachers: Barrett, "Holy Spirit in the Fourth Gospel," 1–15; or teachers (inward inspiration): Porsch, *Pneuma und Wort*. See discussion in Brown, *Spirit in the Writings of John*, 183–85.

22. However, the new commandment is to love one another (cf. 13:34). Also the commandment of the Father is eternal life (12:49). Johannine language is specific yet fluid.

It is significant that "comfort" and "consolation" are also known as "peace." And the peace that Jesus gives is so unlike the peace which the world gives (14:27). In John "peace" fulfills the broader meaning of "comfort" of Isaiah 40:1 (cf. John 20:19–23). Peace occurs frequently with the action that comfort brings—observe the occurrences of "peace" in the farewell chapters and, finally, in the significant section of 20:21–22: "Jesus said to them again, '*Peace* be with you. As the Father has sent me, even so I am sending you.' And when he had said this, he breathed on them and said to them, '*Receive the Holy Spirit.*'"[23] In effect, these verses may reflect the climax of the Paraclete teaching in the Gospel. While breathing indicates the creation motif in the Gospel (i.e., born again and that from Isa 40–55[24] are clearly in view), something else also is emphasized here. This action of Jesus breathing upon the disciples indicates that he is giving them the Paraclete and the peace that comes from Jesus via the Spirit. Jesus, thus, transfers the earthly, mediating activity of himself through (the meaning of Jesus baptizing with the Spirit in John) the Spirit who lives in and among believers, and through them, works in the world. It indicates that by the presence of the Spirit/Paraclete, they, too, become subordinate brokers to the world, as evangelists—either remitting sins or declaring sins unforgiven. The authority of the Father is transferred down the line to the Church; As mediators/brokers they act entirely as the Father wills. Patronage explains this difficult "Johannine" commission. The elevation of the status of believing servants to that of friends in chapter 15, part of this patronage and broker system, anticipates this authority.

Besides love and peace, John emphasizes another Pauline fruit, joy. All three of these words in the Gospel are associated with the mediation of the Spirit. Of all the NT, John proportionately uses "joy" more than any other book except Luke's Gospel: nine times vs. Luke's 12 times.[25] And in the last discourse alone John uses the word six times. It is an attendant reality to "comfort/console" and derives especially from the Paraclete's manifestation.

Another work of the Paraclete is to build faith in the community. It is shown in this discourse in the progression of the disciples as they move from fear to faith: from the continuous warning and comfort given by Jesus, and the increasing tension of the persecution and clarity of those who will persecute the community. The final paragraph proves to be somewhat of a climax, summarizing the entire environment of the Paraclete who will continue the mediating work of Jesus. Believers will experience opposition from the world as did Jesus. The world will treat the followers of Jesus as it treated Jesus. But his followers must be faithful and follow the Way and display love

---

23. For the profound sense of "peace" and its related term, "joy," see the following. Joy is also a profound word in John, especially in these chapters. Conzelmann and Zimmerli, "χαίρω, χαρά, κτλ," *TDNT* 9:363, 370–71; Foerster, "εἰρήνη, εἰρηνεύω, κτλ," *TDNT* 2:402.

24. Note: use of *bara*, "create" for the promise of restoration, see also Genesis.

25. Both Gospels derive this from Isaiah.

towards the Father, the Son, the Paraclete, and one another. The Paraclete is important in building faith in this life-long venture.

Important in this respect also is that the accompanying word "dwell," used in conjunction with the Spirit's dwelling on Jesus and in and among his follower, indicates that this is the sign that they are the true believers in contrast to the claims of all imposters. This was indicated by the presence of the Paraclete who would testify that Jesus was who he claimed to be and that believers would be consoled in their faith. Moreover, the key verses of the Gospel, 20:30–31, should be understood for believers to keep on believing, rather than for non-believers to become believers: "that you may believe" should be read "that you may keep on believing" as opposed to "that you may begin to believe." In 20:19–23, the disciples were fearful of the Jewish leaders and bolted themselves behind closed doors; Jesus came and gave them the Comforter, resulting in peace.

## The Paraclete and Spiritual Ministries[26]

Another way the Spirit works is through spiritual ministries. It is through the ministry of prophecy that characterizes the Paraclete's work. For example, that this Paraclete community was a prophetic one is supported by other texts. In first Corinthians 14:3 the noun *paraklēsin* occurs: "the one who prophesies speaks to people for their upbuilding and encouragement [*paraklēsin*] and consolation."[27] The ESV translates the noun here as "encouragement" although the Greek is the same word in other contexts for consolation. All three nouns in this verse overlap in meaning, suggesting emphasis and extended effects of Spirit ministry. Certainly, the effect of prophecy in the Pauline community was to be the same as in the Johannine one. Paul spends quite some time in first Corinthians 14 on the importance of prophecy to build up the community. Furthermore, the verb (parakaleō) and noun (*paraklēsin*) occur 29 times in second Corinthians; especially so, the word clusters together in chapter 1 ten times and in the same context as that of the farewell chapters of John. Consolation like this indicates a prophetic community where the Spirit consoles them through prophetic speech, for that is how the Spirit works among Jesus's followers.

In first Corinthians 14:3 "comfort" is the result of the ministry of prophecy; in Romans 12:8a it is a "distinct" ministry (cf. Barnabas was known as the son of Consolation). The ESV translates the sentence as "the one who exhorts, in his exhortation"; the verb "exhorts" and the noun "exhortation" are from the same stem. This probably

---

26. I prefer "ministries" rather than "gifts" for methodological reasons—"ministries" is a preferred and better way to translate Gr. word *charisma*. The primary way that the Paraclete worked in this category is through a variety of prophetic ministries. "Prophetic" means more than just inspired speech, although it has it particularly in mind.

27. Admittedly, this noun does not occur in John; however, it is shortsighted semantically to disassociate different forms of the same root, the result (comfort) from the giver (Paraclete). See Brown, *Spirit in the Writings of John*, 184.

emphasises this task in some manner. The word can be translated several ways: to exhort or encourage. The Paraclete, then, through prophecy in its varied manifestations in ministry worked in numerous ways: such as knowledge, wisdom, exhortation, conviction, and consolation, and where his work in and among the community produced godly traits.

Another work of the Spirit/Paraclete is to convict (*elegxein*) the world (John 16:8–11). "Conviction" is rather complicated to understand, for the way these verses are constructed. In the immediate context, the reader is not told how the Spirit will "convict," just that he will. Yet, this is followed by the grounds of his conviction (expressed by *hoti* (because) in the following verses). This Greek word, however, appears in a similar context in first Corinthians 14:22–26 where the prophecy brings "conviction" to the unbeliever. What is relevant in both cases is that "conviction" is operative.

Another example of the work of the Spirit is to intercede and this is significant for understanding the central role of broker. Broker, especially in this way, occurs in Romans 8:26–27 where the Spirit intercedes on behalf of the saints because of their weaknesses, for they do not know what/how to pray as they ought. The Spirit prays according to God's will because he knows the will of the Father.[28] The context reflects that this action happens amid suffering and groaning—the same context as that of John 14–16. We mention also in this same context (Rom 8:16) that the "Spirit himself bears witness with our spirit that we are children of God."

First Corinthians 14 is the Pauline chapter for prophecy and edification of the Church. The purpose of prophecy in its various forms is to build up the church. In 14:6 the "building up" (*oikodomeō*) of 14:4–5 is connected to several ministries—all connected with prophecy:[29] "How will I benefit you unless I bring you some *revelation* or *knowledge*[30] or *prophecy* or *teaching*?" John 14:26 states that the Paraclete "will *teach* you all things and *bring to your remembrance* all that I have said to you." The underlined words above in John 14:26 come from *didaskō*. "Bring to remembrance" hides the meaning somewhat of the verb. The verb form of "teach" in John is the same stem as the noun form in First Corinthians 14:6. The Paraclete will teach, i.e., either through inspired teachers and/or by means of a prophecy, and its content will focus on Jesus. This teaching will contain a variety of things—such as theology, meaning, and application, and they will all focus on Jesus, what he taught, and the theological and practical applications. Prophecies should always follow this principle—and applications may change with situations and generations.

---

28. My paraphrase.

29. Cf. "The one who prophesies speaks to people for their upbuilding [*oikodomēn*] and encouragement [*paraklēsis*] and consolation [*paramythian*]" (14:3). The last two words overlap in meaning but may have specific application in context.

30. Note the Pauline ministries of "word of knowledge" and "word of wisdom."

## Receiving the Paraclete

John gives directives about receiving the Paraclete in the farewell discourse. These directives point to the responsibility of Jesus's followers. For example: Be obedient to Jesus's word. Love one another, which is keeping Jesus's commandment (14:15–6; cf. 15:7–8, 12). Then when the believer does, Jesus will ask the Father and he will send the Spirit of truth. Abide in the vine (cf. ch. 15) and remain in unity with the Father, Son, and Spirit; and of course, other believers. Prayer is important, too, for Jesus said in 16:23–24: "In that day you will ask nothing of me [instead of that—do this]. Truly, truly, I say to you, whatever you ask of the Father in my name, he will give it to you. Until now you have asked nothing in my name. Ask, and you will receive, that your joy may be full." The context of "whatever" refers to the reception of the Paraclete. In other places, however, receiving the Paraclete is a gift of God through Jesus. Only the Father and the Son give life, which is also perceived as being created new, born again. It is like the water changed into wine, the nobleman's son healed, the blind man receiving sight for the first time, and Lazarus coming back to life. These identify Jesus as Son of God and depict what God does.

So, it seems that tension exists in receiving the Paraclete. Proper faith is necessary and John's Gospel deals with that. The Paraclete is received at new birth when faith focuses on Jesus. As followers, regress can happen, like disobedience, and this prevents the Paraclete/Spirit from working as he would. Also, personal circumstances can precipitate a cry for help and the Paraclete responds.[31] This scene in John depicts real life in his community, and in all Christianity, for it is not unlike that behind the writings of Luke.

## Conclusion

The Paraclete title arose out of the confrontation between Jesus and the synagogue, and later between Church and synagogue. In John, the Paraclete focuses attention on the Church's maintenance and health in a hostile environment of the world. What is different about this attempt to climb the summit is that the background, meaning, and function arise from Isaiah's new exodus prophecies. Isaiah's prophecy intends to bring God's eschatological, consolatory new exodus salvation in restoring his people. Also, adding the Gentiles in Isaiah provided the engine that drove such an expression of the Spirit. In like manner, Lukan writings derive the new exodus consolation from Isaiah. But Luke has a different emphasis. Acts 2 is certainly a fulfillment of Simeon's

---

31. Lincoln notes: "In the Fourth Gospel, it is not so much that the disciples must ask for the help of the Spirit. Since it is assumed that the Spirit has already been sent or given to believers and is at work, it is more that the Spirit enables believers to speak and act as faithful witnesses and makes their testimony the vehicle of the Spirit's own witness (cf. 15:26–27)" (Lincoln, *Truth on Trial*, 462). And I submit that it is through prophetic inspiration that this happens.

proclamation in Luke 2:25–32 where he cried out that the consolation (*paraklēsis*) of Israel had arrived. Acts 9:31 records that indeed this is the case: "So the church throughout all Judea and Galilee and Samaria had *peace* and was being *built up*. And walking in the fear of the Lord and in the *comfort* [*paraklēsis*] of the Holy Spirit, it multiplied."[32]

---

32. Luke's community, too, was a prophetic one.

# Chapter 21

## What Does It Mean—According to the Book of Acts and the Letter to the Ephesians—to Be "Filled with" / "Full of" the Holy Spirit?

SVEN SODERLUND[1]

I often hear and read about the importance for Christians to be Spirit-filled. But what does this mean? What does it mean theologically and practically? By studying how both Luke and Paul use the phrase "filled with the Holy Spirit" and (in the case of Luke) its complementary adjectival phrase "full of the Holy Spirit," I hope to find some answers to these probing questions.

To be sure, exploration of this theme is not new. Our honoree himself has explored in some detail the language of "filled with the Spirit" as found in the Gospel of Luke and the book of Acts.[2]

---

1. When I came to teach at Western Pentecostal Bible College (now Summit Pacific College) in 1968, Roger was in the middle of his undergraduate studies at the College. He reminds me that after he graduated in 1971, I recommended that he pursue graduate studies at Regent College in Vancouver. It was there he wrote his thesis on the subject of Luke's pneumatology that eventually became his breakout book, *The Charismatic Theology of St. Luke*. Having kept in touch with Roger in various ways over the years, it is a joy to contribute this article in honor of my friend and brother.

2. See Stronstad, *Charismatic Theology*, 53–55. Those initial observations were expanded in 1984 in a paper presented to the Society for Pentecostal Studies under the title "'Filled with the Holy Spirit' Terminology in Luke-Acts." Three years later, in 1987, the paper served as the lead article in a collection of essays presented to Dr. Leslie Holdcroft (Stronsad and Van Kleek, *Holy Spirit*, 1–13), before finally being included as chapter 4 in an anthology of Stronstad's essays (Stronstad, *Spirit, Scripture, and Theology*, 79–98). On the basis of these studies and the observation that the phrase "filled with the Holy Spirit" stands "unrivalled as the center of [Luke's] pneumatology," Stronstad concluded that it is this phrase even more than the parallel phrase "baptized with the Holy Spirit" that should form "the center of [Pentecostal] pneumatology" (Stronstad, *Spirit, Scripture and Theology*, 83, 98).

## PART IV—READING ST. LUKE'S PNEUMATOLOGY WITH OTHER TEXTS

Other scholars such James B. Shelton,[3] Max Turner,[4] John Michael Penney,[5] Andreas J. Köstenberger,[6] Ju Hur,[7] Gonzalo Haya-Prats[8] and John R. Levison[9] have also discussed the subject in articles or in shorter sections embedded within larger works. These writers, and others, have summarized for us the basic data pertaining especially to Luke's use of the phrases to be "filled with" or "full of" the Holy Spirit" and, in the process, have offered many helpful observations based on the data. Given this fact, what remains to be done?

What remains, I think, is to review some of the data once more to see what can be affirmed and what may need to be modified in light of ongoing research. What also remains to be done is to explore further the significance of Paul's use of similar "filling" language in Ephesians 5:18, namely, in his exhortation for believers to be filled with the Holy Spirit. This is not to say that others have failed to notice that Paul on this one occasion uses language otherwise thought to be uniquely Lukan. But in my experience such observations have more often than not been perfunctory, mentioned in passing without stopping to reflect on what significance this might have for the relation, if any, between Luke and Paul.[10]

In his first book, *The Charismatic Theology of St. Luke*, Stronstad broached the subject of the inappropriate use of Ephesians 5:18 by some scholars for the interpretation of Luke's pneumatology.[11] Yet of special interest for this article is the fact that in his most recent essay, "The Rebirth of Prophecy,"[12] Stronstad closes his wide-ranging review of biblical prophecy with a substantial section on "The Witness of Paul" in which he affirms Paul as one of the great "exemplars of a Spirit-filled prophetic ministry."[13] In the case of the apostle's letters, Stronstad notes the evidence for Paul ministering not only in powerful "deeds" but also in powerful "words" of the Spirit, "words" that were often marked by a strong prophetic and communal character. One illustration of this, Stronstad observes, is when Paul exhorts the Ephesians to "be filled

---

3. In the first instance, as a Stirling University PhD dissertation (Shelton, "Filled with the Holy Spirit"), then as a chapter in Elbert, *Faces of Renewal* (Shelton, "'Filled with the Holy Spirit' and 'Full of the Holy Spirit,'" 81–107), followed by observations on the same theme in Shelton's book (Shelton, *Mighty in Word and Deed*, 136–148, 157–164).

4. Turner, "Spirit Endowment in Luke-Acts," esp. 53–55; "Empowerment," esp. 108–110; *Power from on High*, 165–69, 408–12.

5. See Penney, *Missionary Emphasis*, 96–100.

6. Köstenberger, "What Does it Mean?"

7. Hur, *Dynamic Reading*, esp. 165–71.

8. Haya-Prats, *Empowered*, esp. 155–67.

9. Levison, *Filled*, esp. 317–65.

10. An exception to this pattern is the article by Köstenberger, "What Does it Mean?"

11. Stronstad, *Charismatic Theology*, 10–11.

12. Initially published in *JBPR*, but later included as the last essay in the second edition of Stronstad's collected essays. See Stronstad, *Spirit, Scripture and Theology*, 159–91.

13. Stronstad, "Rebirth," 23.

with the Spirit, speaking to one another in psalms and hymns and spiritual songs, singing and making melody with your heart to the Lord" (Eph 5:18–19).[14]

This is a tantalizing remark given what we know about Stronstad's lifetime engagement with the writings of Luke-Acts and the debate that has arisen around Luke and Paul's distinctive emphases on the work of the Spirit.[15] In the latter part of this essay I wish to draw out the lines of Stronstad's observations from the above mentioned article and probe even further the significance of the "filling" language employed in the book of Acts and in Ephesians 5:18. Finally, I want to touch on, however briefly, the implications of all this for the life of Christian believers, who in these apostolic writings are exhorted, both by example and precept, to demonstrate what it means to be "filled with" / "full of" the Holy Spirit.

## The Language of "Filled with the Holy Spirit" and "Full of the Holy Spirit" in the Book of Acts

When referring to the experience of being filled with or full of the Holy Spirit, Luke in the book of Acts employs the verb *pimplēmi* five times, the adjective *plērēs* four times, and the verb *plēroō* once, all distributed within the first thirteen chapters of the book.[16]

### The Verb *pimplēmi* in Association with the Holy Spirit in the Book of Acts

As noted, Luke uses the verb *pimplēmi* five times in the book of Acts, namely, in 2:4; 4:8, 31; 9:17; 13:9. In these passages Luke documents how the disciples were empowered by the Spirit for bearing inspired witness to the gospel, both in Jerusalem and beyond. That Luke understood empowerment as the primary intention of the Pentecost event is clear from his citation of Jesus's commission in Acts 1:8. Jesus did not say that the Holy Spirit would come upon the disciples to make them regenerate or to make them Christians, but to empower them for witness in Jerusalem, Samaria and to the end of the world. It was the experience of being "clothed with power from on high" (Luke 24:49) that transformed the fearful band that met behind closed doors in Jerusalem into a potent force for proclaiming the gospel by means of word and deed.[17]

---

14. Stronstad, "Rebirth," 24–25.

15. I refer here to the debate occasioned by the publication of Dunn, *Baptism in the Holy Spirit*, a debate well documented by William Atkinson and Martin Mittelstadt. See Atkinson, *Baptism*, esp. 1–91; Mittelstadt, *Reading Luke-Acts*, 46–63.

16. As for the Third Gospel, it uses the phrase "filled with the Holy Spirit" (*eplēsthē pneumatos hagiou*) with reference to John the Baptist (1:15), Elizabeth (1:41) and Zechariah (1:67), while the expression "full of the Holy Spirit" (*plērēs pneumatos hagiou*) is applied to Jesus in Luke 4:1. Although I have not been able to engage in extended discussion of these Gospel passages, they do not materially affect the thesis of the essay.

17. For this reason, the language of empowerment (what Stronstad calls "Pneuma discourse"

The immediate impact on the disciples of being filled with the Spirit on the day of Pentecost was the experience of glossolalia whereby they were enabled to declare "the wonders of God" in the peoples' own languages (2:11), followed by Peter's Spirit-empowered address to the crowd gathered in Jerusalem that day (2:14–39). In the same way, Peter's fearless witness before the Sanhedrin (4:8) and the disciples' bold proclamation of the word of God following Peter and John's release from prison (4:31) all demonstrate the new power and authority with which those filled with the Spirit bore witness to the resurrection. Similarly, Ananias's prophecy over Paul (at the time, Saul) in Damascus that he would be filled with the Holy Spirit (9:17) was fully vindicated when the new convert "at once" began to preach in the synagogues with manifest power and conviction that Jesus was both Son of God and Jewish Messiah (9:20–22). Paul later demonstrated the same empowerment in the city of Paphos on the island of Cyprus when, "filled with the Holy Spirit," he sharply rebuked Elymas the sorcerer with a prophetic word resulting in the latter's blindness and in the conversion of the local Roman governor, Sergius Paulus (13:9–12).

In these passages, all employing the verb *pimplēmi* in some form,[18] Luke is showing what being filled with the Spirit meant for the early disciples. It meant a new order of prophetic enablement to testify to Jesus's resurrection and divine Sonship with signs following.[19] As has frequently been pointed out, the pattern of Spirit fillings documented in the book of Acts was iterative or episodic; that is, the filling in question occurred as each new episode required special endowment by the Spirit for the exercise of prophetic speech.[20]

## The Adjective *plērēs* in Association with the Holy Spirit in the Book of Acts

But Luke used not only the verb *pimplēmi* when referencing the disciples' experience of having been encountered by the Spirit in this special way. In the book of Acts he also uses the adjective *plērēs* ("full of") in the phrase *plērēs pneumatos hagiou*, "full of the Holy Spirit" (Acts 6:3 [the verse omits *hagiou*], 5; 7:55; 11:24). Scholars have inquired whether there is a difference of meaning or nuance in the way the two expressions "filled with the Holy Spirit" and "full of the Holy Spirit" are used in the

---

[Stronstad, *Spirit, Scripture, and Theology*, 92, 98]) better explains what happened on the day of Pentecost than any alternative explanation of the event defined as an experience of conversion-initiation. For a succinct critique of the conversion-initiation interpretation applied to Luke-Acts, see Shelton, *Mighty in Word and Deed*, 128.

18. Whether full verb (aorist indicative, *eplēsthēsan*, 2:4, 4:31; aorist subjunctive, *plēsthēs* 9:17) or aorist participle (*plēstheis*, 4:8, 13:9).

19. This observation is entirely consistent with what scholars such as Hermann Gunkel, Eduard Schweitzer and David Hill from the late nineteenth to the mid-twentieth century had already discerned about the empowering role of the Spirit in the writings of Luke, as helpfully summarized in Menzies, *Empowered*, 18–27.

20. See, for example, Stronstad, *Spirit, Scripture and Theology*, 89; Turner, "Spirit Endowment," 54–55; *Power from on High*, 167–68.

book of Acts. Some have discerned no substantial difference in the way Luke employs these phrases;[21] others have observed a variety of nuanced differences[22] or have cautioned against "imposing dogmatic claims . . . or distinguishing connotations for each expression."[23] For my own part I have found the differences between Luke's use of the verb *pimplēmi* and the adjective *plērēs* to be both striking and significant. In support of this conclusion I will look in detail at the ministry of the so-called seven "deacons" in 6:3, at Stephen as one of The Seven in 6:5 and 7:55, as well as at the ministry of Barnabas in Syrian Antioch in 11:23–24.

Of special interest in these passages (apart from 7:55 on which see more below) is Luke's use of the double genitive of content following the adjective *plērēs*. The select Seven were to be full not just of the Spirit but of the Spirit *and* "wisdom" (*plēreis pneumatos kai sophias*, 6:3). Similarly, Stephen in 6:5 is described as "full of faith and the Holy Spirit" (*plērēs pisteōs kai pneumatos hagiou*) and Barnabas in 11:24 as "full of the Holy Spirit and faith" (*plērēs pneumatos hagiou kai pisteōs*). But do these examples of double genitive expressions signify being full of two separate entities, that is, full of "the Spirit" *and* full of "wisdom" (in the case of The Seven) or full of "faith" *and* "the Holy Spirit" (in the case of Stephen and Barnabas), or are the two items related in some significant way, perhaps even as a kind of hendiadys, that is, making a single point through the use of two coordinated nouns?

In an important contribution to this study, Spanish scholar Gonzalo Haya-Prats has argued that these double expressions in the genitive "are not equivalent members duplicated for mere similarity of sound." On the contrary, "they complete and clarify one another"—or put even more strongly—they signify a "cause-and-effect" relationship between them.[24] Thus, in the case of The Seven, it is the Spirit who is the source of the wisdom needed for the sensitive work of table administration in the community (6:3).[25] Similarly, when Stephen in 6:5 is described as "a man full of faith and of the Holy Spirit" this is best explained as the Spirit being the source of his faith. But of what kind of faith? Of saving faith? More likely in this context it is "faith that confers the power to work miracles."[26] Such an understanding of faith in 6:5 is in keeping with Luke's subsequent description of Stephen as a man "full of God's grace and power"

---

21. For example, Craig Keener, when commenting on the passages in question, seems to treat both phrases alike. See Keener, *Acts*, 2:1273–77, 1279–84, 1440–43, 1844–46.

22. Stronstad has argued that "'full of the Spirit' describes the Spirit's enabling, while 'filled with the Spirit' describes prophetic inspiration" (Stronstad, *Charismatic Theology*, 55; cf. *Spirit, Scripture and Theology*, 95).

23. Hur, *Dynamic Reading*, 168.

24. Haya-Prats, *Empowered*, 158–59.

25. The same kind of inter-relationship between the two terms is discerned by other scholars, e.g., "A wisdom inspired by the Spirit" (Marshall, *Acts*, 126–27). Similarly, see Shelton, "Filled," 101n5.

26. Haenchen, *Acts*, 263–64. Similarly, see Haya-Prats, *Empowered*, 161.

(6:8) who, in debate with his opponents, explained the gospel in such a compelling way that they could not counter the "wisdom or the Spirit by which he spoke" (6:10).[27]

In the same way, when the almost identical phrase "full of the Holy Spirit and faith" is applied to Barnabas in 11:24 we are not to think of "faith" in this context as saving faith but the kind of faith that had confidence in the power of God to embrace the hitherto suspect Gentiles. Someone other than Barnabas might have arrived in the predominantly Gentile city of Antioch and tried to shut the work down for not abiding by Jewish-Christian scruples. But Barnabas when he arrived in the Syrian city, full of that far-seeing and boundary-breaking faith born of the Holy Spirit, instead of being upset "was glad" and with his generous pastoral disposition "encouraged them all to remain true to the Lord with all their hearts" (11:23). It may even be that the reference to Barnabas's "goodness" in 11:24 is a reflection of the latter being "full of the Spirit," even though, as acknowledged by Haya-Prats, the term itself falls outside the two-part genitive construction in the sentence "he was a good man, full of the Holy Spirit and faith."[28]

An even wider application of the phrase "full of the Spirit" can be seen when applied to Stephen who, at the point of being stoned by his accusers, nonetheless "full of the Holy Spirit" looked up to heaven and in a vision saw the glory of God with Jesus standing at his right hand. Understanding the phrase "full of the Holy Spirit" as applying primarily to the vision rather than to Stephen's report of the vision,[29] we see that Stephen's experience of Spirit fullness on this occasion is one step further removed from the Spirit-resourced qualities of wisdom and practical faith noted in 6:3, 5 and 11:24, not to speak of the radically different impact of the Spirit associated with the verb *pimplēmi* in 2:4; 4:8, 31; 9:17; 13:9.

On the basis of the above observations it seems legitimate to draw the conclusion that the phrase, "full of (*plērēs*) the Holy Spirit" in the book of Acts, has a considerably wider range of application than does the verbal phrase "filled with the Holy Spirit" derived from the verb *pimplēmi*. While empowerment for mission was for Luke perhaps the most telling feature of being filled with the Spirit, as attested by his use of the verb *pimplēmi* in the first thirteen chapters of Acts, the use of the phrase "full of (*plērēs*)

---

27. Turner nicely describes Stephen's "evangelistic skill and adroitness" exemplified in 6:10 as a more specialized instance of the wisdom referenced in 6:3, namely, the wisdom "that facilitates the application of the Gospel pastorally to the day-to-day praxis of the church" (Turner, *Power from on High*, 411).

28. Haya-Prats, *Empowered*, 162. Turner supports the view that Barnabas's goodness should be understood in the context of his being full of the Holy Spirit. See Turner, *Power from on High*, 408.

29. Cf. "The Holy Spirit opens the eyes of Stephen . . . to the heavenly Reality so infinitely raised above all earthly polemics" (Haenchen, *Acts*, 292). Similarly, see Levison, *Filled*, 244; Haya-Prats, *Empowered*, 156. Others—such as Shelton—see the phrase "full of the Holy Spirit" as applying just as much to Stephen's words addressed to his hostile audience in 7:56 (Shelton, "Filled," 83–84; *Mighty in Word and Deed*, 138), a reading critiqued by Turner both in "Empowerment," 108, 113n14, as well as in *Power from on High*, 168.

the Spirit" in those same chapters suggests his pneumatology was not restricted to the notion of prophetic empowerment.[30]

## The Verb *plēroō* in Acts 13:52

We turn next to consider the sole use of the verb *plēroō* in conjunction with the Holy Spirit in Acts 13:52. In this passage Luke records that "The disciples were filled (*eplērounto*, imperfect passive) with joy and the Holy Spirit." This is the last sentence in the account of Paul and Barnabas's visit to Pisidian Antioch during what is traditionally known as Paul's first missionary journey. The apostles had preached the gospel in the synagogue of that city to which there had been a positive response by many "Jews and God fearers" (13:43). But when on the following Sabbath almost the whole city gathered to hear "the word of the Lord," some Jews "were filled with jealousy" and contradicted what Paul had said (13:45), and in the process, stirred up persecution against the missionaries, forcing them to leave the region (13:50). But as for the disciples who were left in the city, they "were filled with joy and with the Holy Spirit."

It is obvious that the verb *plēroō* employed here is formally related to the adjective *plērēs*. The use of the durative imperfect (*eplērounto*) suggests a kind of extended fullness (as reflected in the NASB [over] translation, "the disciples were continually filled"), different from the episodic fillings associated with the use of *pimplēmi* in the aorist. Important to note, too, is the fact that the verb *eplērounto* on this occasion is followed by the double genitive of content just as was the case with the double genitives following the adjective *plērēs* in 6:3, 5 and 11:24, only that in this instance the entities in the genitive are "joy and the Holy Spirit."

In the case of the *plērēs* passages we found a special relationship to exist between the two entities in the double genitives.[31] We need to ask now if the same is true in 13:52, that is, whether here, too, there exists a close relationship between the disciples' experience of "joy" and the "Holy Spirit." Are they two separate entities or is there a cause-and-effect relationship between them? We should not be far wrong in suggesting that the joy experienced by the recent converts had its source in the Holy

---

30. It is interesting to observe that even someone like Hermann Gunkel—for whom the role of the Spirit was primarily about supernatural empowerment—had to acknowledge that in such passages as Acts 6:3, 5, 10, Luke showed he was not totally indifferent to "the moral-religious sphere" of the Spirit (Gunkel, *Influence*, 18). Other scholars—such as von Baer, Bovon, and Wenk—adopt a similar position. See von Baer, *Der heilige Geist* (as reported by Menzies, *Empowered*, 35; Turner, *Power from on High*, 32–35); Bovon, *Luke the Theologian*, 247–48; Wenk, *Community-Forming Power*, 291. Menzies, however, argues that in the book of Acts the Spirit is exclusively the agent of inspired speech and not the source of the religious and ethical life of the Christian (Menzies, *Empowered*, 258–59). With respect to Stronstad's position on this issue, Wenk summarizes it well when he says that although Stronstad views the Spirit as primarily the Spirit of prophecy linked to inspired speech and witness, "he [Stronstad] does not deny any ethical dimension of the Spirit in Luke-Acts" (Wenk, *Community-Forming Power*, 37n125).

31. See above.

Spirit.³² If this is so, we note how different is Luke's use not only of the adjective *plērēs* (as previously observed) but now also of the verb *plēroō* in comparison with his use of *pimplēmi* in contexts where prophetic speech is to the fore. Here, then, is another testimony to the fact that while Luke's pneumatology in the book of Acts initially highlights the Spirit's empowerment for prophetic speech, it is not limited to or confined by that aspect of the Spirit's work.

## Summary of Luke's Use of *pimplēmi*, *plērēs* and *plēroō* in the Book of Acts

On the basis of the above analysis of Luke's vocabulary employed in the phrases "filled with" and "full of" the Holy Spirit, I conclude that when Luke wants to give prominence to the role of the Spirit in empowering the disciples for courageous and articulate witness to the gospel he uses the verb *pimplēmi*. When he wants to speak about the role of the Spirit in equipping the disciples for extended administrative and pastoral work, or in privileging a person like Stephen with a vision of heaven, or in inspiring conversion joy in a new community of disciples, however, he prefers to use the adjective *plērēs* and the verb *plēroō*. To acknowledge this is not to question Luke's perspective on the empowering/missionary impulse of the Spirit, but it is to observe that Luke had an appreciation for the role of the Spirit broader than that manifested in passages employing the verb *pimplēmi*.

## Paul's Use of the Verb *plēroō* in Ephesians 5:18

We need now to look at the apostle Paul's use of the verb *plēroō* in Eph 5:18, the same verb that Luke used in Acts 13:52. The traditional translation of Eph 5:18, "Do not get drunk on wine . . . but be filled with the Spirit (*plērousthe en pneumati*)," seems straightforward enough, yet there is a question whether the apostle's exhortation can legitimately be translated "be filled *with* the Spirit" or whether it should be translated—as some insist—"be filled *by* the Spirit." Without going into great detail surrounding the debate, given that both translations can be defended grammatically I will sometimes employ the inclusive phrase "with/by the Spirit."³³

What, then (according to Paul) does it mean for believers to be "filled with/by the Spirit"? How is the evidence of that filling expressed? Thankfully we do not have far to look, since, as has often been observed, in four parallel participial constructions in

---

32. As suggested by Bruce when he says that the disciples were filled with the joy "begotten by the indwelling Spirit of Christ" (Bruce, *Acts*, 269) or the joy "inspired by the Holy Spirit" (Bruce, *Acts, Greek Text*, 316). Similarly, Turner, *Power from on High*, 408, 411; Cullen, "Euphoria," 22.

33. The argument for a dative of means translation is strongly advocated by Daniel Wallace (Wallace, *Grammar*, 93n62, 170–71, 374–75n55) while the counter argument that both a dative of means ("*by* the Spirit") and a dative of content ("*with* the Spirit") are legitimate translations is represented by Gordon Fee (Fee, *Empowering*, 721n196).

verses 19–21 Paul spells out fairly clearly what it would look like for the Ephesians to be filled with/by the Spirit. It would mean:

- *speaking* (*lalountes*) to one another in psalms, hymns and songs of/from the Spirit (v. 19a),
- *singing* and *making music* (*aidontes kai psallontes*) from your heart to the Lord (v. 19b),
- *giving thanks* (*eucharistountes*) always to God the Father . . . (v. 20),
- *submitting* (*hypotassomenoi*) to one another out of reverence for Christ (v. 21)

The above participial constructions focus in turn on corporate worship (vv. 19–20) and mutual relationships (v. 21), the latter applied in the subsequent paragraphs to household relationships, that is, to relationships between wives and husbands, children and parents, slaves and masters (5:22–6:4). In effect, therefore, the Ephesian believers are to demonstrate their having been "filled by/with the Spirit" by their quality of worship in the assembly (vv. 19–20) and by their mutual submission in a broad range of relationships at home and beyond (5:21–6:4). The fact that the Greek participles in question are all in the present continuous tense suggests an ongoing or repeated state of being filled.

## Significance of the above Observations

Two questions now remain for us: What are the implications of the above findings for (1) the relationship between Luke and Paul on the question of being filled with/by the Spirit and (2) the practical implications of the fact that in different contexts in the book of Acts believers are described as "filled with" or "full of" the Holy Spirit, and of Paul's exhortation for the Ephesians to be "filled with" (or "filled by") the Holy Spirit?

### The relationship between Luke and Paul

Comparing Acts 13:52 and Ephesians 5:18 we note that in these verses Luke and Paul have a number of things in common. Both passages contain the writers' only use of the verb *plēroō* in association with the Holy Spirit. Both passages employ the verb in the passive voice and both use either the imperfect or present continuous tense (not the aorist as was the case with Luke's use of *pimplēmi*). Also, both involve an experience of the Spirit's fullness in a community setting. In these small but, nonetheless, significant ways, Luke and Paul bear testimony to similar understandings of the Spirit's filling in the lives of believers. If Luke in Acts 13:52 saw a close connection between the disciples' experience of Spirit fullness and conversion joy, so Paul in Ephesians 5:18–33 saw a close relationship between being filled with the Spirit and community formation.

Admittedly, Paul was very sparse (only one recorded instance!) in his use of explicit "filling" language in comparison with that of Luke. But if, for a moment, we consider Spirit passages in other Pauline contexts we can readily document a number of areas where the two writers had overlapping perspectives. For instance, Paul is not averse to using the language of empowerment with reference to the Spirit.[34] Likewise, he can affirm the role of the Spirit in providing wisdom both in communication and practical matters,[35] just as he can associate the Spirit with conversion joy.[36]

This is not to say that Luke and Paul have identical pneumatologies. Of course not! Paul's rich and diverse understanding of the person and work of the Spirit is well documented[37] and unstintingly acknowledged by Stronstad himself in the closing section of his last essay, "The Rebirth of Prophecy."[38] If we ask whether there is an analogous diversity in Luke's understanding of the role of the Spirit in the life of the church, the answer is probably "No," at least when it comes to comparing breadth and variety of pneumatic expression. Yet—and here is the big *yet*—is it possible that we have to allow for more overlap in the pneumatologies of Luke and Paul than we have been willing to do? Is it at all significant that both Luke and Paul could use the same vocabulary in describing the impact of the Spirit's fullness on a group of recent believers in Pisidian Antioch (in the case of Luke), and (in the case of Paul) in exhorting the Ephesians to experience the same Spirit's fullness in their community life? My analysis of both Luke and Paul's use of filling/fulness language, however narrowly focused, inclines me to think that the question is worth posing.

Pentecostal studies on Luke-Acts have flourished in the wake of redaction and narrative criticism. Both disciplines have been absolutely critical in giving legitimacy to Luke as a biblical and pastoral theologian in his own right with his own distinctive emphases. The gains in our understanding of Luke's pneumatology have been monumental and no one would want to go back to an era of Pentecostal scholarship that predated Stronstad's pioneering work. But now the question presses on us whether the time has come to build on those solid gains and dare to look not only for distinctives, but also for continuities in the various NT perspectives on the Holy Spirit. Here one thinks of what exciting overlaps one may find arising from a thoroughgoing

---

34. Note phrases such as "through the power of the Spirit" (Rom 15:19); by "demonstration of the Spirit and of power" (1 Cor 2:4); "gifts of healing [given] by the one Spirit" (1 Cor 12:9); it is God who supplies the Spirit and works miracles among the Galatians (Gal 3:5).

35. Note the following: "to one is given through the Spirit the word of wisdom" (1 Cor 12:8); "that God may give you the Spirit of wisdom and revelation" (Eph 1:17); "the help given by the Spirit of Jesus Christ" (Phil 1:19); "asking God to fill you with the knowledge of his will through all the wisdom and understanding that the Spirit gives" (Col 1:9).

36. He does this when writing to the Thessalonians, who received the word in great affliction with joy "given by the Holy Spirit" (1 Thess 1:6). In Romans, Paul speaks of "peace and joy in the Holy Spirit" (Rom 14:17).

37. Here we need look no further than to Gordon Fee's comprehensive study, *Empowered*, or his shorter *Paul, the Spirit, and the People of God*.

38. Stronstad, "Rebirth," 22–28.

comparison and contrast of the pneumatologies of Luke, Paul and John. In his own way, Stronstad has contributed to that project in his essay on "The Rebirth of Prophecy" by discussing, in turn, "The Witness of Luke," "The Witness of John," and the "Witness of Paul."[39] Further studies of this type could lead to new and groundbreaking insights.[40]

## What It Means in Practical Terms to Be Filled with the Spirit

Whatever we may think of the challenge articulated above, there is one challenge that none of us dare neglect, namely, what it means for all of us to demonstrate a Christian life "filled with" and "full of" the Holy Spirit. If it is true that being "filled with the Spirit" is a metaphor, as James Dunn says, for being "taken over or controlled" by the Spirit,[41] how is that ideal being reflected in our professional endeavors no less than in our personal relationships? The passion in our witness and scholarship is fine as long as it is rooted in a manner of expression consistent with both Luke and Paul's perspectives on the Spirit-filled life. It is understandable if, at times, we have been tempted to focus more on those contexts in which Luke uses the verb *pimplēmi* for empowered Spirit fillings at the expense of his equally important choice of the words *plērēs* and *plēroō* for pastoral related work, not to speak of Paul's choice of *plēroō* language in Eph 5:18 for the critical function of community formation. It remains for us to seek an integration of these and all other Spirit metaphors to which the biblical writers bear witness. Along these lines is where the next phase of Spirit research could profitably lie.

---

39. Stronstad, "Rebirth," 6–28.

40. Levison's book, *Filled with the Spirit*, which burst on the scene in 2009 with a kind of tour de force, could be regarded as an exercise of this type, but the reception has been mixed. See the articles assessing the work in the *Journal of Pentecostal Theology* (Levison, "Filled with the Spirit"; Stronstad, "Review"; Turner, "Levison's *Filled with the Spirit*"; Waddell, "Holy Spirit of Life").

41. Dunn, *Baptism*, 171.

## Chapter 22

# The Spirit in the Book of Revelation
## *A Narrative Hearing*

### JOHN CHRISTOPHER THOMAS[1]

In the study that follows I offer a narrative hearing of the Spirit in the Book of Revelation.[2] An initial understanding of the Spirit's role at the macro-structural level offers a helpful backdrop for this hearing. The book begins with a prologue (1:1–8) that includes the first mention of the seven Spirits before the throne (1:4) and concludes with an epilogue (22:6–21) that contains the final reference to the Spirit (22:17). Standing between this beginning and ending are four "in the Spirit" phrases (1:10; 4:2; 17:3; 21:10) around which the book appears to be structured.[3] Within each of these major sections various references to the Spirit are to be found. Taken together these macro-structural details reveal something about the way in which pneumatology is part of the very theological fabric of the book.

---

1. When first reading Roger Stronstad's *The Charismatic Theology of St. Luke*, I was immediately convinced that it was, at that time, the most important contribution to biblical studies made by a Pentecostal scholar. As with so many seminal pieces, its incredible significance and impact was out of all proportions to its relative short length. In many ways, Roger's little book marked a sea change in the way Pentecostal biblical scholars would navigate the world of biblical scholarship from that point on as a self-consciously Pentecostal undertaking. His pioneering work would facilitate the way in which the theological task would be conceived and envisioned for a large swath of biblical scholars in the tradition who would follow his lead. If he had never written another word, this contribution would have been the kind that most of scholars dream of making, but there was more to come from his pen—work that has continued to nurture, instruct, and engage a multitude of Pentecostal biblical scholars and beyond. Words are inadequate to express the debt many of us owe to you Roger and I am happy here to acknowledge my own debt publicly. I cannot imagine what Pentecostal biblical studies would have looked like if you, Roger, had not come along! It is an honor for me to be invited to contribute to this *festschrift* in your honor my friend.

2. For a more comprehensive discussion of the passages examined in this study cf. Thomas, *Apocalypse*; Thomas and Macchia, *Revelation*.

3. On the structure of Revelation, see Bauckham, *Climax*, 3–31.

## The Spirit in the Prologue

The first reference to the Spirit comes in the book's prologue as part of the author's greeting addressed to the recipients where the blessings of grace and peace are extended from "the one who is and was and is coming and from the seven Spirits which are before his throne and from Jesus Christ" (1:4). The initial appearance of the seven Spirits within this "divine" context reveals something of the Spirit's significance and identity. Appearing between "the one who is and was and is coming" and "Jesus Christ," the seven Spirits by association appear to be part of this holy community, at the very least suggesting a divine identity for the seven Spirits.[4] This identity is further informed by the order of this listing, as somewhat unexpectedly the seven Spirits occur after reference to the "the one who is and was and is coming," but before reference to "Jesus Christ." Whilst this order may have a variety of theological implications it minimally indicates that the mention of the seven Spirits is anything but perfunctory and prepares the hearers for the Spirit's divine activity as the narrative unfolds. This surprising order also reveals that a close relationship exists between "the one who is and was and is coming" and the seven Spirits, as well as between "Jesus Christ" and the seven Spirits. The location of the seven Spirits "before" the throne indicates the readiness of the seven Spirits to do the bidding of "the one who is and was and is coming," whilst appearing in the listing before "Jesus Christ" may well be in anticipation of the close relationship between the seven Spirits and "Jesus Christ" that awaits the hearers in the narrative to come. Finally, the significance of the number seven in "the seven Spirits" is likely in accord with the use of the number seven previously in v. 4, "the seven churches," and its occurrences later in the book as a whole, where the meaning of completion seems to be the point. On this understanding, reference to the seven Spirits is reference to the Spirit in its fullness.

## In the Spirit

As the hearers move from the Prologue to the body of the document they encounter the first of four "in the Spirit" phrases located throughout the book. The strategic location of these phrases informs the hearers of the text in several ways. First, their locations underscore the way in which the book presents John's revelatory experience as coming by way of the Spirit. As such, the hearers could hardly miss the point that it is by means of John's extraordinary experience of the Spirit that he receives these incredible visions. Since John is instructed to write what he sees (1:19), it appears that what he writes is that which is revealed by means of the Spirit.[5]

Second, the fact that John is regularly said to be "in the Spirit" conveys something about the nature of John's pneumatic experience. Whether or not his experience of the

---

4. Molina, *El Espíritu*.
5. Koester, *Revelation*, 270.

PART IV—READING ST. LUKE'S PNEUMATOLOGY WITH OTHER TEXTS

Spirit is viewed as an ecstatic experience in the classical sense, it is self-evident that John does not lose control of his abilities to observe the visions given, nor to interact with agents of discernment along the way, whether divine, angelic, or human. John's pneumatic experience appears to be understood as on the order of prophetic experience witnessed in the Hebrew Bible, including transportation via the Spirit.

Third, the appearance of each individual "in the Spirit" phrase at various places both, on the one hand, conveys a sense of a change of scene and subject matter; and, on the other hand, literally moves the hearers progressively through the narrative—from Patmos, to heaven, to the wilderness, and finally to the New Jerusalem. The fact that the narrative lacks any indication that John is no longer "in the Spirit" may also reveal something of John's own ongoing experience of the Spirit—perhaps as a model for the community.

Fourth, the "in the Spirit" phrases also underscore the close relationship between the Spirit and worship in the Apocalypse, as worship appears to be the context that makes being "in the Spirit" possible.[6] It is this context that opens the worshipper to the vicarious reception of visions of the resurrected Jesus, to hearing and keeping the prophetic words given by the Spirit, as well as creating the context for discerning reflection as a community.

The significant role the Spirit plays structurally within the book as a whole, is supplemented by the fact that within each of the four major sections introduced by an "in the Spirit" phrase (1:9—3:22; 4:1—16:21; 17:1—21:8; 21:9—22:9) are found multiple references to the Spirit indicating that the Spirit is indeed deeply embedded in the book's theological cloth.

## In the Spirit on the Lord's Day (Rev 1:10)

After having been introduced to the seven Spirits before the throne in the book's prologue (1:4), within the first major section marked by John being "in the Spirit" on the Lord's day (1:9—3:22), one finds seven calls to pneumatic discernment—"the one who has an ear let that one hear what the Spirit is saying to the churches" (2:7, 11, 17, 29; 3:6, 13, 22). Rather than mere repetition, these invitations provide additional concrete information about the role and identity of the Spirit in the book. First, the inaugural appearance of this formula (and later ones as well) indicates that the discerning process to which the hearers are called is not simply a Christological one (1:20), but a pneumatological one as well.[7]

Second, while this refrain indicates that the words to be heard—and thus obeyed—are the words of the Spirit, they are also rather clearly the words that the resurrected Jesus himself is speaking. That is to say, the words the Spirit is saying are

---

6. Archer, "I Was in the Spirit," 130–31.

7. On the subject of pneumatic discernment in the Apocalypse, see Johnson, *Pneumatic Discernment*.

coterminous with the words prophetically spoken by Jesus. The fact that Jesus and the Spirit speak with one voice, without losing their individual identities (14:13), reveals that the relationship between them is closer than their appearance together in the prologue initially suggests (1:4–5).

Third, it would be clear to the hearers that the Spirit who is heard speaking to the church is the same Spirit who enables John's revelatory experience when he is "in the Spirit" and is the same Spirit as the seven Spirits who are before the throne, indicating that the relationship between the Spirit, "the one who is and was and is coming," and Jesus Christ is an especially intimate one.

Fourth, these formulae are concrete calls for discerning reflection on the part of the hearer about how to keep the words of this prophecy with regard to each individual prophetic message as well as the prophetic messages as a whole. The entire interpretive process of discernment appears to be a pneumatic one.

There is also in this first major section a reference to the resurrected Jesus "having the seven Spirits of God" (3:1). This phrase not only further underscores the intimate relationship between Jesus and the Spirit, but it also highlights by extension the relationship between the resurrected Jesus and the one who sits on the throne before whom the seven Spirits are located.

## In the Spirit in Heaven (Rev 4:2)

The second major section of the book, marked by John being "in the Spirit" in heaven (4:1–16:21), is the longest of the book's four parts and contains multiple references to the Spirit. John's description of again being "in the Spirit" would not only function as a structural marker indicating that a change of venue—in this case to heaven—has taken place, but also would suggest that John does not stop being "in the Spirit" as the book moves from Patmos to the heavenly throne room.

The next reference to the Spirit comes fast on the heels of the "in the Spirit" phrase where in a description of the heavenly throne room of God reference is made to "seven lamps of fire sitting before the throne" (4:5), which are immediately identified as "the seven Spirits of God." Mention of these seven lamps of fire would contribute to the sacred context of the heavenly temple reminding of the seven lamps set in the tabernacle (Exod 25:31–40; 40:4, 24–25), as well as the seven lamps that set on Zechariah's golden lampstand (Zech 4:1–14). The lamps being described as "of fire" further connects the activity of the Spirit to that of Jesus, whose eyes of fire say something about the purity and clarity of his vision. At the same time, the close proximity of these seven lamps to the throne reinforces the intimate connection that exists between God and the Spirit, as does the fact that these lamps are explicitly identified as "the seven Spirits of God," further emphasizing the close relationship between God and Jesus who both seem to be in possession of the seven Spirits (3:1).

Still in the heavenly throne room scene, the pneumatological story continues when, in the midst of the description of the initial appearance of the Lamb that looks as though he has been slaughtered, the Lamb is described as having "seven horns and seven eyes which are the seven Spirits of God sent into all the earth" (5:6). Paired with the image of the seven horns—indicating that the Lamb is all-powerful—is the new imagery of the Lamb's seven eyes. Such an image provides additional details of the emerging picture of the Spirit's identity. First, the description of the seven eyes as belonging to the Lamb continues the emphasis upon the extraordinarily close relationship that exists between Jesus and the Spirit, pushing this intimacy even further than before. One of the implications of such an embodied depiction of the seven eyes is that when the Lamb is subsequently worshipped by every creature in the universe, the Spirit is in some way involved in the reception of such worship. Such an implication makes clearer the divine identity of the Spirit that was earlier hinted in the divine context in which the seven Spirits were originally introduced (1:4). Second, the numerical depiction of seven eyes underscores the fact that the Lamb has perfect, one might say, discerning vision as earlier revealed in Revelation 2–3. Mention of these seven eyes underscores yet again the fact that the Spirit's work of discerning knowledge is coterminous with that of the Lamb. Third, the explicit identification of the seven eyes as the seven Spirits of God, not only removes any confusion over the identity of the seven eyes, but also reinforces once again the intimate relationship of the Spirit to both God and the Lamb and in turn their relationship to one another. Fourth, while the description of the seven Spirits of God as being sent out into all the earth would bring added definition to the extent and/or scope of the vision and knowledge of the slaughtered Lamb, it would also prepare the hearers for the book's pneumatological center.

Standing at the book's physical, if not theological, center is a text in which a number of pneumatological emphases converge both thematically and intertextually. With John's commission "to prophesy again" just described (10:11), the instruction is given to carry out the prophetic activity of measuring the sanctuary *naōn* of God (11:1). Within this context the story of the two witnesses is recounted (11:3–12). These virtual identical prophetic twins are divinely enabled to prophesy (11:3), being identified as the two olive trees and two lampstands who stand before the Lord of the earth, indicting their roles as the anointed servants of the Lord (11:4). Endowed with what appear to be the cumulative powers of a variety of Old Testament prophets, these two witnesses are protected from any opposition until their witness is complete, when the beast from the Abyss arises and is victorious over them and kills them (11:5–8). While their body (described in the singular, for their witness is singular) lies upon the street of the Great City, the universal city's identity is revealed to be Sodom, Egypt, and the place where their Lord was crucified (11:8). This trans-geographical and trans-temporal identification comes via pneumatic discernment, as the Greek word *pneumatikōs* indicates. While translations of the term as "figuratively," "metaphorically," "symbolically," "allegorically," or even "spiritually" are philologically possible, they obscure the fact that this kind of discernment is clearly connected to the work of the Spirit, as the term *pneuma* stands at its root. For the hearers, who have experienced various kinds of divine interpretive assistance throughout the Apocalypse, this additional assistance would remind of their call to such discerning reflection at every step of the interpretive journey. The importance of this theme is further underscored by this text's location within the book. As Waddell notes, "In the center of the Apocalypse, John places the story of the two witnesses, and in the center of this brief narrative, John describes the spiritual insight of the church discerning the reality of the great city."[8] In close textual proximity to the description of this pneumatic interpretive event, stands the next occurrence of the Spirit in the book (11:11). After the two witnesses' death, they are denied burial with everyone witnessing their complete humiliation and even rejoicing over their death by the exchanging of gifts to mark the occasion. But when three and a half days had passed, "a Spirit of life from God" entered into them and stood them upon their feet. It is self-evident that this statement affirms yet again the intimate relationship between God and the Spirit that has been observed throughout the text. At the same time, it would not be lost on the hearers that the same Spirit who anoints the two witnesses for their prophetic witness is the same Spirit who raises them to life after their death and enables their ultimate ascension to heaven. The Spirit's activity confirms their prophetic anointing and—along with other divine activities—leads to the conversion of 90 percent of the Great City's population with only a remnant not surviving (11:13), an inversion of Old Testament ideas regarding a remnant.

In Revelation 12–14, which appears to reveal the content of the opened scroll, the hearers encounter the evil triumvirate of the dragon, the beast, and the second beast who, in many ways, parody the figures and activities of God, the Lamb, and the Spirit. It is within the description of these activities that the next occurrence of the word "spirit" appears (13:15). At this point in the narrative, the second beast uses his derived authority to give *pneuma* to the image of the beast in order that the image might speak and cause those who do not worship the image of the beast to be killed. Coming on the heels of the account of the two witnesses, and their pneumatic experience, it is difficult not to see here a parody of the Spirit's action. If the words the image is enabled to speak are deemed to be prophetic words, the parody is made all the greater.

Coming near the climax of Revelation 12–14 the Spirit speaks. On this occasion John says, "And I heard a voice from out of heaven saying, 'Write: Blessed are the dead who die in the Lord from now on.'" To this, the book's second beatitude, the Spirit adds his own affirmation, "Yes . . . in order that they might rest from their labor, for their works follow after them" (14:13). In contrast to those who worship the beast and find no eschatological rest day or night (14:11), those who die in the Lord enter into rest from their labor as faithful witnesses. Just as the two witnesses are vindicated by the Spirit after their death, so those who die in the Lord are reassured that the fruit of their labor is not confined to the time of their earthly life, but the fruit of their faithful

---

8. Waddell, *Spirit*, 182.

labor will continue to follow them even after death. The fact that the Spirit speaks in such a clearly demarcated way, and in close association with the voice from heaven, provides additional definition to the Spirit's individual identity in the book as well as the Spirit's close relationship with God.

Before this second and longest section of the book closes, reference is made for the first time to other kinds of spirits aside from the divine Spirit. As the sixth bowl of final plagues is being poured out, John saw coming from the mouths of the dragon, the beast, and the false prophet, three unclean spirits as frogs who are identified as demonic spirits who perform signs and go out to all the kings of the earth to gather them to the war of the great day of God the all-powerful one (16:13–14). In this text the triumvirate of evil (the dragon, the beast, and the false prophet), who are mentioned here together for the first time in the book, providing a further parody of God, the Lamb, and the Spirit. With the introduction of "unclean spirits" for the first time in the whole of the Johannine literature, the parody of the work of the Spirit by the false prophet—previously known as the beast from the earth—in particular becomes clearer. Although demons that inspire idolatrous worship have been mentioned earlier in the book (9:20), the emphasis here is upon the uncleanness of these spirits, made clear not only by means of their explicit description as such, but also in the imagery of the frogs, a ritually unclean animal according to the Torah (Lev 11:9–12), used to describe them. Specifically, these unclean spirits parody the work of the Spirit by the doing of signs and by going out. But whereas the seven Spirits of God go out into all the earth to inspire faithful witness, these unclean spirits go out to inspire the kings of the whole inhabited world to gather for the war to end all wars with God. In keeping with the depiction of the demonic, antichrists, deceivers, and other spirits throughout the Johannine literature, the work of these unclean demonic spirits is also focused on deception.[9]

## In the Spirit in the Wilderness (Rev 17:3)

The third major section of the book (17:1—21:8) is marked by John being "in the Spirit" in the wilderness (17:3). As the hearer has learned, John's description of again being "in the Spirit" not only functions as a structural marker indicating the change of venue, this time to the wilderness, but also by this point it would imply even more strongly than before that John appears constantly (to be) "in the Spirit" (17:3).

This third "in the spirit" phrase is followed by another reference to unclean spirits in the words from the strong voice of the mighty angel that announces the fall of Babylon the Great (18:2). In this context Babylon is identified as a place of idolatrous worship as the phrase "habitation of demons" implies, owing to the previous role of demons in the book (9:20; 16:13–14) and the way in which the verbal form of the

---

9. Thomas, "Role and Function," 27–47.

noun here translated "habitation" has often appeared in Revelation in association with those who oppose God or his people (3:10; 6:10; 8:13; 11:10; 13:8, 12, 14; 17:2, 8). For the second time in the book, demons and unclean spirits are connected (16:13–14), as Babylon is now identified as a "prison of every unclean spirit." Such language would likely suggest that Babylon, which had dominated or imprisoned so many others—as she was "sitting upon the many waters" (17:1), is now herself a prison full of unclean spirits, spirits that have been associated with deception and idolatry. The focus on uncleanness continues in the next words that identify the other occupants as "every unclean and hateful bird." Such descriptions make clear that these unclean spirits stand in diametric opposition to the Spirit of God in the Apocalypse.

The final reference to the Spirit in this section is one of the most significant in the entire book. It occurs in the context of great rejoicing in heaven by the redeemed, which includes reference to the bride of the Lamb, who is divinely given "fine linen, bright and pure" linen that is at the same time described as "the righteous acts of the saints" (19:8). When John is given the command to write, "Blessed are those who are called to the marriage supper of the Lamb," by one of the righteous ones—who seems to represent the chorus of the redeemed (19:9), John attempts to worship this fellow servant and brother who also has the testimony of Jesus. But the figure refuses the worship instructing John, "Worship God, for the witness of Jesus is the Spirit of prophecy" (19:10). In this compact, concise statement a number of pneumatological and related themes converge in what is one of the most important statements about the Spirit in the book, with several aspects worthy of specific mention. First, the Greek text indicates that the statement about the Spirit of prophecy is rooted and grounded in the command to worship God, made clear by the Greek word translated as "for" that stands at the beginning of the phrase. Such a distinct connection fits well within a book that has emphasized the witness of Jesus, its intimate connection to the work of the Spirit, and its constant focus on the worship of God and avoidance of idolatrous worship.

Second, while the phrase "the witness of Jesus" can grammatically be taken as either emphasizing the witness which Jesus offers or the witness offered about Jesus, it is unlikely that the hearers would make a distinction between these grammatical options as both dimensions of Jesus's witness appear in a very integrated fashion throughout the book.

Third, the book has underscored Jesus as the faithful witness *par excellence* who has been slaughtered for bearing witness (1:5), a witness to which others who follow him are called. These include, but are not limited to, Antipas whom Jesus calls "my faithful witness" who dies as does his Lord (2:13), the souls under the altar who had been slaughtered (6:9–11), the two prophetic witnesses who die and experience resurrection (11:3, 7), as well as those who follow the Lamb wherever he goes (14:4).

Fourth, it should be abundantly clear by this point that the witness of Jesus and the Spirit of prophecy are so intricately connected that it is impossible to understand them apart from one another in the book. The words of Rev 19:10 do not make a simple or static equation between the witness of Jesus and the Spirit of prophecy, for in the Apocalypse the witness of Jesus is quintessentially pneumatic, prophetic, dynamic, and active. The same is true for the witness of the church inspired by the Spirit of prophecy. The seven Spirits of God sent out into all the earth is the same Spirit that empowers the church's prophetic witness. The same Spirit that speaks prophetically to the church is the same Spirit that speaks prophetically to the world. For the hearers of the Apocalypse, the Spirit of prophecy fuels participation in the faithful witness of Jesus. It, too, is an active and dynamic witness that is directed by pneumatic discernment. It is the kind of pneumatic witness that is very much at home in a prophetic community, a community where the prophethood of all believers seems to be a basic understanding.

## In the Spirit in the New Jerusalem (Rev 21:10)

The fourth major section of the book (21:8—22:5) is marked by John being "in the Spirit" in the New Jerusalem (21:10). In this, the shortest of the book's four sections, the only explicit mention of the Spirit comes in this "in the Spirit" phrase, though there is likely an allusion to the Spirit in the reference to "the river of the water of life" that comes from the throne in 22:1. Again, the "in the Spirit" phrase serves as a structural marker indicating another change of venue—the last description of John's pneumatic transportation, this time to the New Jerusalem. As before, John seems always to be "in the Spirit."

## The Spirit in the Epilogue

The book closes with an epilogue that encompasses Rev 22:6–21, though 22:6–7 seems to function as a hinge that both concludes the final major section that precedes and introduces the following epilogue. Even as the book draws to a close, the hearers discover that the pneumatological story continues unabated. Near the end of the description of the New Jerusalem when the revelatory angel says to John, "These words are faithful and true," the hearers not only would be reminded that the same words appeared earlier near the end of the description of the fallen Babylon the Great (21:5), but also that the words of this prophecy are faithful and true and are intended to be kept. It is in this context that the next mention of the Spirit occurs in the continuing words of the revelatory angel, "The Lord, the God of the S/spirits of the prophets sent his angel to show to his servants what is necessary to take place soon" (22:6). Here, a convergence occurs between the theme of the seven Spirits of God who inspire the prophets and the spirits of the prophets who are so anointed. Both the divine and human S/spirits seem to merge in these words. The mention of other prophets in the community would not necessarily come as a surprise to the hearers, for the entire community has been called to offer faithful prophetic witness for which they are equipped by the Spirit. Nor would the mention of other prophets be inconsistent with what follows in the epilogue where the angel informs John that he is John's fellow servant and that "of your brother prophets and those who keep the words of this book" (22:9). The mention of John's brother prophets would confirm something of the extent of the community's prophetic identity for, rather clearly, these prophets are recipients along with John of the visionary details the angel has made known in the Apocalypse. Taken together with the book's previous pneumatological emphases such words would go some way toward leading the hearers to the conclusion that not only is the community, envisioned by the text, a prophetic community, but it might also even be thought of as a community that affirms the prophethood of all believers for those who are part of the community.

Further on in the epilogue, and very near the book's conclusion (22:17), in the final appearance of the Spirit, the Spirit and the bride join together and issue the invitation, "Come." Standing near the close of the book these words would be informed by all those that have preceded with regard to the Spirit and the bride. For by this point the hearers would be more fully informed about the identity and activities of the Spirit which include: the Spirit's intimate relationship to God, the Lamb, and the churches; the way in which the seven Spirits are send out into all the earth; and the role the Spirit plays in the inspiration of the prophetic witness of the church. This Spirit, which speaks to the church and beyond it, now joins voices with the bride, earlier identified with the saints (19:8), in issuing the salvific invitation to any other potential hearers to "come" in response to the prophetic message for the conversion of the nations. This united invitation reveals that the prophetic pneumatically inspired message of the bride is here coterminous with the message that comes from the Spirit. Just as Jesus and the Spirit speak coterminously, though retaining separate identities, so now the bride and the Spirit speak in a coterminous fashion, perhaps bringing additional clarity to the statement, "the witness of Jesus is the Spirit of prophecy" (19:10).

## Major Theological Implications of This Narrative Hearing

A variety of theological themes emerge from this hearing of Revelation's pneumatological story. The following may capture some of the important dimensions:

First, perhaps the most significant foundational element of the Spirit's theological identity in the Apocalypse is rooted and grounded in the unique relationship the Spirit shares with God and Jesus Christ. From the book's beginning, the Spirit appears in what might be called "divine," often triadic, contexts. Whether located before the throne (1:4; 4:5), described as belonging to God and/or Jesus (3:1; 5:6), speaking the words of Jesus in a coterminous fashion with him (2:7, 11, 17, 29; 3:6, 13, 22), being the seven eyes of the Lamb (5:6), acting on God's behalf (5:6; 11:11), and/or speaking with divine authority (14:13; 22:17), the Spirit's intimate relationship with God and/or the Lamb reveals a variety of divine associations that suggest something of the Spirit's own divine identity.

Second, the role faithful prophetic witness plays in the book is extraordinarily important. Built upon the foundation of the witness of Jesus, the faithful witness *par excellence*, believers are called upon to offer faithful prophetic witness in the face of a hostile world. This kind of faithful witness, which often results in the death of the witnesses, (12:11) is fueled by the activity of the Spirit. Explicit examples of this phenomenon are seen in the story of the two prophetic witnesses in 11:1–13 and in the pronouncement in 19:10 that "the witness of Jesus is the Spirit of prophecy."

Third, throughout the book John and his hearers are called to and aided in the process of discernment. On occasion such assistance is offered from the resurrected Jesus himself (1:20), one of the elders (7:13–14), and angelic beings (14:6–13), but clearly, the Spirit plays a significant, if not the most significant, role. In addition to the seven distinct calls in the seven prophetic messages for the one who has an ear to hear what the Spirit is saying to the churches, this aspect of the Spirit's role and function is most readily seen in the account of the two prophet witnesses where the identity of the great city is revealed *pneumatikōs* "by means of the Spirit."

Fourth, in the Apocalypse the experience of the Spirit seems to permeate community life at nearly every level. The extent and variety of Spirit activity within the community implied from the narrative suggests it to be a pneumatic community, comprised of individual members for whom a significant role for Spirit activity would appear to be an ongoing, normative expectation. The "in the Spirit" phrase might even be regarded as a cypher for the community's Spirit experiences.

# Bibliography

Aalen, Sverre. "'Reign' and 'House' in the Kingdom of God in the Gospels." *NTS* 8 (1962) 215–40.

Abrahams, I. *Studies in Pharisaism and the Gospels*. Second Series. Cambridge: Cambridge University Press, 1924.

Albrecht, Daniel E. *Rites in the Spirit: A Ritual Approach to Pentecostal/Charismatic Spirituality*. Sheffield: Sheffield Academic, 1999.

Albright, William Foxwell, and C. S. Mann. *Matthew*. AB 26. Garden City, NY: Doubleday, 1971.

Alexander, Kimberly Ervin. *Pentecostal Healing: Models in Theology and Practice*. Cleveland, TN: Deo, 2006.

Allen, A. A. *God Will Heal You*. Miracle Valley, AZ: A. A. Allen Revivals, n.d.

———. "Private Letter to Patricia Pickard, April 28, 1989." Retrieved from International Flower Pentecostal Heritage Center, August 22, 2017.

———. *A Prosperity Blest Cloth for You: From God's Man of Faith and Power*. Miracle Valley, AZ: A. A. Allen Revivals, n.d.

Allen, Ronald B. *Numbers*. Vol. 2. Expositor's Bible Commentary. Grand Rapids: Zondervan, 1990.

Anderson, Allan. *An Introduction to Pentecostalism*. Cambridge: Cambridge University Press, 2004.

———. "Pentecostalism in East Asia: Indigenous Oriental Christianity." *Pneuma* 22.1 (2000) 115–32.

Anderson, Gordon. "Pentecostal Hermeneutics Part I." *Paraclete* 28.1 (1994) 1–11.

Angus, S. *The Mystery-Religions and Christianity*. New York: Scribner, 1925.

Archer, Kenneth J. *A Pentecostal Hermeneutic for the Twenty-First Century: Spirit, Scripture, and Community*. JPTSup 28. London: T. & T. Clark, 2004.

———. *A Pentecostal Hermeneutic: Spirit, Scripture and Community*. Cleveland: CPT, 2009.

———. "Pentecostal Hermeneutics: Retrospect and Prospect." *JPT* 8 (1996) 63–81.

———. *Pentecostal Story: The Hermeneutical Filter for the Making of Meaning*. Paper presented to the Annual Meeting of the Society for Pentecostal Studies, Lakeland, FL, March 8–10, 2001.

Archer, Kenneth, and William Oliverio Jr., eds. *Constructive Pneumatological Hermeneutics in Pentecostal Christianity*. London: Palgrave Macmillian, 2016.

Archer, Melissa L. *"I Was in the Spirit on the Lord's Day": A Pentecostal Engagement with Worship in the Apocalypse*. Cleveland, TN: CPT, 2015.

Arokiasamy, S. "Sinful Structures in the Theology of Sin, Conversion, and Reconciliation." In *Social Sin: Its Challenges to Christian Life*, edited by S. Arokiasamy and F. Podimattom, 90–115. Bangalore: Claretian, 1991.

Arrington, French L. *Christian Doctrine: A Pentecostal Perspective*. Vol. 2. Cleveland, TN: Pathway, 1993.

———. "The Use of the Bible by Pentecostals." *Pneuma* 16.1 (1994) 101–8.

Arrington, French L., and Roger Stronstad, eds. *Life in the Spirit New Testament Commentary*. Grand Rapids: Zondervan, 1999.

Asamoah-Gyadu, J. Kwabena. *African Charismatics: Current Developments within Independent Indigenous Pentecostalism in Ghana*. Leiden: Brill, 2006.

Ashbrook, James B., and Carol Rausch Albright. *The Humanizing Brain: Where Religion and Neuroscience Meet*. Cleveland: Pilgrim, 1997.

Ashley, Timothy R. *The Book of Numbers*. NICOT. Grand Rapids: Eerdmans, 1993.

Atkinson, William, P. *Baptism in the Spirit: Luke-Acts and the Dunn Debate*. Eugene, OR: Pickwick, 2011.

———. "Pentecostal Responses to Dunn's *Baptism in the Holy Spirit*: Luke-Acts." *JPT* 6 (1995) 87–131.

———. "Pentecostal Responses to Dunn's *Baptism in the Holy Spirit*: Pauline Literature." *JPT* 7.4 (1995) 9–72.

Au, Connie. "Pentecostalism as Suffering: House Churches in China (1949–2012)." In *The Many Faces of Global Pentecostalism*, edited by Harold D. Hunter and Neil Ormerod, 73–99. Cleveland, TN: CPT, 2013.

Aune, David. *The New Testament in Its Literary Environment*. Philadelphia: Westminster, 1987.

Badcock, Gary. *Light of Truth and Fire of Love: A Theology of the Holy Spirit*. Grand Rapids: Eerdmans, 1997.

Bailey, Kenneth Ewing. *Poet and Peasant: A Literary-Cultural Approach to the Parables in Luke*. Grand Rapids: Eerdmans, 1976.

Ball, David Mark. *'I AM' in John's Gospel: Literary Function, Background, and Theological Implications*. Sheffield: Sheffield Academic, 1996.

Bandstra, Andrew J. "The Original Form of the Lord's Prayer." *CTJ* 16 (1981) 15–37.

Barnett, P. W. "The Jewish Sign Prophets—AD 40–70—Their Intentions and Origin." *NTS* 27 (1981) 679–97.

Barrett, C. K. *The Holy Spirit and the Gospel Tradition*. 1947. Reprint, London: SPCK, 1966.

———. "The Holy Spirit in the Fourth Gospel." *JTS* 1 (1950) 1–15.

Bartholomew, Craig G. *Introducing Biblical Hermeneutics: A Comprehensive Framework for Hearing God in Scripture*. Grand Rapids: Baker Academic, 2015.

Bauckham, Richard. *The Climax of Prophecy*. New York: T&T Clark, 1993.

Baum, Gregory. *The Jews and the Gospel: A Re-examination of the New Testament*. London: Bloomsbury, 1961.

Beasley-Murray, G. R. *John*. Vol. 36. Logos edition. Dallas: Word, 2002.

Beaton, Richard. *Isaiah's Christ in Matthew's Gospel*. SNTMS 123. Cambridge: Cambridge University Press, 2002.

Bennema, Cornelis. "The Giving of the Spirit in John—A New Proposal?" *Evangelical Quarterly* 74 (2002) 185–213.

Benson, Alphonsus. *The Spirit of God in the Didactic Books of the Old Testament*. New York: Catholic University of America Press, 1949.

Best, Ernest. *Mark: The Gospel as Story*. Edinburgh: T&T Clark, 1983.
———. *The Temptation and the Passion: The Markan Soteriology*. SNTSMS 2. Cambridge: Cambridge University Press, 1965.
Betz, Otto. *What Do We Know about Jesus?* Philadelphia: Westminster; London: SCM, 1968.
Bietenhard, Hans. "ὄνομα." In *TDNT* 5:242–83.
Black, Matthew. *An Aramaic Approach to the Gospels and Acts*. Oxford: Clarendon, 1967.
Blenkinsopp, Joseph. *Isaiah 56–66*. AB 19B. New York: Doubleday, 2003.
Bloomberg, Craig. "Baptism of the Spirit." In *Evangelical Dictionary of Biblical Theology*, edited by W. A. Elwell. Logos edition. Grand Rapids: Baker, 1996.
Blumhofer, C. M. "Luke's Alteration of Joel 3:1–5 in Acts 2:17–21*." *NTS* 62 (2016) 499–516.
———. *Proclamation from Prophecy and Pattern: Lukan Old Testament Christology*. JSOTSup 12. Sheffield: Sheffield Academic, 1987.
Bock, Darrell L. *A Theology of Luke and Acts: Biblical Theology of the New Testament*. Grand Rapids: Zondervan, 2015.
Boda, Mark J. "Renewal in Heart, Word, and Deed: Repentance in the Torah." In *Repentance in Christian Theology*, edited by Mark J. Boda and Gordon T. Smith, 3–25. Collegeville, MN: Liturgical, 2006.
Boling, Robert G. *Judges: Introduction, Translation, and Notes*. AB. Garden City, NY: Doubleday, 1975.
Bonhoeffer, Dietrich. *Letters and Papers from Prison*. Edited by C. Gremmels, et al. Translated by Isabel Best, et al. Vol. 8. Dietrich Bonhoeffer Works in English. Minneapolis: Fortress, 2010.
Bonsirven, Joseph. *Palestinian Judaism in the Time of Jesus Christ*. New York: Holt, Rinehart & Winston, 1964.
Boring, M. E. "The Influence of Christian Prophecy on the Johannine Portrayal of the Paraclete and Jesus." *NTS* 25 (1978–79) 113–23.
Botha, F. J. "Recent Research and the Lord's Prayer." *Neot* 1 (1967) 42–50.
Bovon, François. *Luc le théologien: Vingt-cinq ans de recherches (1950–1975)*. Paris: Delachaux et Niestle, 1978.
———. *Luke the Theologian: Thirty-Three Years of Research (1950–1983)*. Translated by Ken McKinney. Princeton Theological Monograph Series 20. 1987. Reprint, Allison Park, PA: Pickwick, 2006.
Bowman, John, ed. *Samaritan Documents Relating to Their History, Religion, and Life*. Translated by John Bowman. POTTS 2. Pittsburgh: Pickwick, 1977.
Bradnick, David. "A Pentecostal Perspective on Entropy, Emergent Systems, and Eschatology." *Zygon: Journal of Religion and Science* 43 (2008) 925–42.
Brinsmead, Bernard Hungerford. *Galatians, Dialogical Response to Opponents*. SBLDS 65. Chico, CA: Scholars, 1982.
Brown, Colin. *Miracles and the Critical Mind*. Grand Rapids: Eerdmans, 1984.
Brown, Raymond. *The Message of Numbers*. Downers Grove, IL: InterVarsity, 2002.
Brown, Schuyler. "'Water-Baptism' and 'Spirit-Baptism' in Luke-Acts." *ATR* 59 (1977) 135–51.
Brown, Tricia Gates. *Spirit in the Writings of John: Johannine Pneumatology in Social-Scientific Perspective*. London: T&T Clark, 2003.
Brownlee, William H. "A Comparison of the Covenanters of the Dead Sea Scrolls with Pre-Christian Jewish Sects." *BA* 13.3 (1950) 49–68.

Bruce, F. F. *The Acts of the Apostles: Greek Text with Introduction and Commentary*. 3rd rev. and enlarged ed. Grand Rapids: Eerdmans, 1990.

———. *The Book of Acts*. Rev. ed. NICNT. Grand Rapids: Eerdmans, 1988.

———. *The Books and the Parchments*. Rev. ed. Old Tappan, NJ: Fleming H. Revell, 1963.

———. "The First Church Historian." In *Church, Word, and Spirit*, edited by James E. Bradley and Richard A. Muller, 1–14. Grand Rapids: Eerdmans, 1987.

———. "Holy Spirit in the Qumran Texts." *ALUOS* 6 (1966) 49–55.

———. *The Time Is Fulfilled*. Grand Rapids: Eerdmans, 1978.

Brueggemann, Walter. *The Prophetic Imagination*. 2nd ed. Minneapolis: Fortress, 2001.

———. *Texts Under Negotiation: The Bible and Postmodern Imagination*. Minneapolis: Fortress, 1993.

Bruner, Frederick Dale. *A Theology of the Holy Spirit: The Pentecostal Experience and the New Testament Witness*. Grand Rapids: Eerdmans, 1970.

Büchsel, F. *Der Geist Gottes im Neuen Testament*. Güttersloh: C. Bertlesmann, 1926.

Budd, Philip J. *Numbers*. WBC. Waco, TX: Word, 1984.

Bultmann, Rudolf. *The History of the Synoptic Tradition*. Translated by John Marsh. 2nd ed. Oxford: Blackwell, 1968.

———. *Primitive Christianity in Its Contemporary Setting*. Translated by Reginald H. Fuller. New York: Meridian, 1956.

Burgess, Richard. "Nigerian Pentecostal Theology in Global Perspective." *PentecoStudies* 7.2 (2008) 29–63. http://www.glopent.net/pentecostudies/2008-vol-7/no-2-autumn/burgess-2008.

Burkert, Walter. *Greek Religion*. Translated by John Raffan. Cambridge, MA: Harvard University Press, 1985.

Butticaz, Simon David. *L'identité de l'Église dans les Actes des apôtres: De la restauration d'Israël à la conquête universelle*. Beihefte zur Zeitschrift für die neutestamentliche Wissenschaft und die Kunde der alteren Kirche 174. Berlin: Walter de Gruyter, 2010.

Cantalamessa, Raniero, et al. "Perspectives on Koinonia: The Report from the Third Quinquennium of the Dialogue between the Pontifical Council for Promoting Christian Unity of the Roman Catholic Church and Some Classical Pentecostal Churches and Leaders (1985–1989)." Online. http://www.vatican.va/roman_curia/pontifical_councils/chrstuni/pentecostals/rc_pc_chrstuni_doc_1985-1989_perspectives-koinonia_en.html.

Cargal, Timothy B. "Beyond the Fundamental-Modernist Controversy: Pentecostals and Hermeneutics in a Postmodern Age." *Pneuma* 15.2 (1993) 163–87.

Carson, D. A. *The Farewell Discourse and Final Prayer of Jesus*. Grand Rapids: Baker, 1980.

———. *Showing the Spirit: A Theological Exposition of 1 Corinthians 12–14*. Grand Rapids: Baker, 1987.

———. "Systematic Theology and Biblical Theology." In *New Dictionary of Biblical Theology*, edited by T. D. Alexander, and B. S. Rosner, 89–104. Downers Grove, IL: InterVarsity, 2000.

Carson, D. A., et al., eds. *New Bible Commentary: Twenty-First-Century Edition*. 4th ed. Logos edition. Downers Grove, IL: InterVarsity, 1994.

Cary, M., and T. J. Haarhoff. *Life and Thought in the Greek and Roman World*. 4th ed. London: Methuen, 1946.

Cassidy, Richard J. *Jesus, Politics, and Society: A Study of Luke's Gospel*. 1978. Reprint, Eugene, OR: Wipf and Stock, 2015.

Childs, Brevard S. *The Book of Exodus: A Critical, Theological Commentary.* Philadelphia: Westminster, 1974.

Chilton, Bruce. "Aramaic and Targumic Antecedents of Pauline 'Justification.'" In *The Aramaic Bible: Targums in Their Historical Context*, edited by Derek R. G. Beattie and Martin J. McNamara, 379–97. Sheffield: Sheffield Academic, 1994.

Clark, Albert Curtis. *The Acts of the Apostles.* Oxford: Clarendon, 1933.

Clements, Ronald E. *Exodus.* CBC. Cambridge: Cambridge University Press, 1972.

Clifton, Shane. *Pentecostal Churches in Transition.* Leiden: Brill, 2009.

Collins, John. *The Apocalyptic Imagination.* 3rd ed. Grand Rapids: Eerdmans, 2016.

———. "The Court Tales in Daniel and the Development of Apocalyptic." *JBL* 94 (1975) 218–34.

Conzelmann, Hans. *Acts of the Apostles.* Philadelphia: Fortress, 1987.

———. *An Outline of the Theology of the New Testament.* New York: Harper & Row, 1969.

———. *The Theology of St. Luke.* 1961. Reprint, Philadelphia: Fortress, 1982.

Conzelmann, Hans, and Walther Zimmerli, "χαίρω, χαρά, κτλ." In *TDNT* 9:363, 370–71.

Courey, David J. *What Has Wittenberg to Do with Azusa?: Luther's Theology of the Cross and Pentecostal Triumphalism.* New York: Bloomsbury T&T Clark, 2015.

Cox, Harvey. *Fire from Heaven: The Rise of Pentecostal Spirituality and the Reshaping of Religion in the Twenty-First Century.* Reading: Addison-Wesley, 1995.

Cullen, Peter J. "Euphoria, Praise, and Thanksgiving: Rejoicing in the Spirit in Luke-Acts." *JPT* 6 (1995) 13–24.

Cullmann, Oscar. *Christ and Time.* Translated by Floyd V. Filson. Philadelphia: Westminster, 1950.

Culpepper, R. Allan. *Anatomy of the Fourth Gospel: A Study in Literary Design.* Philadelphia: Fortress, 1983.

Curtis, Byron G. "Charismata as Hermeneutical Help? 'Private Spirits' in Catholic-Protestant Debate (1588–1650) and in *The Westminster Confession of Faith*." Lisle, IL: Evangelical Theological Society Annual Meeting, 1994.

Dahms, John V. "'Lead Us Not into Temptation.'" *JETS* 17 (1974) 223–30.

Dalman, Gustaf. *Jesus-Jeshua: Studies in the Gospels.* New York: Macmillan, 1929.

Danby Herbert, trans. *The Mishnah: Translated from the Hebrew with Introduction and Brief Explanatory Notes.* Oxford: Oxford University Press, 1933.

Danker, Frederick W. "Benefactor." In *Dictionary of Jesus and the Gospel*, edited by Joel Green, et al., 58–60. Downers Grove, IL: InterVarsity, 1992.

———. *A Greek-English Lexicon of the New Testament and Other Early Christian Literature.* Rev. 3rd ed. based on *BDAG*. Chicago: University of Chicago Press, 2000.

Darr, John. "'Watch How You Listen' (Luke 8:18): Jesus and the Rhetoric of Perception in Luke-Acts." In *The New Literary Criticism and the NT*, edited by E. McKnight and E. Malbon, 87–107. Harrisburg, PA: Trinity International, 1994.

Dau, Isaiah Majo. *Suffering and God: A Theological Reflection on the War in Sudan.* Nairobi, Kenya: Paulines Africa, 2003.

Daube, David. *The Exodus Pattern in the Bible.* All Souls Studies 2. London: Faber & Faber, 1963.

Davids, Peter. "The Meaning of *APEIRASTOS* in James 1:13." *NTS* 24 (1978) 386–92.

Davies, W. D. *Paul and Rabbinic Judaism: Some Rabbinic Elements in Pauline Theology.* 4th ed. Philadelphia: Fortress, 1980.

Dawkins, Richard. *The Selfish Gene.* New York: Oxford University Press, 1976.

Dayton, Donald W. *Theological Roots of Pentecostalism*. Grand Rapids: Zondervan, 1987.
Deissmann, G. Adolf. *Bible Studies: Contributions Chiefly from Papyri and Inscriptions to the History of the Language, the Literature, and the Religion of Hellenistic Judaism and Primitive Christianity*. Translated by Alexander Grieve. 1923. Reprint, Winona Lake, IN: Alpha, 1979.
———. *Light from the Ancient East*. Grand Rapids: Baker, 1978.
Del Colle, Ralph. "The Outpouring of the Holy Spirit: Implications for the Church and Ecumenism." In *The Holy Spirit, the Church, and Christian Unity: Proceedings of the Conference Held at the Monastery of Bose, Italy (14–20 October, 2002)*, edited by D. Donnelly, et al., 247–65. Leuven: Leuven University Press, 2005.
Delling, Gerhard. "πίμπλημι." In *TDNT* 6:128–31.
———. "πληρόω." In *TDNT* 6:286–98.
Dempster, M. W., et al., eds. *Called and Empowered: Global Mission in Pentecostal Perspective*. Peabody, MA: Hendrickson, 1991.
Depaul, Michael R. *Resurrecting Old-Fashioned Foundationalism*. Lanham, MD: Rowman & Littlefield, 2000.
Derrenbacker, R. A., Jr. *Ancient Compositional Practices and the Synoptic Problem*. BETL 186. Leuven: Leuven University Press, 2005.
Derrett, J. Duncan M. *Jesus's Audience: The Social and Psychological Environment in Which He Worked*. New York: Seabury, 1973.
———. *Law in the New Testament*. London: Darton, Longman & Todd, 1970.
DeSilva, David. *Honor, Patronage, Kinship and Purity: Unlocking New Testament Culture*. Downers Grove, IL: InterVarsity, 2000.
Dibelius, Martin. *Jesus*. Translated by Charles B. Hedrick and Frederick C. Grant. Philadelphia: Westminster, 1949.
Dodd, C. H. *The Parables of the Kingdom*. London: Nisbet, 1936.
Domning, Daryl P., with Monika K. Hellwig. *Original Selfishness: Original Sin and Evil in the Light of Evolution*. Burlington, VT: Ashgate, 2006.
Driver, G. R. *The Judaean Scrolls: The Problem and a Solution*. Oxford: Blackwell, 1965.
Dunn, James D. G. *The Acts of the Apostles*. Grand Rapids: Eerdmans, 2016.
———. *Baptism in the Holy Spirit*. Philadelphia: Westminster, 1970.
———. *Baptism in the Holy Spirit: A Re-examination of the New Testament Teaching on the Gift of the Spirit in Relation to Pentecostalism Today*. SBT 2/15. London: SCM, 1970.
———. "Baptism of Fire." In *BEB*, edited by W. A. Elwell and B. J. Beitzel, 216. Grand Rapids: Baker, 1988.
———. "Baptism of the Spirit." In *BEB*, edited by W. A. Elwell and B. J. Beitzel, 260–63. Grand Rapids: Baker, 1988.
———. *Jesus and the Spirit: A Study of the Religious and Charismatic Experience of Jesus and the First Christians as Reflected in the New Testament*. Philadelphia: Westminster, 1975.
———. *The Oral Gospel Tradition*. Grand Rapids: Eerdmans, 2013.
———. "Spirit and Kingdom." *ExpT* 82 (1970) 36–40.
Durham, John I. *Exodus*. WBC. Waco, TX: Word, 1987.
Elbert, Paul, and Amos Yong. "Christianity, Pentecostalism: Issues in Science and Religion." In *Encyclopedia of Science and Religion*, edited by J. Wentzel van Huysteen, 132–35. vol. 1. New York: Macmillan Reference Library, 2003.
Ellington, Scott. "'Can I Get a Witness': The Myth of Pentecostal Orality and the Process of Traditioning in the Psalms." *JPT* 20 (2011) 1–14.

Ellis, Earle E. *The Gospel of Luke*. NCB. London: Oliphants, 1974.
Erickson, Millard J. *Truth or Consequences: The Promise and Perils of Postmodernism*. Downers Grove, IL: InterVarsity, 2001.
Ervin, Howard M. "Hermeneutics: A Pentecostal Option." *Pneuma* 3.2 (1981) 11–25.
Ewart, Frank. *The Phenomenon of Pentecost*. Rev. ed. Hazelwood, MO: Word Aflame, 1975.
Faupel, William D. *The Everlasting Gospel: The Significance of Eschatology in the Development of Pentecostal Thought*. JPTSup 10. Edited by John Christopher Thomas, et al. Sheffield: Sheffield Academic, 1996.
Fee, Gordon D. "Baptism in the Holy Spirit: The Issue of Separability and Subsequence." *Pneuma* 7 (1985) 87–100.
———. *God's Empowering Presence: The Holy Spirit in the Letters of Paul*. Peabody, MA: Hendrickson, 1994.
———. *Gospel and Spirit: Issues in New Testament Hermeneutics*. Peabody, MA: Hendrickson, 1991.
———. "Hermeneutics and Historical Precedent: A Major Issue in Pentecostal Hermeneutics" In *Perspectives on the New Pentecostalism*, edited by Russell P. Spittler, 118–33. Grand Rapids: Baker, 1976.
———. *New Testament Exegesis: A Handbook for Students and Pastors*. Rev. ed. Louisville: Westminster John Knox, 1993.
———. *Paul, the Spirit, and the People of God*. Peabody, MA: Hendrickson, 1996.
———. *Pauline Christology: An Exegetical-Theological Study*. Peabody: Hendrickson, 2007.
Fee, Gordon D., and Douglas Stuart. *How to Read the Bible for All Its Worth: A Guide to Understanding the Bible*. 3rd ed. Grand Rapids: Zondervan, 2003.
Fensham, F. Charles. "The Legal Background of Matt 6:12." *NovT* 4 (1960) 1–2.
Fenton, J. C. *Saint Matthew*. Philadelphia: Westminster, 1977.
Filson, Floyd V. *A Commentary on the Gospel According to St. Matthew*. New York; Evanston, IL: Harper & Row, 1960.
Finger, Thomas. "Modernity, Postmodernity—What in the World Are They?" *Transformation* 10 (1993) 353–68.
Fitzmyer, J. *The Gospel According to Luke*. Vol. 2. AB 28. New York: Doubleday, 1985.
Foerster, Werner. "εἰρήνη, εἰρηνεύω, κτλ." In *TDNT* 2:402.
Freedman, David Noel. "Pottery, Poetry, and Prophecy: An Essay on Biblical Poetry." *JBL* 96.1 (1977) 5–26.
Fulford, Robert. *The Triumph of Narrative: Storytelling in the Age of Mass Culture*. CBC Massey Lectures. Toronto: House of Anansi, 2011.
Gabriel, Andrew K., et al. "Changing Conceptions of Speaking in Tongues and Spirit Baptism among Canadian Pentecostal Clergy." *Canadian Journal of Pentecostal-Charismatic Christianity* 7 (2016) 1–24.
Gadamer, Hans-Georg. *Truth and Method*. 2nd rev. ed. New York: Continuum, 1997.
Gaffin, Richard B., Jr. "Systematic Theology and Biblical Theology." *WTS* 38 (1976) 281–99.
Gallegos, John. "African Pentecostal Hermeneutics." In *Pentecostal Theology in Africa*, edited by Clifton R. Clarke, 40–57. Eugene, OR: Pickwick, 2014.
Gasque, W. Ward. *A History of the Interpretation of the Acts of the Apostles*. Rev. ed. Peabody: Hendrickson, 1989.
Gaster, Theodor H. *The Dead Sea Scriptures*. Garden City, NY: Doubleday, 1976.
George, A. "Ne nous soumets pas à la tentation . . . Note sur la traduction nouvelle du Notre Père." *Bible et Vie Chrétienne* 71 (1966) 74–79.

Gibb, Tim. "April 23rd AM." *Vimeo* video, 54:15, April 23rd, 2016. Bethel Sarnia, Ontario, Canada. https://vimeo.com/214690498.

Gibson, Jeffrey B. "Jesus's Wilderness Temptation According to Mark." *JSNT* 53 (1994) 3–34.

Giles, Kevin. "The Church in the Gospel of Luke." *Scottish Journal of Theology* 34 (1981) 121–46.

Gillman, John. *Possessions and the Life of Faith: A Reading of Luke-Acts*. Zacchaeus Studies New Testament. Collegeville, MN: Liturgical, 1991.

Gispen, W. H. *Exodus*. BSC. Grand Rapids: Zondervan, 1982.

Gitlin, Todd. "The Postmodern Predicament." *Wilson Quarterly* 13 (1989) 67–76.

Glasson, T. Francis. *Moses in the Fourth Gospel*. SBT. Naperville, IL: Alec R. Allenson, 1963.

Goldin, Judah. "Not by Means of an Angel and Not by Means of a Messenger." In *Studies in Midrash and Related Literature*, edited by Barry Eichler and Jeffrey Tigay, 163–73. Philadelphia: Jewish Publication Society, 1988.

Goodenough, Erwin R. *Jewish Symbols in the Greco-Roman Period*. 13 vols. BollS 37. Vols. 1–12. New York: Pantheon, 1953–65; Vol. 13. Princeton: Princeton University Press, 1968.

Goppelt, Leonhard. *Theology of the New Testament*. Edited by Jürgen Roloff. Translated by John E. Alsup. 2 vols. Grand Rapids: Eerdmans, 1981–82.

Goshen-Gottstein, Alon. "God the Father in Rabbinic Judaism and Christianity: Transformed Background or Common Ground?" *JES* 38.3 (2001) 470–504.

Goulder, Michael D. "The Composition of the Lord's Prayer." *JTS* NS 14 (1963) 32–45.

———. *Midrash and Lection in Matthew*. Speaker's Lectures in Biblical Studies, 1969–71. London: SPCK, 1974.

Grant, Frederick C. *Ancient Judaism and the New Testament*. New York: Macmillan, 1959.

Grant, W. V. "April 28, 1989." Private Letter to Patricia Pickard. Retrieved from International Flower Pentecostal Heritage Center, Assemblies of God Archives, Springfield, MO, August 22, 2017.

Gray, George B. *A Critical and Exegetical Commentary on Numbers*. ICC. London: T&T Clark, 1903.

Green, Chris E. W. *Sanctifying Interpretation: Vocation, Holiness, and Scripture*. Cleveland TN: CPT, 2015.

———. *Toward a Pentecostal Theology of the Lord's Supper: Foretasting the Kingdom*. Cleveland, TN: CPT, 2012.

Green, Joel B., and Max Turner, eds. *Between Two Horizons: Spanning New Testament Studies and Systematic Theology*. Grand Rapids: Eerdmans, 2000.

Grenz, Stanley. *A Primer on Postmodernism*. Grand Rapids: Eerdmans, 1996.

Griffith, R. Marie. "Female Devotional Practices in American Pentecostalism." In *Women and Twentieth-Century Protestantism*, edited by Margaret Bendroth and Virginia Brereto, 184–208. Chicago: University of Illinois Press, 2001.

———. "Prayer Cloths." *Material History of American Religion Project*. 1995–2001. http://www.materialreligion.org/journal/handkerchief.html.

Grigg, Viv. "The Spirit of Church and the Postmodern City." PhD diss., University of Auckland, 2005.

Grossfeld, Bernard, ed. *The Targum Onqelos to Deuteronomy*. Aramaic Bible. Wilmington, DE: Michael Glazier, 1988.

Grudem, Wayne A. *The Gift of Prophecy in 1 Corinthians*. Lanham, MD: University Press of America, 1982.

Guelich, Robert A. *The Sermon on the Mount: A Foundation for Understanding.* Waco, TX: Word, 1982.

Gundry, Robert H. *Matthew: A Commentary on His Literary and Theological Art.* Grand Rapids: Eerdmans, 1982.

Gunkel, Hermann. *The Influence of the Holy Spirit: The Popular View of the Apostolic Age and the Teaching of the Apostle Paul.* Trans. Roy A. Harrisville and Philip A. Quanbeck III. Philadelphia, PA: Fortress, 1979.

Guthrie, W. K. C. *Orpheus and Greek Religion: A Study of the Orphic Movement.* 2nd ed. New York: W. W. Norton, 1966.

Haenchen, Ernst. *The Acts of the Apostles: A Commentary.* Philadelphia: Westminster, 1971.

———. *John: A Commentary on the Gospel of John.* Edited by Robert W. Funk with Ulrich Busse. Translated by Robert W. Funk. 2 vols. Hermeneia. Philadelphia: Fortress, 1984.

Hamilton, Neill Q. *The Holy Spirit and Eschatology in Paul.* SJTOP 6. Edinburgh: Oliver & Boyd, 1957.

Hanson, Paul. *The Dawn of Apocalyptic.* Philadelphia: Fortress, 1975.

Hart, Larry D. *Truth Aflame: Theology for the Church in Renewal.* Rev. ed. Grand Rapids: Zondervan, 2005.

Haya-Prats, Gonzalo. *Empowered Believers: The Holy Spirit in the Book of Acts.* Edited by Paul Elbert. Translated by Scott A. Ellington. Eugene, OR: Cascade, 2011.

Healy, Nicholas M. *Church, World, and the Christian Life: Practical-Prophetic Ecclesiology.* Cambridge Studies in Christian Doctrine 7. Cambridge: Cambridge University Press, 2000.

Hengel, Martin. *Acts and the History of Earliest Christianity.* London: SCM, 1979.

———. *The Atonement: The Origins of the Doctrine in the New Testament.* Translated by John Bowden. Philadelphia: Fortress, 1981.

———. *The Charismatic Leader and His Followers.* New York: Crossroad, 1981.

———. *The Son of God.* Translated by John Bowden. Philadelphia: Fortress, 1976.

Henry, Carl F.H. "Postmodernism: The New Spectre?" In *The Challenge of Postmodernism: An Evangelical Engagement*, edited by David S. Dockery, 34–52. 2nd ed. Grand Rapids: Baker Academic, 2001.

Hertzberg, Hans Wilhelm. *I and II Samuel.* OTL. Philadelphia: Westminster, 1964.

Hildebrandt, Wilf. *An Old Testament Theology of the Spirit of God.* Peabody: Hendrickson, 1995.

Hill, David. *Greek Words and Hebrew Meanings: Studies in the Semantics of Soteriological Terms.* Cambridge: Cambridge University Press, 1967.

Hodge, A. A. *Outlines of Theology: Rewritten and Enlarged.* New York: Hodder and Stoughton, 1878.

Hodges, Melvin L. *The Indigenous Church: A Complete Handbook on How to Grow Your Churches.* Springfield, MO: Gospel, 1953.

———. *Theology of the Church and Its Mission.* Springfield, MO: Gospel, 1977.

Hoekema, Anthony. *Holy Spirit Baptism.* Grand Rapids: Eerdmans, 1972.

Hofmann, Heinz. "Sator Square." In vol. 3 of *Brill's Encyclopedia of the Ancient World: New Pauly*, edited by Hubert Cancik and Helmuth Schneider, 17–19. Leiden: Brill, 2018.

Holladay, William L. *A Concise Hebrew and Aramaic Lexicon of the Old Testament.* 1971. Reprint, Grand Rapids: Eerdmans, 1976.

Hoppe, Leslie. *Joshua, Judges, with Excursus on Charismatic Leadership in Israel.* OTM. Wilmington, DE: Michael Glazier, 1985.

Hornik, Heidi, and Mikeal Parsons. *The Acts of the Apostles Through the Centuries*. Chichester, MA: Wiley & Sons, 2017.

Horsley, Richard. "'Like One of the Prophets of Old': Two Types of Popular Prophets at the Time of Jesus." *CBQ* 47 (1985) 435–63.

Horsley, Richard, and Tom Thatcher. *John, Jesus, and the Renewal of Israel*. Grand Rapids: Eerdmans, 2013.

Hoskyns, Edwyn Clement. *The Fourth Gospel*. Edited and completed by Francis Noel Davey. 2nd rev. ed. London: Faber & Faber, 1947.

Hotrum, Ronald A. "An Inductive Study of the Old Testament on the Divine Spirit." PhD diss., Western Evangelical Seminary, 1971.

Houk, Cornelius B. "*Peirasmos*, the Lord's Prayer, and the Massah Tradition." *SJT* 19 (1966) 216–25.

Hovenden, Gerald. *Speaking in Tongues: The New Testament Evidence in Context*. New York: Bloomsbury T&T Clark, 2002.

Huffard, E. W. "The Parable of the Friend at Midnight: God's Honor or Man's Persistence?" *ResQ* 21 (1978) 154–60.

Huffman, Douglas D., and Jamie N. Hausherr. "Baptism of Spirit." In *The Lexham Bible Dictionary*, edited by J. D. Bomar, et al. Logos edition. Bellingham, WA: Lexham, 2016.

Hughes, J. A. "British Columbia's Indian Believers." *Pentecostal Testimony*, January 1938. 8.

Hughes, John H. "John the Baptist: The Forerunner of God Himself." *NovT* 14 (1972) 191–218.

Hur, Ju. *A Dynamic Reading of the Holy Spirit in Luke-Acts*. JSNTSup 211. 2001. Reprint, London: T&T Clark International, 2004.

Hymes, David C. "Heroic Leadership in the Wilderness, Part 1." *AJPS* 9 (2006) 295–318.

———. "Heroic Leadership in the Wilderness, Part 2." *AJPS* 10 (2007) 2–23.

———. "Numbers 11: A Pentecostal Perspective." *AJPS* 13 (2010) 257–81.

Isaiah, Abraham Ben. *Numbers: The Pentateuch and Rashi's Commentary, A Linear Translation into English*. Brooklyn: S. S. & R., 1949.

Isbell, Charles D. "The Story of the Aramaic Magical Incantation Bowls." *BA* 41 (1978) 5–16.

Jacobsen, Douglas. *Thinking in the Spirit: Theologies of the Early Pentecostal Movement*. Bloomington, IN: Indiana University Press, 2003.

Jaichandran, Rebecca, and B.C. Madhav. "Pentecostal Spirituality in a Postmodern World." *AJPS* 6 (2003) 39–61.

Jeremias, Joachim. *The Central Message of the New Testament*. New York: Scribner's, 1965.

———. *New Testament Theology*. New York: Scribner's, 1971.

———. *The Parables of Jesus*. 2nd rev. ed. New York: Scribner's, 1972.

———. *The Prayers of Jesus*. Philadelphia: Fortress, 1964.

Jervell, Jacob. "Das gespaltene Israel und die Heidenvölken: Zur Motivierung der Heidenmission in der Apostelgeschichte." *ST* 19.1–2 (1965) 68–96.

———. *Theology of Acts of the Apostles*. New Testament Theology. Cambridge: Cambridge University Press, 1996.

Johns, Jackie David. "Pentecostalism and the Postmodern Worldview." *JPT* 7 (1995) 73–96.

Johnson, Alan F. "Assurance for Man: The Fallacy of Translating *Anaideia* by 'Persistence' in Luke 11:5–8." *JETS* 22 (1979) 125–31.

Johnson, David R. *Pneumatic Discernment in the Apocalypse: An Intertextual and Pentecostal Exploration*. Cleveland, TN: CPT, 2018.

Johnson, Luke Timothy. *The Literary Function of Possessions in Luke-Acts.* SBLDS 39. Missoula, MT: SBL, 1977.

———. *Prophetic Jesus, Prophetic Church: The Challenge of Luke-Acts to Contemporary Christians.* Grand Rapids: Eerdmans, 2011.

———. *Sharing Possessions: What Faith Demands.* 2nd. ed. Grand Rapids: Eerdmans, 2011.

Kalu, Ogbu U. "Preserving a Worldview: Pentecostalism in the African Maps of the Universe." *Pneuma* 24 (2003) 110–137.

Kärkkäinen, Veli-Matti. "Are Pentecostals Oblivious of Social Justice: Theological and Ecumenical Perspectives." In *Pfingstkirchen und Ökumene in Bewegung: Ökumenische Rundschau Beiheft 71*, edited by Christoph Dahling-Sander, et al., 50–65. Frankfurt: Lembeck Verlag, 2001.

———. "The Church as the Fellowship of Persons: An Emerging Pentecostal Ecclesiology of Koinonia." *PentecoStudies* 6 (2007) 1–15. http://www.glopent.net/pentecostudies/online-back-issues/2007/karkkainen-2007.pdf/view.

———, ed. *The Ecclesiology of the Pentecostal Churches. International Journal for the Study of the Christian Church* 11.4 (2011).

———. "Full Gospel, Fullness of the Spirit, and Catholicity: Pentecostal Perspectives on the Third Mark of the Church." In *Pentecostal Issues, Ecclesiolgy & Ecumenism: Papers Presented in Theological Positions Colloquiums 2010 & 2011*, edited by C. Donovan Barron and Riku Tuppurainen, 77–99. Sint-Peters-Leeuw, Belgium: Continental Theological Seminary, 2011.

———. "Identity and Plurality: A Pentecostal-Charismatic Perspective." *International Review of Mission* 91.363 (2002) 500–504.

———. *Missiology: An International Review* 29 (2001) 417–31.

———. "Missiology, Pentecostal and Charismatic." In *The New International Dictionary of Pentecostal and Charismatic Movements*, edited by Stanley M. Burgess and Eduard M. van der Maas, 877–85. Rev. and enl. ed. Grand Rapids: Zondervan, 2002.

———. "Mission and Salvation: A Pentecostal Perspective." Paper presented at the Annual Reformed-Pentecostal International Dialogue, Antalya, Turkey, December 2–6, 2015.

———. "Mission, Spirit, and Eschatology: An Outline of a Pentecostal-Charismatic Theology of Mission." *Mission Studies* 16 (1999) 73–94.

———. "Pentecostal Mission: A Theological Appraisal." In *African Pentecostal Missions Maturing: Essays in Honor of Apostle Opoku Onyinah*, edited by Lord Elorm Donkor and Clifton R. Clarke, 28–49. African Christian Series. Eugene, OR: Wipf and Stock, 2018.

———. "Pentecostal Mission and Encounter with Religions." In *The Cambridge Companion to Pentecostalism*, edited by Cecil M. Robeck and Amos Yong, 294–312. Cambridge: Cambridge University Press, 2014.

———. "The Pentecostal Understanding of Mission." In *Pentecostal Mission and Global Christianity*, edited by Wonsuk Ma, et al., 26–44. Regnum Edinburgh Centenary Series 20. Oxford: Regnum International, 2014.

———. "'The Re-Turn of Religion in the New Millennium': Pentecostalisms and Postmodernities." *Swedish Missiological Themes* 95 (2007) 469–96.

———, ed. *The Spirit in the World: Emerging Pentecostal Theologies in Global Contexts.* Grand Rapids: Eerdmans, 2009.

———. *Spiritus Ubi Vult Spirat: Pneumatology in Roman Catholic-Pentecostal Dialogue (1972–1989).* Schriften der Luther-Agricola-Gesellscahft 42. Helsinki: Luther-Agricola Society, 1998.

———. "Theology of the Cross: A Stumbling Block to Pentecostal-Charismatic Spirituality." In *The Spirit and Spirituality: Essays in Honour of Russell P. Spittler*, edited by Wonsuk Ma and Robert P. Menzies, 150–63. London: T&T Clark International, 2004.

Käsemann, Ernst. *Commentary on Romans*. Edited and translated by Geoffrey W. Bromiley. Grand Rapids: Eerdmans, 1980.

Keener, Craig S. *Acts: An Exegetical Commentary*. Vols 1–2. Grand Rapids: Baker Academic, 2012–13.

———. *The Gospel of John: A Commentary*. Vol. 2. Peabody: Hendrickson, 2003.

———. *The Gospel of Matthew: A Socio-Rhetorical Commentary*. Grand Rapids: Eerdmans, 2009.

———. "The Holy Spirit." In *The Oxford Handbook of Evangelical Theology*, edited by Gerald R. McDermott, 158–73. New York: Oxford University Press, 2010.

———. *Spirit Hermeneutics: Reading Scripture in the Light of Pentecost*. Grand Rapids: Eerdmans, 2016.

———. "Why Does Luke Use Tongues as a Sign of the Spirit's Empowerment?" *JPT* 15 (2007) 177–84.

Keil, Karl F. "The Second Book of Moses." In vol. 2 of *Commentary on the Old Testament in Ten Volumes*, edited by Karl F. Keil and Franz Delitzsch, 9–260. Translated by James Martin. Grand Rapids: Eerdmans, 1975.

Keil, Karl F., and Franz Delitzsch. "The Fourth Book of Moses." In vol. 3 of *Commentary on the Old Testament in Ten Volumes*, edited by Karl F. Keil and Franz Delitzsch, 1–268. Translated by James Martin. Grand Rapids: Eerdmans, 1975.

Kelly, Stewart, and James K. Dew, Jr. *Understanding Postmodernism: A Christian Perspective*. Downers Grove, IL: InterVarsity, 2017.

Kittel, Gerhard, and Gerhard Friedrich, eds. *Theological Dictionary of the New Testament*. Translated by Geoffrey W. Bromiley. 10 vols. Grand Rapids: Eerdmans, 1964–76.

Klausner, Joseph. *Jesus of Nazareth: His Life, Times, and Teaching*. Translated by Herbert Danby. Foreword by Sidney B. Hoenig. 1925. Reprint, New York: Menorah, 1979.

Klein, Ralph W. *I Samuel*. WBC. Waco, TX: Word, 1983.

Klink, Edward W., III, and Darian R. Lockett. *Understanding Biblical Theology: A Comparison of Theory and Practice*. Grand Rapids: Zondervan, 2012.

Klinken, Adriaan von. "Homosexuality, Politics and Pentecostal Nationalism in Zambia." *Studies in World Christianity* 20 (2014) 259–81.

Knox, Wilfred L. *St. Paul and the Church of the Gentiles*. Cambridge: Cambridge University Press, 1939.

———. *St. Paul and the Church of Jerusalem*. Cambridge University Press, 1925.

Koester, Craig R. *Revelation*. AYBRL 38A. New Haven; London: Yale University Press, 2014.

Koester, Helmut. *Introduction to the New Testament*. 2 vols. Philadelphia: Fortress, 1982.

Köstenberger, Andreas J. "What Does It Mean to Be Filled with the Spirit? A Biblical Investigation." *JETS* 40 (1997) 229–40.

Kuecker, Aaron J. "The Spirit and the 'Other,' Satan and the 'Self': Economic Ethics as a Consequence of Identity Transformation in Luke-Acts." In *Engaging Economics: New Testament Scenarios and Early Christian Reception*, edited by Bruce W. Longenecker and Kelly D. Liebengood, 81–103. Grand Rapids: Eerdmans, 2009.

Kuzmic, Peter, and Miroslav Volf. "*Communio Sanctorum*: Toward a Theology of the Church as a 'Fellowship of Persons.'" Paper presented at the International Roman Catholic-Pentecostal Dialogue, Riano, Italy, May 21–26, 1985.

Kydd, Ronald. "Healing in the Christian Church." In *New International Dictionary of Pentecostal and Charismatic Movements*, edited by Stanley M. Burgess and Eduard M. van der Maas, 698–711. Rev. and enl. ed. Grand Rapids: Zondervan, 2002.

———. *Healing Through the Centuries: Models for Understanding*. Grand Rapids: Baker Academic, 1995.

———. "The Impact of the Charismatic Renewal on Classical Pentecostalism in Canada." *Pneuma* 18 (1996) 55–67.

Lachs, Samuel Tobias. "On Matthew 6:12." *NovT* 17 (1975) 6–8.

Ladd, George Eldon. *Theology of the New Testament*. Rev. ed. Grand Rapids: Eerdmans, 1993.

Lake, Kirsopp, and Henry J. Cadbury. *The Acts of the Apostles: English Translation and Commentary*. Vol. 4 of *The Beginnings of Christianity*. Edited by F. J. Foakes-Jackson and Kirsopp Lake. 1933. Reprint, Grand Rapids: Baker, 1979.

Lampe, G. W. H. "'Grievous Wolves' (Acts 20:29)." In *Christ and Spirit in the New Testament: Studies in Honor of C. F. D. Moule*, edited by Barnabas Lindars and Stephen S. Smalley, 253–68. Cambridge: Cambridge University Press, 1973.

Land, Steven J. *Pentecostal Spirituality: A Passion for the Kingdom*. JPTSup 1. 1993. Reprint, Cleveland, TN: CPT, 2010.

Lapide, Pinchas E. *Hebrew in the Church: The Foundations of Jewish-Christian Dialogue*. Translated by Erroll F. Rhodes. Grand Rapids: Eerdmans, 1984.

Lategan, B. C. "Current Issues in the Hermeneutical Debate." *Neot* 18 (1984) 1–17.

Laurentin, René. *Structure et Théologie de Luc I-II*. Paris: Gabalda, 1964.

Leaney, A. R. C. *A Commentary on the Gospel According to St. Luke*. London: Adama & Charles Black, 1958.

Leaney, Robert. "The Lukan Text of the Lord's Prayer (Luke 11:2–4)." *NovT* 1 (1956) 103–111.

Lee, Matthew T., and Amos Yong, eds. *The Science and Theology of Godly Love*. DeKalb, IL: Northern Illinois University Press, 2012.

Lee, Samuel Yull. *Grace and Power in Pentecostal and Charismatic Theology*. Apeldoorn: Theologische Universiteit Apeldoorn, 2002.

Levine, Baruch A. *Numbers 1–20: A New Translation with Introduction and Commentary*. AB. New York: Doubleday, 1993.

Levison, John R. *Filled with the Holy Spirit*. Grand Rapids: Eerdmans, 2009.

———. "Filled with the Spirit: A Conversation with Pentecostal and Charismatic Scholars." *JPT* 20.2 (2011) 213–31.

———. "Holy Spirit." In *NIDB* 5:877–78.

———. "Prophecy in Ancient Israel: The Case of the Ecstatic Elders." *CBQ* 65 (2003) 503–521.

Lewis, John J. "The Wilderness Controversy and Peirasmos." *Colloquium* 7 (1974) 42–44.

Licona, Michael R. *Why Are There Differences in the Gospels? What We Can Learn from Ancient Biography*. New York: Oxford University Press, 2017.

Lincoln, Andrew T. *Truth on Trial: The Lawsuit in the Fourth Gospel*. Peabody: Hendrickson, 2000.

Lindars, Barnabas. *New Testament Apologetic*. London: SCM, 1961.

Ling, Tan-Chow May. *Pentecostal Theology for the Twenty-First Century: Engaging with Multi-Faith Singapore*. Aldershot, UK: Ashgate, 2007.

Long, A. A. *Hellenistic Philosophy: Stoics, Epicureans, Sceptics*. New York: Scribner's, 1974.

Longenecker, Richard N. *Biblical Exegesis in the Apostolic Period*. Grand Rapids: Eerdmans, 1975.

———. *The Christology of Early Jewish Christianity*. 1970. Reprint, Grand Rapids: Baker, 1981.

Lord, Andrew M. *Spirit-Shaped Mission: A Holistic Charismatic Missiology*. Studies in Pentecostal and Charismatic Issues Series. Milton Keynes, UK: Paternoster, 2005.

Lord, Andy. *Network Church: A Pentecostal Ecclesiology Shaped by Mission*. Leiden: Brill, 2012.

Louis, Gabriel Reuben. "Response to Wonsuk Ma." *Cyberjournal for Pentecostal-Charismatic Research* 4 (1998). Online. http://www.pctii.org/cyberj/cyberj4/louis.html.

Louw, J. P., and E. A. Nida. *Greek-English Lexicon of the New Testament: Based on Semantic Domains*. 2nd ed. Logos edition. New York: United Bible Societies, 1996.

Luz, Ulrich. *Matthew 1–7: A Commentary*. Translated by Wilhelm C. Linss. 1989. Reprint, Minneapolis: Fortress, 1992.

Ma, Julie C., and Wonsuk Ma. *Mission in the Spirit: Towards a Pentecostal/Charismatic Missiology*. Oxford: Regnum International, 2010.

Ma, Wonsuk. "If It Is a Sign: An Old Testament Reflection on the Initial Evidence Discussion" *AJPS* 2 (1999) 163–75.

———. "Toward an Asian Pentecostal Theology." *Cyberjournal for Pentecostal-Charismatic Research* 1 (1997). Online. http://www.pctii.org/cyberj/cyberj1/wonsuk.html.

Macchia, Frank D. "Babel and the Tongues of Pentecost–Reversal or Fulfilment? A Theological Perspective." In *Speaking in Tongues: Multi-Disciplinary Perspectives*, edited by Mark J. Cartledge, 34–51. Eugene, OR: Wipf & Stock, 2012.

———. *Baptized in the Spirit: A Global Pentecostal Theology*. Grand Rapids: Zondervan, 2006.

———. "The Spirit-Baptised Church." *IJSCC* 11 (2011) 256–68.

MacDonald, William G. "Pentecostal Theology: A Classical Viewpoint." In *Perspectives on the New Pentecostalism*, edited by R.P. Spittler, 58–75. Grand Rapids: Baker, 1976.

MacMullen, Ramsay. *Enemies of the Roman Order: Treason, Unrest, and Alienation in the Empire*. Cambridge, MA: Harvard University Press, 1966.

Mansfield, Robert M. *"Spirit and Gospel" in Mark*. Peabody, MA: Hendrickson, 1987.

Manson, T. W. *The Sayings of Jesus*. 1957. Reprint, Grand Rapids: Eerdmans, 1979.

Marcus, J. *Mark 1–8*. AB 27. New York: Doubleday, 1999.

Marino, Bruce R. "The Origin, Nature, and Consequences of Sin." In *Systematic Theology*, edited by Stanley M. Horton, 255–90. Rev. ed. Springfield, MO: Logion, 1995.

Marmorstein, A. *The Names and Attributes of God*. Vol. 1 of *The Old Rabbinic Doctrine of God*. 1927. Reprint, New York: Ktav, 1968.

Marsh, John. "Numbers." In *The Interpreter's Bible*, edited by George A. Buttrick, 137–310. Nashville: Abingdon, 1952.

Marshall, I. Howard. *Acts*. TNTC. Leicester: InterVarsity, 1980.

———. *The Gospel of Luke: A Commentary on the Greek Text*. NIGTC. Grand Rapids: Eerdmans, 1978.

———. *Kept by the Power of God: A Study in Perseverance and Falling Away*. 1969. Reprint, Minneapolis: Bethany Fellowship, 1974.

———. *Luke: Historian and Theologian*. Exeter: Paternoster, 1970.

———. *New Testament Theology: Many Witnesses, One Gospel*. Downers Grove, IL: InterVarsity, 2004.

Martin, Lee Roy, ed. *Pentecostal Hermeneutics: A Reader*. Leiden: Brill, 2013.

Martin, Ralph P. *The Worship of God*. Grand Rapids: Eerdmans, 1982.

Mayor, Joseph B. *The Epistle of St. James*. 3rd rev. ed. 1913. Reprint, Minneapolis: Klock & Klock, 1977.

McAlister, Robert E. "Difference Between Speaking in Tongues and the Gift of Tongues." *The Good Report*, May 1, 1911. 4.

McCarter, P. Kyle. *1 Samuel: Introduction, Translation, and Notes*. AB. Garden City, NY: Doubleday, 1980.

McClung, L. Grant, Jr. "Pentecostal/Charismatic Perspectives on a Missiology for the Twenty-First Century." *Pneuma* 16.1 (1994) 11–21.

McGee, Gary. *This Gospel Shall Be Preached*. Vol. 2. Springfield, MO: Gospel, 1989.

McKay, John. "When the Veil Is Taken Away: The Impact of Prophetic Experience on Biblical Interpretation." *JPT* 5 (1994) 17–40.

McKim, Donald K., ed. *Historical Handbook of Major Biblical Interpreters*. Leicester: InterVarsity, 1998.

———. *Westminster Dictionary of Theological Terms*. Louisville: Westminster John Knox, 1996.

McLean, Mark. "Toward a Pentecostal Hermeneutic." *Pneuma* 6.2 (1984) 35–56.

McNamara, Martin. *Targum and Testament*. Grand Rapids: Eerdmans, 1972.

Meier, John P. *Matthew*. NTM 3. Wilmington, DE: Michael Glazier, 1980.

Menzies, Robert P. *The Development of Early Christian Pneumatology with Special Reference to Luke-Acts*. JSNTSup 54. Sheffield: Sheffield Academic, 1991.

———. "The Distinctive Character of Luke's Pneumatology." *Paraclete* 25.3 (1991) 17–30.

———. *Empowered for Witness: The Spirit in Luke-Acts*. JPTSup 6. 1991. Reprint, London: T&T Clark, 2004.

———. "Jumping Off the Postmodern Bandwagon." *Pneuma* 16.1 (1994) 115–20.

———. *The Language of the Spirit: Interpreting and Translating Charismatic Terms*. Cleveland, TN: CPT, 2010.

———. *Pentecost: This Story is Our Story*. Springfield, MO: Gospel, 2013.

———. *Speaking in Tongues: Jesus and the Apostolic Church as Models for the Church Today*. Cleveland, TN: CPT, 2016.

Menzies, William W. "The Methodology of Pentecostal Theology: An Essay on Hermeneutics." In *Essays on Apostolic Themes*, edited by Paul Elbert, 1–14. Peabody: Hendrickson, 1985.

———. "Reflections on Suffering: A Pentecostal Perspective." In *The Spirit and Spirituality: Essays in Honour of Russell P. Spittler*, edited by Wonsuk Ma and Robert P. Menzies, 141–49. London: T&T Clark International, 2004.

Menzies, William, and Robert Menzies. "Evidential Tongues." In *Spirit and Power: Foundations of Pentecostal Experience*, 121–32. Grand Rapids: Zondervan, 2000.

———. *Spirit and Power: Foundation of Pentecostal Experience: A Call to Evangelical Dialogue*. Grand Rapids: Zondervan, 2000.

Metzger, Bruce M. "How Many Times Does 'Epiousios' Occur Outside the Lord's Prayer?" *ExpT* 69 (1957) 52–54.

———. *The Text of the New Testament*. New York: Oxford University Press, 1968.

Meyer, Joyce. *Filled with the Spirit: Understanding God's Power in Your Life*. New York: FaithWords, 2002.

Michaels, J. Ramsey. "Evidences of the Spirit, or the Spirit as Evidence? Some Non-Pentecostal Reflections." In *Initial Evidence: Historical and Biblical Perspectives on the Pentecostal Doctrine of Spirit Baptism*, edited by Gary B. McGee, 202–18. Eugene, OR: Wipf & Stock, 2008.

———. "Luke-Acts." In *Dictionary of Pentecostal and Charismatic Movements*, edited by Stanley Burgess, et al., 544–61. Grand Rapids: Zondervan, 1988.
*Midrash Rabbah*. Translated by H. Freedman and Maurice Simon. 10 vols. New York: Soncino, 1983.
Milgrom, Jacob. *Numbers. The Jewish Publication Society Torah Commentary*. Philadelphia: Jewish Publication Society, 1990.
Mitchell, B. K. "Let There Be Life! Toward a Hermeneutic of Biological and Theological Integration." In *Constructive Pneumatological Hermeneutics in Pentecostal Christianity*, edited by L. William Oliverio Jr. and Kenneth J. Archer, 297–314. CHARIS: Christianity and Renewal—Interdisciplinary Studies. New York: Palgrave Macmillan, 2016.
Mittelstadt, Martin William. "Academic and Pentecostal: An Appreciation of Roger Stronstad." *Canadian Journal of Pentecostal-Charismatic Christianity* 1 (2010) 31–64. https://journal.twu.ca/index.php/CJPC/issue/view/3.
———. *Reading Luke-Acts in the Pentecostal Tradition*. Cleveland, TN: CPT, 2010.
———. "Receiving Luke-Acts: The Rise of Reception History and a Call to Pentecostal Scholars." *Pneuma* 40 (2018) 367–88.
———. *The Spirit and Suffering in Luke-Acts: Implications for a Pentecostal Pneumatology*. JPTSup 26. London: T&T Clark International, 2004.
Moessner, David P. *Lord of the Banquet: The Literary and Theological Significance of the Lukan Travel Narrative*. Minneapolis: Fortress, 1989.
———. "Luke 9:1–50: Luke's Preview of the Journey of the Prophet Like Moses of Deuteronomy." *JBL* 102 (1983) 575–605.
———. "The 'Script' of the Scriptures in Acts: Suffering as God's 'Plan' for the World for the 'Release' of Sins." In *History, Literature, and Society in the Book of Acts*, edited by Ben Witherington III, 218–50. Cambridge: Cambridge University Press, 1996.
Molina, Francisco Contreras. *El Espíritu en el libro del Apocalipsis*. Koinonia 28. Salamanca: Secretariado Trinitario, 1987.
Moltmann, Jurgen. *The Church in the Power of the Spirit: A Contribution to Messianic Ecclesiology*. Translated by Margaret Kohl. London: SCM, 1977.
———. *The Source of Life: The Holy Spirit and the Theology of Life*. Translated by Margaret Kohl. Minneapolis: Fortress, 1997.
———. *The Spirit of Life: A Universal Affirmation*. Translated by Margaret Kohl. Minneapolis: Fortress, 1992.
Montague, George T. *The Holy Spirit: Growth of a Biblical Tradition*. New York: Paulist, 1976.
Montefiore, C. G. "Spirit of Judaism." *BegC* 1:35–81.
———. *The Synoptic Gospels*. 2 vols. 2nd ed. 1927. Reprint, New York: Ktav, 1968.
Montefiore, C. G., and Herbert Loewe, eds. *A Rabbinic Anthology*. 1938. Reprint, New York: Schocken, 1974.
Montefiore, Hugh W. "God as Father in the Synoptic Gospels." *NTS* 3 (1956) 31–46.
Moore, George Foot. *Judaism in the First Centuries of the Christian Era*. 3 vols. 1927–30. Reprint, New York: Schocken, 1971.
Morris, Leon. *Apocalyptic*. Grand Rapids: Eerdmans, 1972.
Motyer, Stephen. *Your Father the Devil? A New Approach to John and "the Jews."* Carlisle: Paternoster, 1997.
Moule, C. F. D. "An Unsolved Problem in the Temptation-Clause in the Lord's Prayer." *Reformed Theological Review* 33 (1974) 65–75.

Moyise, Steve, and Maarten J.J. Menken, eds. *Isaiah in the New Testament*. London: T&T Clark, 2005.

Munyon, Timothy. "The Creation of the Universe and Humankind." In *Systematic Theology*, edited by Stanley M. Horton, 215–53. Rev. ed. Springfield, MO: Logion, 1995.

"My Testimony of Healing." *Pentecostal Testimony*, May 1, 1943. 17.

Neusner, Jacob. *Judaism in the Beginning of Christianity*. Philadelphia: Fortress, 1984.

Neve, Lloyd R. *The Spirit of God in the Old Testament*. Centre for Pentecostal Theology Classics Series. Cleveland, TN: CPT, 2011.

Neyrey, Jerome H., ed. *The Social World of Luke-Acts: Models for Interpretation*. Peabody: Hendrickson, 1991.

Nickle, Keith F. *Preaching the Gospel of Luke: Proclaiming God's Royal Rule*. Louisville: Westminster John Knox, 2000.

Niebuhr, Reinhold. *Man's Nature and His Communities: Essays on the Dynamics and Enigmas of Man's Personal and Social Existence*. New York: Scribner's Sons, 1965.

———. *Moral Man and Immoral Society: A Study in Ethics and Politics*. New York: Scribner's Sons, 1932.

Nock, Arthur Darby. *Conversion: The Old and the New in Religion from Alexander the Great to Augustine of Hippo*. Oxford: Clarendon, 1933.

———. *Early Gentile Christianity and Its Hellenistic Background*. New York: Harper & Row, 1964.

Noel, Bradley Truman. "Gordon Fee and the Challenge to Pentecostal Hermeneutics: Thirty Years Later." *Pneuma* 26 (2004) 60–80.

———. *Pentecostal and Postmodern Hermeneutics: Comparison and Contemporary Impact*. Eugene, OR: Wipf and Stock, 2010.

———. *Pentecostalism, Secularism, and Post-Christendom*. Eugene, OR: Wipf and Stock, 2015.

Noordtzij, A. *Numbers*. BSC. Grand Rapids: Zondervan, 1983.

Noth, Martin. *Numbers*. OTL. Philadelphia: Westminster, 1968.

Odeberg, Hugo. *The Fourth Gospel Interpreted in Its Relation to Contemporaneous Religious Currents in Palestine and the Hellenistic-Oriental World*. 1929. Reprint, Amsterdam: B. R. Grüner; Chicago: Argonaut, 1968.

Oeming, Manfred. *Contemporary Biblical Hermeneutics: An Introduction*. Hants: Ashgate, 2016.

O'Keefe, Mark. *What Are They Saying about Social Sin?* Mahwah, NJ: Paulist, 1990.

Oliverio, L. William, Jr. *Theological Hermeneutics in the Classical Pentecostal Tradition: A Typological Account*. Leiden: Brill, 2012.

Onyinah, Opoku. "Deliverance as a Way of Confronting Witchcraft in Contemporary Africa: Ghana as a Case Study." In *The Spirit in the World: Emerging Pentecostal Theologies in Global Contexts*, edited by Veli-Matti Kärkkäinen, 181–202. Grand Rapids: Eerdmans, 2009.

Opp, James. *The Lord for the Body: Religion, Medicine, and Protestant Faith Healing in Canada, 1880–1930*. Montreal: McGill-Queen's University Press, 2007.

Ormerod, Neil. "The Structure of a Systematic Ecclesiology." *TS* 63 (2002) 3–30.

Packer, J. I. "In Quest of Canonical Interpretation." In *The Use of the Bible in Theology/Evangelical Options*, 35–55. Louisville: John Knox, 1997.

Paddison, Agnus. "The History and Reemergence of Theological Interpretation." In *A Manifesto for Theological Interpretation*, edited by Craig G. Bartholomew and Matthew Y. Emerson, 27–32. Grand Rapids: Baker, 2016.

Palma, Anthony. *The Holy Spirit, A Pentecostal Perspective*. Springfield, MO: Gospel, 2001.

Pao, David W. *Acts and the Isaianic New Exodus*. Grand Rapids: Baker Academic, 2002.

"PAOC Eastern District Conference now convening in Calvary Tabernacle. Toronto." *Minutes*, August 23, 1932.

Parham, Sarah. "Earnestly Contend for the Faith Once Delivered to the Saints." In *Selected Sermons of the Late Charles F. Parham, Sarah E. Parham: Co-Founders of the Original Apostolic Faith Movement*, compiled by Robert L. Parham. Baxter Springs, KS: Apostolic Faith Bible College, 1941.

———. *The Life of Charles F. Parham: Founder of the Apostolic Faith Movement*. 1930. Reprint, Joplin, MO: Hunter, 1969.

Parker, James, III. "The Concept of Apokatastasis in Acts: A Study in Primitive Christian Theology." DTh diss., University of Basil, 1978.

Patte, Daniel. *Early Jewish Hermeneutic in Palestine*. SBLDS 22. Missoula, MT: Scholars, 1975.

———. *The Gospel According to Matthew: A Structural Commentary on Matthew's Faith*. Philadelphia: Fortress, 1987.

Penney, John Michael. *The Missionary Emphasis of Lukan Pneumatology*. JPTSup 12. Sheffield: Sheffield Academic, 1997.

Percesepe, Gary J. "The Unbearable Lightness of Being Postmodern." *Christian Scholar's Review* 20 (1990) 118–35.

Perrin, Norman. *The Kingdom of God in the Teaching of Jesus*. Philadelphia: Westminster, 1963.

Peters, Ted. *Sin: Radical Evil in Soul and Society*. Grand Rapids: Eerdmans, 1994.

Phanon, Yuri. "The Work of the Holy Spirit in the Conception, Baptism and Temptation of Christ: Implications for the Pentecostal Christian." *AJPS* 20 (2017) 37–55.

Phillips, Thomas E. *Reading Issues of Wealth and Poverty in Luke-Acts*. Studies in Bible and Early Christianity 48. Lewiston, NY: Mellen, 2001.

Pilgrim, Walter E. *Good News to the Poor: Poverty and Wealth in Luke-Acts*. Minneapolis: Augsburg Fortress, 1981.

Pimental, P. "The 'Unclean Spirits' of St. Mark's Gospel." *ExpT* 99 (1988) 173–75.

Plummer, Alfred. *An Exegetical Commentary on the Gospel According to S. Matthew*. London: Elliot Stock, 1910.

Poirier, John C., and B. Scott Lewis. "Pentecostal and Postmodernist Hermeneutics: A Critique of Three Conceits." *JPT* 15 (2006) 3–21.

Powell, Mark Allan. *What Are They Saying about Acts?* New York: Paulist, 1991.

———. *What Are They Saying about Luke?* New York: Paulist, 1989.

Purdy, Harlyn G. *A Distinct Twenty-First-Century Pentecostal Hermeneutic*. Eugene, OR: Wipf and Stock, 2015.

Purdy, Vernon. "Divine Healing." In *Systematic Theology: A Pentecostal Perspective*, edited by Stanley M. Horton, 489–523. Springfield, MO: Logion, 1999.

Rahlfs, Alfred, ed. *Septuaginta*. Stuttgart, Germany: Deutsche Bibelstiftung, 1935.

Read-Heimerdinger, Jenny. *The Bezan Text of Acts: A Contribution of Discourse Analysis to Textual Criticism*. JSNTSup 236. New York: Sheffield Academic, 2002.

Reitzenstein, Richard. *Hellenistic Mystery-Religions: Their Basic Ideas and Significance*. Translated by John E. Steeley. PTMS 15. Pittsburgh: Pickwick, 1978.

Reynolds, Benjamin E., et al., eds. *Reconsidering the Relationship between Biblical and Systematic Theology in the New Testament: Essays by Theologians and New Testament Scholars*. Wissenschaftliche Untersuchungen Zum Neuen Testament, 2. Reihe 369. Tübingen: Mohr Siebeck, 2014.

Rice, Monte Lee. "Bill Oliverio: Theological Hermeneutics in the Classical Pentecostal Tradition." Review of *Theological Hermeneutics in the Classical Pentecostal Tradition: A Typological Account*, by L. William Oliverio Jr. *Pneuma Review*, April 20, 2015. Online. http://pneumareview.com/bill-oliverio-theological-hermeneutics-in-the-classical-pentecostal-tradition.

Richie, Tony. "Azusa-era Optimism: Bishop J. H. King's Pentecostal Theology of Religions as a Possible Paradigm for Today." *Journal of Pentecostal Tradition* 14 (2006) 247–60.

———. *Speaking by the Spirit: A Pentecostal Model for Interreligious Dialogue*. Lexington: Emeth, 2011.

Ringe, Sharon H. *Jesus, Liberation, and the Biblical Jubilee: Images for Ethics and Christology*. 1985. Reprint, Eugene, OR: Wipf and Stock, 2004.

Rius-Camps, Josep. "The Spelling of Jerusalem in the Gospel of John: The Significance of Two Forms in Codex Bezae." *New Testament Studies* 48.1 (2002) 84–94.

Rivkin, Ellis. *A Hidden Revolution*. Nashville: Abingdon, 1978.

Robbins, Vernon K. *Exploring the Texture of Texts: A Guide to Socio-Rhetorical Interpretation* Valley Forge: Trinity International, 1996.

———. *Tapestry of Early Christian Discourse: Rhetoric, Society and Ideology*. London: Routledge, 1996.

Robins, R. G. *A. J. Tomlinson: Plainfolk Modernist*. Religion in America. 1st ed. Oxford: Oxford University Press, 2004.

Robinson, Anthony B., and Robert W. Wall. *Called to Be Church: The Book of Acts for a New Day*. Grand Rapids: Eerdmans, 2006.

Rodd, Cyril S. "Spirit or Finger." *ExpT* 72 (1961) 157–58.

Rodriguez, Dario Lopez. *The Liberating Mission of Jesus: The Message of the Gospel of Luke*. Pentecostals, Peacemaking, and Social Justice Series. Eugene, OR: Pickwick, 2012.

Romilley, Ellen. "Heart and Limb Healed." *Household of God* 3.11 (1907) 10.

Ropes, James Hardy. *A Critical and Exegetical Commentary on the Epistle of St. James*. ICC. Edinburgh: T. & T. Clark, 1916.

Rosenbaum, M., and A. M. Silbermann, eds. *Numbers*. Pentateuch with Targum Onkelos, Haphtaroth and Rashi's Commentary. Jerusalem: Silbermann Family, 1933.

Roth, Cecil. "The Subject Matter of Qumran Exegesis." *VT* 10 (1960) 51–68.

Rowland, Christopher. *The Open Heaven: A Study of Apocalyptic in Judaism and Early Christianity*. New York: Crossroad, 1982.

Ruthven, Jonathan. "Charismatic Theology and Biblical Emphases." *EvQ* 69 (1997) 217–36.

Rylaarsdam, J. Coert. "Exodus." In *The Interpreter's Bible*, edited by George A. Buttrick, 833–1099. Nashville: Abingdon, 1952.

Sample, Tex. *Ministry in an Oral Culture: Living with Will Rogers, Uncle Remus, and Minnie Pearl*. 1st ed. Louisville, KY: Westminster, 1994.

Sanders, E. P. *Jesus and Judaism*. Philadelphia: Fortress, 1985.

Sanders, James A. "Sins, Debts, and Jubilee Release." In *Luke and Scripture: The Function of Sacred Tradition in Luke-Acts*, edited by Craig A. Evans and James A. Sanders, 84–92. Eugene, OR: Wipf and Stock, 2001.

Sandmel, Samuel. *Judaism and Christian Beginnings.* New York: Oxford University Press, 1978.

Sawyer, John. F. A. *Isaiah.* Vol. 1. Logos edition. Louisville: Westminster John Knox, 1984.

———. "The Role of Reception Theory, Reader-Response Criticism, and/or Impact History in the Study of the Bible: Definition and Evaluation." Paper presented at the Society of Biblical Literature, San Antonio, Texas, November 20–23, 2004. http://bbibcomm.info/?page_id=183.

Schiffman, Lawrence H. *Sectarian Law in the Dead Sea Scrolls: Courts, Testimony, and the Penal Code.* BJS 33. Chico, CA: Scholars, 1983.

Scholem, Gershom G. *Jewish Gnosticism, Merkabah Mysticism, and Talmudic Tradition.* New York: Jewish Theological Seminary of America Press, 1965.

———. *Major Trends in Jewish Mysticism.* 3rd rev. ed. New York: Schocken, 1971.

Schumacher, Steffen. "The Spirit of God in the Torah: A Pentecostal Exploration." PhD diss., Bangor University, 2019.

Schweizer, Eduard. "πνεῦμα." In *TDNT* 6:412.

———. *The Good News According to Matthew.* Translated by David E. Green. Atlanta: John Knox, 1975.

Seo, Pyung-Soo. *Luke's Jesus in the Roman Empire and the Emperor in the Gospel of Luke.* Cambridge: James Clarke, 2015.

Shelton, James, B. "'Filled with the Holy Spirit' and 'Full of the Holy Spirit': Lukan Redactional Phrases." In *Faces of Renewal: Studies in Honor of Stanley M. Horton Presented on his 70th Birthday,* edited by Paul Elbert, 81–107. Peabody, MA: Hendrickson, 1988.

———. "'Filled with the Holy Spirit': A Redactional Motif in Luke's Gospel." PhD diss., Stirling University, 1982.

———. *Mighty in Word and Deed: The Role of the Holy Spirit in Luke-Acts.* Peabody, MA: Hendrickson, 1991.

Siegel, Seymour. "The Meaning of Israel in Jewish Thought." In *Evangelicals and Jews in Conversation on Scripture, Theology, and History,* edited by Marc H. Tanenbaum, et al., 98–118. Grand Rapids: Baker, 1978.

Silberman, Lou H. "Unriddling the Riddle: A Study in the Structure and Language of the Habakkuk Pesher." *RevQ* 3 (1961–62) 323–64.

Silva, Moisés. *New International Dictionary of New Testament Theology and Exegesis.* 5 vols. rev. 2nd ed. Grand Rapids: Zondervan, 2014.

Smith, David E. *The Canonical Function of Acts: A Comparative Analysis.* Collegeville, MN: Liturgical, 2002.

Smith, Henry Preserved. *A Critical and Exegetical Commentary on Samuel.* ICC. Edinburgh: T. & T. Clark, 1899.

Smith, James K. A. *The Fall of Interpretation: Philosophical Foundations for a Creational Hermeneutic.* Grand Rapids: Baker Academic, 2012.

———. *How (Not) To Be Secular: Reading Charles Taylor.* Grand Rapids: Eerdmans, 2014.

Smith, James K. A., and Amos Yong, eds. *Science and the Spirit: A Pentecostal Engagement with Sciences.* Bloomington: Indiana University Press, 2010.

Smith, Morton. *Tannaitic Parallels to the Gospels.* Philadelphia: SBL, 1951.

Solivan, Samuel. *The Spirit, Pathos, and Liberation: Toward an Hispanic Pentecostal Theology.* JPTSup 14. Sheffield: Sheffield Academic, 1998.

Spittler, Russell P. "Scripture and Theological Enterprise." In *The Use of the Bible in Theology: Evangelical Options*, edited by R. K. Johnston, 56–77. Louisville: Westminster John Knox, 1985.

Sri, Edward. "Release from the Debt of Sin: Jesus's Jubilee Mission in the Gospel of Luke." *Nova et Vetera* 9 (2011) 183–94.

Stanford, Matthew S. *The Biology of Sin: Grace, Hope and Healing for Those Who Feel Trapped*. Downers Grove, IL: InterVarsity, 2010.

Stein, Robert, H. *Luke*. NAC 24. Logos edition. Nashville: Broadman & Holman, 1992.

———. *Mark*. BECNT. Grand Rapids: Baker, 2008.

Stott, John R. W. *The Baptism and Fullness of the Holy Spirit*. Downers Grove, IL: InterVarsity, 1964.

Strack, Hermann L. *Introduction to the Talmud and Midrash*. 1931. Reprint, New York: Atheneum, 1969.

Strauss, Mark L. *The Davidic Messiah in Luke-Acts: The Promise and Its Fulfillment in Lukan Christology*. JSNTSup 110. Sheffield: Sheffield Academic, 1995.

Stronstad, Roger. "The Biblical Precedent for Historical Precedent." Paper presented at the annual meeting of the Society for Pentecostal Studies, Springfield, MO, November 12–14, 1992.

———. "The Biblical Precedent for Historical Precedent." *Paraclete* 27.2 (1993) 1–10.

———. "The Charismatic Theology of St. Luke: Revisited." In *Defining Issues in Pentecostalism: Classical and Emergent*, edited by Steven M. Studebaker, 101–122. McMaster Theological Studies Series 1. Eugene, OR: Pickwick, 2008.

———. *The Charismatic Theology of St. Luke: Trajectories from the Old Testament to Luke-Acts*. 2nd ed. Grand Rapids: Baker Academic, 2012.

———. "'Filled with the Holy Spirit' Terminology in Luke-Acts." In *The Holy Spirit in the Scriptures and the Church: Essays Presented to Leslie Thomas Holdcroft on His 65th Birthday*, edited by Roger Stronsad and Laurence M. Van Kleek, 1–13. Clayburn, BC: Western Pentecostal Bible College, 1987.

———. "'Filled with the Holy Spirit' Terminology in Luke-Acts." In *Spirit, Scripture and Theology: A Pentecostal Perspective*, by Roger Stronstad, 79–89. Baguio City, Philippines: Asia Pacific Theological Seminary Press, 1995.

———. "'Filled with the Holy Spirit' Terminology in Luke-Acts." In *Spirit, Scripture and Theology: A Pentecostal Perspective*, by Roger Stronstad, 61–78. 2nd ed. Baguio City, Philippines: Asia Pacific Theological Seminary Press, 2018.

———. "The Hermeneutics of Lukan Historiography." *Paraclete* 22.4 (1988) 5–17.

———. "The Influence of the Old Testament on the Charismatic Theology of St. Luke." *Pneuma* 2 (1980) 32–50.

———. *A Pentecostal Biblical Theology: Turning Points in the Story of Redemption*. Cleveland, TN: CPT, 2016.

———. "Pentecostal Experience and Hermeneutics." *Paraclete* 26 (1992) 14–30.

———. "Pentecostal Hermeneutics: A Review Essay of Gordon D. Fee, *Gospel and Spirit: Issues in New Testament Hermeneutics*." *Pneuma* 15 (1993) 215–22.

———. "Pentecostalism, Experiential Presuppositions and Hermeneutic." Paper presented at the annual meeting of the Society for Pentecostal Studies, Dallas, TX, November 8–10, 1990.

———. *The Prophethood of All Believers: A Study in Luke's Charismatic Theology*. JPTSup 16. 1999. Reprint, Cleveland, TN: CPT, 2010.

———. "The Rebirth of Prophecy: Trajectories from Moses to Jesus and his Followers." In *Spirit, Scripture, and Theology: A Pentecostal Perspective,* by Roger Stronstad, 159–91. 2nd ed. Baguio City, Philippines: Asia Pacific Theological Seminary Press, 2018.

———. "A Review Essay on Amos Yong, *Who Is the Holy Spirit: A Walk with the Apostles.*" *JPT* 22 (2013) 295–300.

———. "Review of John R. Levison's, *Filled with the Spirit* Part III, Early Christian Literature Chapter 3, 'Filled with the Spirit and the Book of Acts.'" *JPT* 20.2 (2011) 201–6.

———. *Signs on the Earth Beneath: A Commentary on Acts 2:1–21.* Springfield, MO: Life International, 2003.

———. *Spirit, Scripture, and Theology: A Pentecostal Perspective.* Baguio City, Philippines: Asia Pacific Theological Seminary Press, 1995.

———. "Some Aspects of Hermeneutics in the Pentecostal Tradition." In *Pentecostals in the Twenty-First Century: Identity, Beliefs, Praxis,* edited by Corneliu Constantineanu and Christopher J. Scobie, 32–58. Eugene, OR: Cascade, 2018.

———. "Trends in Pentecostal Hermeneutics." *Paraclete* 22 (1988) 12.

———. "Unity and Diversity: Lukan, Johannine, and Pauline Perspectives on the Holy Spirit." *Paraclete* 23.3 (1989) 15–28.

Studebaker, Steve. "Christian Mission and the Religions as Participation in the Spirit of Pentecost." In *Global Renewal, Religious Pluralism, and the Great Commission: Towards a Renewal Theology of Mission and Interreligious Encounter,* edited by Amos Yong and Clifton Clarke, 71–95. Lexington: Emeth, 2011.

Synan, Vinson. "The Role of Tongues as Initial Evidence." In *Spirit and Renewal: Essays in Honor of J. Rodman Williams,* edited by Mark Wilson, 67–82. Sheffield: Sheffield Academic, 1994.

Talbert, Charles H. *Literary Patterns, Theological Themes, and the Genre of Luke-Acts.* Missoula, MN: SBL, 2006.

———. *Reading Acts: A Literary and Theological Commentary on the Acts of the Apostles.* New York: Crossroad, 1997.

———. *Reading Luke: A Literary and Theological Commentary on the Third Gospel.* New York: Crossroad, 1982.

Tannehill, Robert C. *The Narrative Unity of Luke-Acts: A Literary Interpretation.* 2 vols. Philadelphia: Fortress, 1986–1990.

———. *The Sword of His Mouth.* SBLSemSup 1. Missoula, MT: Scholars, 1975.

Tarn, William Woodthorpe. *Hellenistic Civilisation.* Revised by W. W. Tarn, and G. T. Griffith. 3rd rev. ed. New York: New American Library, 1974.

Tasker, R. V. G. *The Gospel According to St. Matthew.* Grand Rapids: Eerdmans, 1961.

Taylor, Joan E. *The Immerser: John the Baptist within Second Temple Judaism.* Grand Rapids: Eerdmans, 1997.

Taylor, Richard A., and Ray Clendenen. *Haggai Malachi.* NAC 21A. Nashville: Broadman & Holman, 2004.

Taylor, Vincent. *The Gospel According to St. Mark.* London: Macmillan, 1952.

Thiselton, Anthony C. "The Holy Spirit in 1 Corinthians: Exegesis and Reception History in the Patristic Era." In *The Holy Spirit and Christian Origins: Essays in Honor of James D. G. Dunn,* edited by Graham N. Stanton, et al., 207–238. Grand Rapids: Eerdmans, 2004.

———. "A Retrospective Reappraisal: Reader Response Hermeneutics and Parable Worlds." In *Thiselton on Hermeneutics: Collected Works with New Essays,* by Anthony C. Thiselton, 515–21. Grand Rapids: Eedermans, 2006.

Thomas, John Christopher. *The Apocalypse: A Literary and Theological Commentary.* Cleveland, TN: CPT, 2012.

———. "Reading the Bible from within Our Traditions: A Pentecostal Hermeneutic as Test Case." In *Between Two Horizons: Spanning New Testament Studies and Systematic Theology*, edited by Joel B. Green and Max Turner, 108–122. Grand Rapids: Eerdmans, 2000.

———. "The Role and Function of the Demonic in the Johannine Tradition." In *'But These Are Written': Essays on Johannine Literature in Honor of Professor Ben C. Aker*, edited by C. S. Keener, et al., 27–47. Eugene, OR: Pickwick, 2014.

———, ed. *Toward a Pentecostal Ecclesiology: The Church and the Fivefold Gospel.* Cleveland, TN: CPT, 2010.

———. "Toward a Pentecostal Theology of Anointed Cloths." In *Toward a Pentecostal Theology of Worship*, edited by Lee Roy Martin, 311–43. Cleveland, TN: CPT, 2016.

———. "Women, Pentecostals, and the Bible: An Experiment in Pentecostal Hermeneutics." *JPT* 5 (1994) 41–56.

Tiede, David L. *The Charismatic Figure as Miracle Worker.* SBLDS 1. Missoula, MT: SBL, 1972.

———. *Prophecy and History in Luke-Acts.* Philadelphia: Fortress, 1980.

Tilborg, Sjef Van. "A Form-Criticism of the Lord's Prayer." *NovT* 14 (1972) 94–105.

Tipei, John Fleter. *The Laying on of Hands in the New Testament: Its Significance, Techniques, and Effects.* Lanham, MD: University Press of America, 2009.

Treier, Daniel J. "Biblical Theology and/or Theological Interpretation of Scripture?" *SJT* 61 (2008) 16–31.

Tuppurainen, Riku, P. "The Contribution of Socio-Rhetorical Criticism to Spirit-Sensitive Hermeneutics: A Contextual Example—Luke 11:13." *JBPR* 4 (2012) 38–66.

———. "The Role(s) of the Spirit-Paraclete in John 16:4b–15: A Socio-Rhetorical Investigation." DTh diss., University of South Africa, 2007.

Turner, Max M. B. "Does Luke Believe Reception of the 'Spirit of Prophecy' Makes All 'Prophets'? Inviting Dialogue with Roger Stronstad." *Journal of the European Pentecostal Theological Association* 20 (2000) 3–24.

———. "'Empowerment for Mission'? The Pneumatology of Luke-Acts: An Appreciation and Critique of James B. Shelton's *Mighty in Word and Deed*." *VE* 24 (1994) 103–122.

———. "Holy Spirit." In *DJG* 341–51.

———. "Levison's *Filled with the Spirit*: A Brief Appreciation and Response." *JPT* 20.2 (2011) 193–200.

———. *Power from on High: The Spirit in Israel's Restoration and Witness in Luke Acts.* Sheffield: Sheffield Academic, 1996.

———. "Spirit Endowment in Luke/Acts: Some Linguistic Considerations." *VE* 12 (1981) 45–63.

Turney, H. M. "The Baptism of the Holy Ghost." *The Weekly Evangel*, July 1, 1916.

Twelftree, Graham H. *Jesus the Exorcist: A Contribution to the Study of the Historical Jesus.* Tübingen: Mohr, 1993.

———. *Luke-Acts People of the Spirit.* Grand Rapids: Baker Academic, 2009.

———. *People of the Spirit: Exploring Luke's View of the Church.* Grand Rapids: Baker Academic, 2009.

Urbach, Ephraim E. *The Sages: Their Concepts and Beliefs.* Translated by Israel Abrahams. 2 vols. 2nd ed. Jerusalem: Magnes, 1979.

———. "Self-Isolation or Self-Affirmation in Judaism in the First Three Centuries: Theory and Practice." In *Aspects of Judaism in the Graeco-Roman Period*, edited by E. P. Sanders, et al., 269–98. Vol. 2 of *Jewish and Christian Self-Definition*. Philadelphia: Fortress, 1981.

Van den Toren, Bennie. "Human Evolution and a Cultural Understanding of Original Sin." *Perspectives on Science and Christian Faith* 68 (2016) 12–21.

Van der Horst, Pieter W. "Musonius Rufus and the New Testament." *NovT* 16 (1974) 306–315.

Van Gelder, C. "Postmodernism as an Emerging Worldview." *CTJ* 26 (1991) 412–17.

"Vancouver Campaign." *Pentecostal Testimony*, June 1927. 2.

Vanhoozer, Kevin J. "Introduction: What Is Theological Interpretation of the Bible?" In *Dictionary for Theological Interpretation of the Bible*, edited by Kevin J. Vanhoozer, et al., 19–26. Grand Rapids: Baker Academic, 2005.

———. "Is the Theology of the New Testament One or Many? Between (the Rock of) Systematic Theology and (the Hard Place of) Historical Occasionalism." In *Reconsidering the Relationship Between Biblical and Systematic Theology in the New Testament: Essays by Theologians and New Testament Scholars*, edited by Benjamin E. Reynolds, et al., 17–38. Wissenschaftliche Untersuchungen Zum Neuen Testament 2. Reihe 369. Tubingen: Mohr Siebeck, 2014.

Vansina, Jan. *Oral Tradition as History*. Madison: University of Wisconsin Press, 1985.

Vermes, Geza. *Jesus and the World of Judaism*. London: SCM, 1983. Philadelphia: Fortress, 1984.

Villafañe, Eldín. *The Liberating Spirit: Toward an Hispanic American Pentecostal Social Ethic*. Grand Rapids: Eerdmans, 1993.

Vinson, Richard, *Luke*. Macon, GA: Smyth & Helwys, 2008.

Volf, Miroslav. "Materiality of Salvation: An Investigation in the Soteriologies of Liberation and Pentecostal Theologies." *Journal of Ecumenical Studies* 26 (1989) 447–67.

Von Baer, H. *Der Heilige Geist in den Lukasschriften*. n.p., 1926.

Wacker, Grant. "Functions of Faith in Primitive Pentecostalism." *HTR* 77 (1984) 353–75.

———. *Heaven Below: Early Pentecostals and American Culture*. Cambridge, MA: Harvard University Press, 2001.

Waddell, Robby C. "The Holy Spirit of Life, Work, and Inspired Speech: Responding to John (Jack) R. Levison, *Filled with the Spirit*." *JPT* 20.2 (2011) 207–212.

———. *The Spirit of the Book of Revelation*. JPTSup 30. Blandford Forum: Deo, 2006.

Wadholm, Rick, Jr. *A Theology of the Spirit in the Former Prophets: A Pentecostal Perspective*. Cleveland, TN: CPT, 2018.

Walker, William O., Jr. "Lead Us Not into Temptation." *ExpT* 73 (1962) 287.

———. "The Lord's Prayer in Matthew and in John." *NTS* 28 (1982) 237–56.

Wallace, Daniel. *Greek Grammar Beyond the Basics: An Exegetical Syntax of the New Testament*. Grand Rapids: Zondervan, 1996.

Wallace, Stan. "The Real Issue: Discerning and Defining the Essentials of Postmodernism." *Postmodernism* Sup 1 (2007) 8–14. https://hongmark.com/resource/SummitResearchSupplementals/Postmodernism.pdf

Warrington, Keith. "Healing and Suffering in the Bible." *International Review of Mission* 95.376/77 (2006) 154–64.

———. *Pentecostal Theology: A Theology of Encounter*. London: T. & T. Clark, 2008.

Watson, Duance F. "Why We Need Socio-Rhetorical Commentary and What It Might Look Like." In *Rhetorical Criticism and the Bible*, edited by Stanley E. Porter and Dennis L. Stamps, 128–57. JSNTSup 195. Sheffield: Sheffield Academic, 2002.

Watts, Rikki E. "The Cross: Not the Defeat of Satan, but the Reconciliation of Yahweh and His People." Paper presented at The Atonement Symposium, University of St. Andrews, June 5, 2018.

———. *Isaiah's New Exodus in Mark*. WUNT 2.88. Tübingen: Mohr-Siebeck, 1997.

———. "Mark." In *Commentary on the New Testament Use of the Old Testament*, edited by G. K. Beale and D. A. Carson, 111–249. Grand Rapids: Baker Academic, 2007.

———. "The Psalms in Mark's Gospel." In *The Psalms in the New Testament*, edited by Steve Moyise and Maarten J. J. Menken, 25–45. Edinburgh: T. & T. Clarke, 2004.

———. "The Stronger One and the Dove: Revisiting Two Discarded Images in Mark's Prologue." Paper presented at the Annual Meeting of the OT in the NT Seminar, Hawarden, Wales, March 22, 2018.

Webb, Robert L. *John the Baptizer and Prophet*. JSNTSup 62. Sheffield: JSOT, 1991.

Welch, Bob. "The Acts of the Holy Spirit in Codex Bezae: An Examination of Variants in D05 with Application to Pneumatology." MTh diss., University of Wales, 2006.

———. "Repetitive Prophetical and Interpretative Formulations in Luke's Gospel of Codex Bezae: An Analysis of Readings in D." PhD diss., Bangor University, 2015.

Wenham, Gordon. *Numbers*. TOTC 4, Downers Grove, IL: InterVarsity, 2008.

———. *Numbers: An Introduction and Commentary*. TOTC. Downers Grove, IL: InterVarsity, 1981.

Wenk, Matthias. *Community-Forming Power: The Socio-Ethical Role of the Spirit in Luke-Acts*. 2000. Reprint, London: T. & T. Clark, 2004.

White, R. E. O. *The Biblical Doctrine of Initiation*. Grand Rapids: Eerdmans, 1960.

Wieder, Naphtali. "The Dead Sea Scrolls Type of Biblical Exegesis among the Karaites." In *Between East and West: Essays Dedicated to the Memory of Bela Horovitz*, edited by Alexander Altmann, 75–105. London: East and West, 1958.

Wigglesworth, Smith. *Ever Increasing Faith*. Springfield, MO: Gospel, 1924.

Wilcox, David L. "A Proposed Model for the Evolutionary Creation of Human Beings: From the Image of God to the Origin of Sin." *Perspectives on Science and Christian Faith* 68 (2016) 22–43.

Williams, Catrin H. *I am He: The Interpretation of 'Ani Hu' in Jewish and Early Christian Literature*. Tübingen: Mohr Siebeck, 2000.

Williams, Patricia A. *Doing without Adam and Eve: Sociobiology and Original Sin*. Minneapolis: Augsburg Fortress, 2001.

Williams, Rodman J. *Renewal Theology*. Vol. 1. Grand Rapids: Zondervan, 1988.

Willis, Geoffrey G. "Lead Us Not into Temptation." *Downside Review* 93 (1975) 281–88.

Wilson, Marvin R. "נָחַם" In *TWOT* 2:570–71.

———. "An Evangelical Perspective on Judaism." In *Evangelicals and Jews in Conversation on Scripture, Theology, and History*, edited by Marc H. Tannenbaum, et al., 2–33. Grand Rapids: Baker 1978.

Wilson, R. McL. *The Gnostic Problem*. London: A. R. Mowbray, 1958.

Wilson, Robert R. *Prophecy and Society in Ancient Israel*. Philadelphia: Fortress, 1980.

Witherington, Ben, III. *The Acts of the Apostles: A Socio-Rhetorical Commentary*. Grand Rapids: Eerdmans, 1998.

Wright, N. T. *Jesus and the Victory of God*. Minneapolis: Fortress, 1997.

Yamauchi, Edwin M. "The 'Daily Bread' Motif in Antiquity." *WTJ* 28 (1966) 145–56.

Yates, John Edmund. *The Spirit and the Kingdom*. London: SPCK, 1963.

Yong, Amos. *The Bible, Disability, and the Church: A New Vision of the People of God.* Grand Rapids: Eerdmans, 2011.

———. *The Hermeneutical Spirit: Theological Interpretation and Scriptural Imagination for the Twenty-First Century.* Eugene: Cascade, 2017.

———. *Hospitality and the Other: Pentecost, Christian Practices, and the Neighbor.* Maryknoll, NY: Orbis, 2008.

———. *The Missiological Spirit: Christian Mission Theology in the Third Millennium Global Context.* Eugene, OR: Cascade, 2014.

———. "Pentecostalism and Science: Challenges and Opportunities." In *Proceedings of the Inaugural Faith and Science Conference, Springfield, Missouri, June 27–28, 2011*, edited by David R. Bundrick and Steve Badger, 133–47. Springfield, MO: Gospel, 2012.

———. *Renewing Christian Theology: Systematics for Global Christianity.* Waco, TX: Baylor University Press, 2014.

———. *The Spirit of Creation.* Grand Rapids: Eerdmans, 2011.

———. *Spirit of Love: A Trinitarian Theology of Grace.* Waco, TX: Baylor University Press, 2012.

———. *The Spirit Poured Out on All Flesh: Pentecostalism and the Possibility of Global Theology.* Grand Rapids: Baker Academic, 2005.

———. *Spirit-Word-Community: Theological Hermeneutics in Trinitarian Perspective.* Eugene: Wipf and Stock, 2002.

———. *Who is the Holy Spirit? A Walk with the Apostles.* Brewster, MA: Paraclete, 2011.

———, ed. "Pentecostalism, Science, and Creation: New Voices in the Theology-Science Conversation." *Zygon: Journal of Science and Religion* 43 (2008) 875–989.

———, ed. *Spirit Renews the Face of the Earth: Pentecostal Forays in Science and Theology of Creation.* Eugene, OR: Pickwick, 2009.

York, John O. *The Last Shall Be First: The Rhetoric of Reversal in Luke.* JSNTSup 46. 1991. Reprint, London: Bloomsbury, 2015.

Zehnle, Richard F. *Peter's Pentecost Discourse: Tradition and Lukan Reinterpretation in Peter's Speeches of Acts 2 and 3.* SBLMS 15. Nashville: Abingdon, 1971.

# Abbreviated & Selected Name Index

**Key to Abbreviations**
bibl = bibliography in the book
n = footnote on the page
port = portrait
x = number of times the source appears on the page

Aalen, S., 122n, 265bibl
Abrahams, I., 115n, 124n, 126n, 265bibl, 287bibl
Aker, B., 231, 287
Albrecht, D.E., 178n, 265bibl
Albright, C.R., 128n, 162n, 265bibl
Albright, W.F., 128n, 265bibl
Alexander, K.E., 82, 84n, 265bibl
Alexander, P., xxxibibl
Alexander, T.D., 268bibl
Allen, A.A., 83n, 265bibl(3x)
Allen, R.B., 265bibl
Alsup, J.E., 272bibl
Altmann, A., 289bibl
Anderson, A., 64, 64n, 69, 69n, 87n(2x), 265bibl(2x)
Angus, S., 117n, 265bibl
Archer, G.L., xxiibibl
Archer, K.J., 58n, 63(7x), 63n(3x), 86, 86n(4x), 87n, 90(2x), 90n(2x), 91n(2x), 92, 93n(3x), 94n, 95, 95n, 97n(2x), 265bibl(5x), 280bibl
Archer, M.L., 82n, 256n, 265bibl
Arokiasamy, S., 163n, 266bibl(2x)
Arrington, F., xxxbibl(2x), xxxiii(3x), 3, 8, 9(2x), 9n(5x), 19, 95, 95n(2x), 163n(2x), 266bibl(2x)
Asamoah-Gyadu, J.K., 181n, 266bibl
Ashbrook, J.B., 162n, 266bibl
Ashley, T.R., 188n, 189(2x), 189n, 190, 190n(2x), 202n, 266bibl
Atkinson, W.P., xxxiiibibl, 5n, 58, 104n, 245n(2x), 266bibl
Au, C., 68, 169n, 266bibl
Aune, D., 10n(2x), 266bibl

Badcock, G., 98n, 266bibl
Bailey, K.E., 130n(3x), 131(2x), 131n, 266bibl
Ball, D.M., 232n, 233, 233n,234n, 266bibl
Bandstra, A.J., 115n(2x), 130n, 266bibl
Barnett, P.W., 223n, 266bibl
Barrett, C.K., 124n, 126n, 220n, 227n, 229n, 237, 266bibl
Barrett, D., 39
Bartholomew, C.G., 53n, 266bibl, 282bibl
Bauckham, R., 254n, 266bibl
Baum, G., 124n, 266bibl
Beale, G.K., 289bibl
Beasley-Murray, G.R., 266bibl
Beaton, R., 220n, 266bibl
Beattie, D.R.G., 269bibl
Beitzel, B.J, 270bibl(2x)
Ben Yoḥai, R.S., 119n, 132n
Bennema, A., 266bibl
Benson, A., 193n, 266bibl
Best, E., 127n(2x), 220n, 228n, 267bibl(2x)
Best, I., 267bibl
Betz, O., 122n, 267bibl
Bietenhard, 117n, 122n, 267bibl
Black, M., 127n, 267bibl
Blenkinsopp, C., 222n, 267bibl
Bloomberg, C., 267bibl
Blumhofer, C.M., 107n(3x), 267bibl(2x)
Bock, D.L., 106, 106n, 138n, 267bibl
Boda, M.J., 140n, 267bibl(2x)
Boling, R.G., 192, 192n, 267bibl
Bomar, J.D., 274bibl
Bonhoeffer, D., 112(2x), 112n, 267bibl(2x)
Bonsirven, J., 116, 119n, 123n(2x), 126n, 130n, 267bibl
Boring, M.E., 237n, 267bibl
Botha, F.J., 115n, 116n, 125n, 267bibl
Bovon, F.J., 11(3x), 11n(2x), 125n, 267bibl
Bowden, J., 273bibl(2x)
Bowman, J., 120n, 267(2x)
Bradnick, D., 171n, 267bibl

Brinsmead, B.H., 124n, 267bibl
Bromiley, G.W., xxibibl, 276bibl(2x)
Brown, C., 221n, 267bibl
Brown, J.K., xixbibl
Brown, S., 26n, 27n, 231n(3x), 232(2x), 234, 234n(2x), 236n(2x), 237n, 239n, 267bibl
Brown, T.G., 267bibl
Brownlee, W.H., 124n, 267bibl
Bruce, F.F., 10n(2x), 17, 18, 119n, 125n, 132n(2x), 145n, 154, 154n, 250n(3x), 268bibl(6x)
Brueggemann, W., 48, 48n, 199n, 268bibl(2x)
Bruner, F.D., 4, 4n, 6, 101n, 268bibl
Büchsel, F., 32n, 268bibl
Bultmann, R., 118n, 123n, 131n, 268bibl(2x)
Burgess, R., 268bibl
Burgess, S.M., 174n, 268bibl, 275bibl, 277bibl, 280bibl
Burkert, W., 117n(3x), 268bibl
Busse, U., 273bibl
Butticaz, S.D., 107n, 268bibl

Cancik, H., 273bibl
Cadbury, H.J., 132n, 277bibl
Cantalamessa, R., 268bibl
Cargal, T.B., 66n, 268bibl
Carson, D.A., 10, 10n, 103(2x), 103n, 120, 268(4x), 289bibl
Cary, M., 130n, 268bibl
Cassidy, R.J., 168n, 268bibl
Chan, S., 92
Charette, B., ix, xi, 209
Chesterton, G.K., 19
Childs, B.S., 187(2x), 187n, 269bibl
Chilton, B., 144n
Clark, A.C., 145n, 275bibl
Clarke, C.R., 176n, 271bibl, 275bibl, 284bibl, 286bibl
Clarno, E., xxxbibl(2x)
Clendenen, A., 286bibl
Clifton, S., 108n, 269bibl
Collins, J., 37n, 199, 269bibl
Conzelmann, H., 31n, 40n, 118n, 167n(2x), 238n, 269bibl(4x)
Courey, D., viii, xi, 101, 105n(3x), 269
Cox, H., 178, 178n, 179n(2x), 269bibl
Cullen, P.J., 250n, 269bibl
Cullmann, O., 124n, 269bibl
Culpepper, R.A., 54n, 269bibl
Curtis, B.G., 98n, 269bibl

Dahms, J.V., 129n, 269bibl
Dalman, G., 115n, 269bibl
Danby, H., 115n, 118n, 126n,269bibl, 276bibl

Danker, F.W., xviiibibl, 231, 232n, 269bibl(2x)
Darr, J., 41, 41n, 269bibl
Dau, I.M., 182n, 269bibl
Daube, D., 126n, 269bibl
Davids, P., 129n, 269bibl
Dawkins, R., 161n, 269bibl
Dayton, D.W., 177n, 270bibl
Deeley, A., vii, xi, xvi, xxix
Deissmann, G.A., 117n, 122n, 132n, 270bibl
Del Colle, R., 105, 105n, 106n(2x), 270bibl
Delitzsch, F., 189, 189n(2x), 190n, 276bibl(3x)
Delling, G., 55n, 270bibl(2x)
Demchuk, D., vii, xi, xvi, 17
Dempster, M.W., 174, 270bibl
Depaul, M.R., 89n, 270bibl
Derrenbacker, R.A., 116n, 270bibl
Derrett, J.D.M., 127n, 130n, 270bibl(2x)
DeSilva, D., 23n, 270bibl
Dew, J.K., 276bibl
Dibelius, M., 115n, 122n, 270bibl
Dockery, D.S., 273bibl
Dodd, C.H., 122n, 270bibl
Domning, D.P., 161n, 270bibl
Donnelly, D., 270bibl
Driver, G.R., 128n, 270bibl
Dunn, J.D.G., xxxiibibl, xxxiii, 4(2x), 4n, 5(4x), 5n, 6, 11, 30n(4x), 33n, 41, 45, 45n, 49, 58, 101(2x), 101n, 104n, 116n, 124n, 245n, 253, 253n, 266(2x), 270bibl(8x), 286
Durham, J.I., 187, 187n(4x), 270bibl

Eichler, B., 272bibl
Elbert, P., 164n, 244n, 270bibl, 273bibl, 279bibl, 284bibl
Ellington, S., viii, xi, 61, 270n, 273n
Ellis, E.E., 31n, 271bibl
Elwell, W.A., 270bibl(2x)
Emerson, M.Y., 282bibl
Erickson, M.J., 89n(2x), 94, 94n, 271bibl
Evans, C.A., 283bibl
Ewart, F., 86n, 271bibl

Faupel, W.D., 93n, 271bibl
Fee, G.D., xxxiibibl, 10(5x), 10n(x), 81, 85(2x), 87(2x), 87n(2x), 88, 88n, 92, 111, 149n, 225n, 230n, 250n(2x), 252n, 271bibl(8x), 281bibl, 285bibl
Fensham, F.C., 127n, 271bibl
Fenton, J.C., 125n, 271bibl
Filson, F.V., 125n, 269bibl, 271bibl
Finger, T., 88n, 271bibl
Fitzmyer, J., 31n, 271bibl
Flattery, G.M., xxx

## ABBREVIATED & SELECTED NAME INDEX

Foakes-Jackson, F.J., 277bibl
Foerster, W., 238n, 271bibl
Freedman, D.N., 124n, 271bibl
Freedman, H., 124n, 280bibl
Friederich, G., xxiibibl
Fulford, R., 41, 41n, 271bibl
Funk, R.W., 273bibl(2x)

Gabriel, A.K., 59n, 271bibl
Gadamer, H.-G., 49n, 93, 271bibl
Gaffin, R.B., Jr., 103(5x), 103n, 271bibl
Gallegos, J., 68(2x), 68n, 271bibl
Gasque, W.W., xxxi, 4, 11, 11n, 271bibl
Gaster, T.H., 126n, 271bibl
George, A., 128n, 271bibl
Gibb, T., 79(6x), 79n, 272, 27bibl
Gibson, J.B., 225n, 272bibl
Gilbrant, T., xxxbibl
Giles, K., 45, 45n, 272bibl
Gillman, J., 168n, 272bibl
Gispen, W.H., 187, 187n(2x), 272bibl
Gitlin, T., 88n, 272bibl
Glasson, T.F., 126n(2x), 272bibl
Goldin, J., 222n, 272bibl
Goodenough, E.R., 126n, 272bibl
Goppelt, L., 120n, 125n, 272bibl
Goshen-Gottstein, A., 118n, 272bibl
Goulder, M.D., 115(3x), 115n(2n), 272bibl(2x)
Grant, F.C., 127n, 272bibl
Grant, W.V., 84n(3x), 272bibl
Gray, G.B., 188, 188n, 189, 190, 190n(3x), 272bibl
Green, C.E.W., 82n, 92(4x), 92n(3x), 102n, 272bibl(2x)
Green, D.E., 284bibl
Green, J.B., xixbibl, 92n(3x), 102n, 269bibl, 272bibl, 287bibl
Grenz, S., 89, 89n(3x), 90, 90n(2x), 272bibl
Grieve, A., 270bibl
Griffith, G.T., 286bibl
Griffith, R.M., 80(3x), 80n(3x), 272bibl(2x)
Grigg, V., 89n, 272bibl
Grossfeld, B., 189n, 272bibl
Grudem, W.A., 124n, 272bibl
Guelich, R.A., 116n, 131n, 273bibl
Gundry, R.H., 116n, 119n, 125n, 127n, 128n, 132n(2x), 273bibl
Gunkel, H., 246n, 249n(2x), 273bibl
Guthrie, W.K.C., 117n, 273bibl

Haarhoff, T.J., 130n, 268bibl
Haenchen, E., 122n, 125n, 248n, 273bibl(2x)
Hamilton, N.Q., 124n, 273bibl
Hanson, P., 38n(2x), 273bibl

Harris, R.L., xxiibibl
Harris, R.W., xxxbibl(3x)
Harrisville, R.A., 273bibl
Hart, L.D., 163n, 164n, 273bibl
Haya-Pratz, G., xxxiiibibl, 132n, 244, 244n, 247, 247n(2x), 248, 248(2x), 273bibl
Healy, N.M., 109n(2x), 273bibl
Hein, R., xxxiibibl
Hellwig, M.K., 161n, 270bibl
Hengel, M., 6n, 117n, 118n, 119n, 128n, 220n, 273bibl(4x)
Henry, C.F.H., 89n(2x), 273bibl
Hertzberg, H.W., 195(2x), 195n(2x), 273bibl
Hildebrandt, W., viii, xi, 197, 201n, 273bibl
Hill, D., 246n, 273bibl
Hodge, A.A., 104, 104n, 273bibl
Hodges, M.L., 174, 174n, 273bibl(2x)
Hoekema, A., 149n, 273bibl
Hofmann, H., 115n, 273bibl
Holdcroft, L.T., xxx, xxxiii, 101, 101n, 243n, 286
Holladay, W.L., 189, 189n, 273bibl
Hoppe, L., 192n, 273bibl
Hornik, H., 80n, 83(6x), 274bibl
Horovitz, B., 289
Horsley, R., 223n, 274bibl(2x)
Horton, S.M., 278bibl, 281bibl, 282bibl, 284
Hoskyns, E.C., 125n, 274bibl
Hotrum, R.A., 189, 189n, 274bibl
Houk, C.B., 120n(2x), 129n, 274bibl
Hovender, G., 146n, 274bibl
Huffard, E.W., 131n, 274bibl
Huffman, D.D., 274bibl
Hughes, J.A., 78, 78n, 274bibl
Hughes, J.H., 223n, 274bibl
Hunter, H.D., 266bibl
Hur, J., 244, 244n, 247n, 274bibl
Hymes, D.C., 198n, 274bibl(3x)

Isaiah, A.B., 189n, 274bibl
Isbell, C.D., 274bibl

Jeremias, J., 114n, 115n, 116n(2x), 118, 118n(5x), 119(2x), 119n(8x), 122n, 124n(2x), 125n, 127n(2x), 128, 128n(2x), 129(2x), 129n(3x), 130n(4x), 132n, 274bibl
Johnson, V., vii, xi, xvi, xxi, xxxiibibl, 35
Johnston, R.K., 285bibl

Kärkkäinen, V.-M., viii, xi, 173, 173n(4x), 174n, 176n, 177n, 180n(4x), 181n, 182(2x), 275bibl(16x), 281bibl
Käsemann, E., 121n, 276bibl

Keener, C.S., vii, xii, 53n(2x), 55n, 69n, 92(2x), 92n, 114, 116n, 125n, 247n(2x), 276bibl(6x), 287bibl
Keil, K.F., 187n, 189, 189n(2x), 190n, 276bibl(4x)
Kelly, S., 88n, 276bibl
Kittel, G., xxibibl, 276bibl
Klausner, J., 119, 119n, 276bibl
Klein, R.W., 194, 195, 195n, 276bibl
Klink, E.W., III, 102n, 276bibl
Klinken, A. von, 71(3x), 71n(2x), 276bibl
Knox, W.L., 117n, 124n, 276bibl(2x)
Koester, C.R., 255n, 276bibl
Koester, H., 117n, 276bibl
Köstenberger, A.J., 244n(2x), 276bibl
Kuecker, A.J., 167n, 276bibl
Kuzmic, P., 180n, 276bibl
Kydd, R.A.N., 3, 80(2x), 80n, 81(3x), 81n(2x), 277bibl(3x)

Lachs, S.T., 127n, 277bibl
Ladd, G.E., 18, 122n, 125n, 277bibl
Lake, K., xviii, 132n, 277bibl(2)
Lampe, G.W.H., 125n, 277bibl
Land, S.J., 40n, 177n, 277bibl
Lapide, P.E., 116n, 277bibl
Lategan, B.C., 52n, 277bibl
Laurentin, R., 137n, 277bibl
Leaney, A.R.C., 125n, 131n(2x)
Leaney, R., 114n, 124n, 277bibl
Lee, M.T., 171n, 277bibl
Lee, S.Y., 178n(2x), 277bibl
Levine, B., 198, 198n, 277bibl
Levison, J.R., xxxiiibibl, 204, 204n(2x), 205n(2x), 244, 244n, 248n, 253(3x), 277bibl, 286, 287, 288
Lewis, B.S., 179n, 282bibl
Lewis, C.S., xv(3x), xxxii(9x), xxxiibibl, xxxiii, xxxiiin, 19(3x)
Lewis, J.J., 129n, 179n, 277bibl
Lewis, S., 282bibl
Licona, M.R., 116n, 277bibl
Liebengood, K.D., 276bibl
Lincoln, A.T., 241n(2x), 277bibl
Lindars, B., 125n, 132n, 277bibl(2x)
Ling, T.-C., 177n, 277bibl
Lockett, D.R., 102n, 276bibl
Long, A.A., 132n, 277bibl
Longenecker, B.W., 276bibl
Longenecker, R.N., 118n, 122n, 124n, 131n, 277bibl
Lord, A., 108n, 278bibl
Lord, A.M., 108n, 278bibl
Louis, G.B., 181n, 278bibl
Louw, J.P., 278bibl

Luz, U., 74, 74n, 278bibl

Macchia, F., 92, 105, 105n, 108n(3x), 166n(2x), 180n, 254n, 278bibl(3x)
MacDonald, G., xxxiibibl, 19
MacDonald, W.G., 9n, 98, 98n, 278bibl
Ma, J.C., 175n, 181n, 278bibl
Ma, W., xxxbibl, 175, 181n, 198n, 275bibl, 278, 278bibl, 279bibl
MacMullen, R., 117n, 278bibl
Malbon, E., 269bibl
Mann, C.S., 128n, 265bibl
Mansfield, R.M., 220n, 278bibl
Manson, T.W., 125n, 127n, 278bibl
Marcus, J., 228n, 278bibl
Marino, B.R., 163n, 278bibl
Marmorstein, A., 118n, 122n, 127n, 132n, 278bibl
Marsh, J., 190n(2x), 268bibl
Marshall, I.H., 6, 128n, 247n, 278bibl(5x)
Martin, J., 276bibl(2x)
Martin, L.R., viii, xii, 47n, 278bibl, 287bibl
Martin, R.P., 119n, 278bibl
May, J.D., xxxibibl
Mayor, J.B., 129n, 279bibl
McAlister, R.E., 43n, 279bibl
McCarter, P.K., 194, 194n, 195, 279bibl
McClung, G., 173
McClung, L.G., 279bibl
McDermott, G.R., 276bibl
McGee, G., 174n, 279bibl
McKay, J., 67n(2x), 95(2x), 95n, 96n, 279bibl
McKim, D.K., 48n, 88n, 279bibl(2x)
McKnight, E., 269bibl
McLean, M., 88, 88n, 279bibl
McNamara, M., 118n, 127n, 132n, 269n, 279bibl
Meier, J.P., 125n(2x), 127n, 128n, 132n, 279bibl
Menken, M.J.J., 232n, 281bibl, 289bibl
Menzies, R.P., vii, xii, xxx, xxxii, xxxiii(2x), 23, 23n, 29n, 41, 41n, 47, 66n, 88, 88n, 92, 104n, 132n, 175(2x), 246n, 249n, 275bibl, 279(9x)
Menzies, W.W., xxx, 10, 88, 88n, 91n, 96(3x), 92n, 96n, 104n, 144n(2x), 181, 181n, 231n, 279(2x)
Metzger, 115n, 125n, 279bibl
Meyer, J., 111, 112n, 279bibl
Michaels, J.R., 9, 56n, 279bibl
Milgrom, J., 202n, 280bibl
Mitchell, B.K., 171n, 280bibl
Mittelstadt, M.W., iii, vii, viii, xii, xvi, 3n, 5n, 10n, 58n, 73, 74n, 81n, 112n, 170n, 181, 181n, 245n(2x), 280bibl
Moessner, D.P., 280bibl(3x)
Montagne, G.E., 280bibl

## ABBREVIATED & SELECTED NAME INDEX

Montefiore, C.G., 118n, 121n, 127n, 129n, 280bibl(2x)
Montefiore, G.T, 118n, 121n, 127n, 129n, 280bibl(3x)
Montefiore, H.W., 119n, 280bibl(2x)
Moore, G.F., 115n, 116, 118n, 121n(2x), 123n, 129n(2x), 132n, 280bibl
Morris, L., 124n, 280bibl
Motyer, S., 127n, 128n, 129, 129n(2x), 280bibl
Moule, C.F.D., 127n, 128n, 129n(2x), 277, 280bibl
Moyise, S., 232n, 281bibl, 289bibl(2x)
Munyon, T., 164n(3x), 281bibl
"My Testimony of Healing", 79n, 281bibl

Neusner, J., 132n, 281bibl
Neve, L.R., 189, 281bibl, 186n(4x), 190n(2x),
Neyrey, J.H., 39n, 281bibl
Nickle, J.H., 29n(2x), 281bibl
Nida, E.A., 278bibl
Niebuhr, R., 161(2x), 161n, 162, 162n, 281bibl(2x)
Nock, A.D., 117n, 132n, 281bibl(2x)
Noel, B.T., viii, xii, 66n, 85n, 88n, 90n, 93n, 95n, 271n, 281bibl(3x)
Noordtzij, A., 189, 189n, 281bibl
Noth, M., 188, 188n, 281bibl

Odeberg, H., 126n, 281bibl
Oeming, M., 52, 52n, 281bibl
O'Keefe, M., 163n, 281bibl
Oliverio, B., 93n, 283
Oliverio, III, L.W., 92(2x), 93(4x), 93n(2x), 265bibl, 280bibl(4x), 281bibl, 283bibl
Onyinah, O., 179n, 275, 281bibl
Opp, J., 79(2x), 80(3x), 80n(4x), 281bibl
Ormerod, N., 109n, 266bibl, 281bibl

Packer, J.I., 102, 102n, 281bibl
Paddison, A., 50n, 282bibl
Palma, A., 282bibl
Pao, D.W., 141n, 282bibl
PAOC, xvi(2x), xxi, 13(3x), 13n(4x), 14, 15, 16, 42, 78(2x), 78n, 79(2x), 282bibl
Parham, R.L., 282bibl
Parham, S., 42n, 86n(2x), 282bibl(2x)
Parker, J., III, 124n, 125n, 282bibl
Parsons, M., 80n, 83(5x), 274bibl
Patte, D., 121n, 129n, 282bibl(2x)
Penney, J.M., 11, 175(2x), 244, 244n, 282bibl
Perrin, Nicholas, xixbibl, 122n, 128n, 282n
Perrin, Norman, 161n, 162n, 282bibl
Percescepe, G.J., 122n, 128n, 282bibl
Peters, Ted, 161n, 162n, 282bibl

Peters, Thomas, xxxiibibl
Phanon, Y., 282bibl
Phillips, S.S., xxxibibl, 168n, 282bibl
Phillips, T., 168n, 282bibl
Pilgrim, W.E., 168n, 282bibl
Pimental, P., 228n, 282bibl
Pinnock, C.H., 3, 4(2x), 98, 98n, 147n(2x)
Plummer, A., 116n, 282bibl
Podimattom, F., 266bibl
Poirer, J.C., 179n, 282bibl
Porter, S.E., 288bibl
Powell, M.A., 11, 11n, 282bibl(2x)
Purdy, H.G., 91(2x), 91n, 178n, 282bibl
Purdy, V., 178n, 282bibl

Quanbeck, P.A., III, 273bibl

Rahlfs, A., 189, 282bibl
Reynolds, B.E., 102n, 283bibl, 288bibl
Rice, M.L., 93n, 283bibl
Richardson, E., xxxibibl
Reid, R.G., xxxibibl
Reid-Heimerdinger, J., 143n, 146n, 282bibl
Reitzenstein, R., 117n, 282bibl
Reynolds, B.E., 102n, 283bibl, 288bibl
Rhodes, E.F., 277bibl
Rice, M.L., 93n, 283bibl
Ringe, S.H., 168n, 283bibl
Ritchie, T., 176(3x), 176n(2x), 283bibl
Rius-Camps, J., 143n, 144n, 283bibl
Rivkin, E., 124n, 283bibl
Robeck, C.M., 92, 275bibl
Robbins, V.K., 40, 49(3x), 49n(3x), 50, 50n, 283bibl(2x)
Robins, R.G.A., 111n(2x), 283bibl
Robinson, A.B., 9n, 283bibl
Rodd, C.S., 147n, 283bibl
Rodriguez, C.S., 168n, 283bibl
Roloff, J., 272bibl
Romilley, E., 76, 76n, 283bibl
Ropes, J.H., 129n, 283bibl
Rosenbaum, M., 188n, 189n, 283bibl
Rosner, B.S., 268bibl
Roth, C., 124n, 283bibl
Rowland, C., 37n, 283bibl
Ruthven, J., 102, 103, 103n, 283bibl
Rylaarsdam, J., 187, 187n, 283bibl

Sample, T., 39n, 283bibl
Sanders, E.P., 124n, 283bibl, 288bibl
Sanders, J.A., 168n, 283bibl
Sandmel, S., 115n, 120n, 124n, 284bibl
Sawyer, J.F.A., 82n, 284bibl
Sayers, D.L., 19

295

Schiffman, L.H., 126n, 284bibl
Schneider, H., 273bibl
Scholem, G.G., 117n, 123n, 284bibl(2x)
Schumacher, S., 192n, 284bibl
Schweizer, E., 26(2x), 128n, 132n, 246, 284bibl(2x)
Seo, P.-S., 284bibl
Shelton, J.B., 5, 11, 58, 244, 244n(4x), 246n, 247n, 248n(2x), 284bibl(3x), 287
Siegel, S., 121n, 284bibl(3x)
Silberman, L.H., 124n, 284bibl
Silbermann, A.M., 188n, 189n, 283bibl(2x)
Simon, M., 280bibl
Smalley, S.S., 277bibl
Smith, D.E., 9n, 284bibl
Smith, G.T., 267bibl
Smith, H.P., 195n, 284bibl
Smith, J.K.A., 42, 42n, 92, 93n, 160n, 284bibl(3x)
Smith, M., 97n, 114n, 116n, 126n, 130n, 284bibl
Soderlund, S., ix, xii, 243
Solivan, S., 182n, 284bibl
Spittler, R.P., 271bibl, 276, 278bibl, 279, 285bibl
Sri, E., 168n, 285bibl
Stamps, D., xxxiiibibl
Stamps, D.L., 288bibl
Stanford, M.S., 162, 162n, 285bibl
Stanton, G.N., 286bibl
Steeley, J.E., 282bibl
Stein, R.H., 228n, 285bibl(2x)
Stott, J.R.W., 4, 4n, 149n, 285bibl
Strack, H.L., 132n, 285bibl
Strauss, M.I., 232n, 233, 233n, 285bibl
Stuart, D., 10n, 271bibl
Stronstad, R.J., [v]port, xxixbibl(6x), xixn(5x), xxxbibl(15x), xxxn(2x), xxxibibl(22x), xxxin, xxxiibibl(29x), xxxiiibibl(14x), xxxiiin(3x), 1n, 280bibl, 285bibl(16x), 286bibl(8x)
Studebaker, S.M., xxxbibl, 285bibl(16x), 286bibl(8x)
Synan, V., 23n, 286bibl

Talbert, C.H., 9n, 35, 124n, 131n, 286bibl(3x)
Tannehill, R.L., 9n, 124, 124n, 130(2x), 13n, 131n(2x), 286bibl(2x)
Tannenbaum, M.H., 289bibl
Tan, S.I., xxxibibl
Tarn, W.W., 117n, 286bibl(2x)
Tasker, R.V.G., 128n, 286bibl
Taylor, C., 84, 84n, 284,
Taylor, J.E., 224n, 286bibl
Taylor, R.A., 286bibl
Taylor, V., 122n, 286bibl
Thatcher, T., 274bibl

Thiselton, A.C., 50, 50n, 74, 74n, 84n, 286, 286bibl(2x)
Thomas, J.C., ix, xii, 92, 97(4x), 97n(2x), 103, 103n, 180n, 254, 254n(2x), 260n, 271, 287
Tiede, D.L., 117n, 124, 287bibl(2x)
Tigay, J., 272bibl
Tilborg, S. van, 115, 115n(2x), 287bibl
Tipei, J.F., 82n, 287bibl
Tolkien, J.R.R., xxxiibibl(2x), 19
Treier, D.J., 102n, 287bibl
Tuppurainen, R.P., i, iii, iv(2x), vii, xii, xvii, 48, 49n, 50n, 53n, 57n, 159n, 275bibl, 287bibl
Turner, M.M.B., 8n(2x), 11, 102n, 104n, 244, 244n, 246n, 248n(5x), 249n, 250n, 253n, 272bibl, 287bibl(7x)
Turney, H.M., 287bibl
Twelftree, G.H., 107n(2x), 228n, 287bibl(3x)

Urbach, E.E., 121n(3x), 122n, 124n, 128, 287bibl(2x), 288bibl

Van den Toren, B., 162n, 288bibl
Van der Horst, P.W., 117n, 288bibl
van der Maas, E.M., 275bibl, 277bibl
Van Gelder, C., 88n, 288bibl
Van Kleek, L.M., xv, xxxbibl, xxxiiibibl, 243n, 285bibl
"Vancouver Campaign", 78n, 288bibl
Vanhoozer, K.J., 103, 103n, 104, 109, 110(6x), 110n, 111(2x), 288bibl(2x)
Vansina, J., 116n, 288bibl
Vermes, G., 116n, 119n, 131n, 288bibl
Villafañe, E., 180n, 288bibl
Vinson, E., 33n, 286bibl, 288bibl
Volf, M., 79, 179n, 180, 180n, 276bibl, 288bibl
Von Baer, H., 249n(2x), 288bibl

Wacher, G., 288bibl(2x)
Waddell, R.C., 253n, 259, 259n, 288bibl(2x)
Wadholm, R., Jr., 195n, 288bibl
Walker, W.O., Jr., 120n, 129n, 288bibl(2x)
Wall, R.W., 9n, 283bibl
Wallace, D., 250n(2x), 288bibl
Waltke, B.K., xxiibibl
Warrington, K., 164n, 181n(2x), 288bibl(2x)
Watson, D.F., 51n, 288bibl
Watts, R.E., ix, xii, 221n, 224n, 225n(3x), 227n, 228n(2x), 229n(2x), 230n, 289bibl(5x)
Webb, R.L., 223n, 289bibl
Welch, B., viii, xii, 135, 135n(2x), 289bibl(2x)
Wells, D., vii, xii, xvi(2x), xxxibibl

## ABBREVIATED & SELECTED NAME INDEX

Wenham, G., 29n, 188, 188n(2x), 189, 189n, 198n, 289bibl
Wenk, M., 11, 168n, 249, 249n(4x), 289bibl
White, R.E.O., 114n, 288bibl
Wieder, N., 124n, 289bibl
Wigglesworth, S., 78(2x), 78n
Wilcox, D.L., 289bibl
Wilcox, N., 76, 78, 162n
Williams, C., 19
Williams, C.H., 169n, 289bibl
Williams, J.R., 163n, 164n, 232n, 286, 289bibl
Williams, P., 289bibl
Willis, G.G., 129n, 289bibl
Wilson, M., 286bibl
Wilson, M.R., 116n, 233n, 289bibl(2x)
Wilson, R.McL., 289bibl
Wilson, R.R., 117, 289bibl

Witherington, Ben, III, 49n, 53n, 280bibl, 289bibl
White, R.E.O., 114n, 289bibl
Wright, N.T., 106(2x), 106n, 280bibl, 289bibl
Wyckoff, B., viii, xiii, xxxi, 147

Yates, J.E., 221n, 289bibl
Yamauchi, E.M., 125n, 289bibl
Yong, A., viii, xiii, xxxiiibibl, 92, 93n, 108n, 109, 109n, 112, 159, 159n, 160n(5x), 164n, 165n(2x), 167n(2x), 170n(2x), 171n(3x), 176, 176n(3x), 179n, 270bibl, 275bibl, 273bibl, 277bibl, 284bibl, 286, 286bibl, 290bibl(13x)
York, J.O., 169, 169n, 290bibl

Zehnle, R.F., 125n, 290bibl
Zimmerli, W., 238n, 269bibl

# Ancient Document Index

**Key to Index of Abbreviations**
§ = section of the source
bibl = bibliography in the book
n = footnote on the page
x = number of times the source appears on the page

## The Old Testament/ Hebrew Bible

### Genesis

| | |
|---|---|
| 1:2 | 210 |
| 2:7 | 55, 210 |
| 10 | 46n |
| 15:13–14 | 199 |
| 16:11 | 136n |
| 16:15 | 136n |
| 17:5 | 136 |
| 17:15 | 136 |
| 17:19 | 142 |
| 20:7 | 199 |
| 21:3 | 136, 136n |
| 22:1 | 128 |
| 27:36 | 189 |
| 29:32–35 | 136 |
| 30:6–24 | 136 |
| 32:29 | 136 |
| 35:10 | 136 |
| 35:23–26 | 29 |
| 37–50 | 200 |
| 39:5 | 199 |
| 41:16 | 199 |
| 41:33–36 | 199 |
| 41:38 | 200n |
| 41:39 | 186 |
| 41:52 | 200 |
| 41:55 | 199 |
| 45:7 | 199 |
| 47:27 | 199 |
| 48:4 | 199 |
| 48:15–16 | 199 |
| 50:21 | 199 |

### Exodus

| | |
|---|---|
| 1:19 | 118n |
| 2:23–25 | 203 |
| 3:11 | 201 |
| 3:16 | 201 |
| 3:16-20 | 201 |
| 3:18, | 201 |
| 4:1–16 | 202 |
| 4:29–31 | 202, 202n |
| 5:14 | 188 |
| 6:7–8 | 199 |
| 7 | 200 |
| 8:19 | 132n |
| 12:21 | 201 |
| 13:21–22 | 56 |
| 14:13–18 | 200 |
| 14:31 | 201n |
| 16:22–23 | 125 |
| 17 | 203 |
| 18 | 202 |
| 18–19 | 201 |
| 18:13–26 | 188n |
| 18:16 | 202 |
| 19:7 | 202 |
| 19:18 | 56 |
| 23:16 | 46n |
| 24 | 201 |
| 24:1–9 | 201n |
| 25:31–40 | 257 |
| 28:3 | 7n, 56, 186, 191 |
| 31:3 | 7n, 56, 186, 191, 223 |
| 32:11–14 | 203 |
| 33:2 | 222n |
| 33:8b | 222n |
| 33:9a | 222n |
| 33:11 | 206 |

## Exodus (continued)

| | |
|---|---|
| 33:14 | 233n(2x) |
| 34:29 | 198 |
| 35:31 | 7n, 56, 186, 187, 191 |
| 35:34 | 187 |
| 36:1–2 | 186 |
| 40:4 | 257 |
| 40:24–25 | 257 |

## Leviticus

| | |
|---|---|
| 11:9–12 | 260 |
| 12:1–8 | 151 |

## Numbers

| | |
|---|---|
| 1 | 201n |
| 1–20 | 198n |
| 1:51–53 | 201 |
| 3:11-23 | 201n |
| 4 | 201n |
| 4:17–20 | 201n |
| 5 | 201n |
| 6:22–27 | 201n |
| 7:89 | 201n |
| 9 | 205 |
| 9:8 | 205 |
| 11 | viii, 29(4x), 46, 190, 190n, 197(3x), 198(6x), 198n, 199, 200, 202(3x), 204(2x), 204n, 20n, 208n, 274bibl |
| 11:1 | 204 |
| 11:4–13 | 202 |
| 11:14 | 188 |
| 11:14–17 | 5 |
| 11:17 | 188, 19(2x), 201n |
| 11:17–29 | 188 |
| 11:18–20 | 202 |
| 11:21–23 | 203 |
| 11:24–30 | 29, 29n |
| 11:25 | 5, 29, 189, 189n, 223n |
| 11:25–29 | 198 |
| 11:27 | 204 |
| 11:27–30 | 204 |
| 11:28 | 190 |
| 11:28–29 | 196 |
| 11:29 | 7, 29, 30, 34, 188n, 190 |
| 11:31–32 | 204 |
| 12:1–2 | 202 |
| 14:1–4 | 202, 207 |
| 15:32–36 | 205 |
| 17:6–7 | 202 |
| 20:2–3 | 202 |
| 21:5 | 202 |
| 24:2 | 223n |
| 27:1–11 | 205 |
| 27:16-17 | 198 |
| 27:16–20 | 5, 191, 206 |
| 27:18 | 191(3x), 223n |
| 36:1–12 | 205 |

## Deuteronomy

| | |
|---|---|
| 1:13–15 | 191 |
| 5:23–29 | 201 |
| 6–8 | 212 |
| 6:13 | 207 |
| 8:3 | 207 |
| 8:18 | 84n |
| 13:13 | 128 |
| 16:18–19 | 201n |
| 18:15 | 198 |
| 18:15–17 | 201 |
| 18:18–19 | 210n |
| 21:1–9 | 201n |
| 21:18–21 | 201n |
| 25:5–10 | 201n |
| 33:24 | 118n |
| 34:9 | 5, 191(2x) |
| 34:10 | 201n |
| 34:12 | 205n |

## Judges

| | |
|---|---|
| 3:10 | 7n |
| 3:11 | 193 |
| 3:30 | 193 |
| 4:5 | 193 |
| 5:31 | 193 |
| 6:12 | 193 |
| 6:34 | 7n |
| 8:28 | 193 |
| 11:29 | 7n |
| 12:7 | 193 |
| 14:6 | 7n |
| 14:19 | 7n |
| 15:14 | 7n |
| 16:31 | 193 |

## 1 Samuel

| | |
|---|---|
| 10 | 196 |
| 10–19 | 198 |
| 10:1 | 194 |

| | | | |
|---|---|---|---|
| 10:2–6 | 194 | 78:25 | 126n |
| 10:6–13 | 189, 194 | 86:17 | 233 |
| 10:7 | 194 | 110 | 229n |
| 10:10 | 5 | 110:1 | 221(2x), 229(2x) |
| 13:14 | 196 | 115 | 134n |
| 16:13 | 195, 223 | 115:1 | 128n |
| 16:13–14 | 5 | 118:22–23 | 229 |
| 16:13–23 | 194 | 118:25–26 | 229 |
| 19:20–24 | 189 | 119:82 | 233 |
| 24:8–13 | 194, 196 | 139:7 | 221, 222, 229 |
| | | 139:10 | 222 |
| | | 145:10–13 | 123(2x) |

## 2 Samuel

| | |
|---|---|
| 6:15 | 137n |
| 7 | 118n |
| 12:7 | 193, 196 |

## Proverbs

| | |
|---|---|
| 20:26 | 191 |

## 1 Kings

| | |
|---|---|
| 3:9 | 195 |
| 3:11–12 | 195 |

## Ecclesiastes

| | |
|---|---|
| 2:10 | 189 |

## Song of Songs
### (Song of Solomon, Canticles)

## 2 Kings

| | |
|---|---|
| 2:9 | 5 |
| 2:15 | 5 |

| | |
|---|---|
| 2:14, | 225 |

## Isaiah

## Job

| | |
|---|---|
| 26:13 | 210 |

## Psalm(s)

| | |
|---|---|
| 2 | 229n(2x) |
| 2:7 | 225 |
| 11:9–10 | 229, 231 |
| 12:10–11 | 229 |
| 12:36 | 229 |
| 14:62 | 229 |
| 15:24 | 229 |
| 15:29 | 229 |
| 15:34 | 229 |
| 22:2 | 229 |
| 22:8 | 229 |
| 22:19 | 229 |
| 33:6 | 220 |
| 37 | 126n |
| 51:11 | 222 |
| 71:21 | 233 |
| 74:19 | 225 |

| | |
|---|---|
| 7:14 | 210 |
| 9 | 118n |
| 9:1–7 | 194 |
| 9:7 | 123 |
| 11:1–3 | 56 |
| 11:1–5 | 194 |
| 11:2 | 191, 235n |
| 11:16 | 126n |
| 12:1 | 233 |
| 24:16 | 144 |
| 29:6 | 56 |
| 32:15 | 141(2x), 223 |
| 34:9 | 56 |
| 40 | 232 |
| 40–55 | 127n, 232–234, 238 |
| 40:1 | 233, 233n(2x), 288 |
| 40:1–2 | 232 |
| 40:1–11 | 228 |
| 40:3 | 126n, 222, 223(2x), 228 |
| 40:3–5 | 138 |
| 40:8–12 | 138 |
| 40:14 | 138 |
| 42 | 132n |

301

## Isaiah (continued)

| | |
|---|---|
| 42:1 | 107, 124n(2x), 218, 225 |
| 42:1–4 | 217, 220 |
| 42:6 | 124n, 169 |
| 43:10–12 | 124n |
| 44:3 | 124n, 223, 225 |
| 44:8 | 124n |
| 44:13 | 144 |
| 49:6 | 124n, 169 |
| 49:13 | 233 |
| 49:24 | 221, 228 |
| 51:3 | 233 |
| 52:5 | 121n |
| 52:7 | 124n |
| 52:9 | 233 |
| 56–66 | 267bibl |
| 57:18 | 233 |
| 59:20–21 | 124n |
| 59:21 | 124n |
| 61:1 | 124n, 194, 223n |
| 61:1–2 | 219 |
| 61:1–2a | 44, 151, 168 |
| 61:1–7 | 217n, 219n |
| 61:2 | 233 |
| 63 | 200, 223(2x), 225 |
| 63–64 | 223 |
| 63:1–6 | 223 |
| 63:3 | 223 |
| 63:3–6 | 223 |
| 63:7–14 | 223 |
| 63:9 | 222 |
| 63:9–12 | 229 |
| 63:10 | 223, 229 |
| 63:10–11 | 222 |
| 63:10–14 | 124n |
| 63:11 | 223 |
| 63:11–14 | 205 |
| 63:14 | 225 |
| 63:16 | 223, 225 |
| 63:17 | 128n |
| 64 | 223 |
| 64:3 | 23 |
| 65:1—66:6 | 223 |
| 66:6 | 56 |
| 66:14b–16 | 223 |
| 66:16 | 59 |
| 66:24b | 223 |

## Jeremiah

| | |
|---|---|
| 8:7 | 225n |
| 8:7 | 225 |
| 15:1 | 224 |
| 16:4–15 | 126n |

## Ezekiel

| | |
|---|---|
| 11:17–21 | 225 |
| 11:19 | 223 |
| 36:23 | 121 |
| 36:24–31 | 225 |
| 36:26–27 | 124, 253 |
| 37 | 56 |
| 37:5–6 | 55 |
| 37:11–14 | 55n |
| 37:14 | 124, 253 |
| 38:23 | 121 |
| 39:7 | 121 |
| 39:25–29 | 225 |
| 39:27 | 121 |
| 39:29 | 124(2x), 253 |

## Daniel

| | |
|---|---|
| 1:1 | 124n |
| 4 | 37 |
| 5:11 | 191 |
| 5:14 | 191 |
| 7:14 | 123 |

## Hosea

| | |
|---|---|
| 2:14–15 | 126n |
| 7:9–11 | 225 |
| 7:11 | 225 |
| 11:8 | 233 |
| 11:11 | 126n |

## Joel

| | |
|---|---|
| 2:3 | 56 |
| 2:28 | 189, 190 |
| 2:28–29 | 7, 124n(2x), 223(2x) |
| 2:28–32 | 26, 30, 34 |
| 2:29 | 234 |
| 2:32c | 141 |
| 2:32d | 141(2x) |
| 2:32e | 147 |
| 3:1-2 | 223 |
| 3:1-5 | 107n(2x), 267bibl |

## Haggai

| | |
|---|---|
| 2:1 | 118n |

## Zechariah

| | |
|---|---|
| 1:63 | 136 |
| 1:67 | 245n |
| 4:1–14 | 257 |
| 13:2 | 215n |
| 14 | 144 |

## Malachi

| | |
|---|---|
| 3:1 | 223 |
| 3:5–6 | 223 |
| 4:1 | 223 |
| 4:3 | 223 |
| 4:5 | 221 |
| 4:5–6 | 221 |
| 4:6b | 223, 224 |

# The New Testament

## Matthew

| | |
|---|---|
| 1:1 | 210 |
| 1:8 | 220(3) |
| 1:10 | 220(3) |
| 1:12 | 220(3) |
| 1:18 | 209, 210, 220 |
| 1:20 | 210, 220 |
| 1:23 | 220(2) |
| 1–7 | 74n, 278bibl |
| 3:1 | 214 |
| 3:8 | 211 |
| 3:15 | 211 |
| 3:16 | 212n, 214 |
| 3:29 | 220 |
| 4:7 | 130 |
| 4:12 | 151 |
| 5:16 | 118n |
| 5:17 | 138n |
| 5:22 | 211n |
| 5:45 | 118n |
| 5:48 | 118n |
| 6:1 | 118n |
| 6:5–15 | 114n |
| 6:9 | 123n |
| 6:9–13 | 120n |
| 6:12 | 127n(2x), 271bibl |
| 6:13 | 127n |
| 6:14 | 118n |
| 6:25–34 | 125 |
| 6:26 | 118n |
| 6:27 | 130 |
| 6:32 | 118n |
| 7:9 | 130 |
| 7:9–10 | 33n, 126 |
| 7:11 | 31, 118n |
| 7:12 | 138n |
| 7:21 | 118n |
| 7:22–23 | 216n |
| 8:16 | 214 |
| 8:28–34 | 214 |
| 9:2–7 | 215 |
| 9:32–34 | 214 |
| 10:1 | 214 |
| 10:6 | 138n |
| 10:8 | 214 |
| 10:32–33 | 118n |
| 10:41 | 216n |
| 11:13 | 138n |
| 11:15 | 138n |
| 12:17–21 | 219, 220 |
| 12:22–24 | 214 |
| 12:28 | 132n, 212n, 214(2x) |
| 12:29 | 214 |
| 12:31 | 220 |
| 12:39 | 215 |
| 12:43–45 | 215 |
| 12:50 | 118n |
| 13:9 | 138n |
| 13:11 | 220 |
| 13:15 | 215 |
| 13:17 | 216n |
| 13:36–43 | 215 |
| 13:43 | 138n |
| 13:57 | 216 |
| 15:8 | 215 |
| 15:13 | 118n |
| 15:19 | 215 |
| 15:22–28 | 214 |
| 15:24 | 138n |
| 16:1–4 | 214, 214n |
| 16:4 | 215 |
| 16:17 | 118n |
| 16:21–23 | 214n |
| 16:27 | 185n |
| 17:14–18 | 214 |
| 17:17 | 215 |
| 18:10 | 118n |
| 18:14 | 118n |
| 18:19 | 118n |
| 18:23–35 | 127(2x) |
| 18:35 | 118n |

303

## Matthew (continued)

| | |
|---|---|
| 22:40 | 138n |
| 23:9 | 118n |
| 23:13 | 214n |
| 23:15 | 214n |
| 23:29 | 216n |
| 24:9–14 | 217n |
| 25:41 | 215 |
| 26:41 | 127n |

## Mark

| | |
|---|---|
| 1–8 | 278bibl |
| 1:2–3 | 221, 230 |
| 1:3 | 222, 226 |
| 1:3b | 222 |
| 1:4–8 | 222 |
| 1:6 | 221 |
| 1:7 | 222 |
| 1:7–8 | 222, 226, 230 |
| 1:8 | 220, 220n, 221, 222, 226n, 228, 293bibl |
| 1:10 | 220, 221, 223 |
| 1:11 | 225, 226, 226n, 229n, 230 |
| 1:12 | 220 |
| 1:12–13 | 221 |
| 1:14 | 151 |
| 1:21–45 | 227 |
| 1:23-26 | 226 |
| 1:23–28 | 226 |
| 1:24 | 226n |
| 1:26 | 239 |
| 1:27 | 225 |
| 1:27–28 | 225 |
| 1:34 | 226 |
| 1:39 | 226 |
| 2:1—3:6 | 227 |
| 2:6 | 227 |
| 2:16 | 227 |
| 2:25 | 222n |
| 3:6 | 227 |
| 3:11–12 | 226 |
| 3:15 | 225 |
| 3:20 | 227n |
| 3:20–35 | 227 |
| 3:21 | 227n |
| 3:22 | 226, 227 |
| 3:22–27 | 226 |
| 3:23–29 | 227n |
| 3:23b | 227 |
| 3:24 | 228 |
| 3:24–25 | 228 |
| 3:26a | 227, 228 |
| 3:24–29 | 228 |
| 3:27 | 221, 226, 228 |
| 3:28–30 | 227 |
| 3:29 | 220, 220n, 221(2x) |
| 3:30 | 227n |
| 3:31–35 | 227 |
| 3:32-35 | 227n |
| 4:1–34 | 227 |
| 4:12 | 228 |
| 5:6–10 | 226 |
| 5:17 | 225 |
| 6 | 45 |
| 6:13 | 225 |
| 6:16–29 | 221 |
| 7 | 45 |
| 7:3 | 115 |
| 7:6 | 222n |
| 7:6–7 | 222n |
| 7:10 | 222n |
| 9:7 | 229n |
| 9:13 | 221 |
| 10:19 | 222n |
| 10:38–39 | 224 |
| 11:1–14 | 224 |
| 11:13 | 224 |
| 11:17 | 224 |
| 11:25 | 118n(2x) |
| 12:31 | 220, 221 |
| 12:36 | 220n, 229n |
| 12:37 | 230 |
| 12:38–44 | 230 |
| 13 | 230, 235, 241 |
| 13:11 | 217n, 220, 220n, 221, 230 |
| 14:27 | 223n |
| 14:36 | 119, 120 |
| 14:62 | 229n |

## Luke

| | |
|---|---|
| 1 | 169n |
| 1:1–4 | 9 |
| 1:13 | 136 |
| 1:14 | 218 |
| 1:15 | 5n, 150 |
| 1:15–17 | 207 |
| 1:17 | 218 |
| 1:28 | 137 |
| 1:35 | 155, 218 |
| 1:39–56 | 207 |
| 1:41 | 5n, 150 |
| 1:41–45 | 218 |
| 142 | 137(4x), 154 |
| 1:52–53 | 169n |

| | | | |
|---|---|---|---|
| 1:53 | 132n | 4:43 | 44 |
| 1:60 | 136 | 5:17 | 42, 46, 218 |
| 1:63 | 136 | 5:20–24 | 167n |
| 1:67 | 5n, 136 | 5:26 | 43 |
| 1:67–79 | 151, 207, 218 | 6:9 | 208 |
| 1:68 | 208 | 6:21 | 207 |
| 1:76 | 136 | 6:25 | 208 |
| 1:77 | 144n, 167n | 7:16 | 43 |
| 1:80 | 207 | 7:28 | 136 |
| 2:25 | 233 | 7:48 | 137 |
| 2:25–26 | 151 | 7:50 | 137 |
| 2:25–27 | 46n | 8:18 | 138n, 269bibl |
| 2:25–32 | 242 | 8:44 | 82n |
| 2:25-35 | 207 | 9:1 | 46 |
| 2:27–32 | 151 | 9:1–17 | 208 |
| 2:30–32 | 169 | 9:1–50 | 232n, 280bibl |
| 2:33–35 | 151 | 9:15 | 208 |
| 2:36–38 | 151, 207 | 9:51—22:53 | 9 |
| 2:40, | 191 | 10 | 46(2x), 152(2x) |
| 3:3 | 144n, 167n | 10:1 | 24, 28, 29, 208n |
| 3:3–14 | 138 | 10:1–12 | 9 |
| 3:4 | 148 | 10:1–16 | 28(3x) |
| 3:7 | 137 | 10:2 | 46 |
| 3:10 | 137 | 10:9–13 | 31 |
| 3:12 | 137 | 10:17 | 208n |
| 3:14 | 137 | 10:19 | 46 |
| 3:15—4:30 | 151 | 10:21 | 33, 34, 152 |
| 3:16 | 5n, 56, 151, 206 | 10:42 | 132n |
| 3:16–17 | 189 | 11 | 56, 152 |
| 3:21 | 32, 133 | 11:1 | 31, 114 |
| 3:21–22 | 34, 151, 152 | 11:1–13 | 114(2x) |
| 3:22 | 6, 27n, 155 | 11:2 | 56 |
| 4 | 107 | 11:2–4 | 277bibl |
| 4:1 | 151, 152, 245n | 11:3 | 208 |
| 4:1a | 151 | 11:4 | 167n |
| 4:1b | 151 | 11:5–8 | 274bibl |
| 4:1–13 | 168 | 11:11 | 130 |
| 4:2 | 9 | 11:11–12 | 33n |
| 4:2–4 | 126, 207 | 11:11–13 | 152 |
| 4:3 | 137 | 11:13 | viii, 6, 24, 31(2x), 32n, 33, |
| 4:9 | 137 | | 34, 118n(2x), 120, 132, 133, |
| 4:12 | 130, 207 | | 287bibl |
| 4:13 | 226n | 11:13b | 56 |
| 4:14 | 27n, 42, 46, 151, 157, 218 | 11:14–28 | 33n |
| 4:16–18 | 168n | 11:15 | 33n |
| 4:16–19 | 218 | 11:17 | 143 |
| 4:16–30 | 9 | 11:19 | 32 |
| 4:17–19 | 151 | 11:21–22 | 33 |
| 4:18 | 144n, 149n | 11:25 | 146 |
| 4:18–19 | 27n, 32, 42, 44, 168 | 12 | 133, 152 |
| 4:18–21 | 5, 206 | 12:4–12 | 130 |
| 4:24–30 | 207 | 12:10 | 217n |
| 4:31—8:56 | 9 | 12:11–12 | 217n |
| 4:36 | 42, 152, 218 | 12:12 | 6 |

## Luke (continued)

| | |
|---|---|
| 12:19 | 132n |
| 12:22–34 | 125, 126 |
| 12:25 | 130 |
| 13:30 | 169 |
| 14:5 | 130 |
| 14:8 | 130 |
| 14:11 | 169 |
| 14:35 | 138n |
| 15:4 | 130 |
| 16:1–15 | 168n |
| 17:3–4 | 167n |
| 17:7 | 130 |
| 18 | 131 |
| 18:9–11 | 168n |
| 18:9–12 | 127 |
| 18:14 | 169 |
| 18:21 | 146 |
| 18:27 | 146 |
| 18:43 | 43 |
| 19:1–10 | 168n |
| 19:3 | 137 |
| 19:11–27 | 168n |
| 20:9–26 | 168n |
| 21:1–4 | 168n |
| 21:14–15 | 6 |
| 22 | 140 |
| 22:18 | 123, 126 |
| 22:28 | 130 |
| 22:32 | 139, 143 |
| 22:34 | 139(2x), 140 |
| 22:44–53 | 152 |
| 22:49–51 | 152 |
| 22:61 | 139, 140 |
| 23:42 | 123 |
| 23:51 | 123 |
| 24:19 | 8 |
| 24:47 | 144n, 167n |
| 24:48 | 7 |
| 24:49 | 36n, 54, 111, 141, 149n, 152, 218, 245 |

## John

| | |
|---|---|
| 14–16 | 237, 240 |
| 14:15–16 | 241 |
| 14:16 | 234 |
| 14:17 | 235(2x) |
| 14:23 | 237 |
| 14:26 | 240(2x) |
| 15 | 237 |
| 15:7–8 | 241 |
| 15:12 | 241 |
| 15:26 | 235(2x) |
| 16:4b–15 | 287bibl |
| 16:7 | 236 |
| 16:8–11 | 240 |
| 16:13 | 235(2x) |
| 17 | 120n |
| 17:17 | 122n |
| 20:19–23 | 238 |
| 20:22 | 236 |

## Acts

| | |
|---|---|
| 1 | 54 |
| 1:1 | 8, 45, 84 |
| 1:1–2 | 153 |
| 1:1–5 | 5 |
| 1:3 | 44 |
| 1:4 | 53, 133 |
| 1:4–5 | 6, 7, 54(2x), 55, 224 |
| 1:4–8 | 124 |
| 1:5 | 221 |
| 1:8 | 53n, 68, 109, 111, 125, 133, 141, 153, 155, 165, 167, 173n, 190, 193, 218(2x) |
| 1:9–10 | 153 |
| 1:12–26 | 53 |
| 1:14 | 32n, 114, 133, 153 |
| 1:45 | 206 |
| 1–2 | 107 |
| 2 | 26(2x), 30, 36, 41, 42(3x), 43, 45(2x), 46(3x), 47, 54, 57, 58, 125, 141, 146, 160, 165, 165n, 166, 167(2x), 290bibl |
| 2 and 3 | |
| 2:1–4 | vii, 6, 9, 48, 49(2x), 53(3x), 54(3x), 55(2x), 56, 57(2x), 58(3x), 59(4x), 60(2x) |
| 2:1–13 | 62 |
| 2:1–21 | xxix, 5, 286bibl |
| 2:2–4 | 165 |
| 2:4 | 26(3x), 27, 27n, 28, 32n, 33, 34, 56, 153, 154, 189, 208 |
| 2:5 | 25 |
| 2:5–6 | 26 |
| 2:5–13 | 154 |
| 2:6 | 25, 55 |
| 2:7–8 | 25 |
| 2:10 | 165 |
| 2:11 | 25(3x), 56, 246 |
| 2:11b | 55, 166 |
| 2:12 | 125n |
| 2:12b | 166 |
| 2:13 | 26, 125n |

| | | | |
|---|---|---|---|
| 2:14 | 154 | 5:31 | 144n, 165n |
| 2:14–40 | 9 | 5:32 | 55, 57, 140, 142 |
| 215 | 125n | 5:36 | 53 |
| 2:15–17 | 26 | 6 | 208 |
| 2:16 | 125n | 6:1–4 | 208 |
| 2:16–18 | 125n, 132 | 6:1–6 | 206 |
| 2:17 | 124, 173, 190, 208 | 6:3 | 6, 114, 191, 218, 246, 247(3x), 248, 248n, 249, 249n |
| 2:17a | 165 | | |
| 2:17–18 | 26, 27(2x), 29, 166 | 6:5 | 6, 114, 218, 247(2x) |
| 2:17–21 | 30, 31, 281n | 6:6 | 114 |
| 2:18 | 26 | 6:7 | 53n |
| 2:19–20 | 166 | 6:8 | 218(2x), 248 |
| 2:22–36 | 56 | 6:10 | 191, 248 |
| 2:24 | 166 | 7:55 | 259 |
| 2:25–28 | 166 | 7:60 | 165n |
| 2:26 | 126 | 8 | 30, 142 |
| 2:29–30 | 166 | 8–10 | 42 |
| 2:31 | 166 | 8:2–25 | 170n |
| 2:33 | 26(2x), 133 | 8:9–24 | 33n |
| 2:33–36 | 30, 166 | 8:14–19 | 62 |
| 2:34–41 | 230 | 8:15 | 27n, 32n(2x), 114, 133 |
| 2:36 | 26 | 8:15–16 | 190 |
| 2:37–38 | 58 | 8:17 | 24, 32n(2x), 216 |
| 2:38 | 26n, 60, 140(3x), 144n, 165n | 8:18 | 6, 27n |
| 2:38c | 140 | 9:1—22:21 | xxxibibl |
| 2:38–39 | 58(2x), 135, 140(3x) | 9:11 | 114, 133 |
| 2:39 | 47, 108, 141 | 9:17 | 27n, 32n, 133, 208 |
| 2:41 | 6, 112 | 9:17–18 | 62 |
| 2:42 | 126 | 9:17–19 | 24(2x) |
| 2:42–44 | 175 | 9:20 | 27n |
| 2:42–47 | 167, 208 | 9:31 | 53n, 242 |
| 2:42–48 | 27 | 9:36 | 218 |
| 3:1-12:17 | 9 | 10 | 45, 46 |
| 3:13 | 219n | 10:9 | 114 |
| 3:19 | 140(3x), 141(6x), 165n | 10:17 | 114 |
| 3:19–20 | 141 | 10:30 | 114, 133 |
| 3:26 | 219n | 10:38 | 107, 218 |
| 3:38–39 | 58 | 10:42–43 | 27 |
| 4:7–8 | 142 | 10:42–48 | 27 |
| 4:8 | 5n, 193, 208 | 10:43 | 165n |
| 4:8–12 | 218, 230 | 10:44 | 27, 133, 155 |
| 4:25 | 219n | 10:44–46 | 62, 142 |
| 4:27 | 219n | 10:44–48 | 30 |
| 4:29–31 | 133 | 10:45 | 6 |
| 4:30 | 219n | 10:45–46 | 27 |
| 4:31 | 6, 29, 32, 114, 193, 208, 218 | 10:46 | 24, 25(2x), 26(2x), 27n, 28, 33, 34, 56 |
| 4:32–35 | 208 | | |
| 4:33 | 230 | 10:47 | 28, 30 |
| 5:1–10 | 167n | 10:47–48 | 27 |
| 5:9 | 130 | 11 | 142, 146 |
| 5:12 | 145 | 11:1–2 | 139, 140, 142 |
| 5:15 | 79, 82n | 11:2 | 133 |
| 5:28 | 135, 141 | 11:15 | 27, 155, 206 |
| 5:29–32 | 58 | 11:15–16 | 224 |

## Acts (continued)

| | |
|---|---|
| 11:15–18 | 27 |
| 11:16 | 5n, 221 |
| 11:17 | 27, 142 |
| 11:18 | 143 |
| 11:24 | 6, 112, 218 |
| 12:24 | 53n |
| 13 | 45, 208 |
| 13:1 | 8(2x) |
| 13:1—19:20 | 9 |
| 13:9 | 5n, 8n, 157, 193, 208, 245, 246n, 248 |
| 13:9–12 | 218 |
| 13:19 | 157 |
| 13:38 | 144n |
| 13:38–39 | 165n |
| 13:47 | 122, 169 |
| 13:52 | 8, 208, 249(3x), 250, 251(2x) |
| 13:58 | 144n |
| 14:3 | 8 |
| 15 | 97(3x), 143 |
| 15:1–2 | 142 |
| 15:2 | 143 |
| 15:4 | 142 |
| 15:7–9 | 142 |
| 15:8 | 6 |
| 15:16–18 | 122 |
| 15:28 | 84 |
| 16:5 | 53n |
| 16:9 | 112 |
| 16:16–18 | 33n |
| 17:6 | 169 |
| 17:28 | 117, 119 |
| 18:21 | 146 |
| 18:25 | 138 |
| 18:27 | 146 |
| 19 | 42, 135, 146 |
| 19:1 | 145 |
| 19:1–6 | 145 |
| 19:1–7 | 62 |
| 19:2 | 28, 32, 145, 190 |
| 19:5 | 145 |
| 19:6 | 6, 27n, 28(2x), 30, 33, 34, 56, 114, 145 |
| 19:11–12 | viii, 73(3x), 74n, 76, 77, 79, 81, 83(2x), 84n |
| 19:11–20 | 33n |
| 19:12 | 75, 77, 78, 79 |
| 19:13–16 | 77 |
| 19:16 | 155 |
| 19:20 | 53n |
| 19:21—21:26 | 9 |
| 20:19 | 130 |
| 20:29 | 177bibl |
| 21:15 | 111 |
| 26:17–18 | 122 |
| 26:18 | 144n, 165n |
| 28 | 175 |
| 28:30–31 | 53n |
| 28:31 | 44 |

## Romans

| | |
|---|---|
| 1:4 | 166 |
| 1:18 | 129 |
| 1:24 | 129 |
| 1:26 | 129 |
| 1:28 | 129 |
| 2:24 | 121n |
| 5:5 | 237 |
| 8:15 | 120(2x) |
| 8:16 | 240 |
| 8:25 | 125 |
| 8:26–27 | 240 |
| 12:6–8 | 155, 156 |
| 12:8a | 239 |
| 14:17 | 252n |
| 15:13 | 157 |
| 15:19 | 36, 157, 252n |

## 1 Corinthians

| | |
|---|---|
| 2:4 | 252n |
| 8:6 | 225 |
| 10:2 | 223 |
| 10:13 | 129 |
| 10:22 | 224 |
| 12 | 42n |
| 12–14 | 25(3x), 148, 155, 268bibl |
| 12:4–11 | 55 |
| 12:7 | 190 |
| 12:10 | 25n, 189 |
| 12:8 | 252n |
| 12:8–10 | 156 |
| 12:9 | 252n |
| 12:13 | 5, 221 |
| 12:28 | 25n, 156, 191 |
| 12:30 | 25n |
| 13:1 | 25n |
| 13:8 | 25n |
| 14 | 239, 240 |
| 14:2 | 25n |
| 14:3 | 239(2x) |
| 14:4 | 25n |
| 14:6 | 25n, 240 |
| 14:6–19 | 25 |

| | | | |
|---|---|---|---|
| 14:13 | 25n | | |
| 14:14–17 | 43n | ## 1 Thessalonians | |
| 14:18 | 25n | 1:1 | 225 |
| 14:22 | 25n | 1:6 | 252n |
| 14:22–26 | 240 | | |
| 14:23 | 25n | | |
| 14:26 | 25n | ## 2 Thessalonians | |
| 14:27 | 25n | 2:10–12 | 129 |
| 14:28 | 25, 30n | | |
| 14:32 | 30n | | |
| 14:39 | 25n | ## Hebrews | |
| 16:22 | 122 | 13:8 | 178 |

## 2 Corinthians

| | | | |
|---|---|---|---|
| 1:22 | 125 | ## James | |
| 5:5 | 125 | 1:13 | 129n, 269bibl |

## Galatians

| | | | |
|---|---|---|---|
| 2 | 70 | ## 1 John | |
| 3:5 | 252n | 4:6 | 235 |
| 4:6 | 120(2x) | | |
| 5:13–26 | 226n | ## Jude | |
| 5:25 | 157 | 9 | 227 |

## Ephesians

| | | | |
|---|---|---|---|
| 1:13–14 | 125 | ## Revelation | |
| 1:17 | 252n | 1:1–8 | 254 |
| 3:7 | 156 | 1:4 | 254, 255(2x), 258, 263 |
| 4:1—6:9 | 226n | 1:4–5 | 257 |
| 4:11 | 156 | 1:5 | 261 |
| 5:18 | 5, 133, 191, 244(3x), 245, 250(3x), 251, 253 | 1:10 | 254 |
| | | 1:19 | 255 |
| 5:18–19 | 245 | 2–3 | 258 |
| 5:18–33 | 251 | 2:7 | 263 |
| 6:10–20 | 226n | 2:11 | 263 |
| | | 2:17 | 263 |
| | | 2:13 | 261 |
| | | 2:29 | 263 |
| ## Philippians | | 3:1 | 257(2x) |
| 1:19 | 252n | 3:6 | 263 |
| | | 3:10 | 261 |
| | | 3:13 | 263 |
| ## Colossians | | 3:22 | 263 |
| | | 4:1–16:21 | 257 |
| 1:9 | 252n | 4:2 | 254, 257 |
| 2:9 | 225 | 4:5 | 257, 263 |
| | | 5:6 | 258, 263 |
| | | 5:11 | 263 |
| | | 6:9–11 | 261 |

## Revelation (continued)

| | |
|---|---|
| 6:10 | 261 |
| 8:13 | 261 |
| 10:11 | 258 |
| 11:1 | 258 |
| 11:3 | 258, 261 |
| 11:3–12 | 258 |
| 11:4 | 258 |
| 11:5–8 | 258 |
| 11:7 | 261 |
| 11:8 | 258 |
| 11:10 | 261 |
| 11:11 | 259 |
| 11:13 | 259 |
| 12–14 | 259(2x) |
| 13:8 | 261 |
| 13:12 | 261 |
| 13:14 | 261 |
| 13:15 | 259 |
| 14:4 | 261 |
| 14:11 | 259 |
| 14:13 | 257, 259, 263 |
| 16:13–14 | 261 |
| 17:1 | 261 |
| 17:2 | 261 |
| 17:3 | 257 |
| 17:8 | 261 |
| 19:8 | 261, 263 |
| 19:9 | 261 |
| 19:10 | 261, 263 |
| 21:10 | 254 |
| 22:6–21 | 254 |
| 22:9 | 263 |
| 22:17 | 254, 263 |

## LXX (Septuagint)/ Deuterocanonical (Apocryphal) Books

### Genesis LXX

| | |
|---|---|
| 10 | 46 |
| 17:5 | 136 |
| 17:15 | 136 |
| 17:19 | 136 |
| 21:3 | 136 |
| 29:32–35 | 136 |
| 30:6–24 | 136 |
| 32:29 | 136 |
| 35:10 | 136 |

### Exodus LXX

| | |
|---|---|
| 38:8b | 222n |

### 2 Samuel LXX

| | |
|---|---|
| 6:15 | 137n |

### 2 Chronicles LXX

| | |
|---|---|
| 5:13 | 137n |

### Psalms LXX

| | |
|---|---|
| 139[138]:7 | 221, 222 |

### Daniel LXX

| | |
|---|---|
| 5:12 | 222n |
| 6:4 | 222n |

### Isaiah LXX

| | |
|---|---|
| 32:15 | 141 |
| 40:1–2 | 232 |
| 63:8–11 | 221 |
| 63:14a | 225 |
| 64:1–3 | 222 |

### Zechariah LXX

| | |
|---|---|
| 1:63 | 136 |

### Sirach (Eccelsiasticus)

| | |
|---|---|
| 2:1–6 | 128 |
| 7:10 | 129n |
| 28:2 | 127 |
| 48:9–10 | 221n |

### Wisdom of Solomon

| | |
|---|---|
| 2:18 | 124n |
| 5:5 | 124n |

# Old Testament Pseudepigrapha

## 1 Enoch

| | |
|---|---|
| 9:4 | 122n |
| 27:3 | 122n |
| 91:1 | 132n |
| 91:4 | 132n |
| 108:1 | 124n |

## 2 Baruch

| | |
|---|---|
| 1:4 | 121n |
| 13:10 | 127n |
| 76:5 | 124n |

## Jubilees

| | |
|---|---|
| 1:21 | 132n |
| 1:23 | 132n |
| 1:25 | 119n |
| 1:28 | 119n, 123n |
| 2:20 | 119n |
| 5:8 | 132n |
| 19:29 | 119n |
| 31:12 | 132n |

## Letters to Aristeas

| | |
|---|---|
| 98 | 122n |

## Psalm of Solomon

| | |
|---|---|
| 17:28–30 | 119n |

## Sibylline Oracles

| | |
|---|---|
| 1.175 | 131n |
| 2.17–19 | 122n |
| 3.604 | 119n |
| 3.750 | 132n |
| 3.659–60 | 132n |

## Testament of Abraham

| | |
|---|---|
| 4A | 132n |
| 12A | 119n |
| 16A | 119n |
| 16B | 119n |

## Testament of Asher

| | |
|---|---|
| 1:9 | 132n |

## Testament of Benjamin

| | |
|---|---|
| 8:2 | 132n |

## Testament of Simeon

| | |
|---|---|
| 4:4 | 132n |

## Testament of Issachar

| | |
|---|---|
| 3:7–8 | 132n |
| 6:1 | 124n |

## Testament of Joseph

| | |
|---|---|
| 2:7 | 132n |

## Testament of Judah

| | |
|---|---|
| 24:2–3 | 223n |

## Testament of Levi

| | |
|---|---|
| 18:11 | 223n |

# Other Jewish Writings

## Thanksgiving Hymns

| | |
|---|---|
| 9:32 | 132n |

## War Scroll

| | |
|---|---|
| 11:3 | 122n |
| 11:15 | 122n |
| 17:2 | 122n |
| 18:13 | 130n |

## Rule of the Community

| | |
|---|---|
| 3.7 | 132n |
| 4.20–27 | 223n |
| 4.21 | 132n |
| 6.4–5 | 126n |

## Rule of the Community (*continued*)

| | |
|---|---|
| 6.20-21 | 126n |
| 6.27—7.1 | 122n |
| 8.4 | 127n |
| 8.16 | 132n(2x) |
| 11.13 | 129n |

## Pesher Habakkuk

| | |
|---|---|
| 8.1–3 | 128n |

## Qumran cave four fragments

| | |
|---|---|
| Florilegium | 118 |

## Words of the Luminaries

| | |
|---|---|
| F1 2Rv:15 | 223 |

## Messianic Apocalypse

| | |
|---|---|
| 2 III | 221n |

## papVisionb ar

| | |
|---|---|
| 1 II, 4 | 221n |

## Josephus, *Jewish Antiquities*

| | |
|---|---|
| 2.276 | 122n |
| 6.166 | 132n |
| 9.212 | 223n |
| 13.299 | 124n |
| 15.373 | 124n |
| 15.55 | 224n |
| 17.34b | 124n |
| 20.97–8 | 223n |
| 20.167–8 | 223n |
| 20.169–72 | 223n |

## Abodah Zerah

| | |
|---|---|
| 16b | 118 |

## Bava Batra

| | |
|---|---|
| 10a | 118n |

## Ehuaqotai pereq

| | |
|---|---|
| 8.269.2.15 | 118n |

## Berakhot (Babylonian tractate)

| | |
|---|---|
| 4b | 132n |
| 5ab | 131n |
| 7a | 119n |
| 11b | 122n |
| 12b | 126n |
| 19a | 122n |
| 30a | 115n, 118n(2x) |
| 31b | 132n |
| 32b–33a | 115n |
| 33b | 122n |
| 51a | 122n |
| 53b | 225 |
| 60b | 122n |
| 62b | 131n |

## Gittin (Babylonian tractate)

| | |
|---|---|
| 4b | 132n |
| 5ab | 128n |
| 7a | 119n |
| 11b | 122n |
| 12b | 126n |
| 17a | 128n |
| 19a | 119n |
| 30a | 115n |
| 30a, bar | 118n(2x) |
| 31b | 132n |
| 32b–33a, bar | 115n |
| 33b | 122n |
| 51a | 122n |
| 60b | 122n |
| 62b | 131n |
| 63a | 128n |

## Pesahim (Babylonian tractate)

| | |
|---|---|
| 53b | 121n |
| 54a | 126n |
| 118a | 128n |

## Sanhedrin (Babylonian tractate)

| | |
|---|---|
| 11a | 124n |
| 60a | 122n |
| 64a | 129n |

## Shabbat (Babylonian tractate)

| | |
|---|---|
| 11a | 124n |
| 60a | 122n |
| 64a | 129n |

## Taanit (Babylonian tractate)

| | |
|---|---|
| 9a | 126n |

## Yevamot (Babylonian tractate)

| | |
|---|---|
| 63b | 126n |

## Yoma (Babylonian tractate)

| | |
|---|---|
| 75a | 119n, 126(2x) |
| 75b | 126n |
| 86b | 121n |

## Deuteronomy Rabbah

| | |
|---|---|
| 1:6 | 119n |
| 3:15 | 119n |
| 5:15 | 132n |
| 6:14 | 144n |
| 11:6 | 122n |

## Didache

| | |
|---|---|
| 8.2 | 127n, 130n |
| 9–10 | 130n |
| 9.2–3 | 116 |

## Ecclesiastes Rabbah

| | |
|---|---|
| 1:1, §1 | 132n |
| 1:9, §1 | 126n |
| 3:1 | 122n |
| 3:16, §1 | 132n |
| 10:8, §1 | 132n |

## Genesis Apocryphon

| | |
|---|---|
| 21.20–22 | 126n |

## Genesis Rabbah

| | |
|---|---|
| 20:9 | 126n |
| 37:7 | 124n |
| 43:6 | 126n |
| 48:2 | 126n |
| 55:2 | 128n |
| 60:7 | 131n |
| 62:2 (Tanna) | 128n |
| 63:14 | 132n |
| 70:8 | 128n |
| 73:5 | 131n |
| 80:8 | 132n |
| 81:14 | 131n |
| 82:4 | 131n |
| 91:5 | 132n |
| 92:7 | 132n |
| 92:9 | 132n |
| 93:7 NV | 132n |
| 96:5 (Judah ha-Nasi) | 128n |
| 100:6 | 131n |

## Lamentations Rabbah

| | |
|---|---|
| 1:5, §31 | 128n |
| 1:17, §52 | 119n |
| 2:20, §23 | 132n |
| 3:3, §1 | 128n |
| 3:18, §6 | 128n |
| 3:20, §7 | 119n |
| 3:58–60, §9 | 132n |
| 4:22, §25 | 128 |
| Proem 2 | 119n |
| Proem 23 | 119n |

## Leviticus Rabbah

| | |
|---|---|
| 1:3 | 118n(2x), 132n |
| 2:16, §1 | 119n |
| 3:6 | 132n |
| 4:1 | 132n |
| 7:1 | 118n |
| 7:1–2 | 118n |
| 9:1 | 128n |

## Leviticus Rabbah (continued)

| | |
|---|---|
| 9:9 | 132n |
| 10:3 | 119n |
| 25:6 | 131n |
| 27:1 | 128n |
| 27:4 | 126n |
| 30:1 | 126n |
| 31:2 | 131n |
| 35:10 | 118n(2x) |

## Berakhot (Mishnah tractate)

| | |
|---|---|
| 2:2 | 123n |
| 4:4 | 115n |

## Berakhot (Tosefta tractate)

| | |
|---|---|
| 3:14 | 118n |
| 4:16–18 | 114n |

## Mekilta Shirata

| | |
|---|---|
| 3 | 121n |

## Mishna Kiddushin

| | |
|---|---|
| 4:14 | 126n |

## Sanhedrin (Mishnah tractate)

| | |
|---|---|
| 7:5 | 123n |

## Sotah (Mishnah tractate)

| | |
|---|---|
| 9:15 | 118n |

## Numbers Rabbah

| | |
|---|---|
| 1:2 | 126n |
| 4:5–8 | 122n |
| 5:3 | 119n |
| 8:4 | 121n |
| 9:8 | 128n |
| 10:2 | 119n, 132n |
| 11:1 | 132n |
| 11:2 | 126n |
| 11:3 | 117n |
| 12:21 | 121n |
| 13:20 | 126n, 132n |
| 15:10 | 124n |

## Numbers Rabbah

| | |
|---|---|
| 15:12 | 121n |
| 16:7 | 119n |
| 17:2 | 128n |
| 18:8 | 132n |
| 19:15 | 132n |
| 20:18 | 132n |

## Pesahim

| | |
|---|---|
| 7b | 122n |
| 53b | 121n |
| 54a | 126n |
| 85b | 118n |
| 112a | 118n |
| 118a | 128n |

## Pesiqta Rabbati

| | |
|---|---|
| 3:2 | 122n |
| 10:2 | 132n |
| 11:2 | 132n |
| 15:17 | 119n |
| 20:1 | 132n |
| 21:7 | 122n |
| 22:5 | 128n |
| 30:1 | 132n |
| 31:10 | 126n |
| 33:2–3 | 132n |
| 34:1 | 132n |
| 35:1 | 132n |
| 50:1 | 132n |
| 50:4 | 132n |
| 51:8 | 127n |

## Sipra (Sifra) *Quedoshim; pereq*

| | |
|---|---|
| 9.207.2.13 | 118n |

## Tanhuma

| | |
|---|---|
| Exod.6:12 | 221n |

## Temurah

| | |
|---|---|
| 16a | 131n |

## Targumic text

Ps 68:14 — 225

## Targum Neofiti

1 on Deut 33:24 — 118n

## Targum Pseudo-Jonathan

on Exod 1:19 — 118n

## Zevahim

8:2 (cf. 9:5) — 124n
22b — 118n

# Other Christian Writings

## Justin Martyr, *I Apology*

33, 44, 47, 63 — 132n

## Justin Martyr, *Dialogue with Trypho*

1.1.5 — 117
25, 32–34 — 132n

## Dio Chrysostom, *Borysthenitica (Or.36)*

36.36 — 117n

## Old Polycarp, *To the Philippians*

2.3 — 127n
6.2 — 127n
7.2 — 127n

# Other Ancient Literature

## Aratus, *Phaennomena*

151–56 — 117n

## Aristophanes, *Acharnenses*

223–25 — 117n

## Epictetus, *Discourses*

1.3.1 — 117n

## Homer, *Iliad*

3.276, 320, 350, 365;
7.179, 202, 446; 8.236;
12.164; 13.631; 15.372;
17.19, 645; 19.270;
21.273; 24.308 — 117n

## Martial, *Epigrams*

10.28 — 117n

## Meander, *Dyskolos*

192 — 117n

## Philo, *De aeternitate mundi*

13 — 119n

## Philo, *Allegorical Interpretation*

3.18 — 224n

## Philo, *De confusion linguarum*

170 — 119n

## Philo, *De vita contemplative*

90 — 119n

## Philo, *De decalogo*

32, 51, 105 — 119n

Philo, *Quod deterius potiori insidari soleat*
118     126n

Philo, *De fuga et invention*
186     132n

Philo, *Quis reum divinarium heres sit*
191     126n

Philo, *Legum allegoriae*
115, 293     119n

Philo, *De migration Abrahami*
204     224n

Philo, *De vita Mosis*
2.238     119n

Philo, *De opificio mundi*
149     128n

Philo, *De Praemiis et poenis*
24     119n

Philo, *De providentia*
2.67     224n

Philo, *Quaestiones et solutions in Genesin*
2.60     119n

Philo, *De sobrietate*
55–56     119n

Philo, *De specialibus legibus*
1.14, 22     119n

Philo, *De virtutibus*
64, 77, 218     119n

Philo, *That the Worse Attack the Better*
176     224n

Pindar, *Isthmionikai*
642     117n

Pindar, *Nemeonbikai*
8.35; 9.53; 10.29     117n

Seneca, *Dialogi*
1.1.5     117n
25     132n
32–34     132n

Sophocles, *Oedipus tyrannus*
6.42     117n

www.ingramcontent.com/pod-product-compliance
Lightning Source LLC
Chambersburg PA
CBHW080728300426
44114CB00019B/2507